THE INTERNATIONAL CRIMINAL COURT
AND NATIONAL COURTS

T0347425

INTERNATIONAL AND COMPARATIVE CRIMINAL JUSTICE

Series Editors:

Mark Findlay, *Institute of Criminology, University of Sydney, Australia*
Ralph Henham, *Nottingham Law School, Nottingham Trent University, UK*

This series explores the new and rapidly developing field of international and comparative criminal justice and engages with its most important emerging themes and debates. It focuses on three interrelated aspects of scholarship which go to the root of understanding the nature and significance of international criminal justice in the broader context of globalization and global governance. These include: the theoretical and methodological problems posed by the development of international and comparative criminal justice; comparative contextual analysis; the reciprocal relationship between comparative and international criminal justice and contributions which endeavor to build understandings of global justice on foundations of comparative contextual analysis.

Other titles in the series:

The Limits of Criminal Law
A Comparative Analysis of Approaches to Legal Theorizing
Carl Constantin Lauterwein
ISBN 978 0 7546 7946 2

Domestic Deployment of the Armed Forces
Military Powers, Law and Human Rights
Michael Head and Scott Mann
ISBN 978 0 7546 7346 0

Democracy in the Courts
Lay Participation in European Criminal Justice Systems
Marijke Malsch
ISBN 978 0 7546 7405 4

The Disruption of International Organised Crime
An Analysis of Legal and Non-Legal Strategies
Angela Veng Mei Leong
ISBN 978 0 7546 7066 7

The International Criminal Court and National Courts
A Contentious Relationship

NIDAL NABIL JURDI
American University of Beirut, Lebanon

Routledge
Taylor & Francis Group

LONDON AND NEW YORK

First published 2011 by Ashgate Publishing

Published 2016 by Routledge
2 Park Square, Milton Park, Abingdon, Oxfordshire OX14 4RN
711 Third Avenue, New York, NY 10017, USA

First issued in paperback 2016

Routledge is an imprint of the Taylor & Francis Group, an informa business

British Library Cataloguing in Publication Data
Jurdi, Nidal Nabil.
  The International Criminal Court and national
  jurisdictions : a contentious relationship.
   -- (International and comparative criminal justice)
  1. International Criminal Court. 2. Criminal
  jurisdiction. 3. Criminal procedure (International
  law) 4. International and municipal law. 5. War crime
  trials. 6. War crimes--Uganda. 7. War crimes--Sudan--
  Darfur.
  I. Title II. Series
  345'.01-dc22

Library of Congress Cataloging-in-Publication Data
Jurdi, Nidal Nabil.
  The International Criminal Court and national jurisdictions : a contentious relationship / by
Nidal Nabil Jurdi.
     p. cm. -- (International and comparative criminal justice)
  Includes bibliographical references and index.
  ISBN 978-1-4094-0916-8 (hardback) 1. International Criminal Court. 2. Jurisdiction
(International law) 3. Criminal liability (International law) 4. Criminal procedure
(International law) 5. International criminal courts. 6. International offenses. 7. Criminal
justice, Administration of-- International cooperation. I. Title.

  KZ6314.J87 2010
  345'.01--dc22

                                                                         2010035142

  ISBN 13: 978-1-138-27220-0 (pbk)
  ISBN 13: 978-1-4094-0916-8 (hbk)

Contents

List of International Instruments

List of Conventions and Statutes

Agreement on Accountability and Reconciliation; Between the Government of the Republic of Uganda and The Lord's Resistance Army/Movement. 29 June 2007. Juba Sudan.

Convention against Torture and Other Cruel, Inhuman or Degrading Treatment or Punishment. 17 December 1984. General Assembly Resolution 39/46, 39 GAOR.

Convention for the Protection of Human Rights and Fundamental Freedoms. Council of Europe, Rome. 1950. Entry into force on 3 September 1953. Cets No.: 005.

Convention for the Suppression of Unlawful Acts against Safety of Civil Aviation. 23 September 1971. 974 U.N.T.S. 177, 10 I.L.M. 1151(1971).

Convention for the Creation of an International Criminal Court. 1936. League of Nations. Supp. No. 156(1936), LN Doc. C. 547(I). M.384(I). 1937. V(1937).

Convention on the Prevention and Punishment of the Crime Genocide, 1948.

Convention With Respect to the Laws and Customs of War on Land. 29 July 1899. Hague, II.

Convention for The Amelioration of The Condition of The Wounded And Sick In The Armed Forces. 12 August 1949. 75 U.N.T.S. 31,62.

Convention for The Amelioration of The Condition of The Wounded, Sick, And Shipwrecked Members of The Armed Forces At Sea. 12 August 1949, 75 U.N.T.S. 85.

Convention Relative to the Treatment of the Prisoners of War, 12 August 1949, 75 U.N.T.S. 135, 236.

Convention Relative to the Protection of Civilian Persons in Time of War. 12 August 1949. 75 U.N.T.S. 287, 386.

Convention for the Suppression of Unlawful Seizure of Aircraft (1971). 16 December 1970.

Convention on the Prevention and Punishment of Crimes against Protected Persons Including Diplomatic Agents. 14 December 1973. General Assembly Resolution 3166 (XXVIII).

International Atomic Energy Agency Convention on the Physical Protection of Nuclear Material. 1980. IAEA.

International Convention against Taking Hostages. 17 December 1979. General Assembly Resolution 34/1146.

International Maritime Organization Convention for the Suppression of Unlawful Acts against the Safety of Maritime Navigation. 10 March 1988. Doc SUA/con/15, 27 ILM. 672/1988.

Maastricht Treaty.

Montreal Convention on Unlawful Acts Against safety of Civil Aviation of 1971.

Protocol I Additional To The Geneva Conventions of 12 August 1949, and Relating To Protection of Victims of Armed Conflict. 10 June 1977.

Protocol II Additional to the Geneva Conventions of 12 August 1949, and Relating to the Protection of Victims of Non-International Armed Conflicts (Protocol II). 1977.

Rules of Procedure And Evidence, Adopted on 29 June 1995. The International Criminal Tribunal for the Prosecution of Persons Responsible for Genocide and Other Serious Violations of International Humanitarian Law Committed in the Territory of Rwanda and Rwandan Citizens Responsible for Genocide and Other Such Violations Committed in the Territory of Neighbouring States, between 1 January 1994 and 31 December 1994. Available at: www.un.org/ictr/rules.html.

Rules of Procedure and Evidence adopted on 11 February 1994, and then amended on 12 July 2007. International Tribunal for the Prosecution of Persons Responsible for Serious Violations of International Humanitarian Law Committed in the Territory of the Former Yugoslavia since 1991, IT/32/Rev. 40. Available at: www.un.org/icty/legaldoc-e/basic/rpe/IT032Rev40e.pdf.

Statute of the International Criminal Tribunal for the Former Yugoslavia, adopted on 25 May 1993 by Resolution 827, and then amended by subsequent Resolutions. November 2007. International Tribunal for the Prosecution of Persons Responsible for Serious Violations of International Humanitarian Law Committed in the Territory of the Former Yugoslavia since 1991. Available at: www.un.org/icty/legaldoc-e/index.htm.

Statute of the International Criminal Tribunal for the Prosecution of Persons Responsible for Genocide and Other Serious Violations of International Humanitarian Law Committed in the Territory of Rwanda and Rwandan Citizens Responsible for Genocide and other Such Violations Committed in the Territory of Neighbouring States, between 1 January 1994 and 31 December 1994, Adopted by Security Council Resolution 955, and then Amended by Security Council Resolutions. 8 November 2004. Available at: www.un.org/ictr/statute.html.

Statute of the Special Court For Sierra Leone. 16 January 2002. Annexed to Agreement between The United Nations And The Government of Sierra Leone on The Establishment of a Special Court For Sierra Leone. Available at: www.sc-sl.org/scsl-statute.html.

The African (Banjul) Charter on Human and Peoples' Rights (1981) OAU Doc. CAB/LEG/67/3 rev. 5, 21 I.L.M. 58. 1982.

The American Convention on Human Rights. 1969. Adopted at the Inter-American Specialized Conference on Human Rights, San José, Costa Rica, 22 November 1969.

The Charter of the United Nations.

The Code of Criminal Procedure, Republic of Germany.

The Convention for the Right of the Child.

The Counterfeiting Convention, 1929.

The European Convention on Extradition, 1957.

The International Convention on the Suppression and Punishment of the Crime of Apartheid (1973). Adopted and opened for signature, ratification by General Assembly Resolution 3068 (XXVIII) of 30 November 1973. Entry into force 18 July 1976.

The International Covenant on Civil and Political Rights (1966), General Assembly Resolution 2200A (XXI), 21 U.N. GAOR Supp. (No. 16) at 52, UN Doc. A/6316 (1966), 999. U.N.T.S. 171.

The International Law Commission Draft Statute in Report of the ILC on the Work of its Forty Sixth Session (1994) UN GAOR.

The Military Criminal Code, the Democratic Republic of Congo.

The Penal Code Act, Republic of Uganda. 1970.

The Rome Statute of the International Criminal Court, UN Doc. A/CONF.183/9. 1998. Entry into force July 2002.

The Rules of Procedure and Evidence of the International Criminal Court, ICC-ASP/1/3.

The Sierra Leone Peace Accord signed at Lomé in July 1999.

The Sudanese Code of Criminal Procedure.

Vienna Convention on the Law of Treaties, 1969. 23 May 1969. Entered into force on 27 January 1980. United Nations, *Treaty Series*, 1155, 331.

Other International Instruments, Declarations, Resolutions and Communications

Basic Principles on the Independence of the Judiciary Adopted by the Seventh United Nations Congress on the Prevention of Crime and the Treatment of Offenders. 26 August – 6 September 1985. Milan. Endorsed by General Assembly Resolutions 40/32 of 29 November 1985 and 40/146 of 13 December 1985.

Council of Europe. October 1994. Council of Europe Recommendation No. R (94) 12 On the Independence, Efficiency and Role of Judges, adopted by the Committee of Ministers on 13 October 1994 at the 518th meeting of the Ministers' Deputies. Available at: www.abanet.org/ceeli/areas/judicial_reform/coe_rec.pdf.

Declaration of Basic Principles of Justice for Victims of Crime and Abuse of Power. Adopted by the General Assembly in the 96th plenary meeting on 29 November 1985. A/RES/40/34.

Draft Code of Crimes against the Peace and Security of Mankind, International Law Commission Report. 1996.

Guiding Principles on Internal Displacement. Available at: www.unhchr.ch/html/menu2/7/b/principles.htm.

Negotiated Relationship Agreement between the ICC and the UN. 4 October 2004. Available at www.icc-cpi.int/library/asp/ICC-ASP-3-Res1English.pdf.

Principles of International Cooperation in the Detection, Arrest, Extradition and Punishment of persons Guilty of War Crimes and Crimes Against Humanity, adopted by The General Assembly. 3 December 1973.

Security Council Resolution 713(1991). UN Doc. S/Res/731. 1991.

Security Council Resolution 827. May 1993. UN Doc. S/Res/827. 1993.

Security Council Resolution 955. 8 November 1994. UN Doc. S/RES/955. 1994.

Security Council Resolution 1422. 2002. UN Doc. S/Res1422. 2002.

Security Council Resolution 1487. 2003. UN Doc. S/Res1487. 2003.

Security Council Resolution 1497. 2004. UN Doc. S/Res1497. 2004.

Security Council Resolution 1556. 30 July 2004. UN Doc. S/RES/1556.

Security Council Resolution 1564. 18 September 2004. S/RES/1564. 2004.

Security Council Resolution 1574. 19 November 2004. S/RES/1574. 2004.

Security Council Resolution 1590. 24 March 2005. UN Doc. S/RES/1590. 2005.

Security Council Resolution 1591. 29 March 2005. UN Doc. S/RES/1591. 2005.

Security Council Resolution 1593. 31 March 2005. UN Doc. S/RES/1593. 2005.

Security Council Resolution 1769. 31 July 2007. UN Doc. S/RES/1769. 2007.

The United Nations Handbook on Justice for Victims. 1999. New York. Available at: www.uncjin.org/Standards/9857854.pdf.

Human Rights Committee. 18 August 1998. Concluding Observations of the Human Rights Committee: Ecuador. CCPR/C/79/Add.92.

United Nations Committee against Torture. 17 November 1998. Conclusions and Recommendations Concerning the Second Periodic Report of Croatia, UN Doc. A/54/44.

United Nations Committee against Torture. November 1999. Conclusions and Recommendations of the Committee against Torture Concerning the Third Periodic Report of Peru, UN Doc. A/55/44.

United Nations Committee against Torture. 17 November 1999. Conclusions and Recommendations of the Committee against Torture concerning the Initial Report of Azerbaijan, UN Doc. A/55/44.

United Nations Committee against Torture. 18 November 1999. Conclusions and Recommendations of the Committee against Torture Concerning the Initial Report of Kyrgyzstan, UN Doc. A/55/44.

United Nations General Assembly GA 3074 (xxviii). 3 December 1973. Principles of International Cooperation in the Detection, Arrest, Extradition and Punishment of persons Guilty of War Crimes and Crimes against Humanity.

United Nations General Assembly Resolution 50/46. 11 December 1995. A/RES/50/46. Available at: www.un.org/documents/ga/res/50/a50r046.htm.

United Nations Human Rights Committee. 7 April 1992. General Comment No. 20, UN Doc. No. CCPR/C/21/Rev.1./Add.3.

United Nations Human Rights Committee. 5 May 1993. Comments of the Human Rights Committee, Uruguay, Consideration of Reports Submitted by States Parties Under Article 40 of the Covenant, UN Doc. CCPR/C/79/Add.19.

United Nations Human Rights Committee. 1995. Comments on Argentina, UN Doc. CCPR/C/79/Add.46.1995.

United Nations Human Rights Committee. 1997. Concluding Observations of the Human Rights Committee – Lebanon, UN Doc. CCPR/C/79/Add.78, 1 April 1997.

United Nations Human Rights Committee. 1999. Concluding Observations of the Human Rights Committee – Chile, UN Doc. CCPR/C/79/Add.104 (1999).

Table of Cases

Table of Legislation

The Criminal Code of 1991. 1991. Republic of Sudan. Available at: www. lawsofsudan.net/modules.php?name=Content&pa=showpage&pid=3.

The Criminal Procedure Act, CPA. 1991. Republic of Sudan. Available at: www. lawsofsudan.net/modules.php?name=Content&pa=showpage&pid=4.

The Criminal Procedure Act, CPA, amended 2002. 2002. Republic of Sudan. Available at: www.lawsofsudan.net/modules.php?name=Content&pa=showp age&pid=6.

The Evidence Act. 2003. Republic of Sudan. Available at: www.unsudanig.org/ docs/The%20Evidence%20Act,%202003.pdf.

The German Constitution. 23 May 1949. Federal Republic of Germany. Available at: www.servat.unibe.ch/law/icl/gm00000_.html.

The International Criminal Court Bill. Draft of 19 April 2004. Republic of Uganda.

The International Criminal Court Bill. Draft of 2006. Republic of Uganda.

The International Criminal Court Law. Adopted on 10 March 2010. Republic of Uganda.

The Lebanese Amnesty Law. 1991. The Lebanese Republic, official Gazette.

The National Security Act of 1999, amended 2001. July 2001. Republic of Sudan.

The National Security Forces Act. 1999. Republic of Sudan. Available at: http:// p076.ezboard.com/fndbfrm20.showPrevMessage?topicID=10.topic.

The Penal Code Act. 1970. Republic of Uganda. Available at: www. ugandaonlinelawlibrary.com/files/free/The_Penal_Code_Act.pdf.

The Police Forces Act. 1999. Republic of Sudan. Available at: www.moi.gov.sd/ ar/lown1.asp.

The Police General Regulations. 2003. Republic of Sudan. Available at: www. unsudanig.org/docs/The%20Police%20General%20Regulation%20Act,%202 003.pdf.

The Prisons Act. 2003. Republic of Sudan. Available at: www.unsudanig.org/docs/ The%20Prisons%20Act,%202003.pdf.

The Ugandan Anti-Terrorism Act. 7 June 2002. Assented to by the President on 21 May 2002 and came into force on 7 June 2002.

List of Abbreviations

ACHR	The African Commission for Human Rights
ADF	Allied Democratic Front
AMIS	African Union Mission in Sudan
ARLPI	Acholi Religious Leaders Peace Initiative
ASP	Assembly of State Paties
CAT	Committee Against Torture
CID	Criminal Investigation Department
CMI	Chieftaincy of Military Intelligence
CSOPNU	Civil Society Organizations for Peace in Northern Uganda
CW	Committee of the Whole in the Rome Conference
DPP	Directorate of Public Prosecutions
ECHR	European Court for Human Rights
ECJ	European Court of Justice
ERC	Emergency Relief Coordinator
FPLC	Forces Patriotiques pour la Libération du Congo
GA	The United Nations General Assembly
HRC	Human Rights Committee
HSM	Holy Spirit Movement
I-ACHR	Inter-American Court for Human Rights
ICC	International Criminal Court
ICCPR	International Covenant for Civil and Political Rights
ICJ	International Court of Justice
ICL	international criminal law
ICTR	International Criminal Tribunal for Rwanda
ICTY	International Criminal Tribunal for the Former Yugoslavia
IDP	internally displaced person
ILC	The International Law Commission
JATF	Joint Anti-Terrorism Task Force
JCCD	Jurisdiction, Complementarity and Cooperation Division
JEM	Justice and Equality Movement
JIC	Judicial Investigations Committee
LDU	Local Defence Units
LRA	Lord's Resistance Army
NATO	North Atlantic Treaty Organizations
NGO	non-governmental organization
NMRD	National Movement for Reform and Development
NRA	National Resistance Army

OAS	Organization of American States
OCHA	UN Office for the Coordination of Humanitarian Affairs
OTP	Office of the Prosecutor – ICC
PP	Public Prosecution
SC	Security Council
SCCED	Special Criminal Court on the Events in Darfur
SCSL	Special Court for Sierra Leone
SLM/A	Sudan Liberation Movement/Army
SOAT	Sudanese Organization against Torture
SPLM	Sudan People's Liberation Army
TRC	Truth and Reconciliation Commission
UHRA	Uganda Human Rights Activists
UHRC	Ugandan Human Rights Commission
UNAMID	United Nations African Union Mission in Darfur
UNLA	Uganda National Liberation Army
UNMIS	United Nations Mission in Sudan
UPC	Union of Congolese Patriot
UPDA	Uganda People's Democratic Army
UPDF	Ugandan Peoples' Defence Forces
UPDM	Uganda People's Democratic Movement
VCCU	Violent Crime Crack Unit

Foreword

David Tolbert[1]

This book addresses a topic which is critically important to the future of international justice. I can think of no more urgent issue facing the international justice movement, which has made such great strides over the past 15 years, than the question of complementarity. While the topic is one of considerable discussion, including one of the key topics addressed at the recently concluded International Criminal Court (ICC) Review Conference held in Kampala, Uganda in June 2010, much more thought, both conceptual and practical, needs to be given to this subject.

Complementarity is indeed at the heart of the Rome Statute system, and it is the key to the fight against impunity. We are moving towards the closure of the *ad hoc* tribunals for the former Yugoslavia and Rwanda as well as the 'hybrid' courts, e.g., the Special Court of Sierra Leone. It is unlikely that there will be future *ad hoc* tribunals and the use of hybrid courts is uncertain. Thus, the enforcement of international humanitarian law will be left primarily to the ICC and to domestic judicial systems.

Against this background, the question of complementarity, that is the relationship between the ICC and domestic courts, is an urgent one. What does the term 'complementarity', which is not a word to be found in English language dictionaries and does not actually appear in the Rome Statute, actually mean in legal terms? What did the drafters of this innovative but somewhat vague term mean? What obligations does the complementarity principle imply with respect to the ICC itself and particularly to the Office of the Prosecutor? What duties does the complementarity principle place, or not place, on State Parties to the ICC Statute? How do supporters of international justice assist in making the complementarity principle operational?

In order to address these and other pertinent questions, Nidal Jurdi, who holds a Ph.D. in International Criminal Justice and Human Rights, University College Cork, National University of Ireland and is currently Human Rights Officer with the Office of the High Commission for Human Rights, has written an impressive

---

1   President, International Center for Transitional Justice; formerly, Deputy Chief Prosecutor, Deputy Registrar, Chef de Cabinet to the President, International Tribunal for the former Yugoslavia; Assistant Secretary General and Special Expert for the Extraordinary Chambers in the Court of Cambodia; Registrar, Special Tribunal for Lebanon; Executive Director, American Bar Association Central European and Eurasian Law Initiative.

and timely book, which systematically examines the legal background and issues that arise with respect to the complementarity principle. He begins with a brief but thorough examination of the key challenges facing international courts, which in the words of the former President of the ICTY and current President of the Special Tribunal for Lebanon Antonio Cassese are 'like giant[s] without any arms or legs', i.e., unlike domestic courts, international courts have no means of enforcement or coercion at their disposal and must rely on the cooperation of others, primarily states.

Using this reality as a point of departure, Dr. Jurdi then closely examines the legal and political background from which the principle of complementarity emerged. While insiders may be aware of the history of how complementarity became part of the Rome Statute, this book is indeed one of the very few places that the story has been told in such a comprehensive manner. This background gives important context to the emergence of the complementarity principle in the Rome Statute. It is as close to 'legislative history' as is available and provides insights into the intention of the drafters, as there is no travaux préparatoire from the Rome Conference, much less the many discussions leading up to it.

Dr. Jurdi then discusses thoroughly the underlying legal theory behind the complementarity idea as well as the issues that it raises, by analyzing those provisions of the Rome Statute in which the complementarity principle is embedded or, as the author terms it, he looks at 'Complementarity in the Abstract'. From this close review of the actual provisions of the Rome Statute, he turns his attention to 'Complementarity in Practice' in which he carefully and systematically examines, respectively, the Uganda case and the matter of Darfur, which came to the ICC through very different paths.

The proceedings related to Uganda originated as a case of 'self-referral', that is Uganda referred itself, i.e., the LRA situation, to the ICC. This approach raises a number of interesting and important issues regarding a state's 'willingness' to prosecute. As the author points out, there are real concerns related to this process as it, in essence, reverses the 'unwillingness' test provided for in the ICC Statute, moving it from an 'unwillingness' to investigate and prosecute to a 'willingness' to transfer. Thus, the author critically examines the Uganda case in detail and carefully discusses the implications of the Prosecutor's policy in this regard as well as the impact that this approach will have on the ICC as an institution, in addition to exploring the obvious questions that are raised regarding the complementarity principle in practice.

Dr. Jurdi also discusses the somewhat different application of the complementarity principle in the case of the Democratic Republic of Congo. He notes that the ICC might have played a more constructive role in that country if it had applied the complementarity principle in a different manner, that is by allowing the domestic authorities to proceed but at the same time carefully monitoring their proceedings and intervening only if needed. Finally, the discussion turns to the case of the Darfur referral by the United Nations Security Council. In this connection, Dr. Jurdi provides a very interesting analysis of the way the Sudanese authorities attempted to use arguments based on the complementarity principle to avoid this referral.

Through this multi-faceted approach, looking at issues of practice and principle as well as also taking account the political context, this book will make an important contribution of our understanding of the complementarity principle, which lies at the heart of the Rome Statute and its effectiveness, both for the short-term and for the long-term. In this important sense, Dr. Jurdi has provided an excellent view into the issues that will no doubt dominate the debate regarding the ICC, both in theory and in practice. Thus, this book will indeed prove its value to practitioners and academics alike.

Acknowledgements

The accomplishment of this book comes after a journey replete with challenges as well as dedication. This work covers the contentious relation between the International Criminal Court and national systems, which combines legal, financial, and political complexities that continue to face the enforcement of international criminal law. The insight and comments of a number of professors and colleagues were decisive in broadening the scope of this work into wider dimensions. I am indebted for their comments and support.

I am particularly grateful to Dr. Siobhan Mullally, Senior Lecturer at the Faculty of Law, University College Cork, Ireland, for her valuable comments and suggestions. I am indebted to David Tolbert, President of the International Centre for Transitional Justice for endorsing this book despite his busy schedule. Special thanks go to Professor Morten Bergsmo, George Town University, and to Dr. Mohammad El-Zeidy, Legal Officer, The International Criminal Court, for their words on this work.

A final thanks to the editorial team of Ashgate Publishing for their professionalism and commitment.

Nidal Nabil Jurdi, 2011

About the Author

Nidal Nabil Jurdi is a Lecturer in International Law and Organizations at the American University of Beirut, Lebanon, and Human Rights Officer at the United Nations Office of the High Commissioner for Human Rights, Middle East Office. Nidal has published widely in this and related areas.

To Nabil, Nahida and Yara with lots of love

Chapter 1

Introduction

Background

The last century witnessed two world wars and a series of international and national conflicts marked by massive atrocities to humanity and human existence. The 'never again' promise of Nuremberg that crimes against humanity and aggression would 'not go unpunished' has not been realized.[1] Many criminals and violators of human rights and humanitarian law escaped legal accountability for their crimes.

The failure of the early attempts to establish a permanent international criminal court to prosecute violators of international humanitarian law and international criminal law[2] placed the burden of implementing international criminal law (ICL) on national judicial systems. In the last 50 years, ICL has relied mainly on the indirect enforcement mechanism, where the primary duty rested on states to implement ICL in their domestic judicial systems.[3] However, the national enforcement of ICL has been generally criticized for its lack of consistency and failure to prosecute many violations of international criminal law. In the last 60 years, numerous factors have hindered the indirect enforcement system from delivering justice systematically and effectively. Domestic courts have had various political and legal reasons to refrain from prosecuting international crimes. For instance, the Bangladeshi attempts to prosecute Pakistani prisoners of war, after the war of independence, were aborted after the Pakistani–Bangladeshi agreement in 1973.[4] Several perpetrators were members of the ruling political elite, which made it difficult, if not impossible, for the local judiciary to prosecute them. It is difficult to imagine, in an authoritarian country (as was Pol Pot's Cambodia) the national courts prosecuting their own head of state. Often rulers provide themselves with permanent domestic immunities to prevent any possible prosecution, such as General Pinochet. Despite the aforementioned obstacles, the indirect enforcement

---

1 Ferencz, B. January 2000. Book Review of *The International Criminal Court: The Making of the Rome Statute – Issues, Negotiations, Results*, edited by R. Lee. *The American Journal of International Law*, 94, 218-221. Available at: www.benferencz.org/arts/38.html [accessed: 14 October 2008].

2 Robertson QC, G. August 2000. *Crimes against Humanity: The Struggle for Global Justice*. United Kingdom: Penguin, 326.

3 Bassiouni, M.Ch. (ed.). 1998. *International Criminal Law; Procedural and Enforcement Mechanism*. New York: Transnational Publishers, second edition, II, 5.

4 Bassiouni, M.Ch. 1992. *Crimes against Humanity*. Dordrecht/Boston/London: Martinus Nijhoff Publishers, 230.

system has witnessed key juridical moments when domestic trials prosecuted such figures as Eichmann,[5] Demanjuk,[6] Barbie,[7] Polyukhovich,[8] Priebke[9] and others.[10] However, these cases are few cases compared to the uncounted instances of impunity.

In principle, the international obligations of national judicial systems to prosecute international crimes arise from ratifying international conventions and treaties that impose such obligation to prosecute or extradite. Additionally, the obligation may rise from international customary laws imposing obligations on states to prosecute crimes that emerge as *jus cogens* in international law generating an *erga omnes* duty on all states belonging to the international community.[11] In state practice, the application of these duties has been far from uniform. Some states have refrained from adjudicating, while others have lacked national laws to implement international obligations. The French judicial system, for example, at one point lacked proper national laws to prosecute war crimes under 1949 Geneva Conventions.[12] In addition, some states have adopted implementing legislations that restrict the scope of obligation stipulated by treaties. The US Military Commissions Act amending the War Crimes Act of 1996 is one example.[13]

Under international customary law, states tend to refrain from initiating proceedings in the absence of a body of law, whether ratified international treaty or national implementation legislation. Genocide is now a *jus cogens* crime under customary international law.[14] However, the Swiss Appellate Military Tribunal

---

5   *Attorney General of Israel* v. *Eichmann*. 1961. District Court of Jerusalem, 36 ILR 18, 50.

6   *United States of America* v. *John Demjanjuk*. 2002. United States District Court Northern District of Ohio, Eastern Division, Case No. 1:99cv1193.

7   The Trial of Klaus Barbie. 11 May 1987. The Jewish Virtual Library. Available at: www.jewishvirtuallibrary.org/jsource/Holocaust/barbietrial.html [accessed: 15 September 2008].

8   *Polyukhovich* v. *The Commonwealth of Australia and Another*. 1991, 172 Commonwealth Law Reports 501 F.C. 91/026.

9   *Haas* and *Priebke* cases. 7 March 1998 to 16 November 1998. Military Court of Appeal of Rome, Supreme Court of Cassation, Italy.

10   McGoldrick, D., Rowe, P. and Donnelly, E. 2004. *The Permanent Criminal Court, Legal and Policy Issues*. Portland: Hart Publishing, 53.

11   Bassiouni, M.Ch. 1992. *Crimes Against Humanity*. Dordrecht/Boston/London: Martinus Nijhoff Publishers, 508.

12   Cassese, A. 2003. *International Criminal Law*. Oxford: Oxford University Press, 304.

13   Military Commissions Act of 2006. 17 October 2006. The United States, Pub. L. No. 109-366, 120 Stat. 2600.

14   Wise, E.M. 1998. Aut Dedare aut Judicare: The Duty to Prosecute or Extradite, in *International Criminal Law; Procedural and Enforcement Mechanism*, edited by M.Ch. Bassiouni. New York: Transnational Publishers, second edition, II, 29.

in the case of Niyonteze held that it could not apply the rules of the Genocide Convention of 1948, as Switzerland had not ratified the Convention.[15]

These shortages should not minimize the primary role of the indirect enforcement mechanism for enforcing international criminal law. ICL is expected to be enforced through national judicial systems. This holds for at least two reasons. First, no international court is independently capable of prosecuting and enforcing ICL against worldwide violations of humanitarian law and human rights. Second, in the current world order, basic principles of legality and sovereignty of the state act in favour of considering the indirect enforcement mechanism as the primary enforcing body of ICL on the national level.[16]

The post-Cold War era has witnessed an increase in the interest in suppressing violations of ICL – it is no coincidence that we witnessed two *ad hoc* Tribunals and a permanent international criminal court in one decade – and this has an impact at various national levels. The Rwandan courts have tried thousands since 1996 for their role in the atrocities of 1994.[17] Moreover, Belgian courts have also initiated prosecutorial steps against Rwandans involved in these massacres. In 1993, Bosnia, after the Dayton agreement, prosecuted and sentenced Sretko Damjanovic and Borislav Herak.[18] The famous case of Tadic has in fact started with the prosecution of Tadic by German courts.[19] These contradicting cases of accountability and impunity indicate that although certain improvements were noticed, systematic and effective global implementation of ICL on the national level remains incomplete.

The idea of establishing a permanent international criminal court for prosecuting violations of international humanitarian law and international criminal law is more than 75 years old.[20] The first attempt to establish a world criminal court dates back to 1937, when a draft statute for a court to try international terrorists was initiated by the League of Nations.[21] After the Second World War, the General Assembly requested that the International Law Commission (ILC) draft a statute

---

15   *Fulgence Niyontez* v. *Public Prosecutor*. 27 April 2001. Tribunal Militaire de Cassation, Switzerland.

16   Bassiouni, M.Ch. 1998. Policy Considerations on Inter-State Cooperation in Criminal Matters, in *International Criminal Law; Procedural and Enforcement Mechanism*, edited by M.Ch. Bassiouni. New York: Transnational Publishers, second edition, II, 3.

17   Schabas, W.A. 2002. The Rwanda Case, Sometimes Its Impossible, in *Post-Conflict Justice*, edited by M.Ch. Bassiouni and M. Ardsley. New York: Transnational Publishers, 499-522.

18   Judgement No. K-I-14/93. 12 March 1993. The District Military Court (Okruzni Vojni Sud), Sarajevo, BiH.

19   Schabas, W.A. 2003. National Courts Finally Begin to Prosecute Genocide, the Crime of Crimes. *Journal of International Criminal Justice*, 39-66, 53.

20   Sadat, L. and Carden, S.R. March 2000. The New International Criminal Court: An Uneasy Revolution. *Georgetown Law Journal*, 88, 381-474, 456.

21   Convention for the Creation of an International Criminal Court. 1936. League of Nations. Supp. No. 156(1936), LN Doc. C. 547(I). M.384(I). 1937. V(1937).

for an international criminal court, and to codify international crimes.[22] Working parallel to the ILC, the General Assembly established a Committee charged with drafting the Statute of an International Criminal Court. The Committee succeeded in submitting a draft statute in 1951,[23] which was subsequently amended in 1953.[24] The effort of the ILC and the Committee, however, did not materialize because of disagreement over the definition of the crime of aggression[25] – the result of the absence of the political will in a world sharply divided by the Cold War.[26]Although a definition of aggression was adopted in 1974, the ILC did not resume its work on the subject until the late 1980s.[27]

The political changes the world witnessed in the 1980s and 1990s opened the door for establishing a permanent criminal court. The end of the Cold War eliminated 40 years of global tension on the international level. This created relief in international relations in general, permitting an atmosphere that allowed progressive steps towards the establishment of the International Criminal Court.

In 1989, Trinidad and Tobago initiated a resolution in the General Assembly asking the ILC to expand its codification role to include drafting a statute for an international criminal court.[28] The end of the Cold War and the establishment of the two *ad hoc* Tribunals for Yugoslavia and Rwanda created both momentum and expectations for the establishment of a permanent international criminal court.

The International Law Commission submitted its Draft in 1994 to the General Assembly, which proceeded by adopting a resolution establishing the *Ad Hoc* Committee with mandate to review the draft.[29] The *Ad Hoc* Committee was succeeded by the Preparatory Committee in 1996. The General Assembly

---

22   Schabas, W. 2001. *An Introduction to the International Criminal Court*. Cambridge: Cambridge University Press, 8.

23   Report of the Committee on International Criminal Court Jurisdiction. 1952. UN Doc.. A/2135.

24   Williams, Sh.A. Summer 2000. The Rome Statute on the International Criminal Court: From 1947-2000 and Beyond. *Osgoode Hall Law Journal*, 38, 2, 297-330, 300.

25   Williams, Sh.A. Summer 2000. The Rome Statute on the International Criminal Court: From 1947-2000 and Beyond. *Osgoode Hall Law Journal*, 38, 2, 297-330, 300.

26   Cassese, A. 2003. *International Criminal Law*. Oxford: Oxford University Press, 334.

27   Williams, Sh.A. Summer 2000. The Rome Statute on the International Criminal Court: From 1947-2000 and Beyond. *Osgoode Hall Law Journal*, 38, 2, 297-330, 300.

28   Overview of the Rome Statute of the International Criminal Court, United Nations Treaty Collection. Available at: http://untreaty.un.org/cod/icc/general/overview.htm [accessed: 17 March 2009].

29   Boos, A. 2002. From the International Law Commission to the Rome Conference (1994-1998), in *The Rome Statute of the International Criminal Court: A Commentary*, edited by A. Cassese, P. Gaeta and J.R.W.D. Jones. Oxford: Oxford University Press, I, 36.

mandated the Preparatory Committee 'to discuss further major substantive and administrative issues arising from the ILC Draft'.[30]

In July 1998, the Rome Diplomatic Conference realized the aims of these efforts by establishing the International Criminal Court (ICC). The conference succeeded after five weeks of intensive negotiations among delegates and heavy lobbying by various non-governmental organizations (NGOs). The Rome Statute of the International Criminal Court was adopted in an emotional vote of 120 to seven, with 21 countries abstaining.[31] The Rome Statute established a permanent international criminal court complementing national judicial systems in exercising jurisdiction over international crimes. In the climax of jubilations at the final ceremony on 18 July, the president of the Drafting Committee asserted that '[t]he world will never be the same after the establishment of the International Criminal Court'.[32] This phrase warrants attention to the extent that the presence of the Court assists in a value-change towards a world order anchored to pursuing global justice and respecting human rights.[33] The Court's establishment will be a yardstick for a world court's effectiveness on ending impunity and prosecuting international crimes on the national and international level.

International Criminal Law: Lacking Effective Enforcement Mechanisms?

The enforcement of international criminal law on the national level has not been satisfactory as states have often either been unable or unwilling to apply the law.[34] Governments, on several occasions, have ignored violations of humanitarian law and human rights.[35] ICL has proven especially difficult to prosecute when governments themselves or high-ranking officials may be culpable. For many, ICL has been a law without an enforcement mechanism. The indirect enforcement system of ICL has been widely criticized for lack of enforcement, whether because

---

30   United Nations General Assembly Resolution 50/46. 11 December 1995. A/RES/50/46. Available at: www.un.org/documents/ga/res/50/a50r046.htm [accessed: 17 February 2009].

31   Sadat, L. and Carden, S.R. March 2000. The New International Criminal Court: An Uneasy Revolution. *Georgetown Law Journal*, 88, 381-474, 383.

32   Bassiouni Speech at The Rome Ceremony on 8 July 1998. Bassiouni, M.Ch. 1999. Symposium: Negotiating the Treaty of Rome on the Establishment of the International Criminal Court. *Cornell International Law Journal*, 443, 445.

33   Falk, R. 2006. Reshaping Justice: International Law and the Third World: An Introduction. *Third World Quarterly*, 27, 711-712, 711.

34   Lee, R. 1999. The Rome Conference and its Contribution to International Law, in *The International Criminal Court, The Making of The Rome Statute. Issues, Negotiations, Results*, edited by R. Lee. The Hague: Kluwer International, 1.

35   Broomhall, B. 2003. *International Justice and the International Criminal Court: Between Sovereignty and the Rule of Law*. Oxford: Oxford University Press, 1.

of lack of political will to adjudicate or due to the absence of the national legal framework to prosecute these crimes.

There are number of contentious issues which remain unresolved after seven years of the entrance of the Rome Statute into force. The complementarity system of the ICC in abstract can assist in the creation of an effective indirect enforcement system of international criminal law, however, the prosecutorial policy of the ICC does not seem to support this direction. Furthermore, the Prosecutor's interpretation of the complementarity principle mainly with respect to cases of inactions on the national level could lead to results that are inconsistent with the intention of the drafters of the Statute as stipulated in its Preamble. The admissibility of cases of inactions for 'able' and 'willing' states contradicts the role allocated to national systems as primary forums for prosecution. Moreover, where the complementarity principle can contribute to creating a positive cooperative system between states and the Court – which could positively affect the application of the Statute at the national level – it is still affected by the weak enforcement system of the ICC.

Based on the above, there is an urge to assess the short experience of application of the complementarity principle to determine the extent of which the ICC, in law or practice, can act as an effective 'checking body' vis-à-vis national judicial systems. This assessment will determine the extent to which the complementarity mechanism plays a decisive factor in encouraging states to consolidate their indirect enforcement system to preserve sovereignty from any court's intervention. It is of paramount importance for practitioners and academics to find an answer on whether the complementary principle in practice can induce national systems to initiate prosecutions of international crimes or not.

Outline

The book first explores the background and history of the principle of complementarity, seeking to answer the question of whether the principle of complementarity has any legal roots in international law or any customary status that binds states to respect it. The legal constituencies of the complementarity principle are discussed in Chapter 3, as this is crucial to analyse the scope of the admissibility mechanism. This work delves extensively into the legal components of the principle of complementarity and Article 17 of the Statute. Related articles, such as Article 20 and Article 53, are covered to the extent required for fully understanding the admissibility requirements. Chapter 3 also covers the application of Articles 17 and 53 in practice, including analysis of the prosecutorial policy in practice. Chapter 4 explores the hurdles that face the complementarity principle vis-à-vis national legal systems. The chapter focuses primarily on whether amnesties can be caught by the complementarity principle, asking whether Article 17 permits their escape. The chapter also addresses the question of whether pardons can render a case admissible before the ICC. The last section focuses on the Security Council's deferrals and their possible impact on indirectly blocking admissibility.

The complementarity principle is analysed practically through the selection of two case studies. Chapter 5 is dedicated to analyse the Ugandan referral, which has been chosen, as a case study, to allow the analysis of the complementarity principle in a state referral scenario. In this case study, this work first analyses the constituencies of the complementarity principle as applied by the Court, and then determines the extent to which the ICC's involvement could encourage the Ugandan national system to prosecute international crimes that are not prosecuted by the ICC. The level of cooperation between the ICC and the referring party is assessed in order to check its impact on a possible division of labour between the ICC and Uganda. In analysing the Ugandan referral, the ICC's experience with the DRC referral is taken into consideration, as both situations entail state referral. Comparison here serves to enrich discussion on the topic. The second case study is the Security Council's Darfur referral. This case study is significant because it permits us to observe the application of the complementarity principle under a Security Council referral. Here the study can examine how the complementarity principle could contribute to the indirect enforcement mechanism when the ICC is acting under the powers of Chapter VII of the UN Charter. The cooperation of Sudan, under Security Council Resolution 1593, is analysed to check if the Sudanese system has been encouraged to reform its judiciary and prosecute crimes that fall under the jurisdiction of the ICC. The conclusion is subsumed in Chapter 7.

Chapter 2

History and Legal Background of the Principle of Complementarity

As a relatively new concept, the principle of complementarity has attracted different stands regarding its origin, development and legal roots in international law, human rights law or international criminal law. The discussion on the nature of the jurisdictional relationship between the ICC and national systems continues to question the nature of complementarity, its impact on the national level, the limits of the relationship between complementarity and state sovereignty, and the extent to which complementarity could overcome states' interests and sovereignty to end impunity. For this purpose, this chapter will cover the history of complementarity, and then it will focus on complementarity in the Rome Statute before delving into the legal background of this principle.

History of the Principle of Complementarity

On 18 July 1998, the Rome Conference adopted the Rome Statute of the International Criminal Court.[1] 'It was the result of 75 years of hard work and false starts'.[2] No doubt, the establishment of the ICC is one of the most significant achievements in the path of development of international criminal law, humanitarian law and human rights. The International Criminal Court will be 'complementary to national jurisdictions'.[3] The Statute affirms that in Article 1, which stipulates:

> An International Criminal Court ('the Court') is hereby established. It shall be a permanent institution and shall have the power to exercise its jurisdiction over persons for the most serious crimes of international concern, as referred to this Statute, and shall be complimentary to national criminal jurisdiction.[4]

---

1   Broomhall, B. 2003. *International Justice and the International Criminal Court: Between Sovereignty and the Rule of Law*. Oxford: Oxford University Press, 1.

2   Sadat, L. and Carden, S.R. March 2000. The New International Criminal Court: An Uneasy Revolution. *Georgetown Law Journal*, 88, 381-474, 383.

3   Preamble of the Rome Statute of the International Criminal Court, UN Doc. A/CONF.183/9.

4   Article 1 of the Rome Statute of the International Criminal Court, UN Doc. A/CONF.183/9.

The first appearance of the principle of complementarity was in the International Law Commission Draft Statute of the International Criminal Court in 1994. The ILC included the principle of complementarity in the Preamble as a basic principle that organizes the jurisdictional relation between the ICC and national courts.[5] Initially, the complementarity principle in the ILC Draft was criticized for lacking a precise definition.[6] The ILC Draft provided that the ICC's jurisdiction would be complementary to the national criminal justice systems in cases 'where such trial procedures may not be available or may be ineffective'.[7] The criticism is well founded, as the 'ineffective' phrase seems subjective. It raised concerns and scepticism among many states. The issue remained pending, and was later addressed in the Preparatory Committee.

Linked to the preambular paragraph, Article 35 of the Draft Statute addressed the question of admissibility of the cases before the court:

> The Court may, on application by the accused or at the request of an interested state or anytime prior to the commencement of the trial, or of its own motion, decide, having regard to the purposes of this Statute set out in the Preamble, that a case before it is inadmissible on the ground that the crime in question (a) has been duly investigated by a state with jurisdiction over it, and the decision of that state not to proceed to a prosecution is apparently well founded; (b) is under investigation by a state which has or may have jurisdiction over it, and there is no reason for the Court to take any further action for the time being with respect to the crime; (c) is not of such gravity to justify further actions by the Court.[8]

The ILC adopted the ICC Draft and forwarded it to the General Assembly, recommending the convention of a conference of plenipotentiaries to study the Draft and to conclude a treaty on the establishment of an International Criminal Court.[9] The General Assembly adopted a resolution for establishing the *Ad Hoc* Committee for further substantive and administrative review of the ILC Draft

---

5 Preamble of The International Law Commission Draft Statute in Report of the ILC On The Work of Its Forty Sixth Session. 1994. UN GAOR, 49th Session, Supp. no. 10, A/49/10.

6 Brown, B.S. Summer 1998. Primacy or Complementarity: Reconciling the Jurisdiction of National Criminal Tribunals. *The Yale Journal of International Law*, 23, 2, 383-436, 417.

7 Preamble of The International Law Commission Draft Statute in Report of the ILC On The Work of Its Forty Sixth Session. 1994. UN GAOR, 49th Session, Supp. no. 10, A/49/10.

8 Article 35 of The International Law Commission Draft Statute in Report of the ILC On The Work of Its Forty Sixth Session (1994) UN GAOR, 49th Session, Supp. no. 10, A/49/10,

9 Boos, A. 2002. From the International Law Commission to the Rome Conference (1994-1998), in *The Rome Statute of the International Criminal Court: A Commentary*, edited by A. Cassese, P. Gaeta and J.R.W.D. Jones. Oxford: Oxford University Press, I, 36.

Statute.[10] The *Ad Hoc* Committee waited until August's session of 1995 to discuss the principle of complementarity extensively. The session was limited to the discussion of the principle of complementarity, and did not engage in negotiation or drafting.[11]

During the August session, there was a common recognition of the importance and sensitivity of the principle of complementarity, as it shapes and defines the relation of the ICC and its member states. It was stressed that the Court is not meant to replace the national jurisdiction.[12] Instead, the primacy of the national system was delineated. However, there was agreement that complementarity should be clearly defined.

Adrian Boos, the chairman of the *Ad Hoc* Committee, considered that the second session of the Committee's meeting succeeded in eliminating the suspicions of many delegates toward the Court's jurisdiction.[13]

The 'unavailable or ineffective' phrase was left to the Preparatory Committee (PrepComm) of 1996, which succeeded the *Ad Hoc* Committee. In the Preparatory Committee, the preliminary debate regarding the principle of complementarity showed that there was disagreement on the approach adopted.[14] The 'unavailability or ineffectiveness' of the national system continued to worry the delegates, and the term continued to be criticized for being too vague. Some considered that Article 35 violated state sovereignty, others considered it too narrow, and that it should cover cases being prosecuted or investigated. The outcome of that divergence was numerous states-proposals adopting different approaches.[15]

It was not before the August 1997 session that the principle of complementarity was addressed again. The aggregation of various proposals assisted to orient the discussion towards defining issues in complementarity. The discussion in the Preparatory Committee focused on the meaning of complementarity, its reflection in the Statute, and the connection of the principle to other Articles in the Statute.

---

10   Boos, A. 2002. From the International Law Commission to the Rome Conference (1994-1998), in *The Rome Statute of the International Criminal Court: A Commentary*, edited by A. Cassese, P. Gaeta and J.R.W.D. Jones. Oxford: Oxford University Press, I, 37.

11   Bassiouni, M.Ch. 1999. Symposium: Negotiating the Treaty of Rome on the Establishment of the International Criminal Court. *Cornell International Law Journal*, 443, 445.

12   Boos, A. 2002. From the International Law Commission to the Rome Conference (1994-1998), in *The Rome Statute of the International Criminal Court: A Commentary*, edited by A. Cassese, P. Gaeta and J.R.W.D. Jones. Oxford: Oxford University Press, I, 44.

13   Boos, A. 2002. From the International Law Commission to the Rome Conference (1994-1998), in *The Rome Statute of the International Criminal Court: A Commentary*, edited by A. Cassese, P. Gaeta and J.R.W.D. Jones. Oxford: Oxford University Press, I, 45.

14   Report of the Preparatory Committee. 1996. I, 36-41. Available at: www.un.org/law/icc [accessed: 14 October 2008].

15   Holmes, J. 1999. The Principle of Complementarity, in *The International Criminal Court: The Making of the Rome Statute, Issues, Negotiations, Results*, edited by R. Lee. The Hague: Kluwer, 1.

Two major proposals were circulated: one from the United States, and the other from Britain.[16] The British proposal emphasized that complementarity applies 'not only to national decisions to prosecute or not, or to conviction or acquittal, but also to decisions by national authorities to seek assistance, including extradition, from another state and decision by another state to cooperate accordingly, particularly when the state is under obligation to do so'.[17] In addition, suggestions were raised to include other Articles on inadmissibility, such as Article 42 on *ne bis in idem* in Article 35.[18]

John Holmes, who presided on the informal consultations on the issue of complementarity in the Rome Conference,[19] played a decisive role in bringing about an acceptable compromise. He conducted informal consultations, in which discussions were divided among a number of substantial issues, such as reference to jurisdiction, and the Court's course of action in the case of inability or unwillingness. The consultations brought a general agreement that the principle of complementarity should be reflected in the Preamble. In addition, it was widely agreed that the gravity of the case should be a determining factor of admissibility.[20]

The coordinator Holmes succeeded in producing a draft article on complementarity, which was clean in the sense that there were no brackets in the text. The draft article was later annotated with several provisos. Firstly, a text box was placed at the beginning of the article explaining its origin. Secondly, footnotes were added to explain the approach used to reach that drafted article. Thirdly, an alternative approach to the one mentioned previously was included.[21] During these consultations, the terms 'unwilling' or 'unable genuinely' were introduced for the first time.[22]

---

16   Boos, A. 2002. From the International Law Commission to the Rome Conference (1994-1998), in *The Rome Statute of the International Criminal Court: A Commentary*, edited by A. Cassese, P. Gaeta and J.R.W.D. Jones. Oxford: Oxford University Press, I, 50.

17   UK Discussion Paper on Complementarity. 29 March 1996. Available at: www.iccnow.org/documents/UKPaperComplementarity.pdf [accessed: 11 October 2008].

18   Report of the Preparatory Committee. 1996. Proceedings of the Preparatory Committee during March April and August 1996. General Assembly 51st Session, Supp. no. 22, A/51/22, 1996, I, 154.

19   Boos, A. 2002. From the International Law Commission to the Rome Conference (1994-1998), in *The Rome Statute of the International Criminal Court: A Commentary*, edited by A. Cassese, P. Gaeta and J.R.W.D. Jones. Oxford: Oxford University Press, I, 59.

20   Holmes, J. 1999. The Principle of Complementarity, in *The International Criminal Court: The Making of the Rome Statute, Issues, Negotiations, Results*, edited by R. Lee. The Hague: Kluwer, 46.

21   Holmes, J. 1999. The Principle of Complementarity, in *The International Criminal Court: The Making of the Rome Statute, Issues, Negotiations, Results*, edited by R. Lee. The Hague: Kluwer, 1.

22   El-Zeidy, M. Summer 2002. The Principle of Complementarity: A Machinery to Implement International Criminal Law. *Michigan Journal of International Law*, 23, 4, 869-978, 894.

With respect to 'inability', the issue of 'total or partial collapse' of the state national judicial system was a major concern. While the 'total collapse' did not need much elaboration, as it was understood as the inability of the national state to exercise effective control over its territories, the partial collapse needed further discussion. It was later agreed that a further definition of partial or total collapse is not needed, since the criterion of 'the state being unable to secure the accused or to obtain the necessary evidence and testimony' was added.[23] The negotiators requested that the two requirements be met for the national judicial system to be considered 'unable'. The result was the inclusion of the phrase 'or otherwise unable to carry out its proceedings'.[24]

As for 'effectively, ineffectively, good faith, and diligently', 'effectively or ineffectively' were rejected for their subjectivity. 'Good faith' seemed to be narrower than 'genuine', the term that the negotiators finally settled on.[25] The term 'genuinely' was attached to both paragraphs, that of 'unwilling' and 'unable'.

The task of defining unwillingness seemed very difficult. Many states did not want the ICC to function as a court of appeal. There was serious concern to minimize any subjective factor in the 'unwilling' criteria, in order to prevent any undesirable consequence. The 'apparently well-founded' phrase in the ILC draft was not acceptable.

As the term 'genuinely' was included, the negotiators agreed that 'unwillingness' would prohibit sham trials aimed at covering or shielding perpetrators and at hampering any process of prosecution on behalf of the Court.

A second criterion for determining 'unwillingness' was the delaying of national procedures with the goal of preventing the Court from exercising its jurisdiction. The delegates agreed on providing guidance for that, and they included 'undue delay' that is 'inconsistent with an intent to bring the person concerned to justice'.[26]

The last criterion was 'impartiality or independence'. Where this was an important development to address the rights of the defendant, many questions were raised in that regard.[27] What if the state is genuinely willing to prosecute, but there are some individuals who manipulate the conduct of the proceedings to

---

23   Holmes, J. 1999. The Principle of Complementarity, in *The International Criminal Court: The Making of the Rome Statute, Issues, Negotiations, Results*, edited by R. Lee. The Hague: Kluwer, 49.

24   Holmes, J. 1999. The Principle of Complementarity, in *The International Criminal Court: The Making of the Rome Statute, Issues, Negotiations, Results*, edited by R. Lee. The Hague: Kluwer, 49.

25   Holmes, J. 2002. Complementarity: National Courts versus the International Criminal Court, in *The Rome Statute of The International Criminal Court: A Commentary*, edited by A. Cassese, P. Gaeta and J.R.W.D. Jones. Oxford: Oxford University Press, I, 674.

26   The Preparatory Committee Decisions. Article 35(3). 1997.

27   The Preparatory Committee Decisions. Article 35(3). 1997.

disrupt the meeting of the 'impartiality' and 'independence' criterion? These were questions left with no answers.

By the end of the discussions of the PrepComm, Article 15 read as follow:

1 Having regard to paragraph 3 of the preamble, the Court shall determine that a case is inadmissible where (a) the case is being investigated or prosecuted by a state which has jurisdiction over it, unless the state is unwilling or unable genuinely to carry out the investigation or prosecution; (b) the case has been investigated by a state which has jurisdiction over it and the decided not to prosecute the person concern, unless the decision resulted from the unwillingness or inability of the state genuinely to prosecute; (c) the person concerned has already been tried for conduct which is the subject of the complaint, and a trial by the Court is not permitted under paragraph 2 of Article 18; (d) the case is not of sufficient gravity to justify further action.

2 In order to determine unwillingness in a particular case, the Court shall consider whether one or more of the following exist as applicable.
   (a) The proceedings were or are being undertaken or the national decision was made for the purpose of shielding the person concerned from criminal responsibility for crimes within the jurisdiction of the Court as set out in Article 5.
   (b) There has been an undue delay in the proceedings which in the circumstances is inconsistent with the intent to bring the person concerned to justice.
   (c) The proceedings were not or are not being conducted independently or partially and they were or are being conducted in a manner, which, in the circumstances, is inconsistent with an intent to bring the person to justice.

3 In order to determine the inability in a particular case, the Court shall consider, whether due to total or partial collapse or unavailability of its national judicial system, the State is unable to obtain the accused or otherwise unable to carry out its proceedings.[28]

The article states that the drafted text is the result of informal consultations on Article 15, and it is intended to facilitate the work on elaborating the Statute of the Court. It was followed by an alternative approach, which the draft included for further negotiations. This approach prohibits the Court from intervening when the national decision has been taken to prosecute or investigate, or has been prosecuted.[29]

---

28   Report of the Preparatory Committee on the Establishment of an International Criminal Court. 14 April 1998. A/conf.183/2/add1, 40-42.

29   Report of the Preparatory Committee on the Establishment of an International Criminal Court. 14 April 1998. A/conf.183/2/add1, 40-42.

The language of this agreed text was not changed in the Zetphen Inter-Sessional draft.[30] The meeting in Zetphen, the Netherlands on 19-30 January 1998 provided some structure and streamlining for the completion of the draft proposal.[31]

Complementarity in the Rome Conference

The negotiations at the Rome Conference built upon the Preparatory Committee's draft Statute.[32] The issue of complementarity was discussed in the Committee of the Whole (CW). The draft article, which was introduced by the Preparatory Committee, faced three main problems during the negotiations.

Firstly, some delegates criticized Article 15(2) for providing the Court with broad discretionary power in determining willingness.[33] States were worried that the determination of 'unwillingness' was still subjective, as the sub-provisions (a) and (b) were not sufficient to limit such discretion. The obstacle was circumvented by adding the phrase in accordance with the norms of 'due process recognized by international law'.[34] This phrase reassured some states, as it limited the freedom of the Court to the recognized standards in international law and human rights.

The second problem was the issue of 'partial collapse'. It was argued that partial collapse is not a sufficient criterion to determine inability. A partial collapse of the national judicial system could occur, and yet the state could still be able to enforce the law in other regions of the country.[35] This was a valid argument, as regional collapse of the state authority may not prevent the national judicial system from functioning in the rest of the country. There were two suggestions during the discussions; either eliminate 'partial', or substitute it with 'substantial'. There was broader support for the latter option. 'Partial' was replaced by 'substantial' in the final package.

---

30 Sadat, L. and Carden, S.R. March 2000. The New International Criminal Court: An Uneasy Revolution. *Georgetown Law Journal*, 88, 381-474, 396.

31 Bassiouni, M.Ch. 1999. Symposium: Negotiating the Treaty of Rome on the Establishment of the International Criminal Court. *Cornell International Law Journal*, 443, 445.

32 Sadat, L. and Carden, S.R. March 2000. The New International Criminal Court: An Uneasy Revolution. *Georgetown Law Journal*, 88, 381-474, 423.

33 Holmes, J. 1999. The Principle of Complementarity, in *The International Criminal Court: The Making of the Rome Statute, Issues, Negotiations, Results*, edited by R. Lee. The Hague: Kluwer, 53.

34 Article 17(2) of the Rome Statute of the International Criminal Court, UN Doc. A/CONF.183/9.

35 Holmes, J. 2002. Complementarity: National Courts versus the International Criminal Court, in *The Rome Statute of The International Criminal Court: A Commentary*, edited by A. Cassese, P. Gaeta and J.R.W.D. Jones. Oxford: Oxford University Press, I, 677.

The third obstacle was the vague phrase 'undue delay'. The term 'undue' raised concerns about its possible interpretation. There was an agreement to substitute it with 'unjustified' delay. Although still subjective, the latter term was supported by the states as it raised the threshold for the Court. It also gave the state an opportunity to provide explanation for any delay.[36]

Meanwhile, the Drafting Committee suggested the inclusion in part one of a reference to the principle of complementarity. It was considered that complementarity, as a fundamental principle in the Statute, should be restated there. That entailed a minor change in Article 17 to refer to Article 1. The three changes and the reference to Article 1 were finalized and incorporated in Article 17, which was adopted as a package at the end of the Rome Conference. The Article is pivotal in the relationship between the Court and national judicial systems.

However, Article 17 was adopted without sorting out other thorny issues, such as pardon, parole and amnesty in relation to complementarity. These are important aspects, which could undermine the complementarity principle of the Court.

Legal Background of the Principle of Complementarity

Complementarity and Not Primacy

The establishment of the two *ad hoc* Tribunals in the 1990s helped in building a momentum for the creation of the ICC. However, the International Criminal Tribunal for the former Yugoslavia (ICTY) and the International Criminal Tribunal for Rwanda (ICTR) enjoyed primacy over national courts according to Article 9 and 10 of their Statute respectively,[37] while the ICC is complementary to the national judicial systems. In analysing the ICC jurisdiction, a simple question arises; why did the primacy of the two *ad hoc* Tribunals not spread to the ICC?

There are numerous reasons that discarded the 'primacy' option for the ICC in favour of 'complementarity'. The primacy of the *ad hoc* Tribunals has been adopted in two exceptional situations that were a threat to world peace and security. Security Council members found that primacy was necessary for the *ad hoc* courts to be able to act swiftly in the Yugoslavian and Rwandan context. Within this context, the impartiality of the national judicial system was highly questionable.[38] In addition, the urgency of both situations required quick action,

---

36   Bassiouni, M.Ch. 1999. Symposium: Negotiating the Treaty of Rome on the Establishment of the International Criminal Court. *Cornell International Law Journal*, 443, 451.

37   See Security Council Resolution 827. S/Res/827 (1993); Security Council Resolution 955. S/Res/955 (1994).

38   Cassese, A. 2003. *International Criminal Law*. Oxford: Oxford University Press, 349.

which is why the Security Council granted primacy to the ICTY and the ICTR.[39] However, statements from permanent Security Council members show how weary and careful these states were in the process of providing restricted primacy to the ICTY.[40] Even with this primacy, Yugoslavia did not acknowledge the legitimacy of the establishment of the Tribunal.[41]

States accepted cautiously the primacy of the two *ad hoc* Tribunals with respect to two specific situations threatening the stability of regional and global order. Yet, they were highly reluctant to accept the existence of such a model on a permanent basis as that would constitute a threat to their sovereignty. This can explain the early dismissal of the idea of 'primacy' from the negotiations for the establishment of the ICC.[42] States saw the primacy of the *ad hoc* Tribunals as an exception to the rule.

One author considered that the decline in jurisdictional priority from 'primacy' in ICTY and ICTR to 'complementarity' in the ICC is an inevitable compromise in order to have a global criminal court acceptable by world states.[43] Complementarity came as a 'realist' option for a workable court in a world order that is still depending on the will of states as main constituencies of international order. The ICC as a treaty-based organization is the result of negotiations and compromises among state participants and the lobbying of various non-governmental organizations. Yet, at the end of the day, the success of the ICC will depend on the cooperation of the states. Hence, it was vital to reach an acceptable formula for the states so that the Court will have a viable opportunity to succeed in ending impunity and pushing for accountability for international crimes. A permanent court with primacy over national courts would not have been acceptable by the states. Complementarity is arguably the maximum the participants of Rome Conference were ready to accept.

While the establishment of an international criminal court has been a very important achievement, it is critical that its jurisdiction is acceptable to world states and societies, as their cooperation remain vital to the success of the ICC. This remains indispensable in an international world order that continues to rest

---

39   Brown, B.S. Summer 1998. Primacy or Complementarity: Reconciling the Jurisdiction of National Criminal Tribunals. *The Yale Journal of International Law*, 23, 2, 383-436, 387.

40   See Provisional Verbatim Record of The Three Thousand Two Hundred And Seventieth Meeting, UN Doc. S/Pv.3217. 1993.

41   Brown, B.S. Summer 1998. Primacy or Complementarity: Reconciling the Jurisdiction of National Criminal Tribunals. *The Yale Journal of International Law*, 23, 2, 383-436, 403.

42   El-Zeidy, M. Summer 2002. The Principle of Complementarity: A Machinery to Implement International Criminal Law. *Michigan Journal of International Law*, 23, 4, 869-978, 887.

43   Brown, B.S. Summer 1998. Primacy or Complementarity: Reconciling the Jurisdiction of National Criminal Tribunals. *The Yale Journal of International Law*, 23, 2, 383-436, 383.

on traditional principles, such as state sovereignty and non-interference in their domestic affairs.

Legal Roots of Complementarity

The complementarity regime is a cornerstone in the mechanism of the ICC.[44] The Rome Statute did not define the complementarity principle. The Preamble and Article 1 were limited to indicate that the Court shall be complementary to national criminal jurisdiction.[45]

The term 'complementarity' is unknown in legal systems.[46] Before its insertion in the International Law Commission Draft of 1994, the term was only used in the Maastricht Treaty, and had a different connotation.[47] Bassiouni, the vice chair of the *Ad Hoc* and the Preparatory Committees, indicated that the term 'complementarity' was a translation from the French term 'complementarite'.[48] Some writers explained complementarity as a word describing a situation 'in which two different things enhance each other to form a balanced whole'.[49]

The drafters of the Rome Statute aimed to establish a court that will supplement the national courts.[50] The *Ad Hoc* Committee of 1995 thought that this term could best describe the relationship between the Court and the national judicial systems. That does not need inspection or analysis, as the fifth paragraph of the Rome Statute Preamble is clear on the matter. It indicates that the state is the basic pillar in adjudicating international crimes.[51] That flows harmoniously with the legal tradition of international law; a law in which states are still the main subjects in

---

44   Holmes, J. 1999. The Principle of Complementarity, in *The International Criminal Court: The Making of the Rome Statute, Issues, Negotiations, Results*, edited by R. Lee. The Hague: Kluwer, 53.

45   Preamble and Article 1 of the Rome Statute of the International Criminal Court, UN Doc. A/CONF.183/9.

46   Boos, A. 2002. From the International Law Commission to the Rome Conference (1994-1998), in *The Rome Statute of the International Criminal Court: A Commentary*, edited by A. Cassese, P. Gaeta and J.R.W.D. Jones. Oxford: Oxford University Press, I, 44.

47   Dashwood, Alan et al. 2000. *European Union Law*. London: Sweet & Maxwell, fourth edition, 156.

48   Bassiouni, M.Ch. 1997. Observations Concerning the 1997-1998 Preparatory Committee Work. Nouvelles, 13, 25, *Denver Journal of International Law and Policy*.

49   Jensen, R. 12-30 August 2001. *Complementarity: the Principle of Complementarity in the Rome Statute of the International Criminal Court*. Submitted at the 15th International Conference of the International Society for the Reform of Criminal Law held at Canberra, Australia, 26-30 August 2001.

50   Brown, B. S. Summer 1998. Primacy or Complementarity: Reconciling the Jurisdiction of National Criminal Tribunals. *The Yale Journal of International Law*, 23, 2, 383-436, 389.

51   Preamble of the Rome Statute of the International Criminal Court, UN Doc. A/CONF.183/9.

forming its norms and implementing them. The Rome Statute came to subsume a language that maintains some traditional features of international law. The hope of an international body for international justice that could add a new dynamic for a changing world order was crafted in a language that rests on conservation of states' sovereignty and interests.

Complementarity seemed a pragmatic formula between realism and idealism: a realist approach favouring the conservation of states' sovereignty and an idealist one establishing an international body that transcends state boundaries to fight impunity. The establishment of the ICC can be seen as a positive step for a change towards a different world order based on respect for human rights and accountability. However, the ICC seems to be constrained by a Statute that was crafted on rigid grounds that respects the current state-system world order. The drafters reasoned that by respecting state sovereignty, and by claiming that the exercise of jurisdiction is related to the enforcement of the law by a coercive body through judicial, executive, administrative and police action, the state will always be the suitable context in which to adjudicate and prosecute on the national level. The former President of the Court, Philip Kirsch, and the Prosecutor of the Court have affirmed this reasoning on a number of occasions.[52]

Simultaneously, in this complex relationship of complementarity the Court is the arbiter of its own jurisdiction.[53] The Court, restricted by the Articles of the Statute, has to be satisfied that it has jurisdiction in any case. The complementarity regime thus acts like a check-and-balance system between the Court and the national systems.

Hence, the complementarity regime came to respect the role of the indirect enforcement system as a primary enforcement mechanism of ICL at the national level. The complementarity system supplements the national system in prosecuting and punishing international crimes.[54] The ICC mechanism rotates around the idea that the national system plays the primary role in adjudicating international crimes, while the ICC jurisdiction prevails when national systems waive their

---

52   The International Criminal Court, Office of the Prosecutor. 2003. *Paper on Some Policy Issues before the Office of the Prosecutor*. ICC-OTP 2003, 1-9, 4. Available at: www.icc-cpi.int/library/organs/otp/030905_Policy_Paper.pdf [accessed: 22 February 2008]. See also President Philippe Kirsch speech to the United Nations General Assembly; Kirsch, Philippe. 9 October 2006. Address to the United Nations General Assembly, 1-5, 5. Available at: www.icc-cpi.int/library/organs/presidency/PK_20061009_en.pdf [accessed: 13 June 2008].

53   Holmes, J. 2002. Complementarity: National Courts versus the International Criminal Court, in *The Rome Statute of The International Criminal Court: A Commentary*, edited by A. Cassese, P. Gaeta and J.R.W.D. Jones. Oxford: Oxford University Press, I, 677.

54   El-Zeidy, M. Summer 2002. The Principle of Complementarity: A Machinery to Implement International Criminal Law. *Michigan Journal of International Law*, 23, 4, 869-978, 896.

own jurisdiction, whether out of their own [un]will or out of their inability to prosecute.[55]

In terms of nature, complementarity is considered a jurisdictional concept, rather than a normative one.[56] That indicates a relationship among various jurisdictional authorities over ICL violations. Complementarity, as a jurisdictional concept, comes to organize any concurrent jurisdiction among these different jurisdictional authorities.[57] It also aims to fill in and prevent gaps of impunity in the enforcement system of the ICL. This is materialized in the treaty-based relationship between the ICC and the member states. Yet, it is hard to speculate in the absence of a binding treaty, how a principle, lacking a firm legal basis, can be invoked between various jurisdictional authorities, here the ICC and non-state parties.

In terms of its legal roots, complementarity has no explicit roots in previous legal instruments in international criminal law. Some writers and jurists consider that its legal basis rests on the maxim *aut dedere aut judicare* (extradite or adjudicate), while others consider that it has similarities with the 'subsidiarity' principle in European law.

To one author, the principle of complementarity has its legal basis in the maxim *aut dedere aut judicare*.[58] He argues that the principle *aut dedere aut judicare* is 'implicitly' in the Preamble and in Articles 1, 12, 15, 17 and 18 of the Rome Statute.[59] Others consider that the complementarity principle has some similarities with the 'subsidiarity' principle, which exists in European Union law.[60] Some writers considered that the subsidiarity principle also has a structural base in human rights law.[61]

In EU law, 'subsidiarity' can be found in the Maastricht Treaty of 1992, where it indicates that 'the functions handed over to the community are those which the member states at the various levels of decision-making can no longer discharge satisfactorily'.[62] The subsidiarity principle is not rigid; it implies that there are

---

55   Smith, A. Summer 2004. Book Review: *From Nuremberg to The Hague: The Future of International Criminal Justice. Harvard International Law Journal*, 563.

56   Bassiouni, M.Ch. 2003. *Introduction to International Criminal Law*. New York: Transnational Publishers, 16.

57   Bassiouni, M.Ch. 2003. *Introduction to International Criminal Law*. New York: Transnational Publishers, 16.

58   Knoops, G.J.A. 2002. *Surrendering To International Criminal Courts: Contemporary Practice and Procedure*. New York: Transnational Publishers, 314.

59   Bassiouni, M.Ch. 2003. *Introduction to International Criminal Law*. New York: Transnational Publishers, 314.

60   Dashwood, A. et al. 2000. *European Union Law*. London: Sweet & Maxwell. Fourth edition, 156.

61   Carozza, P. January 2003. Subsidiarity as a Structural Principle of International Human Rights Law. *The American Journal of International Law*, 97, 1, 38-79, 38.

62   The Principle of Subsidiarity: Communication of The Commission to the Council and European Parliament, SEC (92) 1990 Final Act. Lasok, K.P.E. 2001. *Laws and Institutions of the European Union*. London: Butterworths, 50.

values and rights that states sometimes cannot provide for their citizens, and thus they should avoid these areas, leaving it for the individuals or the community (in the case of the European context) to achieve.[63] The principle rests on the inherent rights of the individual based on human dignity. It recognizes the precedence of human dignity over state sovereignty. Some critics consider that subsidiarity is in opposition to the concept of sovereignty.[64] If the ICC's complementarity rests on this principle, then the ICC's practice could evolve in the direction of prioritizing human dignity over state sovereignty.

The origin of subsidiarity can also be tracked to the philosophy of Aristotle, where it is embedded in his political theory.[65] In Aristotle's vision of the state, the latter serves as a provider for the most favourable conditions for the flourishing of the 'human personality'. Additionally, individual autonomy is to be maximized so long as it conforms to life in a civil society. Aristotle implicitly endorsed the idea of a minimalist state that leaves space for human development through the preservation of self-autonomy.[66] Catholic Christianity elaborated the idea. Thomas Aquinas incorporated Aristotelian reasoning into his notion of Christian faith.[67] This theological incorporation, on the one hand, envisioned the state as part of God's design, while on the other hand, limited its rule to preserve human development.[68] Johannes Althusius developed the principle of subsidiarity in correlation with the idea of a (post-Westphalian) secular state. Subsidiarity also has traces in writings of Montesquieu, Locke, Tocqueville, Lincoln and Proudhon.[69] The 1931 Encyclical Quadragesimo Anno of Pius XII raised the principle of subsidiarity as a protective principle for individuals against of the increased power of the corporate state (especially the communist type).[70] Until that time, the roots of subsidiarity did not seem to rest on a legal base, but rather on a combination of religious

---

63   Carozza, P. January 2003. Subsidiarity as a Structural Principle of International Human Rights Law. *The American Journal of International Law*, 97, 1, 38-79, 39.

64   Endo, K. 2001. *Subsidiarity and its Enemies: To What Extent is Sovereignty Contested in the Mixed Commonwealth of Europe?*, EU Working Paper No. RSC 2001. Available at: http://netec.mcc.ac.uk/WoPEc/data/Papers/erpeuirscp0051.html [accessed: 14 January 2009].

65   Beale, A. and Geary, R. January 1994. Subsidiarity Come of Age? *New Law Journal*, 144, 12-15, 12.

66   Beale, A. and Geary, R. January 1994. Subsidiarity Come of Age? *New Law Journal*, 144, 12-15, 12.

67   Carozza, P. January 2003. Subsidiarity as a Structural Principle of International Human Rights Law. *The American Journal of International Law*, 97, 1, 38-79, 41.

68   Beale, A. and Geary, R. January 1994. Subsidiarity Come of Age? *New Law Journal*, 144, 12-15, 13.

69   Carozza, P. January 2003. Subsidiarity as a Structural Principle of International Human Rights Law. *The American Journal of International Law*, 97, 1, 38-79, 41.

70   Lasok, D. 1992. Subsidiarity and the Occupied Field. *New Law Journal*, 1228, 1228.

and philosophical doctrine.[71] Moreover, for some writers, subsidiarity was neither theological nor philosophical, but a piece of concealed historical wisdom[72] emphasizing the common good of the community. Yet, subsidiarity, which evolved initially as a political and social value, has been transformed into a legal concept.

After the Second World War, former totalitarian European states invoked the idea of providing adequate necessary opportunities for citizens to pursue their own life plans, without state interference.[73] The principle percolated from the political and theological realms into the legal field through sources like European Union law and human rights law.

In the 1970s and 1980s, discussion about the development of the European Community towards a more coherent political unit facilitated the emergence of the principle of subsidiarity within the context of European law. It arose here as a possible compromise since many states were concerned about the impact that developing a more unified European Community might have on their sovereignties.

The principle appeared in Council of Europe's resolutions in the 1970s and 1980s.[74] By 1991, the European Commission's president Jacque Delors spoke of subsidiarity as a vital principle that stemmed out of respect for human dignity.[75] The expansion of the Community following the Single European Act in 1987 led to the appearance of the principle in European law and its subsequent inclusion in the Maastricht Treaty.[76] The Treaty contained a number of Articles related to the principle of subsidiarity, but Article 3b articulates its legal frame best. The Article indicates that, 'The Community shall take action, in accordance with the principle of subsidiarity, only if and in so far as the objectives of the proposed action cannot be sufficiently achieved by the member states and can therefore ... be better achieved by the Community'.[77] The Charter of Fundamental Rights of

---

71   Lasok, K.P.E. 2001. *Laws and Institutions of the European Union*. London: Butterworths, 48.

72   Czaretzky, J.M. and Rychlack, R.J. December 2003. An Empire or Law? Legalism and the International Criminal Court. *Notre Dame Law Review*, 79, 55-126, 75.

73   Beale, A. and Geary, R. January 1994. Subsidiarity Come of Age? *New Law Journal*, 144, 12-15, 13.

74   Policy and Operation Department of the Dutch Ministry of Foreign Affairs. *The Definitions of Complementarity and their Evolution*, Working Document. Available at: www.euforic.org/iob/publ/workdocs/complimentarity_3.html [accessed: 10 February 2009].

75   Beale, A. and Geary, R. January 1994. Subsidiarity Come of Age? *New Law Journal*, 144, 12-15, 13.

76   Estella, A. 2002. *The EU Principle of Subsidiarity and Its Critique*. Oxford: Oxford University Press, 82-89.

77   See Article 3b, under Title II. Available from http://europa.eu.int/en/record/mt/title2.html [accessed: 11 February 2009].

the European Union, adopted in 2000, also invoked the principle of subsidiarity to balance the relationship between European supra-nationalism and local identity.[78]

The insertion of subsidiarity into the EU treaty aimed at preserving two main concepts: integration and diversity.[79] The principle of subsidiarity comes from history as a political and theological concept that has been transformed into a legal one in the EU legal instruments.

Like complementarity, subsidiarity has more of a jurisdictional character than a normative one. It delineates the authority of the nation, the individual and the community, approximating the typology of complementarity of the ICC as Bassiouni described previously.[80]

The inclusion of the subsidiarity principle in Maastricht realized the theoretical notion as a legal principle, justifiable before the European Court of Justice (ECJ).[81] Although the ECJ has not thus far applied the principle in exercising its jurisdiction,[82] we can still notice the principle implemented tacitly in ECJ case law on fundamental rights. That was through judicially reviewing member states' acts of alleged violations of the Community fundamental rights.[83]

While functioning to delineate jurisdiction, writers such as Paolo Carozza also argue that subsidiarity is a structural principle in international human rights law.[84] Carozza builds his argument on similar historical bases as those locating subsidiarity within the European legal order. The language of the Universal Declaration of Human Rights bypasses inter-state relations to address the 'people' of the world, hence penetrating borders and sovereignties to grant the 'individual' inalienable rights that stem from human dignity and humanity.

Contra those supporting subsidiarity, Martti Koskenniemi considers it a challenge to sovereignty because its foundations are based on a vision of a social life of humanity and common good directed towards the dignity of the social

78   Carozza, P. January 2003. Subsidiarity as a Structural Principle of International Human Rights Law. *The American Journal of International Law*, 97, 1, 38-79, 53.

79   Syrpis, P. June 2004. In Defence of Subsidiarity. *Oxford Journal of Legal Studies*, 24, 323, 324.

80   Bassiouni, M.Ch. 2003. *Introduction to International Criminal Law*. New York: Transnational Publishers, 16.

81   Beale, A. and Geary, R. January 1994. Subsidiarity Come of Age? *New Law Journal*, 144, 12-15, 15.

82   Carozza, P. January 2003. Subsidiarity as a Structural Principle of International Human Rights Law. *The American Journal of International Law*, 97, 1, 38-79, 55.

83   *Hellmut Marshall* v. *Land Nordrhein-Westfalen*. 11 November 1997. European Court of Justice, Case C-409/95. See also, *E. Kalanke* v. *Freie Hansestadt Bremen*. 11 October 1995. European Court of Justice, Case C-450/93 E.C.R. I-3051. See also, Carozza, P. January 2003. Subsidiarity as a Structural Principle of International Human Rights Law. *The American Journal of International Law*, 97, 1, 38-79, 55.

84   Carozza, P. January 2003. Subsidiarity as a Structural Principle of International Human Rights Law. *The American Journal of International Law*, 97, 1, 38-79.

human being, and towards overriding man-made concepts of political order, including especially sovereignty.[85]

The above analysis highlights a number of similarities, which the principle of subsidiarity shares with the complementarity of the ICC. Firstly, both principles function when states are not able to provide certain rights or protection for their citizens. Secondly, these rights stem from human dignity and humanity (ultimate values of human rights and humanitarian law). One can cite the Martens Clause in the Hague Convention of 1899 in that regard.[86] Thirdly, both principles endorse the priority of human dignity over sovereignty. It gives human beings precedence over any political or legal concept that might potentially obstruct or violate their human rights (such as sovereignty).

On the other hand, one can also explore to what extent complementarity could have grounds in the maxim *aut dedere aut judicare* (extradite or prosecute). The maxim *aut dedere aut judicare* is a modern adoption of the Grotian concept meaning to either extradite or punish.[87] It indicates that a state should either prosecute or extradite to another state, if the latter state is willing to prosecute international crimes.

Historically, there has been no consensus among legal scholars as to whether *aut dedere aut judicare* imposes a legal customary duty upon states. Grotius, Heineccius, Burlmaqui, Vattel, Rutherforth, Schmelzing and Kent endorse the existence of a duty to extradite, while others, such as Pufendorf, Voet, Martens, Kluber, Leyser, Kluit, Saalfeld, Schmaltz, Mittermayer and Heffler, consider it an 'imperfect obligation', incomplete without a binding treaty.[88]

The duty has evolved to the point whereby international law, in the last century, has come to recognize *aut dedere aut judicare* as customary. However, there is still no agreement on whether this crystallization is for all international crimes or only for certain more serious ones. A general distinction separates a narrow from a broad approach. The narrow approach considers the duty to extradite or prosecute solely of a customary nature, applicable to crimes defined by treaties. The broad approach (endorsed by Bassiouni), indicates that the maxim applies to international crimes in their entirety.[89] Bassiouni invokes Christian Wolff's *civitas maxima* to demonstrate the existence of a society of states who have a shared

---

85   Koskenniemi, M. 1991. The Future of Statehood. *Harvard International Law Journal*, 32, 397-410, 397.

86   Preamble of Convention With Respect To the Laws and Customs of War on Land. 29 July 1899. Hague, II. In Avalon Project, Yale University. Available at: www.yale.edu/lawweb/avalon/lawofwar/hague02.htm [accessed: 10 March 2008].

87   Grotius, H. 1624. *De Jure belli Ac Pacis*. Book 2, ch. XXI. Sections 3, 4, 5(1) and 5(3).

88   Wheaton, H. 1866. *Elements of International Law*. London: R.H. Dana, eighth edition, 181.

89   Knoops, G.J.A. 2002. *Surrendering To International Criminal Courts: Contemporary Practice and Procedure*. New York: Transnational Publishers, 22.

interest in fighting all crimes.[90] This echoes ideas on which Grotius based the maxim *aut dedere aut punire.*

State practice with respect to *aut dedere aut judicare* has been inconsistent. Until recently, it was difficult to infer a general practice,[91] because judicial systems in many countries are reluctant to apply a duty to extradite in the absence of a treaty. In certain cases, national courts have not applied the maxim even for ratified treaties due to a lack of national implementation of these treaties. For the cases of *Nulyarimma* v. *Thompsonthe*[92] *and Buzzacott* v. *Hill,*[93] both held before the Federal Court in Australia in 1999, the court refrained from applying the Genocide Convention, contending that there is no legislative act in the domestic law for the Convention's application.[94] In the *Qaddafi case,* the Paris Court of Appeal cited the duty to prosecute for international crimes. Yet, the Court of Cassation overruled that decision, stating that international customary law prohibits the exercise of criminal jurisdiction over foreign heads of state in office.[95]

However, the customary nature of this maxim emerges from the numerous ratified treaties subsuming it, confirmed by *opinion juris.* The duty to extradite or prosecute is accepted for certain serious international crimes only.[96] *Aut dedere aut judicare* imposes a duty towards certain international crimes of a *jus cogens* character, and not all international crimes.[97]

The duty to prosecute or extradite is found in a large number of treaties and conventions. The first treaty imposing such an obligation is the Convention for the Suppression of Counterfeiting of 1929.[98] In addition, the Convention on the

90   Knoops, G.J.A. 2002. *Surrendering To International Criminal Courts: Contemporary Practice and Procedure.* New York: Transnational Publishers, 29.

91   Kelly, M. Fall 2003. Cheating Justice by Cheating Death, the Doctrinal Collision for Prosecuting Foreign Terrorist – Passage of Aut Dedere Aut Judicare into Customary International Law and Refusal to Extradite on the Death Penalty. *Arizona Journal of International and Comparative Law,* 20, 491-532, 495.

92   *Nulyarimma* v. *Thompson.* 1 September 1999. Federal Court of Australia, FCA 1192.

93   *Buzzacott* v. *Hill, Minister for the Environment and others.* 1999. The Federal Court of Australia, FCA 639.

94   Cassese, A. 2003. *International Criminal Law.* Oxford: Oxford University Press, 304.

95   *Arrêt of the Cour de Cassation,* No. 1414. 13 March 2001. Cour de Cassation, France. See also, Zappalà, S. 2001. Do Heads of State in Office Enjoy Immunity from Jurisdiction for International Crimes? The Ghaddafi Case Before the French Cour de Cassation. *European Journal of International Law,* 12, 3, 595-612, 607.

96   Knoops, G.J.A. 2002. *Surrendering To International Criminal Courts: Contemporary Practice and Procedure.* New York: Transnational Publishers, 49.

97   Knoops, G.J.A. 2002. *Surrendering To International Criminal Courts: Contemporary Practice and Procedure.* New York: Transnational Publishers, 313.

98   Wise, E.D. 1998. Aut Dedare aut Judicare: The Duty to Prosecute or Extradite, in *International Criminal Law; Procedural and Enforcement Mechanism,* edited by M.Ch.

Illicit Traffic in Dangerous Drugs of 1936, the Convention on Terrorism of 1937, the Convention on Traffic in Persons (white slavery) of 1950, include prosecution or extradition of these crimes.[99] All of these stipulate that a state that refrains from extraditing should prosecute before its national courts. The common Article 4 of the Geneva Conventions of 1949 imposes an alternative duty on high contracting states to search for persons who committed 'grave breaches' and bring such persons before their courts or otherwise hand them over for trial by another state party that has made a *prima facie* case. Variations with the same spirit can be found in conventions related to terrorism and combating terrorism,[100] such as The Hague Convention for The Suppression of Unlawful Seizure of Aircrafts of 1970;[101] the single Convention on psychotropic substances of 1971; and the Montreal Convention on Unlawful Acts Against the Safety of Civil Aviation in 1971. In fact, the 1970 Hague Convention for The Suppression of Unlawful Seizure of Aircrafts' language on *aut dedere aut judicare* (Article 7) was adopted as a model for later treaties, including other treaties relating to terrorism. In addition, the principle is included in other treaties and conventions, with some variations: the New York Convention on Crimes against Protected Persons of 1973;[102] the Hostage Convention of 1979;[103] the Convention on the Physical Protection of Nuclear Material of 1980;[104] the Torture Convention of 1984;[105] the Rome Convention of The Safety of Maritime Navigation of 1988;[106] and the Mercenaries Convention of 1989.[107] Regional Instruments include similar or modified version of *aut dedere*

Bassiouni. New York: Transnational Publishers, second edition, II, 17.

99   Wise, E.D. 1998. Aut Dedare aut Judicare: The Duty to Prosecute or Extradite, in *International Criminal Law; Procedural and Enforcement Mechanism*, edited by M.Ch. Bassiouni. New York: Transnational Publishers, second edition, 18.

100   Knoops, G.J.A. 2002. *Surrendering To International Criminal Courts: Contemporary Practice and Procedure*. New York: Transnational Publishers, 314.

101   Convention for the Suppression of Unlawful Seizure of Aircraft (1971) Dec. 16, 1970, 860 U.N.T.S 105, 10 I.L.M. 133.

102   Convention on the Prevention and Punishment of Crimes against Protected Persons Including Diplomatic Agents. 14 December 1973. General Assembly Resolution 3166 (XXVIII). Available at: http://untreaty.un.org/English/Terrorism/Conv4.pdf [accessed: 23 April 2009].

103   International Convention against Taking Hostages. 17 December 1979. GA Resolution 34/1146, UN. GAOR.

104   International Atomic Energy Agency Convention on the Physical Protection of Nuclear Material. 1980. IAEA. Legal Series no. 12. 1982.

105   Convention against Torture and Other Cruel, Inhuman or Degrading Treatment Or Punishment. 17 December 1984. GA Resolution 39/46, 39 GAOR. UN Doc. A/39/51. 1984.

106   International Maritime Organization Convention for the Suppression of Unlawful Acts Against The Safety of Maritime Navigation. 10 March 1988. Doc SUA/con/15, 27 ILM. 672/1988.

107   International Convention against the Recruitment, Use, Financing and Training of Mercenaries. GA Resolution 44/34 adopted Dec. 1989. UN Doc. A/Res/44/34. 11

aut judicare, such as the European and American conventions on issues like terrorism and torture.[108]

The problem in these treaties is that although all of them include the maxim *aut dedere aut judicare*, there is considerable difference in the language adopted.[109] It is unclear whether the maxim *aut dedere aut judicare* prioritizes extradition or prosecution.[110] The difference is not only technical, but includes variations in determining what obligation takes precedence. Some conventions include a legal language that binds state parties to cooperate; take measures to suppress prohibited conduct; take necessary measures for implementing the treaty content in national laws; adopt measures for prohibiting the crime; impose penalties or administrative sanctions; enact legislation necessary for ensuring that penalties are being implemented; take all measures to investigate, prosecute and punish offenders; make prohibited conduct subject to legal proceedings; submit the case to competent authorities to prosecute; or bring offenders before the courts.[111] While the language used in these instruments suggests an overlapping meaning, it is not possible to infer a clear meaning from the numerous international conventions. Since 1970, the language of the Hague Convention on Unlawful Seizure of Aircrafts has been recycled in a number of subsequent conventions. The structure of obligations in the 1970 convention has been replicated in a number of subsequent agreements, such as the Montreal Convention on Unlawful Acts Against Safety of Civil Aviation of 1971,[112] the New York Convention on Crimes against Internationally Protected Persons of 1972,[113] the Hostage Convention of 1979, and others.[114]

Variations in the languages of these conventions spread to the maxim *aut dedere aut judicare*. Bassiouni and Edward Wise discuss three categories. Firstly, a category which provides for local prosecution if the state denies extradition. Here extradition is ordered first, and if states refuse to extradite, then they are

---

December 1989. ILM. 672. 1988.

108   Wise, E.D. 1998. Aut Dedare aut Judicare: The Duty to Prosecute or Extradite, in *International Criminal Law; Procedural and Enforcement Mechanism*, edited by M.Ch. Bassiouni. New York: Transnational Publishers, second edition, 19.

109   Bassiouni, M.Ch. and Wise, E. 1995. *Aut Dedere Aut Judicare, the Duty to Extradite or Prosecute in International Law*. Dordrecht: Martinus Nijhoff Publishers, 8.

110   Bassiouni, M.Ch. 1992. *Crimes against Humanity*. Dordrecht/Boston/London: Martinus Nijhoff Publishers, 501.

111   Knoops, G.J.A. 2002. *Surrendering To International Criminal Courts: Contemporary Practice and Procedure*. New York: Transnational Publishers, 9.

112   Convention for the Suppression of Unlawful Acts Against Safety of Civil Aviation. 23 September 1971, 974 U.N.T.S. 177, 10 I.L.M. 1151(1971).

113   Convention On The Prevention And Punishment of Crimes Against Internationally Protected Persons, Including Diplomatic Agents. 14 December 1973. 1035 U.N.T.S 167, 13 I.L.M. 1456 (1974).

114   International Convention against the Taking of Hostages. 17 December 1979. G.A. Res. 34/146, U.N. G.A.O.R. Supp. (no. 46), at 245, UN Doc. A/34/46 (1980), 18 I.L.M. 1419 (1979).

obliged to prosecute cases themselves. The European Convention on Extradition 1957 is an example. The 1929 Counterfeiting Convention additionally indicates that the obligation to take proceedings is subject to rejection of the request of extradition, and thus the country to which the request has been made should initiate proceedings.

The 1970 Hague Convention formula is the precedent for the second group. Treaties using this formula stipulate an obligation to extradite or prosecute. They indicate that national jurisdiction has to exercise that jurisdiction if extradition is not granted. Therefore, extradition is prioritized. If extradition is denied for other valid reasons, the national authorities are under obligation to prosecute. This formula has been repeated in various subsequent treaties replicating The Hague Convention model, mentioned earlier.[115]

The last category is constituted by treaties that incorporate an obligation to either prosecute or extradite. This obligation is embodied in the Geneva Conventions of 1949.[116] There is no preference indicated between prosecution or extradition. The language used stipulates that high contracting parties shall bring persons alleged to have committed 'grave breaches' of the Convention before their national courts or, if they prefer, in accordance with their national laws, hand them to another concerned high contracting party.[117] The language used gives the member states discretion to decide whether to prosecute or extradite, taking into consideration national preference and law.

---

115   Convention on the Prevention and Punishment of Crimes against Protected Persons Including Diplomatic Agents. 14 December 1973 General Assembly Resolution 3166 (XXVIII). Available at: http://untreaty.un.org/English/Terrorism/Conv4.pdf [accessed: 23 April 2009]. International Convention against Taking Hostages. 17 December 1979. GA Resolution 34/1146, UN. GAOR. International Atomic Energy Agency Convention on the Physical Protection of Nuclear Material. 1980. IAEA. Legal Series no. 12 (1982). Convention against Torture and Other Cruel, Inhuman or Degrading Treatment Or Punishment. 17 December 1984. GA Resolution 39/46, 39 GAOR. UN Doc. A/39/51. 1984. International Maritime Organization Convention for the Suppression of Unlawful Acts Against The Safety of Maritime Navigation. 10 March 1988. Doc SUA/con/15, 27 ILM. 672/1988. International Convention against the Recruitment, Use, Financing and Training of Mercenaries. GA Resolution 44/34 adopted Dec. 1989. UN Doc. A/Res/44/34. 11 December 1989. ILM. 672. 1988.

116   Knoops, G.J.A. 2002. *Surrendering To International Criminal Courts: Contemporary Practice and Procedure*. New York: Transnational Publishers, 11-15.

117   See Article 49 of the Convention For The Amelioration of The Condition of The Wounded And Sick In The Armed Forces, 12 August 1949, 75 U.N.T.S. 31, 62; Article 50, Convention For The Amelioration of The Condition of The Wounded, Sick, And Shipwrecked Members of The Armed Forces At Sea, 12 August 1949, 75 U.N.T.S. 85, 116; Article 129, Convention Relative To The Treatment of The Prisoners of War, 12 August 1949, 75 U.N.T.S. 135, 236; Convention Relative To The Protection of Civilian Persons In Time of War, 12 August 1949, 75 U.N.T.S. 287, 386; Article 85 of Protocol I Additional To The Geneva Conventions of 12 August 1949, And Relating To Protection of Victims of Armed Conflict, 10 June 1977, 16 I.L.M. 1391(1977).

The legal roots of the complementarity principle could be traced to this model of *aut dedere aut judicare*. There are definite similarities. Firstly, in both concepts it is up to the national state to decide explicitly or implicitly whether to prosecute or extradite. In the Geneva Conventions model, it is clear that the state's action is decisive, while in the complementarity principle, the national state's 'unwillingness' or 'inability' also may warrant the Court's jurisdiction. While 'unwillingness' or 'inability' is officially for the ICC to assess, the state's implicit or explicit decisions and behaviour ultimately render the case admissible before the Court. While this point is clear with respect to 'unwillingness', it is vague in terms of 'inability'. Unwillingness is a voluntary decision on behalf of the state, whereby the state refuses to prosecute. When such a scenario materializes, the state is obligated to extradite (surrender) to the Court. In cases of inability, the volition of the state may not be at stake, but, all the same, the 'inability' of the judicial system to prosecute leaves the state obligated to surrender (extradite) to the Court. This is confirmed in Article 90 of the Statute, which stipulates that if the member state does not prosecute, then it is under obligation to surrender to the Court.[118] In case of concurrent requests between surrender to the Court and extradition to another state, the priority is to the Court's request, unless the member state is under previous international obligations (Articles 90(2) and 90(4)). The aim of the principle of complementarity is primarily the prosecution of core international crimes by the national judicial system, and if not, then through surrender to the ICC. It is important to note that vis-à-vis legal nature, extradition and surrender are similar.[119] The term 'surrender' is used in relation to international courts–state relations to indicate that the relation between these international courts and states are vertical, and thus different from horizontal inter-state extradition. Nonetheless, surrender and extradition are conceptually equivalent, 'as they merely reflect the same action of transferring the jurisdiction of a person from one legal entity to another legal entity endowed with criminal proceedings'.[120]

Furthermore, the Convention on the Prevention and Punishment of the Crime of Genocide also includes traits of the principle of complementarity. Article VI states that the prosecution of the perpetrators 'shall be tried by a competent tribunal of the state on the territory of which the act was committed, or by such international penal tribunal that shall have jurisdiction with respect to these contracting parties which shall have accepted its jurisdiction'.[121] The Article stipulates that the

---

118   Article 90 of the Rome Statute of the International Criminal Court, UN Doc. A/CONF.183/9.

119   Knoops, G.J.A. 2002. *Surrendering To International Criminal Courts: Contemporary Practice and Procedure*. New York: Transnational Publishers, 13.

120   Knoops, G.J.A. 2002. *Surrendering To International Criminal Courts: Contemporary Practice and Procedure*. New York: Transnational Publishers, 314.

121   Convention on the Prevention and Punishment of the Crime of Genocide, 1948, in *Blackstone's International Human Rights Documents*, edited by P.R. Ghandi. 2002, third edition, 20.

national courts and the international tribunal will have alternative jurisdiction, without specifying any criteria of preference. However, mentioning the national courts at the beginning of Article VI before indicating the jurisdiction of the tribunal could imply that there is a preference for the national court followed by the international tribunal. The *travaux préparatoires* of the Convention seems in favour of such a supposition. The discussions in drafting the Convention show states affirming their primary right to exercise their jurisdiction over the crime of genocide. The Soviet position was robust in that regard.[122] The chair of the *Ad Hoc* Committee, John Maktos of the United States, endorsed the idea of establishing an international penal tribunal to prosecute perpetrators of genocide based on a rule of subsidiarity or complementarity. Through this mechanism, the tribunal would only have jurisdiction if the territorial state could not or failed to act.[123] The proposal was adopted by the *ad hoc* committee unanimously.[124]

These various international instruments and treaties show that complementarity has some legal basis in international treaty law. Complementarity is not verbatim in these treaties, though it does find grounds in their implementation mechanisms.

Conclusion

While the duty of *aut dedere aut judicare* is a customary international rule pertaining to some international crimes, it does not pertain to all. Some writers and jurists assert its customary rule towards all international crimes,[125] others do not support this view.[126] There is more consensus with respect to certain

---

122   El-Zeidy, M. Summer 2002. The Principle of Complementarity: A Machinery to Implement International Criminal Law. *Michigan Journal of International Law*, 23, 4, 869-978, 877.

123   Basic Principle of Convention on Genocide. UN ESCOR. Ad Hoc Committees on Genocide. Seventh meeting. UN Doc. E/AC.25/SR-7. 1948.

124   El-Zeidy, M. Summer 2002. The Principle of Complementarity: A Machinery to Implement International Criminal Law. *Michigan Journal of International Law*, 23, 4, 869-978, 878.

125   Professor Bassiouni tends to endorse the maxim *aut dedere aut judicare* with respect to all international crimes. Bassiouni, M.Ch. 1987. *International Extradition: United States Law and Practice*. US: Oceana Publications, fourth edition, 22-24. Bassiouni, M.Ch. 1992. *Crimes against Humanity*. Dordrecht/Boston/London: Martinus Nijhoff Publishers, 499-510. Also, Judge Weermantry in his opinion descended in the Lockerbie Case. 1992 ICJ Reports 3, 69 (Libya vs USA).

126   Antonio Cassese does not approve that there is a recognized general rule to prosecute or extradite all international crimes. Cassese, A. 2003. *International Criminal Law*. Oxford: Oxford University Press, 301. See Robertson, G. 1999. *Crimes against Humanity*. New York: Penguin, 366.

international crimes, namely *jus cogens* crimes.[127] It is more generally accepted that the maxim *aut dedere aut judicare* is a customary general rule pertaining to *jus cogens* crimes such genocide, war crimes, crimes against humanity[128] and torture.[129] This is because treaties addressing these crimes have been ratified by most states belonging to the international community. These treaties are thus part of a customary norm in international law that imposes an obligation not only on member states, but *erga omnes*, on all members of the international community.

Despite the lack of a final assertion, among legal scholars, that *aut dedere aut judicare* is a *jus cogens* principle applicable to all international crimes, most crimes under the Statute of the ICC are widely considered to be *jus cogens* crimes (namely genocide, war crimes and crimes against humanity). The Geneva Conventions and the Genocide Convention of 1948 are now part of customary international law. These treaties insist on the punishment of the perpetrators, whether through prosecution, through extradition to other states (Geneva Conventions), or by an international tribunal (Genocide Convention). By now, crimes against humanity are widely accepted as *jus cogens* crimes that entail prosecution by states.[130]

The principle of complementarity emerges from the community's intention to end impunity for these heinous crimes. If the state is unwilling or unable, then the Court will fill the gap. Through complementarity, either the member state or the Court is able to fulfil an international duty to prosecute these crimes.

At the same time, the above analysis shows differences between complementarity, as a jurisdictional concept, and *aut dedere aut judicare*. For the latter, there is no priority between prosecuting and extraditing, while for the former, priority goes to the national judicial system. Complementarity imposes a duty on states to surrender the accused to the Court if the primary jurisdictional authority (the member state) does not prosecute.

However, this difference is of a procedural nature and not substantive. In substance, the principle of complementarity and *aut dedere aut judicare* rest on common basis, as both aim to prosecute the perpetrators of international crimes through national courts or via extradition/surrender to international courts.

The above discussion is aimed at analysing the possible legal background and roots of complementarity in international law in general. Yet, with respect to the relationship between states and the ICC, it is the Rome Statute, as an international treaty, that provides the fundamental legal basis for the complementarity principle to be implemented.

---

127   Knoops, G.J.A. 2002. *Surrendering To International Criminal Courts: Contemporary Practice and Procedure*. New York: Transnational Publishers, 315.

128   Mueller, G. 1983. International Criminal Law: *Civitas Maxima* – An Overview. *Case Western Reserve Journal of International Law*, 1.

129   Knoops, G.J.A. 2002. *Surrendering To International Criminal Courts: Contemporary Practice and Procedure*. New York: Transnational Publishers, 315.

130   Bassiouni, M.Ch. 1992. *Crimes against Humanity*. Dordrecht/Boston/London: Martinus Nijhoff Publishers, 489-499.

Chapter 3

Complementarity in Abstract

Introduction

A substantial analysis of the complementarity principle is necessary for understanding the basic elements of this new principle vis-à-vis the functions of the ICC.

The aim of this chapter is to analyse the basic components of the complementarity principle as set out in Article 17 of the Rome Statute, to shed light on the effective aspects and deficiencies of the complementarity principle. Analysis will also clarify the relation between the Court and national legal systems. This assists in understanding the impact of the ICC on national legal systems, and on investigations and prosecutions of international crimes at domestic level. Article 17 is not to be analysed alone. The following also looks at Article 20 (and particularly section 3), since it is closely linked with Article 17. In addition, the chapter proceeds to scrutinize complementarity in practice by analysing the prosecutorial policy of the ICC since its adoption by the Rome Statute.

With respect to the relation between the Court and national legal systems, complementarity is the pivotal concept. Clearly the product of a compromise, the principle of complementarity emerged in the formative negotiations for the ICC and services the delicate balance between the competing interests of state sovereignty,[1] judicial independence and accountability for grave violations of human rights and humanitarian law. During the Rome Conference, this issue was both politically sensitive and legally complex, and some states were not ready to accept the primacy of the Court over their national jurisdictions.[2]

The Statute recognizes the primary responsibility of the states to prosecute international crimes; and the ICC may only exercise jurisdiction when national legal systems fail to do so, including cases where they are inactive, unwilling or unable genuinely to carry out proceedings. The principle of complementarity

---

1 Several international conventions describing the legal norms which regulate conflict embody the recognition of a legal right of a state to prosecute enemy citizens who violate those norms, as well as its own nationals: Convention on the Prevention and Punishment of the Crime of Genocide, Article 6; Geneva Convention relative to the treatment of prisoners of war, Articles 85, 89 and 102.

2 Williams, Sh.A. 1999. Article 17: Issues of Admissibility, in *Commentary on the Rome Statute of the International Criminal Court: Observer's Note, Article by Article*, edited by O. Triffterer. Baden-Baden: Nomos Verlagsgesellschaft, 383-394, 375.

is based on two basic pillars: the respect for the primary jurisdiction of states, and considerations of efficiency and effectiveness. This is a reflection of states generally having the best access to evidence and witnesses, along with the resources to carry out proceedings. Furthermore, the ICC, as a single institution with limited resources,[3] may not be able to conduct more than a limited number of prosecutions at any given time.

The complementarity regime serves as a system to encourage and facilitate the compliance of states with their responsibility to investigate and prosecute international core crimes. The ICC Prosecutor must be ready to initiate proceedings where states fail to carry out genuine proceedings out of inability or lack of willingness. Such procedures must be independent and impartial, and demonstrate the international community's determination to prosecute international crimes. The ICC Statute reflects this determination by primarily encouraging national prosecutions.[4] The ICC Prosecutor states, in his *Paper on Some Policy Issues before the Office of the Prosecutor*, that 'the principle of complementarity represents the express will of States Parties to create an institution that is global in scope while recognising the primary responsibility of States themselves to exercise criminal jurisdiction'.[5]

Legal Analysis of Article 17

The principle of complementarity is stipulated in the Preamble and Article 17 of the Rome Statute. The language of Article 17 implies that state parties maintain the primary jurisdiction while the ICC's jurisdiction is the exception. The negative language of the Article supports such an argument. It is only when national courts refrain from taking any actions, or are unwilling or unable to conduct investigations and prosecutions, that the ICC will render the situation admissible.[6] Article 17 of the Rome Statute stipulates the following:

    1. Having regard to paragraph 10 of the Preamble and Article 1, the Court shall determine that a case is inadmissible where:

---

    3   International Criminal Court, Office of the Prosecutor. 2003. *Paper on Some Policy Issues before the Office of the Prosecutor*. ICC-OTP 2003, 1-9, 2. Available at: www.icc-cpi.int/library/organs/otp/030905_Policy_Paper.pdf [accessed: 20 February 2009].

    4   International Criminal Court, Office of the Prosecutor. 2003. *Informal Expert Paper: The Principle of Complementarity in Practice*. ICC-OTP 2003, 1-38, 2. Available at: www.icc-cpi.int/library/organs/otp/complementarity.pdf [accessed: 11 August 2009].

    5   International Criminal Court, Office of the Prosecutor. 2003. *Paper on Some Policy Issues before the Office of the Prosecutor*. ICC-OTP 2003, 1-9, 2. Available at: www.icc-cpi.int/library/organs/otp/030905_Policy_Paper.pdf [accessed: 20 February 2009].

    6   Article 17 of the Rome Statute of the International Criminal Court, UN Doc. A/CONF.183/9.

a. The case is being investigated or prosecuted by a State which has jurisdiction over it, unless the State is unwilling or unable genuinely to carry out the investigation or prosecution;

b. The case has been investigated by a State which has jurisdiction over it and the State has decided not to prosecute the person concerned, unless the decision resulted from the unwillingness or inability of the State genuinely to prosecute;

c. The person concerned has already been tried for conduct which is the subject of the complaint, and a trial by the Court is not permitted under Article 20, paragraph 3;

d. The case is not of sufficient gravity to justify further action by the Court.

2. In order to determine unwillingness in a particular case, the Court shall consider, having regard to the principles of due process recognized by international law, whether one or more of the following exist, as applicable:

a. The proceedings were or are being undertaken or the national decision was made for the purpose of shielding the person concerned from criminal responsibility for crimes within the jurisdiction of the Court referred to in Article 5;

b. There has been an unjustified delay in the proceedings which in the circumstances is inconsistent with an intent to bring the person concerned to justice;

c. The proceedings were not or are not being conducted independently or impartially, and they were or are being conducted in a manner which, in the circumstances, is inconsistent with an intent to bring the person concerned to justice.

3. In order to determine inability in a particular case, the Court shall consider whether, due to a total or substantial collapse or unavailability of its national judicial system, the State is unable to obtain the accused or the necessary evidence and testimony or otherwise unable to carry out its proceedings.[7]

A legal analysis of Article 17 requires a precise and elaborate analysis of basic legal concepts within the Article. That will be elaborated *infra*.

The Case being Investigated or Prosecuted

One could start by asking the valid question of whether the term 'investigation' must be criminal in nature or if it should imply a broader meaning to include a 'diligent, methodical effort to gather the evidence and to ascertain the facts relating to the conduct in question, in order to make an objective determination

---

7   Article 17 of the Rome Statute of the International Criminal Court, UN Doc. A/CONF.183/9.

in accordance with pertinent criteria'.[8] Some assert that the drafters of the Statute intended the word to refer only to criminal investigations,[9] while others consider 'investigation's' meaning to be broader and include non-criminal investigations.[10] The latter, more expansive meaning, counts various sorts of proceedings as 'investigations'. Proceedings from Truth and Reconciliation Commissions (TRC) are a prime example here, and ultimately serve to discount the validity of the latter interpretation. The original aim of the drafters leans more towards a definition whereby 'investigation' refers to criminal investigations. This is evident in Article 17(2)(b) and (2)(c) where reference to 'an intent to bring the person concerned to justice' is made. Since TRC proceedings and amnesties have been widely regarded as inconsistent with the intention to bring someone to justice,[11] hence contradicting the aforementioned quote, the broader interpretation of 'investigation' is invalidated. This is also in conformity with the duty to prosecute as recognized by the preamble of the Rome Statute[12] and human rights treaties.[13]

---

8   Robinson, D. June 2003. Serving the Interest of Justice: Amnesties, Truth Commissions and The International Criminal Court. *The European Journal of International Law*, 481-509, 481, 500.

9   Roht-Arriaza, N. 2000. Amnesty and the International Criminal Court, in *International Crimes, Peace, and Human Rights: The Role of the International Criminal Court*, edited by D. Shelton. Ardsley: Transnational, 77, 79. Also, Scharf, M. 1999. The Amnesty Exception to the Jurisdiction of the International Criminal Court. *Cornell International Law Journal*, 32, 507, 525.

10   Della Morte, G. 2002. Les Frontières De La Compétence De La Cour Pénale Internationale: Observations Critiques. *Revue Internationale De Droit Penal*, 73, 24, 33.

11   Gavron, J. 2002. Amnesties in the Light of Developments in International Law and the Establishment of the International Criminal Court. *International and Comparative Law Quarterly*, 51, 91-126, 111.

12   Paragraph 6 of the Preamble of the Rome Statute of the International Criminal Court, UN Doc. A/CONF.183/9.

13   Article 2 of International Covenant on Civil and Political Rights. 1996. G.A. res. 2200A (XXI), 21 U.N. GAOR Supp. (no. 16) at 52, UN Doc. A/6316. 1966. 999 U.N.T.S. 171, entered into force 23 March 1976. Article 1 of the American Convention On Human Rights. 1969. Adopted at the Inter-American Specialized Conference on Human Rights, San José, Costa Rica, 22 November 1969. Available at: www.oas.org/juridico/english/Treaties/ b-32.htm [accessed: 25 June 2008]. Article 1 of the Convention for the Protection of Human Rights and Fundamental Freedoms. 1950. Entry into force on 3 September 1953. Cets no.: 005. Available at: http://conventions.coe.int/treaty/EN/cadreprincipal.htm [accessed: 26 January 2008]. Article 1 of the African (Banjul) Charter on Human and Peoples' Rights. 1981. OAU Doc. CAB/LEG/67/3 rev. 5, 21 I.L.M. 58. 1982, entered into force 21 October 1986. Available at: www.africaunion.org/Official_documents/Treaties_%20Conventions_ %20Protocols/Banjul%20Charter.pdf#search='African%20charter%20on%20Human%20 Rights [accessed: 27 January 2008].

Inaction by State Authorities

The opposite situation to the above scenario would trigger the ICC's jurisdiction, that is, if the state does not initiate any investigation or prosecution, then the case will be admissible before the Court. To one author, this means the ICC can trigger its jurisdiction if national courts do not take action.[14] The Office of the Prosecutor itself indicates in its Policy Paper that '[t]here is no impediment to the admissibility of a case before the Court where no State has initiated any investigation. There may be cases where inaction by States is the appropriate course of action'.[15] The ICC jurisdiction is activated primarily when there is lack of action by the national courts of those states that have a direct nexus with a defined situation, such as the territorial state, the state of nationality of the alleged perpetrators, or the state of nationality of the victims.[16] The case will be admissible where the relevant state is neither investigating nor prosecuting.[17] These are cases of so-called uncontested jurisdiction, in which a case of 'no action' will discard the application of Article 17 and the case will become admissible before the ICC.

Unwilling Genuinely to Investigate or Prosecute

Under Article 17, the ICC will exercise jurisdiction when no action is taken by the state or when the state is unwilling or unable genuinely to carry out the investigation or prosecution. The issues of 'unwilling' and 'genuine' arise, *inter alia*, when a state has initiated an investigation or prosecution and there are reasons to believe that the proceedings will not result in delivering justice.[18] Clearly, the terms 'unwillingness' and 'genuinely' need to be defined and analysed extensively.

---

14   Olasolo, H. 26 March 2004. *The Triggering Procedure of the International Criminal Court, Procedural Treatment of the Principle of Complementarity, and the Role of Office of the Prosecutor*. Guest Lecture Series of the Office of the Prosecutor, The Hague, 1-22, 14.

15   International Criminal Court, Office of the Prosecutor. 2003. *Paper on Some Policy Issues before the Office of the Prosecutor*. ICC-OTP 2003, 1-9, 2. Available at: www.icc-cpi.int/library/organs/otp/030905_Policy_Paper.pdf [accessed: 20 February 2009].

16   Olasolo, H. 26 March 2004. *The Triggering Procedure of the International Criminal Court, Procedural Treatment of the Principle of Complementarity, and the Role of Office of the Prosecutor*. Guest Lecture Series of the Office of the Prosecutor, The Hague, 1-22, 15.

17   International Criminal Court, Office of the Prosecutor. 14 September 2006. *The Office of the Prosecutor Report on Prosecutorial Strategy*, The Hague, 1-11. Available at: www.icc-cpi.int/library/organs/otp/OTP_Prosecutorial-Strategy-20060914_English.pdf [accessed: 2 June 2009].

18   International Criminal Court, Office of the Prosecutor. 2003. *Informal Expert Paper: The Principle of Complementarity in Practice*. ICC-OTP 2003, 1-38, 7. Available at: www.icc-cpi.int/library/organs/otp/complementarity.pdf [accessed: 11 August 2009].

Determining 'unwillingness' is a technically complex process subject to considerable political sensitivity.[19] According to the Office of the Prosecutor:

> A State is *unwilling* if the national decision has been made and proceedings are or were being undertaken for the purpose of shielding the person concerned from criminal responsibility; there has been an unjustified delay which is inconsistent with an intent to bring the person concerned to justice; or the proceedings were not, or are not being conducted independently or impartially.[20]

The test of 'willingness' as embedded in Article 17(2) is in fact a test of the 'intentions' and the good faith of national authorities. The Court is to determine a state's unwillingness by assessing both normative and empirical factors.[21] This is reflected in the drafters' intention to establish objective criteria to help the Court in assessing 'unwillingness'.[22] As for the normative factors, the Court will focus on the general institutional features of national systems, which includes laws, procedures, practices and standards, as developed by case law. The assessment of these institutional features shall be complemented with empirical factors. The specific attitude and behaviour of the state authorities in connection with a given case is to be analysed objectively. For instance, in assessing an 'unjustified delay' or 'non impartial and non independent proceedings', the Court will use institutional features while taking into account empirical factors to determine the intention of a state whose behaviour is 'inconsistent with intent to bring the person concerned to justice'.[23]

Article 17(2) stipulates that the principles of due process recognized by international law will be taken into consideration when assessing 'unwillingness'. Rule 51 of the Rules of Procedure and Evidence of the ICC permits the state that is invoking complementarity to provide information showing that 'its courts meet internationally recognized norms and standards for the independent and

---

19   International Criminal Court, Office of the Prosecutor. 2003. *Informal Expert Paper: The Principle of Complementarity in Practice*. ICC-OTP 2003, 1-38, 14. Available at: www.icc-cpi.int/library/organs/otp/complementarity.pdf [accessed: 11 August 2009].

20   International Criminal Court, Office of the Prosecutor. 2003. *Informal Expert Paper: The Principle of Complementarity in Practice*. ICC-OTP 2003, 1-38, 4. Available at: www.icc-cpi.int/library/organs/otp/complementarity.pdf [accessed: 11 August 2009].

21   International Criminal Court, Office of the Prosecutor, 2003. *Working Group on Complementarity Issues, Final Document, Experts Group Reflection Paper for The Principle of Complementarity in Practice*. ICC-OTP, 10.

22   Holmes, J. 1999. The Principle of Complementarity, in *The International Criminal Court: The Making of the Rome Statute, Issues, Negotiations, Results*, edited by R. Lee. The Hague: Kluwer, 49.

23   Article 17(2)(c) of the Rome Statute of the International Criminal Court, UN Doc. A/CONF.183/9.

impartial prosecution of similar conduct' in order to help the Court in assessing the unwillingness of the states.[24]

The requirement of respect for 'the principles of due process recognized by international law'[25] and the term 'genuinely' restricts any margin of discretion for the Court to assess any unwillingness. Such objective normative criteria limit the grounds for the possibility of subjective assessments. Some delegations aimed during the Rome Conference to restrict Article 17(2) in order not to give the Court too much freedom in determining a state's unwillingness. The insertion of the statement 'in accordance with the norms of due process recognized by international law' in the criteria of unwillingness reflects this intention.[26]

For instance, the criteria of respect for 'the principles of due process recognized by international law' imply the implementation of international human rights standards. The application of human rights principles of fair trial and due process is pivotal in the application of the complementarity principle. This is not based solely on the language of Article 17, but also on Article 21, which stipulates in paragraph 3 that 'application and interpretation of law pursuant to this Article [sources of applicable law by the Court] must be consistent with internationally recognized human rights'.[27] These include Articles 14 and 26 of the ICCPR, Article 6 of the ECHR, Article 8 of I-ACHR and Article 7 of the African Charter on Human and Peoples' Rights. The right to a fair trial, as subsumed in these treaties, provides for a number of procedural rights including: the right of legal aid and a counsel of one's own choice; to equality of arms between prosecution and defence; not to be compelled to testify against him/herself; to expeditiousness of proceedings; the right to examine and cross-examine witnesses; to the publicity of the proceedings; to be promptly and adequately informed of the charges in a language understood by the accused; and the right to have an interpreter if he/she cannot understand the language of the proceedings.[28]

This raises the question of whether the ICC acts, in certain aspects, as a human rights court. If the Court does not respect human rights and rights of due process, that will be inconsistent with the intention of 'bringing the person to justice' as delineated in paragraph 2 of Article 17. The role of the Court, as an international

---

24   Rule 51 of the Rules of Procedure and Evidence. ICC-ASP/1/3, 1-107, 38.

25   Article 17(2) of the Rome Statute of the International Criminal Court, UN Doc. A/CONF.183/9.

26   Discussion Paper of the Bureau of the Committee of the Whole and the Bureau Proposal. See Discussion Paper of the Bureau of the Committee of the Whole, Part 2. Jurisdiction, Admissibility and Applicable Law, A/CONF.183/C.1/L.53, 6 July 1998, Article 15, 16; Bureau Proposal, Committee of the Whole, Part 2. Jurisdiction, Admissibility and Applicable Law, A/CONF.183/C.1/L.59, 10 July 1998, Article 15, 14.

27   Article 21 of the Rome Statute of the International Criminal Court, UN Doc. A/CONF.183/9.

28   See Article 14 of the International Covenant on Civil and Political Rights (1966), G.A. res. 2200A (XXI), 21 U.N. GAOR Supp. (no. 16) at 52, UN Doc. A/6316. 1966. 999 U.N.T.S. 171.

body complementing national jurisdictions in meting out fair trial for the most serious crimes by abiding by the highest international human rights standards,[29] supports the argument *supra*. Hence, in case where an accused has been convicted in national court proceedings that breached his or her due process rights, the Court could theoretically step in, since the phrase suggests an assessment of the quality of justice from the standpoint of procedural and perhaps even substantive fairness.[30] A combined reading with Article 20(3) supports this position.

As a result, the Court may declare a case admissible under the 'unwillingness test', 'in case of any violation of internationally recognized principles that is inconsistent with delivering a fair judgment for the accused'.[31]

In terms of the meaning of 'genuinely', analysis can begin by noting that the Rome Statute does not define the term 'genuinely' stipulated in Article 17. Moreover, there is no precedent in international law that defines the term 'genuine'.[32] One should resort to Article 21 of the Statute for possible definition of the term, as human rights law can provide a source for defining the term. The case law of the European Court of Human Rights and the Inter-American Court of Human Rights holds in many cases that an effective investigation should be able to identify and punish those responsible.[33] Effectiveness was initially used during the negotiations in the Rome Conference, but was later replaced by the term 'genuinely'.[34] *Black's Law Dictionary* defines 'genuine' as authentic or real, as opposed to false.[35] The *Oxford English Dictionary* defines it as having the supposed character, not sham or feigned. The term 'genuinely'[36] in Article 17 more likely applies to the phrase

---

29   International Criminal Court, Office of the Prosecutor. 2003. *Informal Expert Paper: The Principle of Complementarity in Practice*. ICC-OTP 2003, 1-38, 24. Available at: www.icc-cpi.int/library/organs/otp/complementarity.pdf [accessed: 11 August 2009].

30   Schabas, W. 2001. *An Introduction to the International Criminal Court*. Cambridge: Cambridge University Press, 68.

31   Schabas, W. 2001. *An Introduction to the International Criminal Court*. Cambridge: Cambridge University Press, 24.

32   Holmes, J. 2002. Complementarity: National Courts versus the International Criminal Court, in *The Rome Statute of The International Criminal Court: A Commentary*, edited by A. Cassese, P. Gaeta and J.R.W.D. Jones. Oxford: Oxford University Press, I, 674.

33   See ECHR cases: *Yasa* v. *Turkey*, ECHR App. no. 22281/93, 27 June 2002, not published, para. 98; *Assenov* v. *Bulgaria*, ECHR App. no. 24760/94, 28 October 1998, ECHR 1998-VIII, para. 102. Also, I-ACHR cases: *Velasquez Rodriguez* v. *Honduras*, 29 July 1988, I-ACHR Series C, no. 4, para 174.

34   El-Zeidy, M. Summer 2002. The Principle of Complementarity: A Machinery to Implement International Criminal Law. *Michigan Journal of International Law*, 23, 4, 869-978, 882.

35   *Black's Law Dictionary*. 1999. St Paul: West, seventh edition, 695.

36   Terms such as 'effectively', proposed in earlier drafts, were unacceptable to several delegations, due to fear that the ICC might 'judge' and monitor a legal system against ideal standards. See International Criminal Court, Office of the Prosecutor 2003. *Informal Expert*

'to carry out an investigation or prosecution'. Article 17, paragraph 1(b) clarifies any confusion on whether the term 'genuine' modifies 'unable' and 'unwilling' or if it modifies 'to carry out' and 'to prosecute'.[37] Such an interpretation is widely supported by the *travaux préparatoires*, since earlier drafts ('to genuinely carry out') were adjusted on grammatical grounds to avoid violating the rule against split infinitives.[38] The French version of the Rome Statute more explicitly confirms this.[39]

The issue of genuineness arises whenever the state claiming jurisdiction over a crime does not appear to be willing or able to set up meaningful investigations or prosecutions. This allows the application of defined criteria in assessing national proceedings. Through these criteria, the term 'genuine' restricts the class of national proceedings admissible by the ICC.[40] The inclusion of these criteria is the outcome of a compromise within the Rome Statute that established a balance between giving the ICC the power to assess the objective quality of a national proceeding and restricting the ICC's assessment by a number of criteria, including 'genuineness' of proceedings.[41]

To conclude, the notion of genuineness of proceedings should be understood in conjunction with paragraphs 2 and 3 of Article 17, which define the terms 'unwillingness' and 'inability'.[42] National proceedings could be considered not genuine if they intend to shield the person concerned from justice, to violate the principle of impartiality and independence, or cause an unjustified delay in the proceedings.

In order to avoid giving broad discretionary powers to the Court in determining the 'unwillingness' of national authorities, the Rome Statute included an

---

Paper: The Principle of Complementarity in Practice. ICC-OTP 2003, 1-38, 8. Available at: www.icc-cpi.int/library/organs/otp/complementarity.pdf [accessed: 11 August 2009].

37   International Criminal Court, Office of the Prosecutor. 2003. *Informal Expert Paper: The Principle of Complementarity in Practice.* ICC-OTP 2003, 1-38, 8. Available at: www.icc-cpi.int/library/organs/otp/complementarity.pdf [accessed: 11 August 2009].

38   International Criminal Court, Office of the Prosecutor. 2003. *Informal Expert Paper: The Principle of Complementarity in Practice.* ICC-OTP 2003, 1-38, 8. Available at: www.icc-cpi.int/library/organs/otp/complementarity.pdf [accessed: 11 August 2009].

39   See Article 17 in French copy of the Rome Statute. The French version has the same authenticity according to Article 33, paragraph 3 of the Vienna Convention on the Law of Treaties.

40   International Criminal Court, Office of the Prosecutor. 2003. *Informal Expert Paper: The Principle of Complementarity in Practice.* ICC-OTP 2003, 1-38, 8. Available at: www.icc-cpi.int/library/organs/otp/complementarity.pdf [accessed: 11 August 2009].

41   Williams, Sh.A. 1999. Article 17: Issues of Admissibility, in *Commentary on the Rome Statute of the International Criminal Court: Observer's Note, Article by Article*, edited by O. Triffterer. Baden-Baden: Nomos Verlagsgesellschaft, 383–394, 392.

42   El-Zeidy, M. Summer 2002. The Principle of Complementarity: A Machinery to Implement International Criminal Law. *Michigan Journal of International Law*, 23, 4, 869-978, 884.

exhaustive list of factors that are to be taken into consideration by the Court. Some arguments were raised afterwards concerning whether or not the list is exhaustive. However, the *travaux préparatoires* and the intention of the drafters clearly favour the stand that the list is exhaustive.[43] The three listed criteria restrict the Court's power of assessment through forcing the ICC to conduct empirically the test of 'unwillingness'. The list of criteria for determining 'unwillingness' constitutes the following: 'shielding', 'unjustified delay' and lack of independent or impartial proceedings.[44]

Proceedings for shielding   Article 17(2), paragraph (a) is an important provision as it is intended to assist in determining 'unwillingness' by inserting a defined criterion that should be taken into consideration by the Court when applying the 'unwillingness test'. This provision intends, *inter alia*, to prevent any possible sham trials from obstructing ICC jurisdiction. Sham trials occur in situations where the state appears to be prosecuting international crimes but in reality aims to ensure impunity for the crime.[45] This process remains delicate in spite of the objectivity of this provision because the Court is in these cases forced to delve into the intention of the national authorities to detect bad faith. Article 17(2)(a) allows the ICC to challenge the good faith of a state if there is evidence that the state's proceedings or prosecutions are a sham, designed solely to defeat the ICC's jurisdiction.

John Holmes argues that the ICC is also be able to rely on objective facts to presume the bad faith of a state. These include, among others, the presence of investigations or prosecutions of some perpetrators that lead to sham proceedings or obvious departures from the legal procedures of the state.[46]

Human rights law, as a source of law for the Court under Article 21, could be of help in clarifying possible shortages in defining some of the terms included in Article 17(2)(a). The decisions of the Inter-American Commission of Human Rights and the jurisprudence of the Inter-American Court of Human Rights provide

43   El-Zeidy, M. Summer 2002. The Principle of Complementarity: A Machinery to Implement International Criminal Law. *Michigan Journal of International Law*, 23, 4, 869-978, 890.

44   Article 17(2)(a) and (b) and (c) of the Rome Statute of the International Criminal Court, UN Doc. A/CONF.183/9.

45   The International Law Commission stated that if the national judicial system has not functioned independently or impartially or the proceedings were aimed to shield the accused from international criminal responsibility, then 'the International community should not be required to recognize a decision that is the result of such a serious transgression of the criminal justice process'. See Report of the International Law Commission. 6 May-26 July 1996. 48th session. UN Doc. A/51/10, 1996, 67.

46   Holmes, J. 2002. Complementarity: National Courts versus the International Criminal Court, in *The Rome Statute of The International Criminal Court: A Commentary*, edited by A. Cassese, P. Gaeta and J.R.W.D. Jones. Oxford: Oxford University Press, I, 667-675.

examples and scenarios of objective facts that can be taken into consideration when determining whether a state's intention is to shield persons from criminal responsibility.

The Inter-American Commission stated in the case of the extra-judicial execution of Jesuit priests that the concealing of the identity of the authors by the senior official officers in charge of the investigation is to be considered an objective fact in determining the state's intention to shield the authors from criminal responsibility.[47] The senior officer's steps taken to shield the perpetrators included: ordering weapons from the crime switched to prevent identification of the perpetrators; the destruction of evidence indicating any responsibility of the armed forces; alteration of statements submitted in the investigation; and the deletion of any referral to some officers.[48]

Additionally, the Inter-American Court stated in the case of *Street Children* v. *Guatemala* that restricting investigation to the crime of murder, while excluding the crimes of abduction and torture from any investigation, is an indicator of the state's intention to shield the perpetrators from criminal responsibility.[49]

Proof of shielding may also be deduced through proving the politicized nature of the national system concerned. Also, proof of shielding could be obtained through one of the following means: through a testimony from an insider within the system; through evidences included in documents such as legislation, orders, amnesty decrees, instructions and correspondence; or through procedural gaps and malfunctions such as unjustified delay, lack of impartiality, longstanding knowledge of crimes without action.[50]

The objective criteria that are imposed on the ICC while evaluating 'unwillingness' represent a serious step by state parties to create a balance between the ICC powers to monitor and observe national proceedings, and any possible misuse of such powers. Article 17(2)(a) imposes certain empirical criteria to use in determining 'unwillingness', which are pivotal for determining any attempt to shield perpetrators from criminal responsibility, and can assist in determining empirically the existence of a state of 'unwillingness'.

---

47 *Ignacio Ellacuria et al.* v. *El Salvador* (Jesuit Case). 22 December 1999. Inter American Commission of Human Rights. Case 10.488, 22 December 1999, Report no. 136/99, para. 81-82. Available at: www.oas.org [accessed: 11 September 2008].

48 *Ignacio Ellacuria et al.* v. *El Salvador* (Jesuit Case). 22 December 1999. Inter American Commission of Human Rights. Case 10.488, 22 December 1999, Report no. 136/99, para. 81-82. Available at: www.oas.org [accessed: 11 September 2008].

49 *Street Children Case (Caso Villagran Morales y Otros)*. 19 November 1999. Inter-American Court of Human Rights, Judgment of 19 November 1999.

50 The International Criminal Court, Office of the Prosecutor. 2003. *Informal Expert Paper: The Principle of Complementarity in Practice*. ICC-OTP 2003, Annex 4, 1-38, 27-28. Available at: www.icc-cpi.int/library/organs/otp/complementarity.pdf [accessed: 11 August 2009].

Unjustified delay   'Unjustified delay' is the second criterion that is taken into consideration in determining 'unwillingness'. Within this criterion, three factors are to be considered: Firstly, the existence of a delay, secondly, how the delay is unjustified, and thirdly, how the delay is inconsistent with an intent to bring the person to justice.[51]

Firstly, the existence of delay is a necessary but not a sufficient requirement. Delay could occur in various stages of the proceedings, during the investigative stages or the prosecution stages.[52] The determination of 'delay' is not conducted in abstract, but rather in comparison to similar processes in the concerned state. In other words, the question raised is whether or not the proceedings are longer than the usual proceedings in similar cases within the same judicial system. If the answer is affirmative, then 'delay' has occurred.[53]

Detection of delay will therefore take place by a comparative analysis of the judicial system's practice and the defined case. The Court will assess delay on a case-by-case basis, but consistent with the jurisprudence of international human rights law that assesses delay on a case-by-case basis.[54] Article 21 of the Rome Statute remains applicable here, and standards of international law and international human rights law should be taken into consideration. The body of international human rights law defines the right of fair trial and the right to be tried without 'undue delay'[55] and 'within a reasonable time'.[56]

Secondly, for delay to be unjustified it must reflect 'unwillingness' by the national authorities. The term 'unjustified delay' replaced the term 'undue delay'

---

51   Article 17(2)(b) of the Rome Statute of the International Criminal Court, UN Doc. A/CONF.183/9.

52   The International Criminal Court, Office of the Prosecutor. 2003. *Informal Expert Paper: The Principle of Complementarity in Practice*. ICC-OTP 2003, Annex 4, 1-38, 29. Available at: www.icc-cpi.int/library/organs/otp/complementarity.pdf [accessed: 11 August 2009].

53   Holmes, J. 2002. Complementarity: National Courts versus the International Criminal Court, in *The Rome Statute of The International Criminal Court: A Commentary*, edited by A. Cassese, P. Gaeta and J.R.W.D. Jones. Oxford: Oxford University Press, I, 676.

54   *W* v. *Switzerland*. 26 January 1993. ECHR App. no. 14379/88, ECHR Series A, no. 254-A, para. 30.

55   Article 14 of the International Covenant on Civil and Political Rights (1966), G.A. res. 2200A (XXI), 21 U.N. GAOR Supp. (no. 16) at 52, UN Doc. A/6316 (1966), 999 U.N.T.S. 171.

56   Art. 9, para. 3 of the International Covenant on Civil and Political Rights. 1966, G.A. res. 2200A (XXI), 21 U.N. GAOR Supp. (no. 16) at 52, UN Doc. A/6316 . 1966. 999 U.N.T.S. 171. Art. 5, para. 3 ECHR, Art. 6 of the Convention for the Protection of Human Rights and Fundamental Freedoms. Council of Europe, Rome, 4.XI.1950. Available at: www.echr.coe.int/NR/rdonlyres/D5CC24A7-DC13-4318-B4575C9014916D7A/0/ EnglishAnglais.pdf [accessed: 11 September 2008]. Article 5(1), para (c) of ECHR insists on the right of the detainees to be tried 'within a reasonable time'.

during the negotiation process of the Statute.[57] Substantially, the replacement does not alter the standard, although 'justified' is more in conformity with state sovereignty, as it grants the state the right to verify any delay before the Court determines that a case is admissible. This change allows the involvement of the state concerned in this process, as opposed to leaving the Court to determine delay alone. It sets a higher standard than the term 'undue' on the procedural level.[58] This reflects states' concern to preserve their interests and sovereignty versus this international body.

The last requisite for determining delay stipulates that delay must be inconsistent with the intention to bring the person to justice. Again, the body of human rights law assists in defining this requisite. Here, the Court's role is not that of a human rights court, but rather to evaluate any possible bad faith on behalf of the state. The invocation of human rights law in the process permits the use of the objective criteria within this process,[59] which in turn holds national courts liable for sham trials and attempts to shield possible perpetrators.[60]

Proceedings not conducted independently or impartially   The third prerequisite for determining 'unwillingness' is that proceedings must have not been conducted in an independent or impartial manner and in circumstances inconsistent with an intent to bring the person concerned to justice. This prerequisite includes three factors: independent proceedings, impartiality of proceedings, and inconsistence with an intent to bring the person concerned to justice. The first two factors are alternative; the requisite is fulfilled if one of the two factors has occurred. The proceedings need to be conducted either without impartially or in a non-independent manner. If these factors are fulfilled, then the third prerequisite of the 'unwillingness' test is satisfied. To explore how these factors work, the sources of law for the Court are to be adopted, and Article 21 is to be invoked. The book will turn to international law in general, and international human rights and international criminal law in particular, for the clarification of the terms noted above.

The jurisprudence of human rights law provides a number of legal interpretations of what constitutes an 'impartial' national judicial system. The European Court of

---

57   Williams, Sh.A. 1999. Article 17: Issues of Admissibility, in *Commentary on the Rome Statute of the International Criminal Court: Observer's Note, Article by Article*, edited by O. Triffterer. Baden-Baden: Nomos Verlagsgesellschaft, 383–394, 392. See Bureau Proposal, Committee of the Whole, Part 2. Jurisdiction, Admissibility and Applicable Law, A/CONF.183/C.1/L.59, 10 July 1998, Article 15, 14.

58   Holmes, J. 1999. The Principle of Complementarity, in *The International Criminal Court: The Making of the Rome Statute, Issues, Negotiations, Results*, edited by R. Lee. The Hague: Kluwer, 54.

59   El-Zeidy, M. Summer 2002. The Principle of Complementarity: A Machinery to Implement International Criminal Law. *Michigan Journal of International Law*, 23, 4, 869–978, 901.

60   See Report of the International Law Commission. 6 May-26 July 1996. 48th session. UN Doc. A/51/10, 1996, 67.

Human Rights indicated in the *McGonnell* v. *United Kingdom* case that, in order to detect the impartiality of the national judicial system, two aspects must be taken into consideration. Firstly, the tribunal must fulfil the requirement of impartiality, and that requires offering guarantees that eliminate any legitimate doubt. The UN Human Rights Committee, in its *Concluding Observations Concerning Slovakia*, stated that states must protect judges from any political pressure, and that 'objective legal criteria for judicial appointment and tenure conditions' must be applied. Political interference in the appointment of the judges must also be prevented.[61] Secondly, the proceedings must not be biased, and should thus be free from any bias, or personal prejudice.[62] In addition, the ICC will no doubt look into its own process of selecting the judges and the trial chambers, which guarantees impartiality, to detect if the national systems have similar guarantees. The Statute and the jurisprudence of the Human Rights Committee could be of assistance to the ICC for establishing a method.[63] The Court will look at the process of appointing judges, their qualifications, the duration of their terms in office, the circumstances of their promotion, and the transfer and cessation of their functions. The ECHR added in *Sramek* v. *Austria* that the judiciary must not be subordinated in its duties to one of the parties in a trial.[64] In terms of international criminal law, the case law of the ICTY states that the lack of bias of the judge must be established on a subjective basis, as well as with respect to the objective surrounding circumstances in order to determine that impartiality exists.[65] The ICTY in the *Furundzija case* indicated that there would appear to be a lack of impartiality if there is a financial or material interest for the judge who is a party to the case.[66] According to the Basic Principles on the Independence of the Judiciary, the judiciary shall decide on matters impartially, taking into consideration the facts and in accordance with the law. This process shall be free from any limitations, improper influences, pressures, and direct or indirect threats or interferences.[67] Furthermore, the *Informal Expert Paper: The Principle of Complementarity in Practice* documents many of the elements embedded in the Statute, human rights law and international criminal

---

61   Concluding Observations on Slovakia, HRC, 1997, UN Doc. CCPR/C/79/Add. 79.

62   *McGonnell* v. *United Kingdom*. 8 February 2000. ECHR App. no. 28488/95, ECHR 2000-II, para. 52.

63   Articles 36, 40 and 41 of the Rome Statute of the International Criminal Court, UN Doc. A/CONF.183/9. See also Concluding Observations on Algeria, HRC, 1998, UN Doc. CCPR/C/79/Add. 95.

64   *Sramek* v. *Austria*. 22 October 1984. ECHR App. no. 8790/79, ECHR Series A, no. 54.

65   *Prosecutor* v. *Furundzija*. 21 July 2000. ICTY, IT-95-17/1-A, App. Ch., para. 189.

66   *Prosecutor* v. *Furundzija*. 21 July 2000. ICTY, IT-95-17/1-A, App. Ch., para. 189.

67   Basic Principles on the Independence of the Judiciary Adopted by the Seventh United Nations Congress on the Prevention of Crime and the Treatment of Offenders. 26 August-6 September 1985. Milan. Endorsed by General Assembly Resolutions 40/32 of 29 November 1985 and 40/146 of 13 December 1985.

law that the ICC will take into consideration while assessing the 'impartiality' of the proceedings. This includes commonality of purpose between the suspect perpetrator and the state authority on various levels of investigation, prosecution and adjudication. This can include the following:

- Political objectives of state authority, dominant political party; and
- Coincidence or dissonance in objectives and crime (political gains, territorial goals, subjugation of group).
- Rapport between authorities and suspected perpetrators (this applies only in situations where the investigative, prosecutorial or judicial authorities are not independent of other authorities).
- Statements (condemning or praising actions);
- Awards or sanctions, promotion or demotion;
- Financial support; and
- Deployment or withdrawal of law enforcement, inhibiting or supporting investigation.
- Linkages between perpetrators and judges.[68]

The ICC Prosecutor indicated in one event that 'impartiality' for an international prosecutor means to apply the same criteria to all parties.[69] According to the ICC Prosecutor, it is not necessary to prosecute both sides of conflict. Moreno-Ocampo affirmed his application for such criterion in the investigation in northern Uganda.[70]

To determine what an 'independent proceeding' is, we need to consider the work of human rights treaty bodies, the case law of *ad hoc* international criminal tribunals, and international and non-binding resolutions. The independence of a judicial body is deduced from its method of establishment; the method of appointing and dismissing judges; the degree of subordination to a political body; the degree of separation of power between the judiciary and other branches;[71] the degree of independence of the judiciary and the prosecutors of investigating agencies;[72] and

---

68   International Criminal Court, Office of the Prosecutor. 2003. *Informal Expert Paper: The Principle of Complementarity in Practice*. ICC-OTP 2003, Annex 4, 1-38, 28-29. Available at: www.icc-cpi.int/library/organs/otp/complementarity.pdf [accessed: 11 August 2009].

69   Moreno-Ocampo, L. 2006. Symposium: International Criminal Tribunals in the 21st Century: Keynote Address: Integrating the Work of the ICC into Local Justice Initiatives. *American University International Law Review*, 21, 497-503, 501.

70   Moreno-Ocampo, L. 2006. Symposium: International Criminal Tribunals in the 21st Century: Keynote Address: Integrating the Work of the ICC into Local Justice Initiatives. *American University International Law Review*, 21, 497-503, 501.

71   *McGonnell* v. *United Kingdom*. 8 February 2000. ECHR App. no. 28488/95, ECHR 2000-II.

72   *De Cubber* v. *Belgium*. 26 October 1984. ECHR App. no. 9186/80, ECHR Series A. See also International Criminal Court, Office of the Prosecutor. 2003. *Informal Expert Paper: The Principle of Complementarity in Practice*. ICC-OTP 2003, Annex 4, 1-38, 29.

the degree of interference or threats that face the judiciary from within the state. With respect to the method of appointing and dismissing the judges, the European Court of Human Rights stated in the *Langborger* v. *Sweden* case that 'in order to establish whether a tribunal can be considered as 'independent', regard must be made, *inter alia*, to the manner of appointment of the members and their term of office, the existence of guarantees against outside pressures and the question of whether the body presents an appearance of independence.[73] The UN Human Rights Committee indicated that to determine 'independence' one should take into consideration the manner in which the judges have been appointed; the qualifications and requirement for appointment; the length of terms of office; the conditions governing their promotion; and the transfer and cessation of their functions.[74] The states should apply objective legal criteria for judicial appointment and tenure conditions that will prevent political interference in the functions of the judiciary.[75] As for the degree of interference or threats that face the judiciary, the Human Rights Committee clearly indicated that for the judiciary to be independent it must be protected from threats, reprisals and interferences.[76] Moreover, predetermined outcomes in trials are a strong indicator of lack of independence.[77]

With respect to the criterion of inconsistence with the intention to bring the person to justice, the analysis *supra* on the same concept can be adopted to clarify the term.[78]

Inability

Inability is another criterion for determining whether the state is able to carry out its duty under the Statute. The effectiveness of the national judicial system, vis-à-vis ability to prosecute, will render the case inadmissible.[79] Thus, the 'inability'

Available at: www.icc-cpi.int/library/organs/otp/complementarity.pdf [accessed: 11 August 2009].

73   *Langborger* v. *Sweden*. 22 June 1989. ECHR App. no. 11179/84, ECHR Series A, no. 155, para. 32. *McGonnell* v. *United Kingdom*. 8 February 2000. ECHR App. no. 28488/95, ECHR 2000-II, para. 52.

74   Concluding Observations on Algeria. 1998. Human Rights Committee, HRC, UN Doc. CCPR/C/79/Add. 95.

75   Concluding Observations on Slovakia. 1997. Human Rights Committee, HRC, UN Doc. CCPR/C/79/Add. 79.

76   Concluding Observations on Brazil. 1997. Human Rights Committee, HRC, 1997, UN Doc. CCPR/C/79/Add. 66.

77   International Criminal Court, Office of the Prosecutor. 2003. *Informal Expert Paper: The Principle of Complementarity in Practice*. ICC-OTP 2003, Annex 4, 1-38, 29. Available at: www.icc-cpi.int/library/organs/otp/complementarity.pdf [accessed: 11 August 2009].

78   See *supra* p.45.

79   El-Zeidy, M. Summer 2002. The Principle of Complementarity: A Machinery to Implement International Criminal Law. *Michigan Journal of International Law*, 23, 4, 869-978, 884.

of the national system to prosecute core crimes will open the door for the ICC to render the case admissible. The *travaux préparatoires* shows that the negotiations for 'inability' were less contentious than those of 'unwillingness'.[80] The outcome of the Rome Statute shows that an assessment of 'inability' is less complex than that of 'unwillingness', as it is based on criteria that are more objective.[81] This restricts the prosecutorial discretion, although some writers still consider that a margin of appreciation remains in determining the objective criteria.[82]

The standard for showing 'inability' is a stringent one, as the ICC is not a human rights court, and its primary aim is not to detect violations of the fair trial principle, but rather to discover if the national judicial system is capable of prosecuting the core crimes in the Statute or not.[83]

Article 17(3) includes three criteria that the Court will take into consideration in determining whether the national system is able or not. The first two criteria are: total or substantial collapse of the national judicial system, or unavailability of its national judicial system. The third criterion is that the state is unable to obtain the accused or the necessary evidence and testimony, or is otherwise unable to carry out its proceedings. Some states in the Rome Conference asserted that requiring the two criteria could limit the Court's ability to act,[84] necessitating the addition of the phrase 'or otherwise unable to carry out its proceedings'.[85]

To fulfil the requirements of Article 17(3), the national system should, firstly, be either 'unavailable' or 'collapsed' and, secondly, the state must be unable to obtain the accused or the evidence and testimony, or otherwise unable to carry out proceedings.[86]

---

80   Holmes, J. 2002. Complementarity: National Courts versus the International Criminal Court, in *The Rome Statute of The International Criminal Court: A Commentary*, edited by A. Cassese, P. Gaeta and J.R.W.D. Jones. Oxford: Oxford University Press, I, 677.

81   Kleffner, J. April 2003. The Impact of Complementarity on National Implementation of Substantive International Criminal Law. *Journal of International Criminal Justice*, 1, 86-115, 87.

82   Newton, M.A. 2001. Comparative Complementarity: Domestic Jurisdiction Consistent with the Rome Statute of the International Criminal Court. *Military Law Review*, 167, 20-73, 66.

83   International Criminal Court, Office of the Prosecutor. 2003. *Informal Expert Paper: The Principle of Complementarity in Practice*. ICC-OTP 2003, 1-38, 14. Available at: www.icc-cpi.int/library/organs/otp/complementarity.pdf [accessed: 11 August 2009].

84   Holmes, J. 1999. The Principle of Complementarity, in *The International Criminal Court: The Making of the Rome Statute, Issues, Negotiations, Results*, edited by R. Lee. The Hague: Kluwer, 49.

85   El-Zeidy, M. Summer 2002. The Principle of Complementarity: A Machinery to Implement International Criminal Law. *Michigan Journal of International Law*, 23, 4, 869-978, 884.

86   International Criminal Court, Office of the Prosecutor. 2003. *Informal Expert Paper: The Principle of Complementarity in Practice*. ICC-OTP 2003, 1-38, 14. Available

Total or substantial collapse, or unavailability   With respect to 'total collapse' of the national judicial systems, the drafters of the Rome Statute decided not to define the term. The determination of total collapse of a judicial system according to Article 17(3) was argued to be both logical and self-evident.[87]

The collapse of the national judicial system is usually the outcome of the collapse of the state itself. State collapse can be primarily defined by the absence of effective governmental authority at the domestic level with an external outcome reflected in the incapacity of the state to sustain itself as a member of the international community.[88] The absence of an effective government is characterized by the disappearance of state structures. This translates as an absence of basic organs of the state such as police, judiciary, education and healthcare.

The drafters of Article 17(3) had in mind situations where central government was lacking, such as Somalia, or state chaos due to civil war, such as Lebanon between 1975 and 1990, or in states wrought by natural disaster.[89] Analysis of those disastrous situations may shed light on main features of a 'total collapse'.[90] Rwanda provides an important example of a 'historical instance' of 'total collapse'.[91] In addition, other situations of violent and destructive conflicts, such as Kosovo and East Timor, offer other relevant examples of a total collapse of national judiciary. In the case of Kosovo, the total collapse of the judicial system was the result of an official policy of discrimination against Kosovar Albanians by Serbian authorities. This policy reduced the number of Kosovar Albanian judges and prosecutors to 30 out of 756, and to the mass departure of the non-Albanian population of Kosovo.[92] The total collapse of East Timor was even more intense than Kosovo.

---

at: www.icc-cpi.int/library/organs/otp/complementarity.pdf [accessed: 11 August 2009].

87   Holmes, J. 2002. Complementarity: National Courts versus the International Criminal Court, in *The Rome Statute of The International Criminal Court: A Commentary*, edited by A. Cassese, P. Gaeta and J.R.W.D. Jones. Oxford: Oxford University Press, I, 677.

88   Yannis, A. 1997. State Collapse and Prospects for Political Reconstruction and Democratic Governance in Somalia. *African Yearbook of International Law*, 5, 25.

89   Arsanjani, M.H. May 1999. Reflections on the Jurisdiction and Trigger Mechanism of the International Criminal Court, in *Reflections on the International Criminal Court*, edited by H. von Hebel, J.G. Lammers and J. Schukking. Cambridge: Cambridge University Press, 57, 70.

90   Yemi, O. 1996. Legality in a Collapsed State: the Somali Experience. *International and Comaparative Law Quarterly*, 45, 910-923, 910. Abdulqawi, Y. 1995. Reflections on the Fragility of State Institutions in Africa. *African Yearbook of International Law*, 2, 3

91   International Criminal Court, Office of the Prosecutor. 2003. *Informal Expert Paper: The Principle of Complementarity in Practice*. ICC-OTP 2003, Annex 4, 1-38, 27-28. Available at: www.icc-cpi.int/library/organs/otp/complementarity.pdf [accessed: 11 August 2009].

92   Strohmeyer, H. January 2001. Collapse and Reconstruction of a Judicial System: The United Nations Missions in Kosovo and East Timor. *The American Journal of International Law*, 95, 1, 46-63, 50.

The 'scorched earth' campaign that followed the popular consultation of 30 August 1999 destroyed the existing judicial infrastructure, including courts' equipments and legal materials (law books, case files and archives). The total collapse of the judicial system was also due to the lack of judges, lawyers and judicial support staffs, as most of them fled East Timor.[93]

Based on the criteria set in the Statute, international human rights law and the examples indicated *supra*, the determination of a total collapse of the national judicial system should take into consideration a number of factors. The *Informal Expert Paper: The Principle of Complementarity in Practice* includes the following non-exhaustive list of factors in determining whether there is a total collapse of the national judicial system: 'Lack of necessary personnel, judges, investigators, prosecutor; lack of judicial infrastructure; lack of substantive or procedural penal legislation … lack of access rendering system "unavailable"; obstruction by uncontrolled elements rendering system "unavailable"; amnesties, immunities rendering system "unavailable"'.[94]

With respect to 'substantial collapse' of the national judicial system, the latter will be rendered 'unable' if it has substantially collapsed, and the state is unable to obtain the accused or the necessary evidence and testimony, or otherwise unable to carry out its proceedings. However, neither the Statute, nor the Rules of Procedures and Evidence and the Regulations provide a definition of the term 'substantial'. The *travaux préparatoires* indicates that the term 'substantial collapse' replaced the previous phrase 'partial collapse'. Some delegations expressed the concern that the partial collapse of a national judicial system is not a strong enough threshold to consider the national system unable. The debate turned on substituting 'partial' with 'substantial'.[95]

Both qualitative and quantitative elements will be taken into consideration in determining the existence of a substantial collapse:[96] in terms of the quantitative element, the Court will examine the portion of the judicial system affected by the crisis. Depending on the quantitative element is not enough, and the Court will have to consider other qualitative elements, such as the type of institution

---

93 Strohmeyer, H. January 2001. Collapse and Reconstruction of a Judicial System: The United Nations Missions in Kosovo and East Timor. *The American Journal of International Law*, 95, 1, 46-63, 58.

94 International Criminal Court, Office of the Prosecutor. 2003. *Informal Expert Paper: The Principle of Complementarity in Practice*. ICC-OTP 2003, Annex 4, 1-38, 31. Available at: www.icc-cpi.int/library/organs/otp/complementarity.pdf [accessed: 11 August 2009].

95 Holmes, J. 1999. The Principle of Complementarity, in *The International Criminal Court: The Making of the Rome Statute, Issues, Negotiations, Results*, edited by R. Lee. The Hague: Kluwer, 53-54.

96 International Criminal Court, Office of the Prosecutor. 2003. *Informal Expert Paper: The Principle of Complementarity in Practice*. ICC-OTP 2003, 1-38, 28. Available at: www.icc-cpi.int/library/organs/otp/complementarity.pdf [accessed: 11 August 2009].

or personnel affected by such crisis.[97] For the qualitative elements, the relevance of the partial or substantial collapse will depend on the practical effect of such collapse on the judiciary. Bearing in mind Article 21, paragraph 3, it could be argued that the interpretation of 'substantial collapse' must be consistent with internationally recognized human rights.[98] It can be then argued that if the partial collapse has affected the conformity of the judiciary with due process and human rights, the collapse is then 'substantial' enough to be in contradiction with Article 21 of the Statute.

To conclude, the relation between the quantitative and qualitative element is thin. The quantitative element contributing to the qualitative elements indicates a 'substantial' collapse. For instance, a 'substantial' collapse can occur when a partial collapse (quantitative element) affects the function of the judiciary to deliver justice impartially and independently (qualitative element). Yet a partial collapse that does not affect the judiciary in its process of investigating and prosecuting core crime under the Statute according to Article 17 and 21 will hardly fulfil the 'inability' test.

With respect to unavailability of the national judicial system, 'unavailability' falls among one of the alternative factors within the first set of criteria that are taken into consideration by the Court when determining 'inability'. However, assessing 'unavailability' is more complex as the term is open-ended and could be subject to multiple interpretations.

Prima facie, the system will most likely be considered 'unavailable' simply because the judicial system is non-existent.[99] States that have no criminal judicial system, for instance, will cause a designation of 'unavailable' – hence bringing in the argument about states failing to take the necessary legal measures to incorporate necessary articles of the Statute into the domestic criminal and legal system (including core crimes of the ICC). Additionally, some jurists, like Lattanzi, Kleffner and Condorelli, acknowledge that the defects of domestic codes and laws can render a national system unavailable and that makes the case admissible before the ICC.[100] This has had an impact on some states that decided to incorporate

---

97   International Criminal Court, Office of the Prosecutor. 2003. *Informal Expert Paper: The Principle of Complementarity in Practice*. ICC-OTP 2003, 1-38, 28. Available at: www.icc-cpi.int/library/organs/otp/complementarity.pdf [accessed: 11 August 2009].

98   Article 21 of the Rome Statute of the International Criminal Court, UN Doc. A/CONF.183/9.

99   Cárdenas, C. 25-26 June 2004. The Admissibility Test Before The International Criminal Court Under Special Consideration of Amnesties And Truth Commissions, in *Complementary Views on Complementarity Proceedings of the International Roundtable on the Complementary Nature of the International Criminal Court, Amsterdam 25-26 June 2006*, edited by J. Kleffner and G. Kor. May 2006. Cambridge: Cambridge University Press, 8.

100   Kleffner, J. April 2003. The Impact of Complementarity on National Implementation of Substantive International Criminal Law. *Journal of International Criminal Justice*, 1, 86-115. Lattanzi, F. 2002. Official Capacities and Immunities, in *The*

the crimes of the Statute in their national systems. Some other states, such as Colombia, refused the argument that lack of national legislation to criminalize international crimes would render the system as unavailable.[101] According to this author, the latter opinion does not contradict the Rome Statute when such a defect does not prevent the national judicial systems from prosecuting the core crimes of the Statute as ordinary crimes according to Articles 17 and 20. Nonetheless, there are international crimes that do not have criminalization equivalent to ordinary crimes. For example, many legal systems do not have a matching legal terminology and criminalization for the war crime of forcing a prisoner of war or other protected person to serve in the forces of a hostile power.[102] Based on the above, the absence of criminalization of the ICC core crimes will not render the system unavailable if a corresponding ordinary crime is available at the national level. It is only when there is an absence of any criminalization of the core crimes – whether as international or as ordinary crimes – that the system can be rendered unavailable. The drafters of the Rome Statute accepted the prosecution of international crimes as ordinary crimes as a defence for the principle *ne bis in idem*, and therefore it will be illogical to consider the system unavailable if it is able to prosecute them as ordinary crimes.

The situation becomes more complex when the legal system is generally functional, but not in the particular instance of the defined case. This might be due to factual or legal obstacles related to the particular situation. Despite ambiguity, it seems that the Court will look into the defined case to see if the national judicial system is unavailable in this case, even if the system is generally functional.[103] The latter argument, which has been adopted by the *Informal Expert Paper* published by the ICC, can be criticized on a number of issues. Firstly, these instances need to be defined, as a broad margin of discretion on that may include numerous non-judicial elements beyond the scope of inability or unwillingness. Secondly, if these cases are not defined, then willing and able states could invoke such 'unavailability' to shift the burden to the ICC, and that will be inconsistent with the aim of the drafters to encourage national judicial system to prosecute international crimes.

Rome Statute of The International Criminal Court: A Commentary, edited by A. Cassese, P. Gaeta and J.R.W.D. Jones. Oxford: Oxford University Press, I, 667-678.

101   Declaration made upon ratification of the Rome Statute by Colombia. Available at: http://untreaty.un.org/ENGLISH/bible/englishinternetbible/partI/chapterXVIII/treaty10.asp [accessed: 11 September 2008].

102   Kleffner, J. April 2003. The Impact of Complementarity on National Implementation of Substantive International Criminal Law. *Journal of International Criminal Justice*, 1, 86-115, 88.

103   The International Criminal Court, Office of the Prosecutor. 2003. *Informal Expert Paper: The Principle of Complementarity in Practice*. ICC-OTP 2003, 1-38, 29. Available at: www.icc-cpi.int/library/organs/otp/complementarity.pdf [accessed: 11 August 2009].

'Inability to obtain the accused or the necessary evidence and testimony or otherwise'   In order for the ICC to consider the national judicial system 'unable' it should, firstly, be unavailable or suffering a total or substantial collapse, and secondly, be unable to obtain the accused or the necessary evidence and testimony or to carry out the proceedings.

The *travaux préparatoires* indicates that the 'inability to obtain the accused or the necessary evidence and testimony was then broadened to include "otherwise unable to carry out its proceedings"'.[104] The latter phrasing was introduced during the Preparatory Committee's negotiations for further clarification and completion of the admissibility test.[105] Based on this, the Court would deem a case to be admissible only when the national judicial system is 'unable' due to partial or total collapse and the state is unable to obtain an accused or key evidence and testimony or otherwise unable to carry out its proceedings.

In terms of inability to obtain the accused or the necessary evidence and testimony, many states face problems in bringing the accused to justice. This problem becomes acute and clear in extradition cases, where other states refuse to extradite the accused to the state interested in prosecuting the core crimes. In this situation, the national judicial system may be functional, but the state is nonetheless unable to obtain the accused due to external factors not related to substantial or total collapse of the national judicial system. Some jurists reasoned that in this case it is probable that the ICC could consider the case admissible based on the inability of the government to 'obtain the accused'.[106] This position can be easily criticized, and it can be argued that the system is 'available' and it is neither totally nor substantially collapsed, and therefore the first requirement for inability is not fulfilled. The legal language of the Statute clearly stipulates that the inability of a state to obtain extradition of an accused is not enough by itself to consider the case admissible under Article 17(3). The admissibility of the Ugandan referral could here be criticized, as we will see later in Uganda's case study.

Moreover, Article 17(3) includes the criterion 'otherwise unable to carry out its proceedings'. Without inserting such a statement, Article 17(3) would have constrained the power of the ICC to assess 'inability'. If not for this phrase, the Court would not have been able to look into cases where states are unable to prosecute core crimes due to factors other than inability to obtain the accused or the necessary evidence and testimony. This criterion opens the door to covering

---

104   Holmes, J. 1999. The Principle of Complementarity, in *The International Criminal Court: The Making of the Rome Statute, Issues, Negotiations, Results*, edited by R. Lee. The Hague: Kluwer, 49.

105   Holmes, J. 1999. The Principle of Complementarity, in *The International Criminal Court: The Making of the Rome Statute, Issues, Negotiations, Results*, edited by R. Lee. The Hague: Kluwer, 49.

106   Morris, M. 2000. Complementarity and Its Discontents: States, Victims and The International Criminal Court, in *International Crimes, Peace, and Human Rights: The Role of The International Criminal Court*, edited by D. Shelton, 189-190.

instances beyond the state's inability to obtain the accused or the necessary evidence or testimony.[107] This phrase empowers the ICC to look into other instances that hamper national judicial systems from prosecuting the crimes of the Statute such as: lack of judicial infrastructure; denial or obstruction of access to the system;[108] lack of legal framework; absence of correctional system; or insufficiency of qualified personnel.[109]

Gravity

The whole of the Statute rests on the idea of gravity. The ICC was established with the aim of creating an international court that can hear only the most serious cases of an international nature,[110] filling the gap left by embryonic international courts, which, due to practical, logistic and financial limitations, cannot prosecute all international crimes regardless of their gravity and mass.

Although the working group on complementarity did not differentiate between the gravity of the case and the gravity of the crime, the Statute makes this distinction. Article 17(1)(d) requires that the Court take into consideration the gravity of the case, while Article 53 raises the issue of taking into consideration the gravity of the crime.

The Statute does not include a definition for 'gravity'. The ILC draft included the gravity criterion by empowering the Court to find the case inadmissible if it is not of sufficient gravity.[111] The issue was not raised later during the negotiations. Again, in the Rome Conference it proved less contentious than other terms during the *travaux préparatoires* of the Rome Conference. There is no definition of 'gravity' in the Statute, but the chapeaus of Articles 6, 7 and 8 provide some guidance for interpreting the notion: Article 8 of the Statute requires the occurrence of war crimes to be part of a plan or policy or to be committed on a large scale for it to be prosecuted by the Court. Article 7 stipulates that the Court will prosecute

---

107   Holmes, J. 2002. Complementarity: National Courts versus the International Criminal Court, in *The Rome Statute of The International Criminal Court: A Commentary*, edited by A. Cassese, P. Gaeta and J.R.W.D. Jones. Oxford: Oxford University Press, I, 667-678.

108   International Criminal Court, Office of the Prosecutor. 2003. *Informal Expert Paper: The Principle of Complementarity in Practice*. ICC-OTP 2003, 1-38, 28. Available at: www.icc-cpi.int/library/organs/otp/complementarity.pdf [accessed: 11 August 2009].

109   Holmes, J. 2002. Complementarity: National Courts versus the International Criminal Court, in *The Rome Statute of The International Criminal Court: A Commentary*, edited by A. Cassese, P. Gaeta and J.R.W.D. Jones. Oxford: Oxford University Press, I, 667-678.

110   Preamble of the Rome Statute of the International Criminal Court, UN Doc. A/CONF.183/9.

111   Holmes, J. 1999. The Principle of Complementarity, in *The International Criminal Court: The Making of the Rome Statute, Issues, Negotiations, Results*, edited by R. Lee. The Hague: Kluwer, 1-54, 47.

crimes against humanity when committed 'as part of (a) wide spread or systematic attack'. Article 6 delineates the concept of the 'group' in prosecuting crimes of genocide.[112]

For further elaboration on the notion of 'gravity', Article 21 of the Statute is invoked again, and thus the practice of international courts could provide a source of practice for the ICC. Under the 'completion strategy' of the *ad hoc* Tribunals, the ICTY Appeals Chamber, in the case of *Prosecutor* v. *Zlatko Aleksovski*, indicated that the gravity of an offence is the result of the combined analysis of circumstances of the case and of the form and degree of participation of the accused in the crime.[113]

As for the gravity of a case, this may be assessed, firstly, according to the particular circumstances of each of the crimes committed (gravity in *concreto*) and secondly, according to the person concerned (gravity in *personam*). Rule 11 *bis* of the ICTY Rules of Procedure and Evidence indicates that in the process of referring back to national courts, the element of gravity of the crimes and the level of responsibility of the accused will be taken into account.[114]

In addition, the ICTR, in the *Prosecutor* v. *Laurent Semanza* case, upheld a position similar to that of the ICTY by stating that the gravity of a crime must go 'beyond the abstract gravity of the crime to take into account the particular circumstances of the case, as well as the form and degree of the participation of the accused in the crime'.[115] The analysis *supra* of the Statute and the ICTY jurisprudence falls mainly under the umbrella of Article 53, as it tackles the 'gravity of the crime' rather than 'gravity of the case'. However, the 'gravity of the case' itself includes the assessment of the 'gravity of the crimes' and 'those bearing the greatest responsibility' for those crimes.[116] This will be further elaborated *infra*.

Gravity is the most important factor for selecting cases and evaluating situations.[117] The notion of 'gravity' is pivotal in the function of the ICC, as the

---

112   El-Zeidy, M. Summer 2002. The Principle of Complementarity: A Machinery to Implement International Criminal Law. *Michigan Journal of International Law*, 23, 4, 869-978, 885.

113   *Prosecutor* v. *Zlatko Aleksovski*. 24 March 2000. ICTY, Case No IT-95-14/1-A, App. Ch., para. 182.

114   Rule 11 *bis* of Rules of Procedure And Evidence of The International Criminal Tribunal for the former Yugoslavia. Revised 30 September 2002, amended 28 July 2004, amended 11 February 2005. IT/32/Rev. 37. Available at: www.un.org/icty/legaldoc-e/index-t.htm [accessed: 24 January 2006].

115   *Prosecutor* v. *Laurent Semanza*. 15 May 2003. ICTR, Case no. ICTR-97-20-T, para. 555.

116   International Criminal Court, Office of the Prosecutor. 2003. *Paper on Some Policy Issues before the Office of the Prosecutor*. ICC-OTP 2003, 1-9, 7. Available at: www.icc-cpi.int/library/organs/otp/030905_Policy_Paper.pdf [accessed: 20 February 2009].

117   Moreno-Ocampo, L. 2006. Symposium: International Criminal Tribunals in the 21st Century: Keynote Address: Integrating the Work of the ICC into Local Justice Initiatives. *American University International Law Review*, 21, 497-503, 499.

ICC cannot look into all cases related to committing war crimes, crimes against humanity and genocide in the world. If this had been the case, the Court would have been flooded with cases that exceed its capability to handle.[118] The Court as a single institution with a limited budget cannot but adjudicate a small number of cases based on defined criteria, and here the criterion of 'gravity' becomes crucial. This criterion will restrict the Court to looking into cases of grave impact and outcome, while cases of lower gravity will be deferred to the national judicial system. However, the problem of an 'impunity gap' could materialize if the national system does not prosecute cases of a low gravity.[119]

As mentioned earlier, 'gravity' under Article 17(1)(d) covers the gravity of the case. That includes the assessment of the 'gravity of the crimes' and 'those bearing the greatest responsibility' for those crimes. This gravity threshold does not relate to the crimes alone, but also to the role of the accused.[120]

The Office of the Prosecutor indicated that the factors relevant in assessing the 'gravity' threshold include 'the scale of the crimes, the nature of the crimes, the manner of commission of the crimes, the impact of the crimes',[121] and the number of victims, particularly for the most serious crimes.[122] The Legal Advisory Section of the ICC elaborated on further factors to be taken into consideration as indicative of 'gravity'. They include the number of persons apparently involved in the crime; the level of perpetration of the persons involved; and availability of national proceedings, at least with respect to some of the alleged perpetrators. Hence, a case may be deemed of low gravity level if the perpetrator does not have a high level of responsibility for the crimes, even where such crimes in themselves are grave.[123]

Prosecutor Moreno-Ocampo reasoned that 'gravity' is one of the most important criteria for selection of situations and cases for which to initiate investigations.[124]

---

118 El-Zeidy, M. Summer 2002. The Principle of Complementarity: A Machinery to Implement International Criminal Law. *Michigan Journal of International Law*, 23, 4, 869-978, 885.

119 International Criminal Court, Office of the Prosecutor. 2003. *Paper on Some Policy Issues before the Office of the Prosecutor*. ICC-OTP 2003, 1-9. Available at: www.icc-cpi.int/library/organs/otp/030905_Policy_Paper.pdf [accessed: 20 February 2009].

120 The ICTR jurisprudence in *Laurent Semanza* case has taken into consideration the degree and role of the accused while assessing the element of gravity. See *Prosecutor* v. *Laurent Semanza*. 15 May 2003. ICTR, Case no. ICTR-97-20-T.

121 International Criminal Court, Office of the Prosecutor. 2003. *Paper on Some Policy Issues before the Office of the Prosecutor*. ICC-OTP 2003, 1-9, 5. Available at: www.icc-cpi.int/library/organs/otp/030905_Policy_Paper.pdf [accessed: 20 February 2009].

122 Moreno-Ocampo, L. 2006. Symposium: International Criminal Tribunals in the 21st Century: Keynote Address: Integrating the Work of the ICC into Local Justice Initiatives. *American University International Law Review*, 21, 497-503, 499.

123 International Criminal Court, Office of the Prosecutor, 17 February 2005. *Revised Discussion Paper on ICC-OTP Case Selection Criteria*, 11.

124 Moreno-Ocampo, L. 2006. Symposium: International Criminal Tribunals in the 21st Century: Keynote Address: Integrating the Work of the ICC into Local Justice

The Court, including the Office of the Prosecutor, shall determine that a case is inadmissible where 'the case is not of sufficient gravity to justify further action by the Court'.[125] For assessing situations, Moreno-Ocampo determined the Democratic Republic of Congo as the gravest situation, with Uganda a close second. The Security Council referral of Darfur is no less grave than the former cases.[126]

Finally, one could raise a simple question of whether the Court will depend solely on quantitative criteria to determine 'gravity' or whether the qualitative criteria should be taken into consideration. The analysis of the nature of the factors indicated *supra* will assist us in deducing the degree to which the ICC is dependent on quantitative and qualitative elements in assessing 'gravity' under Article 17. The list indicated *supra* shows that the Court will mainly take into consideration quantitative criteria. Most of the factors – including the scale of the crime; the nature of the crimes; the manner of commission of the crimes; the number of victims; the number of persons apparently involved in the crime; and the level of perpetration of the persons involved – are mainly quantitative in nature, and the Court considers them as such. However, the Court will also take into consideration 'the impact of the crimes' in determining 'gravity'. The last criterion is of a qualitative nature, as the Court will assess the impact of the crimes, considering several questions: will the crimes cause further crimes? Will they affect peace and security of the society? The answers cannot be of a quantitative nature, but rather of qualitative nature.

Hence, assessment of gravity will mainly depend on factors of a quantitative nature, not disregarding the qualitative element counting the 'impact of the crime'.

Complementarity and Article 20(3)

Article 17(1)(c) stipulates that the Court shall determine that a case is inadmissible where, *inter alia*, 'the person concerned has already been tried for conduct which is the subject of the complaint, and a trial by the Court is not permitted under Article 20, paragraph 3'.[127] This brings in the application of Article 20(3), which states that:

Initiatives. *American University International Law Review*, 21, 497-503, 499.

125   International Criminal Court, Office of the Prosecutor. 2003. *Paper on Some Policy Issues before the Office of the Prosecutor*. ICC-OTP 2003, 1-9, 5. Available at: www. icc-cpi.int/library/organs/otp/030905_Policy_Paper.pdf [accessed: 20 February 2009].

126   Moreno-Ocampo, L. 2006. Symposium: International Criminal Tribunals in the 21st Century: Keynote Address: Integrating the Work of the ICC into Local Justice Initiatives. *American University International Law Review*, 21, 497-503, 499.

127   Article 17(1)(c) of the Rome Statute of the International Criminal Court, UN Doc. A/CONF.183/9.

[N]o person who has been tried by another court for conduct also proscribed under Article 6, 7 or 8 shall be tried by the Court with respect to the same conduct unless the proceedings in the other court:

(a) Were for the purpose of shielding the person concerned from criminal responsibility for crimes within the jurisdiction of the Court; or (b) Otherwise were not conducted independently or impartially in accordance with the norms of due process recognized by international law and were conducted in a manner which, in the circumstances, was inconsistent with an intent to bring the person concerned to justice.[128]

Based on the articles above, the *ne bis in idem* principle is connected with the principle of complementarity reflected in Article 17.[129] The complementarity principle takes into consideration the principle of double jeopardy as a cornerstone in the relation between the Court and national courts. The *ne bis in idem* is a commonly recognized principle and a basic human right.[130]

The *ne bis in idem* is a fundamental principle in most legal traditions at the domestic level. It has historically been regarded as merely an internal rule of domestic criminal justice.[131] During the last decades, however, there has been an increasing trend to recognize the principle of *ne bis in idem* at the international level. The *ne bis in idem* maxim has been stipulated in a number of international instruments and courts, such as the International Covenant on Civil and Political Rights,[132] treaties of the Council of Europe and European Union[133] – including the

---

128   Article 20(3) of the Rome Statute of the International Criminal Court, UN Doc. A/CONF.183/9.

129   El-Zeidy, M. Summer 2002. The Principle of Complementarity: A Machinery to Implement International Criminal Law. *Michigan Journal of International Law*, 23, 4, 869-978, 898.

130   Surlan, T. 2005. Ne bis in idem in Conjunction with the Principle of Complementarity in the Rome Statute. The European Society of International Law; 'Agora' Papers presented at the 2005 Florence Founding Conference of the European Society of International Law, 1-8, 1. Available at: www.esil-sedi.eu/english/pdf/Surlan.PDF [accessed: 1 October 2008].

131   Ligenti, K. 2005. Protocol of the Proceedings on Concurrent National and International Criminal Jurisdiction and the Principle of Ne Bis In Idem. *Revue Internationale De Droit Penal*, 751.

132   Article 14(7) of the International Covenant on Civil and Political Rights (1966), G.A. res. 2200A (XXI), 21 U.N. GAOR Supp. (no. 16) at 52, UN Doc. A/6316 (1966), 999 U.N.T.S. 171.

133   Ligenti, K. 2005. Protocol of the Proceedings on Concurrent National and International Criminal Jurisdiction and the Principle of Ne Bis In Idem. *Revue Internationale De Droit Penal*, 751.

Schengen Convention[134] – and the Statutes of the *ad hoc* Tribunals for the former Yugoslavia[135] and Rwanda.[136]

The principle *ne bis in idem* at the domestic level rests on three bases. Firstly, no one should have to face more than one prosecution for the same offence. Secondly, the prosecution normally cannot take actions against the same persons for the same facts after criminally proceedings have been finally ceased. Thirdly, the *ne bis in idem* maxim reflects respect to the judicial decision and *res judicata.*[137]

At the international level, the first rationale for international *ne bis in idem* is, to a certain extent, to protect the individual, as is the case at the domestic level. It is important to note that international human rights instruments do not provide protection beyond the state legal system. The other rationale is to avoid contradictory judgments, even among foreign courts.[138]

The application of the principle *ne bis in idem* in the Rome Statute is somewhat different, in terms of its ambit, from what is commonly known in the national law.[139] The principle in the Statute works at two different levels of law: national and international.

The Court will render the case inadmissible if the person has already been 'tried' for conduct which is the subject of the complaint where the conduct is proscribed under Article 6, 7 or 8 of the statute, 'unless the proceedings were ... for the purpose of shielding the person concerned from criminal responsibility, or ... were not conducted independently or impartially in accordance with the norms of due process recognized by international law and were conducted in a manner which, in the circumstances, was inconsistent with an intent to bring the person concerned to justice'.[140]

---

134 Van den Wyngaert, Ch. and Stessens, G. October 1999. The International Non Bis In Idem Principle: Resolving Some of the Unanswered Questions. *The International and Comparative Law Quarterly*, 48, 4, 779-804, 779, 786.

135 Security Council Resolution 827 (25 May 1993), Article 10(2)(a). S/Res/827(1993).

136 Security Council Resolution 955 (8 November 1994), Article 9(2)(a). S/RES/955 (1994).

137 Van den Wyngaert, Ch. and Stessens, G. October 1999. The International Non Bis In Idem Principle: Resolving Some of the Unanswered Questions. *The International and Comparative Law Quarterly*, 48, 4, 779-804, 779, 780.

138 Van den Wyngaert, Ch. and Stessens, G. October 1999. The International Non Bis In Idem Principle: Resolving Some of the Unanswered Questions. *The International and Comparative Law Quarterly*, 48, 4, 779-804, 782.

139 Surlan, T. 2005. Ne bis in idem in Conjunction with the Principle of Complementarity in the Rome Statute. The European Society of International Law; 'Agora' Papers Presented at the 2005 Florence Founding Conference of the European Society of International Law, 1-8, 6. Available at: www.esil-sedi.eu/english/pdf/Surlan.PDF [accessed: 2 October 2009].

140 Article 20(3) of the Rome Statute of the International Criminal Court, UN Doc. A/CONF.183/9.

A legal analysis for each of the terms within Article 17(1)(c) and Article 20(3) seems indispensable for further understanding the admissibility mechanism of the ICC. This study does not engage in a detailed analysis of Article 20. Instead, it focuses on Article 20(3) as it is related to the admissibility criteria under Article 17.

The Term 'Tried'

To apply the *ne bis in idem* maxim, the person has to have been already tried. Yet does the term 'tried' includes the investigation, prosecution, trial and sentencing or acquittal, or only some of these stages? The ICC will most likely take into consideration the ICTY jurisprudence and practice. In the *Prosecutor* v. *Tadic* case, Decision on the Defence Motion on the principle of *ne bis in idem*, the Trial Chamber dismissed the defence contention that Tadic has been already tried in Germany. The ICTY Trial Chamber contradicted this assertion, stating that the principle *ne bis in idem* is not violated until the accused has been already tried – which was not the case for Tadic – and as there is no judgment yet, there cannot be claims of violation of *ne bis in idem*.[141]

The application of the *ne bis in idem* refers to the final decision or judgment. *Ne bis in idem* may cover situations where misconduct took place at the final stage of the judicial decision even though investigation and prosecution had been carried out appropriately.[142]

The Term 'Conduct' within Articles 17 and 20(3)

The provision uses the term 'conduct' rather than 'crime' for discarding the ICC's admissibility for the case if the conduct has been tried before and certain conditions obtained. The Statute adopted a broad approach in the upward *ne bis in idem*, while it used a restricted downward *ne bis in idem*. In the latter, the Statute prohibits national trials against persons who have been tried by the ICC for the same crime.

Use of the term 'conduct' in the upward *ne bis in idem* is the result of a compromise during the Rome Negotiations.[143] Initially this was not the case with the ILC Draft

---

141   Rodney, D. and Khan, K. 2003. *Archbold, International Criminal Courts Practice, Procedure and Evidence*. London: Sweet & Maxwell Limited, 454.

142   Surlan, T. 2005. Ne bis in idem in Conjunction with the Principle of Complementarity in the Rome Statute. The European Society of International Law; 'Agora' Papers Presented at the 2005 Florence Founding Conference of the European Society of International Law, 1-8, 6. Available at: www.esil-sedi.eu/english/pdf/Surlan.PDF [accessed: 2 October 2009].

143   The final package included two amendments. The first amendment made was in the phrase 'with respect to the same conduct' in the chapeau of paragraph 3. It clarified that the ICC can still try a person even if he/she had already been tried in a national court,

Statute. Article 42 of the 1994 ILC Draft Statute provided an 'ordinary' crimes exception to the *ne bis in idem* principle; the ICC could try a person if the acts for which he or she was tried in another court were characterized by that Court as an 'ordinary crime'. According to the Commission's definition, a situation where the act has been treated as an ordinary crime, and not as an international crime having the special characteristics, would exclude the application of the *ne bis in idem* principle and render the situation admissible before the ICC.

During discussions in the *Ad Hoc* Committee, it was suggested that the ordinary crimes distinction should be abolished since such a distinction was not common to all legal systems and could therefore cause substantial legal problems. Concerns were also expressed that Article 42 of the ILC Draft Statute was problematic because it conferred upon the Court too much of a supervisory role vis-à-vis national systems.[144]

The 'ordinary crimes' issue resurfaced during the negotiations of the Preparatory Committee between 1996 and 1998. Delegates diverged greatly on how to define the concept of 'ordinary crimes' and many therefore questioned whether it should be included at all. The majority argued that if an accused committed some reprehensible offence, it did not matter if that person was tried, convicted and punished pursuant to a national crime as opposed to the crimes listed in the Statute. Arguments were made concerning the deterrent and retributive effects of adjudicating crimes as international, but these points did not sway the majority. Consequently, the concept of 'ordinary crime' was not included.[145]

The issue of an 'ordinary crimes' exception was largely resolved by the time of the Rome Conference. Due to definitional difficulties,[146] such an exception was not included. No further elaboration has been provided in the *travaux préparatoires*.

---

as long as the previous trial was for a different conduct. The second amendment added the phrase 'in accordance with the norms of due process recognized by International law' in the Article regarding admissibility to make the criteria more objective. Since this phrase had been accepted for admissibility, it was believed that it should be made applicable for *ne bis in idem*. Holmes, J. 1999. The Principle of Complementarity, in *The International Criminal Court: The Making of the Rome Statute, Issues, Negotiations, Results*, edited by R. Lee. The Hague: Kluwer, 59.

144   The Report of the *Ad Hoc* Committee does not elaborate upon this but the implication seems to be that the ambiguity of the 'ordinary crimes' exception gave too much power to the Court to ignore national decisions.

145   Holmes, J. 1999. The Principle of Complementarity, in *The International Criminal Court: The Making of the Rome Statute, Issues, Negotiations, Results*, edited by R. Lee. The Hague: Kluwer, 58.

146   Surlan, T. 2005. Ne bis in idem in Conjunction with the Principle of Complementarity in the Rome Statute. The European Society of International Law; 'Agora' Papers Presented at the 2005 Florence Founding Conference of the European Society of International Law, 1-8, 6. Available at: www.esil-sedi.eu/english/pdf/Surlan.PDF [accessed: 2 October 2008].

During the Rome Conference, a technical change was included in the chapeau of paragraph 3: 'with respect to the same conduct'. Holmes says, 'the addition was made to clarify that the Court could try someone even if that person had been tried in a national court, provided that different conduct was the subject of the prosecution'.[147]

The Conduct Proscribed under Articles 6, 7 and 8

The impact of the ICC decision on national courts is much narrower than the effect of a national decision on the ICC.[148] In comparison with national judicial systems, the ICC powers are more restricted and tied to applying the *ne bis in idem* principle.

Article 20(3) stipulates that such conduct or act should meet the specific requirements listed in Articles 6, 7 and 8.[149] The 'conduct' has to be listed among one of conducts identified in the core crimes of the Statute, whether it is under the crime of genocide, crimes against humanity, or war crimes. This correlation limits the phrase 'conduct' and attaches to it specific acts under each of the crimes, leaving us with two interpretations of 'conduct'. Firstly, these conducts should be considered as falling under one of the conducts under Articles 6, 7 and 8. Bassiouni defines the 'same conduct' as identical acts, or a series of acts related to each other by the scheme or intent of the actor, or multiple acts committed in more than one place at different times, but correlated to the actor's criminal design.[150] For instance, Article 7(1)(a) refers to murder as one of the conducts that could qualify as a crime against humanity if its other elements are fulfilled. If national courts try someone for murder (which is proscribed under Article 7(1)(a)), even as an ordinary crime, the ICC is barred from retrying that person again for a crime against humanity. The second interpretation states that such conduct or act should meet the specific requirements listed in Articles 6, 7 and 8. For example, if this interpretation is applied to the conduct under Article 7(1)(a), it requires that murder be 'part of a widespread or systematic attack directed against any

---

147   Holmes, J. 1999. The Principle of Complementarity, in *The International Criminal Court: The Making of the Rome Statute, Issues, Negotiations, Results*, edited by R. Lee. The Hague: Kluwer, 58.

148   Surlan, T. 2005. Ne bis in idem in Conjunction with the Principle of Complementarity in the Rome Statute. The European Society of International Law; 'Agora' Papers Presented at the 2005 Florence Founding Conference of the European Society of International Law, 1-8, 6. Available at: www.esil-sedi.eu/english/pdf/Surlan.PDF [accessed: 2 October 2008].

149   El-Zeidy, M. Summer 2002. The Principle of Complementarity: A Machinery to Implement International Criminal Law. *Michigan Journal of International Law*, 23, 4, 869-978, 899.

150   Bassiouni, M.Ch. 1996. *International Extradition: United States Law and Practice*. Dobbs Ferry: Oceana, 602.

civilian population, with knowledge of the attack'.[151] According to this position, the elements of the core 'crime' are required from the conduct itself, and entails that the conduct constitute the 'crime'. Thus, according to this view, the intention of the drafters was 'crime' and not 'conduct'. Despite some jurists upholding the second interpretation by building a joint correlation between Article 20(3)(a) and Article 22(1),[152] the first interpretation is more appropriate, and the intention of the drafters was for the term 'conduct' 'proscribed under Article 6, 7 or 8'. If states adjudicate and convict a person for an ordinary crime with no intention of shielding that person from criminal responsibility, then this judicial action bars the ICC from retrying the person for a core crime within the Statute.[153] Thus, the Rome Statute does not provide any exception from the *ne bis in idem* principle for ordinary crimes.[154]

A legal reading of Article 20, as it refers specifically to 'conduct' rather than 'crimes', suggests that the characterization of crimes is not relevant to the application of the *ne bis in idem* principle. If the relevant conduct has been prosecuted then the Court is precluded from conducting its own prosecution. Support for this conclusion may also be garnered from the *travaux préparatoires* on Article 20, as well as secondary accounts of the negotiations.[155]

Based on the above, the characterization of crimes does not seem to have an impact on the application of the *ne bis in idem* principle. Furthermore, it appears that states are not under any obligation to implement legislation mirroring the content of the Rome Statute. The investigations and prosecutions for core international crimes as ordinary ones will most likely render the case inadmissible under Article 20(3).[156]

---

151   Article 7(1) of the Rome Statute of the International Criminal Court, UN Doc. A/CONF.183/9.

152   El-Zeidy, M. Summer 2002. The Principle of Complementarity: A Machinery to Implement International Criminal Law. *Michigan Journal of International Law*, 23, 4, 869-978, 900.

153   Kleffner, J. April 2003. The Impact of Complementarity on National Implementation of Substantive International Criminal Law. *Journal of International Criminal Justice*, 1, 86-115, 92.

154   Surlan, T. 2005. Ne bis in idem in Conjunction with the Principle of Complementarity in the Rome Statute. The European Society of International Law; 'Agora' Papers Presented at the 2005 Florence Founding Conference of the European Society of International Law, 1-8, 6. Available at: www.esil-sedi.eu/english/pdf/Surlan.PDF [accessed: 2 October 2008].

155   Working Group on Complementarity and Trigger Mechanism. 13 August 1997. Preparatory Committee on the Establishment of an International Criminal Court. 4-15 August 1997.A/Ac.249/1997/Wg.3/Crp.2, 2. Available at: www.iccnow.org/documents/ IssuesofAdmissibility.pdf [accessed: 3 July 2008].

156   Van den Wyngaert, C. and Ongena, T. 2002. Ne bis in idem Principle, Including the Issue of Amnesty, in *The Rome Statute of The International Criminal Court: A Commentary*,

Proceedings for the Purpose of Shielding

The final agreement in the Rome Conference was to discard the 'ordinary crime' exception. It was replaced with 'shielding the person'. Despite the differences, both approaches are based on the same idea, that is, 'the necessity of proper law qualification, proper punishment and satisfaction of victims, justice, and preventive effect'.[157]

Each of these safeguards provided under Article 20(3) has been discussed extensively earlier, and from the above we can glean that the Court considers it imperative that these safeguards to *ne bis in idem* exist when the national system is either unwilling or unable. However, the application of *ne bis in idem* is precluded in the total absence or collapse of the national system as no trials will take place and no judgments will be reached. Thus, the only remaining exception to *ne bis in idem* is the 'unwillingness' of national authorities to behave independently or impartially with the intention of shielding the accused. If the proceedings were for the purpose of shielding the person concerned, then the trial is a sham trial, and the ICC can try the accused. Furthermore, if the proceedings are not conducted independently or impartially, then this is an exception to the *ne bis in idem* principle under Article 20 and the ICC will retry the person concerned. The only possible room for considering the system 'unable' is when an inadequate sentence is applied to the matching ordinary crime. For example, instead of imposing the war crime sentence for pillage, a much lighter sentence would be imposed for normal theft. According to one author, it is possible to consider 'the system unavailable' in the absence of an adequate sentence for the crime.[158] However, this may have less to do with *ne bis in idem*, but rather with the complementarity principle and the availability of the national judicial system under Article 17(3). Hence, proceedings (acquittal or conviction in continental system) for the purpose of shielding the person concerned, or that were not conducted independently or impartially, are exceptions to the *ne bis in idem* principle under Article 20(3), and render the national system 'unwilling' to prosecute under the complementarity principle. Based on the *supra* argument, the case will be admissible before the ICC, and retrial is allowed as an exception to Article 20.

---

edited by A. Cassese, P. Gaeta and J.R.W.D. Jones. Oxford: Oxford University Press, I, 724-726.

157   Surlan, T. 2005. Ne bis in idem in Conjunction with the Principle of Complementarity in the Rome Statute. The European Society of International Law; 'Agora' Papers Presented at the 2005 Florence Founding Conference of the European Society of International Law, 1-8, 6. Available at: www.esil-sedi.eu/english/pdf/Surlan.PDF [accessed: 2 October 2009].

158   Kleffner, J. April 2003. The Impact of Complementarity on National Implementation of Substantive International Criminal Law. *Journal of International Criminal Justice*, 1, 86-115, 93.

To conclude, the *ne bis in idem* principle, as adopted in Article 20 of the ICC Statute, is more 'diluted' than what was adopted in the ICTY and ICTR Statutes. The adoption of 'conduct' instead of 'crime' has unfortunate implications for the national implementation of the Rome Statute in national systems. Since states can still prosecute core crimes as ordinary crimes (if proscribed under Articles 6, 7 and 8) without triggering the ICC's jurisdiction, then pressure or legal obligation on state parties to incorporate ICC core crimes into national criminal codes is relaxed.

However, there is still hope that states remain compelled to prosecute certain international crimes for fear that the ICC will render the case admissible. In addition, some of the ICC crimes have no matching ordinary crime. For example, there is no ordinary crime available for prosecuting the war crime of compelling a prisoner of war or other protected person to serve in the forces of a hostile power. In addition, there is no matching ordinary crime for crime of denial of quarter in the customs and laws of war. In this instance, the states must be compelled to investigate and prosecute for the same crime and not conduct, otherwise the principle *ne bis in idem* cannot be invoked, and the case will be admissible before the ICC.

Complementarity in Practice

The Prosecutorial Policy of the OTP

The application of complementarity in practice has been elaborated through the policy paper published by the Office of the Prosecutor (OTP), as well as through the application of the admissibility criteria in cases before the Court. These cases will be discussed in the coming chapters. This section will discuss the elaboration of the complementarity principle through the Prosecutor's policy.

The Prosecutor has stipulated in the *Paper on Some Policy Issues before the Office of the Prosecutor* that the Office will function on two levels.[159] At the first level, it will target those who bear most responsibility for the crimes. At the second level, it will encourage national prosecutions for the lower-ranking perpetrators through positive cooperation between the Court and the national systems.[160] The element of gravity of the case is pivotal in the selection of cases for the Prosecutor.[161] The Office also invoked a 'sequenced' approach in the selection of

---

159   International Criminal Court, Office of the Prosecutor. 2003. *Paper on Some Policy Issues before the Office of the Prosecutor*. ICC-OTP 2003, 1-9, 3. Available at: www. icc-cpi.int/library/organs/otp/030905_Policy_Paper.pdf [accessed: 20 February 2009].

160   International Criminal Court, Office of the Prosecutor. 2003. *Paper on Some Policy Issues before the Office of the Prosecutor*. ICC-OTP 2003, 1-9, 3. Available at: www. icc-cpi.int/library/organs/otp/030905_Policy_Paper.pdf [accessed: 20 February 2009].

161   International Criminal Court, Office of the Prosecutor. 2003. *Paper on Some Policy Issues before the Office of the Prosecutor*. ICC-OTP 2003, 1-9, 7. Available at: www.

cases according to their gravity.[162] The Court will prosecute those who bear the most responsibility for grave crimes that are admissible. Nevertheless, the issue of less serious perpetrators also stands. The Prosecutor employs a kind of division of labour within the complementarity principle: it is the duty of national judicial systems to prosecute this category of crimes and perpetrators. In the absence of such prosecutions, the 'impunity gap' may materialize. This is a real case scenario, and it presents a problem for the complementarity system. While the ICC Statute does impose a duty on the states to prosecute international crimes,[163] in instances where states lack the will to prosecute, the ICC is to prosecute under the complementarity principle. The primacy of the state to prosecute is forfeited when the state refrains from exercising jurisdiction.

The restriction of the prosecutorial policy to those most responsible may, however, lead to impunity for low-level perpetrators if states do not take action against them. The Prosecutor has stressed on cooperation between the Court and the concerned state to encourage and facilitate national prosecutions, but the Prosecutor has not explained how the Court would impose cooperation in relation to 'non-cooperative' states. The terms 'encouraging' or 'facilitating' are inadequate; if states remain determined to refuse to prosecute, the 'impunity gap' becomes a reality. This is a serious lacuna for the whole complementarity principle in particular and for ending impunity – as stated in the preamble of the Statute – in general.

Furthermore, the Office of the Prosecutor developed three core principles that constitute essential constituencies of the prosecutorial strategy: positive complementarity, focused investigations and prosecutions, and maximizing the impact.[164]

With respect to the positive approach to complementarity, the Prosecutor indicated that the Court will 'encourage genuine national proceedings where possible; relies on national and international networks; and participates in a system of international cooperation'.[165] There are two guiding principles that clarify the

---

icc-cpi.int/library/organs/otp/030905_Policy_Paper.pdf [accessed: 20 February 2009]. See also Moreno-Ocampo, L. 2006. Symposium: International Criminal Tribunals in the 21st Century: Keynote Address: Integrating the Work of the ICC into Local Justice Initiatives. *American University International Law Review*, 21, 497-503, 499.

162　International Criminal Court, Office of the Prosecutor. 14 September 2006. *The Office of the Prosecutor Report on Prosecutorial Strategy*, The Hague, 1-11, 4. Available at: www.icc-cpi.int/library/organs/otp/OTP_Prosecutorial-Strategy-20060914_English.pdf [accessed: 2 June 2009].

163　Preamble of the Rome Statute of the International Criminal Court, UN Doc. A/CONF.183/9.

164　International Criminal Court, Office of the Prosecutor. 14 September 2006. *The Office of the Prosecutor Report on Prosecutorial Strategy*, The Hague, 1-11, 4. Available at: www.icc-cpi.int/library/organs/otp/OTP_Prosecutorial-Strategy-20060914_English.pdf [accessed: 2 June 2009].

165　International Criminal Court, Office of the Prosecutor. 14 September 2006. *The Office of the Prosecutor Report on Prosecutorial Strategy*, The Hague, 1-11, 5. Available

OTP approach to complementarity: 'partnership' and 'vigilance'. 'Partnership' is necessary in exercising the complementarity principle among the ICC and state parties, and such partnership should be positive and constructive. As for 'vigilance', the ICC must diligently apply various levels of scrutiny to detect whether the national judicial system is willing and able to exercise its duty to prosecute core international crimes. In the case of *indicia* that the national process is not genuine, the prosecutor is to carry out his responsibilities under the Statute.[166]

A positive approach to complementarity – in order to encourage national proceedings – requires involvement in external diplomatic and political negotiations and consultation with states. The allocation of a separate division within the Office of the Prosecutor reflects this approach. The formation of the Jurisdiction, Complementarity and Cooperation Division (JCCD) indicates the importance of the non-judiciary role of the Prosecutor on various levels.

Prosecutor Moreno-Ocampo has confirmed on a number of occasions the importance of establishing cooperation and consultation with state parties. On one occasion he stated that 'a prosecutor in the United States does not have to convince the Senate to support his activities, nor convince the chief of police to follow his instructions. He has a police force at his disposal. I have none of this. In effect, I am a stateless prosecutor'.[167]

A considerable part of the work of the OTP of the ICC is hence not of judicial nature. Such function differs from the role of similar OTPs of *ad hoc* Tribunals. There are no similar JCCD divisions within the ICTY and ICTR.[168]

As for focused investigations and prosecutions, the Prosecutor will concentrate on the most serious crimes and on those agents bearing the greatest responsibility.[169]

---

at: www.icc-cpi.int/library/organs/otp/OTP_Prosecutorial-Strategy-20060914_English.pdf [accessed: 2 June 2009].

166   International Criminal Court, Office of the Prosecutor. 2003. *Informal Expert Paper: The Principle of Complementarity in Practice*. ICC-OTP 2003, 1-38, 3. Available at: www.icc-cpi.int/library/organs/otp/complementarity.pdf [accessed: 11 August 2009].

167   Moreno-Ocampo, L. 2006. Symposium: International Criminal Tribunals in the 21st Century: Keynote Address: Integrating the Work of the ICC into Local Justice Initiatives. *American University International Law Review*, 21, 497-503, 501.

168   The ICTY and ICTR are based on Security Council Resolutions 827 and 955 under Chapter VII. The two *ad hoc* tribunals' jurisdictions enjoy primacy over national courts that are obliged to cooperate with these courts under Chapter VII of the UN Charter. There is no necessity for organizing cooperation or jurisdiction between these international courts and national courts, on the contrary to the ICC–state parties' relation.

169   International Criminal Court, Office of the Prosecutor. 14 September 2006. *The Office of the Prosecutor Report on Prosecutorial Strategy*, The Hague, 1-11, 4. Available at: www.icc-cpi.int/library/organs/otp/OTP_Prosecutorial-Strategy-20060914_English.pdf [accessed: 2 June 2009].

According to the OTP, this strategy will shortlist cases and investigations, and enhance the possibility of expeditious trials.[170]

The third principle in the Prosecutor's strategy is to maximize the impact of the investigations and prosecutions of the Office.[171] Prosecutor Moreno-Ocampo confirms this strategy: 'We must therefore discuss how to maximize the impact of trials because my real duty is to investigate and prosecute in order to contribute to the prevention of future crimes'.[172] Moreover, the ICC maximizes its impact not only by exercising its own jurisdiction, but also by encouraging states to prosecute and further cooperate with the Court.[173] However, the ICC's recent prosecutorial policy in the Democratic Republic of Congo case seems to be inconsistent with the positive complementarity approach, as instead of encouraging the DRC judicial system to prosecute – when able and willing – it has requested the surrender of one of the suspects to the ICC.[174] This will be elaborated further in later chapters.

It is within these parameters that the ICC prosecutorial policy functions vis-à-vis admissibility issues. Further testing of this prosecutorial policy in practice will be elaborated in the coming two case studies within this research. One should notice that the ICC will function within the traditional parameters of international law with the cooperation (and consent) of the states. This implies a contest between political interests and the Court's legal duties to fight impunity. States have been keen to preserve their sovereignty to prevent the creation of a state-transcending court that moves world order towards respecting human rights. Despite the achievement of establishing the ICC, the language of the Statute, in a

---

170   International Criminal Court, Office of the Prosecutor. 14 September 2006. *The Office of the Prosecutor Report on Prosecutorial Strategy*, The Hague, 1-11, 4. Available at: www.icc-cpi.int/library/organs/otp/OTP_Prosecutorial-Strategy-20060914_English.pdf [accessed: 2 June 2009].

171   International Criminal Court, Office of the Prosecutor. 2003. *Paper on Some Policy Issues before the Office of the Prosecutor*. ICC-OTP 2003, 1-9, 4. Available at: www.icc-cpi.int/library/organs/otp/030905_Policy_Paper.pdf [accessed: 20 February 2009].

172   Moreno-Ocampo, L. 2006. Symposium: International Criminal Tribunals in the 21st Century: Keynote Address: Integrating the Work of the ICC into Local Justice Initiatives. *American University International Law Review*, 21, 497-503, 498.

173   International Criminal Court, Office of the Prosecutor. 2003. *Informal Expert Paper: The Principle of Complementarity in Practice*. ICC-OTP 2003, 1-38, 3. Available at: www.icc-cpi.int/library/organs/otp/complementarity.pdf [accessed: 11 August 2009].

174   Decision on the Prosecutor's Application for a Warrant of Arrest, Article 58, *Prosecutor* v. *Thomas Lubanga Dyilo*, Pre-Trial Chamber, ICC-01/04-01/06. 10 February 2006. However, the Trial Chamber I ordered on 2 July 2008 the release of Thomas Lubanaga Dyilo as the Chamber found that it would be impossible to secure a fair trial for the accused due to non-disclosure of exculpatory materials covered by Article 54(3)(e). See *Prosecutor* v. *Thomas Lubanga Dyilo*, Trial Chamber I ordered the release of Thomas Lubanga Dyilo – Implementation of the decision is pending. 2 July 2008. ICC-CPI-20080702-PR334-ENG. Available at: www.icc-cpi.int/press/pressreleases/394.html [accessed: 4 March 2009].

number of aspects, is a disappointment for those who envisage a stronger role for international law and international courts.

Limitations and Challenges to Admissibility

Political constraints As the ICC Prosecutor is a stateless prosecutor,[175] his success depends on state cooperation.[176] One author indicated that the Court has 'no policing power or enforcement agencies and cannot seize evidentiary material, execute arrests, make searches or compel witnesses to give testimony without the co-operation of national authorities'.[177] Therefore, while states are under legal obligation to cooperate with the Court,[178] the Court is nonetheless under pressure to enter into political negotiations to secure cooperation from states. The experience of the ICTY, which functions under a more stringent cooperation system under Chapter VII, shows that if state cooperation is not secured the Court will find it increasingly difficult to function effectively and deliver justice.[179] Antonio Cassese, the then president of the ICTY, observed that the ICTY is like an 'armless and legless giant' that 'needs artificial limbs to act and move'.[180] These limbs are state authorities.

Another author adds, '[s]tatutory powers are no match for states unwilling to cooperate with international prosecutors to secure state cooperation'.[181] State cooperation remains a political issue, and the level of cooperation depends on the state's political and economic interest. The experience of Republika Srpska remains a vivid example.[182]

---

175   Moreno-Ocampo, L. 2006. Symposium: International Criminal Tribunals in the 21st Century: Keynote Address: Integrating the Work of the ICC into Local Justice Initiatives. *American University International Law Review*, 21, 497-503, 501.

176   Katz Cogan, J. 2002. International Criminal Courts and Fair Trials: Difficulties and Prospects. *Yale Journal of International Law*, 27, 119.

177   Brubacher, Matthew R. 2004. Prosecutorial Discretion within the International Criminal Court. *Journal of International Criminal Justice*, 2, 1, 71-95, 74.

178   See Part 9 of the Rome Statute of the International Criminal Court, UN Doc. A/CONF.183/9.

179   Wartanian, A. Summer 2005. The ICC Prosecutor's Battlefield: Combating Atrocities While Fighting For States' Cooperation Lessons from the U.N. Tribunals Applied To the Case of Uganda. *Georgetown Journal of International Law*, 36, 1289-1314, 1294.

180   Kalinauskas, M. 2002. The Use of International Military Force in Arresting War Criminals: The Lessons of the International Criminal Tribunal for the Former Yugoslavia. *The University of Kansas Law Review*, 50, 383-429, 399.

181   Wartanian, A. Summer 2005. The ICC Prosecutor's Battlefield: Combating Atrocities While Fighting For States' Cooperation Lessons from the U.N. Tribunals Applied To the Case of Uganda. *Georgetown Journal of International Law*, 36, 1289-1314, 1293.

182   Will Not Give Up War Crimes Suspects, Bosnian Serb President Tells U.N., *Toronto Star*, 9 January 1997, 14.

Article 16 of the Statute, as will be indicated in Chapter 4,[183] allocates a political role for the Security Council to 'freeze' the ICC's complementarity regime pertaining to specified situations.[184]

The power of the ICC to monitor and apply the complementarity principle will no doubt be affected by the political support of the states.[185] The Assembly of State Parties, to which the Court turns in instances of lack of cooperation, consists of entities with political interests.[186] *Realpolitik* will remain a decisive factor affecting the effectiveness and efficiency of the ICC. The effect of the complementarity principle will depend on the power of enforcement of the ICC, which itself depends on the support of powerful states. Even in terms of the Security Council Darfur referral, the reluctance of influential states to cooperate with the Court is negatively affecting the implementation of the arrest warrants against Kushayeb, Harun and President al-Bashir. The Court continues to find serious difficulty in securing Sudan's cooperation in the first place.

In this author's view, states have thus far remained vigilant in creating a court that lacks independent powers of enforcement. Such a fact could have an immense effect on the success of the ICC in achieving the goals it was designed to achieve. Reaching a world where human dignity is preserved and human rights are maximized has more chance with a more powerful Court enjoying an independent enforcement mechanism. This is not the case yet in the Rome Statute.

Financial constraints   The financial aspect is a crucial factor in the functionality of the Court, its investigations and prosecutions, as a restricted budget will decide the number of investigations and prosecutions. Limited resources restrain the ICC.[187] The programme budget for 2007 was €93,458,300.[188] The approved budget for 2010 is €103,623,300.[189] One quick note is that the Court's budgets

---

183   See *infra* the section on Complementarity and Security Council, p. 116.

184   Brubacher, Matthew R. 2004. Prosecutorial Discretion within the International Criminal Court. *Journal of International Criminal Justice*, 2, 1, 71-95, 82.

185   See Wartanian, A. Summer 2005. The ICC Prosecutor's Battlefield: Combating Atrocities While Fighting For States' Cooperation Lessons from the U.N. Tribunals Applied To the Case of Uganda. *Georgetown Journal of International Law*, 36, 1289-1314, 1289-1314.

186   Brubacher, Matthew R. 2004. Prosecutorial Discretion within the International Criminal Court. *Journal of International Criminal Justice*, 2, 1, 71-95, 83.

187   Wartanian, A. Summer 2005. The ICC Prosecutor's Battlefield: Combating Atrocities While Fighting For States' Cooperation Lessons from the U.N. Tribunals Applied To the Case of Uganda. *Georgetown Journal of International Law*, 36, 1289-1314, 1295.

188   Annex I. Draft Resolution of The Assembly of States Parties On The Proposed Program Budget for 2007. ICC-ASP/5/32.

189   Programme budget for 2010, the Working Capital Fund for 2010, scale of assessments for the apportionment of expenses of the International Criminal Court, financing appropriations for the year 2010, the Contingency Fund, conversion of a GTA psychologist post to an established one, Legal aid (defence) and the Addis Ababa Liaison

are relatively small for a permanent criminal court, and this is a major setback to the Court. The OTP stated, in the *Report on Prosecutorial Strategy*, that one of the objectives of the OTP is 'to conduct four to six new investigations of those who bear the greatest responsibility in the Office's current or new situations'.[190] This means that if, hypothetically, grave crimes occurred in more than six situations, and the states were unwilling or unable to prosecute, the ICC prosecutorial strategy and the limited budget will prevent the Court from initiating investigations and prosecutions beyond this number. This is another problem in the complementarity regime.

In conclusion, all the above factors leave no doubt that the decision of the Prosecutor and the Pre-Trial Chamber in determining admissibility will take into consideration a number of complex variables[191] that exceed the statutory legal parameters of the complementarity regime. The limits of the Rome Statute are evident in Articles 17, 20, 21 and 53, as well as external non-legal elements, such as peace versus justice, ongoing conflicts, and budgetary limitations. *Realpolitik* balances within the Assembly of States and the Security Council will directly or indirectly affect the admissibility of the case.

This chapter has explored the contributions and shortcomings of the complementarity principle *in abstracto* and in the emerging prosecutorial policy. The complementarity principle will be analysed extensively in the following two case studies: northern Uganda and Darfur to analyse further the application of the complementarity principle in practice.

Office Resolution ICC-ASP/8/Res.7, Adopted at the 8th plenary meeting, on 26 November 2009, by consensus. Available from www.icc-cpi.int/iccdocs/asp_docs/Resolutions/ICC-ASP-8-Res.7-ENG.pdf [accessed: 2 March 2010].

190   International Criminal Court, Office of the Prosecutor. 14 September 2006. *The Office of the Prosecutor Report on Prosecutorial Strategy*, The Hague, 1-11, 5. Available at: www.icc-cpi.int/library/organs/otp/OTP_Prosecutorial-Strategy-20060914_English.pdf [accessed: 2 June 2009].

191   Sarooshi, D. December 2004. Editorial Comments: The ICC Takes Off – Prosecutorial Policy and the ICC – Prosecutor's *Proprio Motu* Action or Self-Denial? *Journal of International Criminal Justice*, 2, 4, 940-944, 943.

Chapter 4

Possible *de Jure* and *de Facto* Hurdles to Complementarity

There are number of factors that could constitute possible obstacles to the complementarity principle. Although some of these obstacles may not fall directly under the complementarity principle, their effect on the application of the complementarity mechanism remains significant. For, to the extent that the jurisdiction of the Court is moot, the complementarity *ab initio* will not be implemented, and the exclusion of the ICC jurisdiction will preclude the applicability of the complementarity principle. This in itself will most probably restrict the Court's impact on the indirect enforcement mechanism. The exclusion of the ICC jurisdiction will deprive the ICC from its role as a 'complement' to the concerned national system. Under such restrictions, concerned states may be less encouraged to exercise their duty to prosecute the international core crimes.

This chapter will initially tackle the issue of amnesties and their impact on the complementarity principle. The first section of the chapter will analyse if amnesties fall under Article 17 or other articles of the Statute, such as Article 53. It will also analyse the impact of amnesties on the complementarity principle and the jurisdiction of the Court. The second section will shed light on the effect of pardons on the complementarity principle. It will study whether or not pardons pass the admissibility test. The last section will focus on the relation between the Security Council and the ICC under Article 16. The Security Council deferral will be analysed to determine its impact on the jurisdiction of the Court, and on its complementarity principle.

Amnesty as a Possible Hurdle to the Complementarity Principle

Black's Law Dictionary defines 'amnesty' as an act of forgiveness that a sovereign state grants to individuals who committed offensive acts.[1] Amnesty could be an act or decree, which precludes the criminal prosecution of the perpetrator of certain crimes, and that is done mostly for the purpose of reconciliation and peace.[2] This phenomenon is not new in the world. Monarchs and kings granted amnesties to their

---

1 Henry Campbell, B. 1991. *Black's Law Dictionary*. St Paul: West, sixth edition, 1113.

2 Young, Gwen. January 2002. Amnesty and Accountability. *University of California Davis Law Review*, 35, 427-486, 429.

citizens as well as to enemy combatants.[3] Thus, amnesty has long been considered a sovereign act, free of external interference, and a prerogative endowed to the state by its nature as a sovereign entity. Until recently, the international community rarely, if ever, scrutinized national amnesties. Instead they were always viewed as part of the right of the state to exercise its sovereignty over its land and citizens, as a domestic issue outside the reach of international law.

In recent years, amnesties have acquired a specific meaning in the context of transitional justice. Amnesty can serve a positive purpose: it can be used as a political tool for encouraging peace and reconciliation, as was the case with Sierra Leone,[4] and it has served in certain instances as a method of transition from an authoritarian regime to democracy. The South African model is a good example.[5]

With the emergence of human rights law and humanitarian law, violating human rights and committing serious international crimes became a concern to the entire international community. Hence, states can no longer rely on the principle of non-interference in domestic affairs as an excuse for violating human rights.[6]

This section aims to analyse amnesty as a possible obstacle to the complementarity principle of the ICC. This requires exploring whether amnesty falls under Article 17 or Article 53 for a better understanding of whether amnesty could block the complementarity principle of the Court or whether it could fall outside the ambit of Article 17, and thus within the Prosecutor's discretion under Article 53.

The first part of this chapter will start with a short analysis of amnesties in national and international laws. This entails exploring and enumerating various conventional and customary international and national laws, as well as various state practices. The second part will discuss amnesty in the Rome Statute, its relation with Article 17, and then its relation to Article 53. It will also shed light on the Prosecutor's policy towards Articles 17 and 53. The third part will focus on prosecutorial discretion. It is necessary to understand the margin of

---

3   Gavron, J. 2002. Amnesties in the Light of Developments in International Law and the Establishment of the International Criminal Court. *International and Comparative Law Quarterly*, 51, 91-126, 91.

4   The Lome Peace agreement promised the establishment of a Truth and Reconciliation Commission which practically lead to amnesty for perpetrators of international crimes in favour of disclosure of the historical record of the conflict and human rights and humanitarian law violations, and that was considered as a response to the needs of the victims. See Schabas, W. December 2004. The Special Court for Sierra Leone: Testing the Waters – Conjoined Twins of Transnational Justice? – The Sierra Leone Truth and Reconciliation Commission and the Special Court. *Journal of International Criminal Justice*, 1082-1092, 1084.

5   Gallagher, K. Fall 2000. No Justice, No Peace: The Legalities and Realities of Amnesty in Sierra Leone. *Thomas Jefferson Law Review*, 23, 149-195, 158.

6   The prosecutions of Nazi perpetrators for crimes against humanity against their own citizens are significant examples in that regard.

discretion of the ICC Prosecutor in the Statute and in practice with respect to amnesties. The fourth part presents the conclusion of this section.

Amnesty in International and National Laws

Writers and jurists are divided on whether there exists a customary rule in international law that prohibits amnesty in international law. Where some consider that such a rule exists,[7] others disagree with such a generalization.[8]

This part focuses on amnesty within the area of human rights law and international humanitarian law, as the core crimes of the ICC Statute fall mainly under these two bodies of law. In terms of human rights law and humanitarian law, most treaties include an implicit duty to investigate and punish violations of human rights. The state parties are under the obligation to respect these rights, as well as punish their violations.[9] However, these treaties entail obligations on states and not individuals.

The Genocide Convention requires, in states in which the crime has occurred, state parties to prosecute or punish the offenders. Articles 4 and 6 explicitly put stress on the prosecution and punishment of the perpetrators regardless of their official capacity.[10] Clearly, the language of the Genocide Convention does not tolerate any amnesty for this grave crime.

The four Geneva Conventions impose an obligation on state parties to bring those responsible for breaches of humanitarian law before their courts and to provide penal sanctions accordingly. The *aut dedere aut judicare* is indicated explicitly in Articles 49 and 54 of the Convention for Amelioration of the

---

7   Newman, D.G. 2005. The Rome Statute, Some Reservations Concerning Amnesties, and a Distributive Problem. *American University International Law Review*, 293-246, 299.

8   Dugard, J. 2002. Possible Conflicts of Jurisdiction with Truth Commissions, in *The Rome Statute of The International Criminal Court: A Commentary*, edited by A. Cassese, P. Gaeta and J.R.W.D. Jones. Oxford: Oxford University Press, I, 699.

9   Article 2 of International Covenant on Civil and Political Rights (1996), G.A. Res. 2200A (XXI), 21 U.N. GAOR Supp. (no. 16) at 52, UN Doc. A/6316 (1966), 999 U.N.T.S. 171, entered into force 23 March 1976. Article 1 of the American Convention On Human Rights (1969) Adopted at the Inter-American Specialized Conference on Human Rights, San José, Costa Rica, 22 November 1969. Available at: www.oas.org/juridico/english/Treaties/b-32.htm [accessed: 25 January 2008]. Article 1 of the Convention for the Protection of Human Rights and Fundamental Freedoms (1950), entry into force on 3 September 1953. Cets no.: 005. Available at: http://conventions.coe.int/treaty/EN/cadreprincipal.htm [accessed: 26 January 2008]. Article 1 of African (Banjul) Charter on Human and Peoples' Rights (1981) OAU Doc. CAB/LEG/67/3 rev. 5, 21 I.L.M. 58 (1982), entered into force 21 October 1986. Available at: www.africa-union.org/Official_documents/Treaties_%20Conventions_%20Protocols/Banjul%20Charter.pdf#search='African%20charter%20on%20Human%20Rights [accessed: 26 January 2008].

10   Article 4 and 6 of the Genocide Convention on the Prevention and Suppression of the Crime of Genocide (1948) 78, U.N.T.S 277.

Conditions of the Wounded and the Sick in Armed Forces in the Field.[11] The legal language of the Geneva Convention leaves no room for amnesty for grave breaches that are enlisted in Article 8(2)(a) of the Rome Statute. However, the Second Protocol of the Geneva Conventions of 1977 states in Article 6 that at the end of hostilities the authorities in power shall grant the broadest possible amnesty to people who were involved in conflict.[12] This Protocol explicitly recognizes amnesty within the context of an internal armed conflict. The scope of this Article is controversial. The head of the legal division of the International Committee of the Red Cross stated that this amnesty is restricted to the lawful combatant and does not apply to persons who violate international humanitarian law.[13]

The ambiguity becomes clearer when encountering crimes against humanity, as most of these crimes are not subject to any convention, except for torture and the crime of apartheid. An obligation to prosecute acts of torture can be derived from Article 7 of the Convention against Torture, which indicates that states are required to submit cases of torture to competent national authorities for the purpose of prosecution when committed on their territories.[14]

With respect to apartheid, the International Convention on the Suppression and Punishment of the Crime of Apartheid does not tolerate impunity. Article I of the Convention indicates, 'The States Parties to the present Convention declare criminal those organizations, institutions and individuals committing the

---

11   Article 49 and 54 of Convention for Amelioration of the Conditions of the Wounded and the Sick in Armed Forces in the Field (1949). 75U.N.T.S 31. Also see Article 50 of the Convention for Amelioration of the Conditions of the Wounded, Sick and Shipwrecked Members of the Armed Forces at Sea (1949). 75U.N.T.S.85. Also, see Article 129 of Convention (III) relative to the Treatment of Prisoners of War. Geneva (1949) Diplomatic Conference of Geneva of 1949, entered into force 21 October 1950. The Geneva Conventions of 12 August 1949, International Committee of the Red Cross, Geneva, 75-152.

12   Article 6 of Protocol Additional to the Geneva Conventions of 12 August 1949, and relating to the Protection of Victims of Non-International Armed Conflicts (Protocol II). 1977. Diplomatic Conference on the Reaffirmation and Development of International Humanitarian Law applicable in Armed Conflicts, entry into force 7 December 1978. Protocols additional to the Geneva Conventions of 12 August 1949, International Committee of the Red Cross, Geneva, 1977, 89-101.

13   Letter to Dr Toni Pfanner to Cassel, 15 April 1997, in J. Gavron. January 2002. Amnesties in the Light of Developments in International Law and the Establishment of the International Criminal Court. *International and Comparative Law Quarterly*, 51, 1, 91-118, 114.

14   Article 7 of The United Nations Convention against Torture and Other Cruel, Inhuman or Degrading Treatment or Punishment (1984) G.A. Res. 39/46, annex, 39 U.N. GAOR Supp. (no. 51) at 197, UN Doc. A/39/51, entered into force 26 June 1987.

crime of apartheid'.[15] Article IV imposes a duty on member states to criminalize apartheid and to prosecute, bring to trial and punish the persons responsible.[16] There is no room for amnesty under this convention.

As a result, the obligation to prosecute (or extradite for prosecution) applies to treaty-based crimes, such as the crime of genocide, for war crimes, the crime of apartheid and torture, with the exception of Protocol II of the Geneva Conventions that tolerates amnesties in non-international armed conflicts. Yet even on this point, it is ambiguous whether the recognition of amnesty is related to combatant activity or to international crimes. As for customary crimes within the Statute, the vision is further blurred and there is no consensus in international law.[17]

As the crystallization of international law requires state practice and *opinio juris*, then state practice on amnesties is hybrid and lacks consistency.[18] Modern history is full of cases of granting amnesties.[19] State amnesties range in type, from self and blanket amnesties, like the Chilean model, to conditional types of amnesties, such as the South African model, and to the targeted prosecution model, which prosecutes only the persons most responsible. Self-amnesty usually occurs when the executive issues self-amnesty to ensure that once he steps down from power he will be immune from prosecution.[20] Self-amnesties target specific individuals, but they are blanket at the same time, since they cover all the perpetrated crimes without requiring any precise condition or act from persons granted amnesty. A classic example is the self-amnesty of the

---

15   Article I of The International Convention on the Suppression and Punishment of the Crime of Apartheid (1973). Adopted and opened for signature, ratification by G.A. Res. 3068 (XXVIII) of 30 November 1973, entered into force 18 July 1976. Available at: www.unhchr.ch/html/menu3/b/11.htm [accessed: 20 February 2008].

16   Article IV of The International Convention on the Suppression and Punishment of the Crime of Apartheid (1973). Adopted and opened for signature, ratification by G.A. Res. 3068 (XXVIII) of 30 November 1973, entered into force 18 July 1976. Available at: www.unhchr.ch/html/menu3/b/11.htm [accessed: 20 February 2009].

17   Newman, D.G. 2005. The Rome Statute, Some Reservations Concerning Amnesties, and a Distributive Problem. *American University International Law Review*, 293-246, 299.

18   Slye, R. Fall 2002. The Legitimacy of Amnesties under International Law and General Principles of Anglo-American Law: Is a Legitimate Amnesty Possible? *Virginia Journal of International Law*, 173-241, 175.

19   Dugard, J. 2002. Possible Conflicts of Jurisdiction with Truth Commissions, in *The Rome Statute of The International Criminal Court: A Commentary*, edited by A. Cassese, P. Gaeta and J.R.W.D. Jones. Oxford: Oxford University Press, I, 699.

20   Dugard, J. 2002. Possible Conflicts of Jurisdiction with Truth Commissions, in *The Rome Statute of The International Criminal Court: A Commentary*, edited by A. Cassese, P. Gaeta and J.R.W.D. Jones. Oxford: Oxford University Press, I, 699.

Chilean president in Decree 2191 covering crimes committed between 1973 and 1978.[21]

State practice shows numerous examples of granted amnesties, including the cases of Lebanon,[22] Haiti, Guatemala,[23] Uganda and many states in South America.[24] This serves to show that practice still favours factors like state interest, security and stability, on the expense of accountability against human rights violations.

The Human Rights Committee has expressed concern about various national amnesties covering grave human rights violations. For example, it noted a 'deep concern' over Uruguay's expiry law that prevented the prosecution of police and military officials, and dismissed pending prosecutions. The Human Rights Committee recommended the amendment of the law to permit victims access to an effective remedy for human rights violations.[25] It has also criticized amnesties in Argentina by stating the following:

> The Committee is concerned that amnesties and pardons have impeded investigations into allegations of crimes committed by the armed forces and agents of national security services and have been applied even in cases where there exists significant evidence of such gross human rights violations as unlawful disappearances and detention of persons, including children. The Committee expresses concern that pardons and general amnesties may promote an atmosphere of impunity for perpetrators of human rights violations belonging to the security forces. Respect for human rights may be weakened by impunity for perpetrators of human rights violations.[26]

With respect to Chile, The Human Rights Committee observed that:

---

21   Chile Report. 1999. Human Rights Watch. Available at: www.hrw.org/reports/1999/chile/Patrick-03.htm#P422_160352 [accessed: 23 January 2008].

22   Lebanese Amnesty Law of 1991, which grants a general amnesty, with a few exceptions, for crimes committed before 28 March 1991.

23   Young, Gwen. January 2002. Amnesty and Accountability. *University of California Davis Law Review*, 35, 427-486, 427.

24   The Amnesty Act. 2000. The Ugandan Amnesty Act. Available at: www.c-r.org/accord/uganda/accord11/downloads/2000_Jan_The_Amnesty_Act.doc [accessed: 11 May 2008].

25   United Nations Human Rights Committee. Comments of the Human Rights Committee, Uruguay, Consideration of Reports Submitted by States Parties Under Article 40 of the Covenant, UN Doc. CCPR/C/79/Add.19, 5 May 1993; Views of 19 July 1994, Hugo Rodriguez, Communication no. 322/1988, UN Doc. CCPR/C/51/D/322/1988 (Uruguay). See also General Comment no. 20, UN Doc. no. CCPR/C/21/Rev.1./Add.3, 7 April 1992, para. 4, concerning torture.

26   United Nations Human Rights Committee (1995) Argentina, UN Doc. CCPR/C/79/Add.46, reprinted in UN Doc. A/50/40 (1995), para. 146.

Amnesty Decree Law, under which persons who committed offences between 11 September 1973 and 10 March 1978 are granted amnesty, prevents the State party from complying with its obligation under Article 2, paragraph 3, to ensure an effective remedy to anyone whose rights and freedoms under the Covenant have been violated. The Committee reiterated the views expressed in its General Comment 20, in which amnesty laws covering human rights violations are generally incompatible with the duty of the State party to investigate human rights violations, to guarantee freedom from such violations within its jurisdiction and to ensure that similar violations do not occur in the future.[27]

The Human Rights Committee also considered the Lebanese blanket amnesty law of 1991 to prevent the appropriate investigation and punishment of the perpetrators of past human rights violations, and to undermine efforts to establish respect for human rights, as constituting an impediment to efforts undertaken to consolidate democracy.[28]

The Human Rights Committee had similar views towards amnesties in El Salvador, Croatia and Haiti.[29] Moreover, the Committee against Torture criticized amnesties in several countries, including Azerbaijan, Croatia, Kyrgyzstan and Peru, and recommended that they not apply to torture.[30]

---

27   United Nations Human Rights Committee. 1999. Concluding Observations of the Human Rights Committee – Chile, UN Doc. CCPR/C/79/Add.104 (1999), para. 7

28   United Nations Human Rights Committee (1997) Concluding Observations of the Human Rights Committee – Lebanon, UN Doc. CCPR/C/79/Add.78, 1 April 1997, para. 12.

29   United Nations Human Rights Committee. UN Doc. CCPR/C/79/SLV, 22 August 2003, para. 6 (reiterating the same concerns expressed in 1994), Haiti, UN Doc. CCPR/C/79/Add.34, 21 September 1994, reprinted in UN Doc. A/49/40 (1994), para. 215. Croatia, UN Doc. CCPR/CO/71/HRV, 30 April 2001, para. 11.

30   Conclusions and Recommendations of the Committee against Torture Concerning the Initial Report of Azerbaijan, UN Doc. A/55/44, 17 November 1999, para. 68 (3) (expressing concern about '[t]he use of amnesty laws that might extend to the crime of torture') and para. 69 (c) (recommending that, '[i]n order to ensure that perpetrators of torture do not enjoy impunity, the State party ... ensure that amnesty laws exclude torture from their reach'); Conclusions and Recommendations Concerning the Second Periodic Report of Croatia, UN Doc. A/54/44 (17 November 1998), para. 66 (expressing concern that 'the Amnesty Act adopted in 1996 is applicable to a number of offences characterized as acts of torture or other cruel, in human or degrading treatment or punishment within the meaning of the Convention'); Conclusions and Recommendations of the Committee against Torture Concerning the Initial Report of Kyrgyzstan, UN Doc. A/55/44, 18 November 1999, para. 74 (e) (expressing concern about '[t]he use of amnesty laws that might extend to torture in some cases') and para. 75 (c) (recommending that, '[i]n order to ensure that the perpetrators of torture and ill-treatment do not enjoy impunity, the State party ... ensure that amnesty laws exclude torture from their reach'); Conclusions and Recommendations of the Committee against Torture Concerning the Third Periodic Report of Peru, UN Doc. A/55/44, 15 November 1999, para. 59 (g) (expressing concern about '[t]he use of, in

The Inter-American Court of Human Rights has found that amnesties in Honduras and Peru for crimes under international law violate the American Convention on Human Rights.[31] Similarly, the Inter-American Commission on Human Rights has found that amnesties in Argentina, Chile, Colombia and Uruguay violate the Convention.

Mary Robinson, the then United Nations High Commissioner for Human Rights, has indicated her concern about the issue of amnesty laws, especially with respect to gross violations of human rights and international humanitarian law.[32]

Amnesty in the Rome Statute

The issue of amnesty was raised in the meetings of the Preparatory Committee preceding the Rome Conference, but was not seriously considered.[33] Many experts indicated that this avoidance was deliberate.[34] During the drafting of the Statute, there was lengthy debate over non-prosecutorial programmes, including amnesties. The South Africans were the most insistent on the recognition of such alternatives. On the other hand, many delegations, despite being sympathetic with the South African model, considered the South American models of amnesties intolerable[35] and incompatible with the aim of ending impunity for human rights violations. While they condemned the Chilean model of self-amnesties, some delegations strongly resisted the inclusion of an article on amnesties. Other delegations argued

---

particular, the amnesty laws which preclude prosecution of alleged torturers who must, according to Articles 4, 5 and 12 of the Convention, be investigated and prosecuted where appropriate') and para. 61 (d) (recommending that 'amnesty laws should exclude torture from their reach').

31   *Barrios Altos Case*, Inter-American Court for Human Rights. 20 March 2001. (Reparations), para. 41; *Loayza Tamayo Case*, Inter-American Court for Human Rights (Ser. C). 27 November 1998. Case no. 42, (Reparations), paras 165-171; *Castillo Paez Case*, Inter-American Court for Human Rights (Ser. C). 27 November 1998. Case no. 43, (Reparations), paras 98-108; *Velasquez Rodriguez Case*, Inter-American Court for Human Rights Rts (Ser. C), no. 4 (1988) (judgment), para. 174 ('The State has a legal duty to take reasonable steps to prevent human rights violations and to use the means at its disposal to carry our serious investigation of violations committed within its jurisdiction, to identify those responsible, to impose the appropriate punishment and to ensure the victim adequate compensation').

32   Robinson, M. 2001. The Principles on Universal Jurisdiction, Program in Law and Public Affairs, Princeton University. Princeton, New Jersey, 17.

33   Dugard, J. 2002. Possible Conflicts of Jurisdiction with Truth Commissions, in *The Rome Statute of The International Criminal Court: A Commentary*, edited by A. Cassese, P. Gaeta and J.R.W.D. Jones. Oxford: Oxford University Press, I, 700.

34   Hafner, G., Boon, K., Rbesame, A. and Huston, J. March 1999. A Response to the American View as Represented by Ruth Wedgwood. *The European Journal of International Law*, 10, 108-128, 112.

35   Schabas, W. 2001. *An Introduction to the International Criminal Court*. Cambridge: Cambridge University Press, 68.

that the proposal was unnecessary, that the admissibility articles in the Statute are sufficient to permit the Court to consider issues like amnesties and pardons.[36] As a result, the Rome Statute stayed silent on the issue of amnesty.[37]

The fourth paragraph of the Preamble of the Statute affirms that most serious crimes (of which the core crimes of the Statute are constituted) 'must not go unpunished and their effective prosecution must be ensured by taking measures at the national level'.[38] Furthermore, it emphasizes ending impunity and delineates the duty of every state to exercise criminal jurisdiction over those most responsible for international crimes.[39]

Article 17 and amnesty   Article 17 determines the admissibility of the case before the ICC. The Court will determine admissibility according to defined criteria. The case is inadmissible if:

- The case is being investigated or prosecuted by a state having jurisdiction.
- A state, which has jurisdiction over the case, has investigated the case and decided not to initiate a prosecution.
- The person concerned has already undergone a trial for the conduct in question subject to Article 20, paragraph 3.
- The case is not of sufficient gravity.[40]

However, if the decision to investigate and prosecute (or not) indicates that the state did not take action or was either 'unwilling' or 'unable' to genuinely carry out an investigation or prosecution, then the case is admissible before the Court. Hence, an investigation or prosecution by national authorities could render the case inadmissible before the Court. Yet, the provision does not state what type of investigation or prosecution is required.[41] If the term 'investigation' or 'prosecution' is read in conjunction with the preambular paragraph, which states that international crimes should not go unpunished, then 'investigation' or 'prosecution' should be of criminal nature and not affiliated to non-prosecutorial programmes. Subsection

---

36   Holmes, J. 1999. The Principle of Complementarity, in *The International Criminal Court: The Making of the Rome Statute, Issues, Negotiations, Results*, edited by R. Lee. The Hague: Kluwer, 41.

37   Dugard, J. 2002. Possible Conflicts of Jurisdiction with Truth Commissions, in *The Rome Statute of The International Criminal Court: A Commentary*, edited by A. Cassese, P. Gaeta and J.R.W.D. Jones. Oxford: Oxford University Press, I, 700.

38   The Preamble, paragraph 4, The Rome Statute of the International Criminal Court, UN Doc. A/CONF.183/9.

39   The Preamble, paragraph 5 and 6, The Rome Statute of the International Criminal Court, UN Doc. A/CONF.183/9.

40   Article 17 of the Rome Statute of the International Criminal Court, UN Doc. A/CONF.183/9.

41   Young, Gwen. January 2002. Amnesty and Accountability. *University of California Davis Law Review*, 35, 427- 486, 434.

2 of Article 17 suggests that genuine investigation is a reflection of whether or not proceedings are 'inconsistent with an intent to bring the person concerned to justice'.[42] Such a phrase could be interpreted as requiring criminal proceedings.[43] In other words, according to Article 17(1)(a), the case is inadmissible if criminal investigation or prosecution is taking place and the outcome of such process is not previously determined. Based on this analysis, non-criminal prosecutions or investigations of truth and reconciliation commissions do not fall under the ambit of Article 17(1)(a).[44]

As amnesty is the preclusion of criminal prosecution of the perpetrators, it is difficult for it to fall under Article 17(1)(a). Under certain amnesty programmes, investigation becomes an aim in itself rather than a mean, since such an investigation will not lead to prosecutions.[45]

Article 17(1)(b) addresses decisions by national authorities not to proceed after an investigation is conducted. Yet, the nature of such investigation is not clear. As the decision not to investigate will hamper prosecution, we cannot but imagine a criminal investigation that has the option of prosecution. Such an argument is strengthened if correlated to paragraph four of the Preamble, which delineates 'effective prosecutions' aiming to punish perpetrators of these crimes.[46] This implies that amnesties do not fall under the ambit of Article 17(1)(b). Amnesty, whether blanket or conditional, leaves no room for prosecution. In blanket amnesties, the preclusion of punishment is granted before any investigation or prosecution.[47] In conditional amnesties, such as truth and reconciliation commissions, investigation is an aim in itself and the possibility of prosecutions is absent. Therefore, these *supra* scenarios can hardly fulfil the requirements of Article 17(1)(b). The matter becomes even more complex when amnesty programmes leave a slim option for prosecution if certain requirements by alleged perpetrators are not fulfilled. An example of such a situation is the South African model where prosecution is at least an option. In South Africa, the truth and reconciliation commission could

---

42   Article 17(2) of the Rome Statute of the International Criminal Court, UN Doc. A/CONF.183/9.

43   Scharf, M. 1999. Symposium: The American Exception to the Jurisdiction of the ICC. *Cornell International Law Journal*, 32, 507-531, 518.

44   Robinson, D. June 2003. Serving the Interest of Justice: Amnesties, Truth Commissions and The International Criminal Court. *The European Journal of International Law*, 14, 481-509, 492.

45   The South African Amnesty could be a model in that regard. Act 200: Interim Constitution of South Africa. 1993. Assented to 25 January 1994. Available at: www.polity.org.za/govdocs/legislation/1993/consti0.html [accessed: 12 October 2008].

46   The Preamble, paragraph 4, The Rome Statute of the International Criminal Court, UN Doc. A/CONF.183/9.

47   Young, G. January 2002. Amnesty and Accountability. *University of California Davis Law Review*, 35, 427-486, 431.

have denied amnesty,[48] even though granting or denying amnesty did not depend on the gravity of the crime or other criminal aspect, but rather on the degree of disclosure of information.[49]

Article 17(1)(c) considers cases inadmissible when the person concerned has been tried for the same conduct before. This is in conjunction with Article 20 and the *ne bis in idem* principle, and this keeps amnesties outside the umbrella of Article 20. Article 17(1)(c) deals with cases where trials have already taken place and verdicts, whether of conviction or acquittal, have been issued, while amnesties are usually granted before trials. This may not prevent persons in the process of being tried benefiting from amnesty laws.[50]

If the case is not of sufficient gravity, then any granted amnesty will remain outside the jurisdiction of the Court under Article 17(1)(d). This is not due to the legality of the amnesty, but rather to a level of gravity not meeting the threshold required under Article 17(1)(d). This seems the case in Uganda as discussed in Chapter 5.

In analysing Article 17(1), it seems that in general as amnesties preclude certain persons from criminal prosecution, the state cannot claim to be investigating or prosecuting these persons for crimes falling under the jurisdiction of the Court. Hence, Articles 17(1)(a) and Article 17(1)(b) cannot plausibly be raised with regard to the amnestied persons, as no criminal prosecution or trial occurred. In addition, granting amnesty can be construed as a 'decision not to prosecute' under Article 17(1)(b). Such an interpretation faces two problems. Firstly, when amnesty is granted automatically, which is usually the case, no actual decision is made in any specific case as required by Article 17(1)(b). Secondly, the decision not to prosecute, in such a situation, is not taken after investigating the case.

Important questions can be raised via the analysis of Article 17(1)(d) as to which cases of less sufficient gravity will be considered inadmissible by the Court. The 'sufficient gravity' item is not defined in the Statute. The Prosecutor indicated that several factors determine the gravity of the crime, the most obvious being the

---

48   Robinson, D. June 2003. Serving the Interest of Justice: Amnesties, Truth Commissions and The International Criminal Court. *The European Journal of International Law*, 14, 481-509, 493.

49   Section 20(7) of the Promotion of National Unity and Reconciliation Act: Act 200: Interim Constitution of South Africa. 1993. Assented to 25 January 1994. Available on the South African Government's website at: www.polity.org.za/govdocs/legislation/1993/consti0.html [accessed: 12 October 2008]. The Act permits the Committee on amnesty established by the Act to grant amnesty in respect to any act, omission or offence provided that the applicant concerned has made full disclosure of all relevant facts as long as these acts are affiliated to a political objective prior to 6 December 1993.

50   The Lebanese Amnesty Law includes such clause. The Lebanese Amnesty Law of 1991 grants a general amnesty, with a few exceptions, for crimes committed before 28 March 1991.

number of people killed or tortured. The impact of the crime is another factor in determining the gravity of the crime.[51]

Based on the argument *supra*, blanket amnesties, or even conditional ones, do not fall under the ambit of Article 17(1). It is hard for national authorities to invoke the inadmissibility clauses under Article 17(1) in such a case.

Amnesties could constitute a state of unwillingness to prosecute alleged perpetrators if granted under certain specific conditions. Article 17(2) requires of these conditions the existence of one of the following criteria: the proceedings of amnesty are being undertaken or were undertaken for the purpose of shielding the person from criminal responsibility; or the proceedings are delayed to an extent that they are inconsistent with an intent to bring the alleged perpetrator to justice; or the lack of independence or impartiality of proceedings; and they were conducted in a manner which is inconsistent with the intent to bring the alleged perpetrators to justice.[52] There is also the possibility that amnesty may not be the result of unwillingness as defined by Article 17(2). Paragraph 1 of Article 17 will be applicable in that case. In summary, the Statute resolves the dilemmas of amnesties reflecting unwillingness in Article 17(2); and blanket amnesty or conditional amnesty in Article 17(1).

Based on the above, amnesties most probably will not escape Article 17, and they will be, in most cases, admissible before the ICC. As amnesties deny the possibility for criminal prosecution in general, then they do not fulfil the conditions of Article 17 for inadmissibility. The case will also be admissible in instances of 'unwillingness' on the part of the national authorities. 'Inability' will also be admissible. Hence, in all scenarios, amnesties will not escape Article 17 and will remain admissible before the Court. Cases of amnesty will not evade the jurisdiction of the Court as falling under either 'inaction', 'unwillingness' or 'inability'.

The ICC's prosecutorial policy   The Prosecutor indicated that due to financial and logistic limitations, the OTP would focus on those most responsible for core crimes of the Statute.[53] This has been restated in a number of documents published by the OTP and in statements from the Prosecutor himself. For instance, Prosecutor Moreno-Ocampo indicated in his statement in one meeting that the ICC will prioritize its effort to prosecute groups that are most

---

51   The International Criminal Court, Office of The Prosecutor. December 2005. *Informal Meeting of Legal Advisors of Ministries of Foreign Affairs in New York, 24 October 2005*; Statement by Luis Moreno-Ocampo, Prosecutor of the International Criminal Court. ICC-02/04-01/05-67, 1-31, 6.

52   Article 17(2)(a) and (b) and (c) of the Rome Statute of the International Criminal Court, UN Doc. A/CONF.183/9.

53   International Criminal Court, Office of the Prosecutor. 2003. *Paper on Some Policy Issues before the Office of the Prosecutor*. ICC-OTP 2003, 1-9, 3. Available at: www.icc-cpi.int/library/organs/otp/030905_Policy_Paper.pdf [accessed: 20 February 2009].

responsible for the gravest crimes.[54] Moreno-Ocampo admits that his elaborated strategy depends on important elements in which the focus of the investigation and prosecutorial efforts is on those who bear the greatest responsibility for the most serious crimes, as it is not feasible for the ICC to bring charges against all alleged perpetrators.[55] The first arrest warrant, which the ICC has unsealed, affirms this approach. On 13 October 2005, the Pre-Trial Chamber unsealed the arrest warrants for the case of northern Uganda that were previously requested by the Prosecutor. The warrants were for the arrest of the five senior leaders of the Lord's Resistance Army (LRA).[56] The Prosecutor designated the five leaders as those most responsible. The following indictments of a number of leaders in various situations including President al-Bashir are in the same direction.

Such a prosecutorial policy does have a number of justifications. Firstly, from a practical standpoint, the Court is incapable financially and logistically to prosecute thousands of perpetrators.[57] In the Ugandan case, for instance, bringing before the Court all the members of the LRA involved in perpetrating numerous crimes is simply impossible. Secondly, from a legal standpoint, a number of experts argue that customary law limits the duty to prosecute to those persons most responsible.[58] One author argues that customary law does not require the prosecution of every person, but it urges the prosecution of those who are most responsible for human rights atrocities.[59] Thirdly, from a common sense standpoint, it is normal to prosecute those most responsible if the Court is to choose between those most responsible and other low-level perpetrators. If the ICC cannot prosecute all perpetrators, and this is currently the case, then international justice

---

54   International Criminal Court, Office of the Prosecutor. December 2005. *Informal Meeting of Legal Advisors of Ministries of Foreign Affairs in New York, 24 October 2005*; Statement by Luis Moreno-Ocampo, Prosecutor of the International Criminal Court. ICC-02/04-01/05-67, 1-31, 2.

55   International Criminal Court, Office of the Prosecutor. December 2005. *Informal Meeting of Legal Advisors of Ministries of Foreign Affairs in New York, 24 October 2005*; Statement by Luis Moreno-Ocampo, Prosecutor of the International Criminal Court. ICC-02/04-01/05-67, 1-31, 2.

56   International Criminal Court. 14 October 2005. *Warrants of Arrest Unsealed Against Five LRA Commanders*. Press Release. The Hague. ICC20051410.056-En. Available at: www.icc-cpi.int/press/pressreleases/114.html [accessed: 9 December 2008].

57   Robinson, D. June 2003. Serving the Interest of Justice: Amnesties, Truth Commissions and the International Criminal Court. *The European Journal of International Law*, 14, 481-509, 489.

58   Kritz, N.J. Autumn 1996. Coming to Terms with Atrocities: a Review of Accountability Mechanism for Mass Violations of Human Rights. *Law and Contemporary Problems*, 59, 4, 127-152; Morris, M. Autumn 1996. International Guidelines against Impunity: Facilitating Accountability. *Law and Contemporary Problems*, 59, 29-39.

59   Orentlicher, D.F. June 1991. Symposium: International Law: Article: Settling Accounts: The Duty to Prosecute Human Rights Violations of a Prior Regime. *Yale Law Journal*, 2537-2630, 2599.

should pursue those most responsible for planning and executing international crimes. Individuals responsible for ordering or perpetrating the killing of hundreds and thousands are more responsible than individuals who are involved in a single killing.[60]

The prosecutorial policy raises question about the ICC's position on the accountability of low-level perpetrators. The Prosecutor's Policy Report indicates that, in cases of low-level perpetrators, the ICC will defer to national prosecutions systems or programmes. Yet, in the case of inaction, inability or unwillingness of the national judicial system, when neither the ICC nor the national system will prosecute low-level perpetrators, an impunity gap emerges. Low-level criminals escape accountability. This dilemma, however, is not the core issue of our discussion in this section. The problem here concerns national amnesties when granted for low-level perpetrators. What will the ICC's stand towards amnesties for such perpetrators be? Will an amnesty granted for low-level perpetrators fall outside the ambit of ICC articles in general and Article 17 in particular? The answer to these questions is relatively clear: amnesties to low-level perpetrators escape the complementarity principle of the ICC. The ICC prosecutorial policy towards the Ugandan Act[61] supports this argument.

The Ugandan Amnesty Act precludes criminal prosecutions and any form of punishment for crimes committed during the armed rebellion. The amnesty is open to persons who have engaged or have been engaging in war or armed rebellion against the Ugandan government since 26 January 1986.[62] The amnesty covers only members or rebel forces of Ugandan nationality. The *ratione materiae* of the Act is any crime committed in the course of the war or the armed rebellion. The crimes covered by the Act fall under the scope of the core crimes of the Statute. The scope of the Amnesty Act is not limited to amnesty, but also covers pardon. In other words, the Ugandan Act is not limited to criminal prosecutions, but also includes amnesty from punishment.[63] Amnesty in this Act is defined 'as pardon, forgiveness, exemption or discharge from criminal prosecution or any

---

60   Robinson, D. June 2003. Serving the Interest of Justice: Amnesties, Truth Commissions and the International Criminal Court. *The European Journal of International Law*, 14, 481-509, 489.

61   The Amnesty Act. 2000. The Ugandan Amnesty Act. Available at: www.c-r.org/accord/uganda/accord11/downloads/2000_Jan_The_Amnesty_Act.doc [accessed: 12 May 2008].

62   Part II, Section 3(1), The Amnesty Act. 2000. The Ugandan Amnesty Act. Available at: www.c-r.org/accord/uganda/accord11/downloads/2000_Jan_The_Amnesty_Act.doc [accessed: 12 May 2008].

63   Part I, Section 2, The Amnesty Act. 2000. The Ugandan Amnesty Act. Available at: www.c-r.org/accord/uganda/accord11/downloads/2000_Jan_The_Amnesty_Act.doc [accessed: 12 May 2008].

other form of punishment by the state'.[64] The Act covers 'any Ugandan ... who is engaged or is engaging in war or armed rebellion'.[65]

The Amnesty Act of 2000 does not preclude any specific category of combatants or fighters, such as commanders or senior leaders. In that respect, it is close to blanket amnesty for all members of the rebel movements, including the LRA.[66] The only conditions are: reporting to the nearest army or police unit, renouncing and abandoning involvement in the war or armed rebellion, and surrendering weapons. When all these conditions are met, the minister officiates a certificate of amnesty.[67]

In December 2003, amendments were introduced to the Amnesty Act that exclude leaders of terrorist organization, commanders of units of terrorist organizations, and financiers of terrorist organizations from the purview of amnesty.[68] The LRA falls under the definition of the terrorist organizations under the Amendment Act of 2003.

The following could summarize the OTP policy towards the Ugandan Amnesty Act: firstly, the Prosecutor announced on a number of occasions that prosecutions will target those most responsible for the crimes committed in northern Uganda.[69] The ICC remained silent on the Amnesty Act in Uganda. However, as the Prosecutor indicted five senior leaders of the LRA – those labelled the 'most responsible' – the ICC ignored the Amnesty Act with respect to those 'most responsible'. One can argue that the Amnesty Act did not preclude the ICC from acting on those most responsible. Through this policy, the ICC did not respect the Amnesty Act in its initial form. The original version of the Amnesty Act contradicts the ICC prosecutorial policy.[70] Yet, the subsequent amendments

---

64 Part I, Section 2, The Amnesty Act. 2000. The Ugandan Amnesty Act. Available at: www.c-r.org/accord/uganda/accord11/downloads/2000_Jan_The_Amnesty_Act.doc [accessed: 12 May 2008].

65 Part II, Section 3, The Amnesty Act. 2000. The Ugandan Amnesty Act. Available at: www.c-r.org/accord/uganda/accord11/downloads/2000_Jan_The_Amnesty_Act.doc [accessed: 12 May 2008].

66 Hovil, L. and Lomo, Z. February 2005. Whose Justice? Perceptions of Uganda's Amnesty Act 2000: The Potential for Conflict Resolution and Long-Term Reconciliation. Refugee Law Project Working Paper No. 15. Faculty of Law of Makerere University, 1-30, 6. Available at: www.refugeelawproject.org [accessed: 2 July 2009].

67 Part II, Section 4, The Amnesty Act. 2000. The Ugandan Amnesty Act. Available at: www.c-r.org/accord/uganda/accord11/downloads/2000_Jan_The_Amnesty_Act.doc [accessed: 12 May 2009].

68 Amendments to The Amnesty Act 2000. 2003. Available at: www.c-r.org/accord/uganda/accord11/downloads/2000 Jan The Amnesty Act.doc [accessed: 12 May 2009].

69 International Criminal Court. 14 October 2005. *Warrants of Arrest Unsealed Against Five LRA Commanders*. Press Release. The Hague. ICC20051410.056-En. Available at: www.icc-cpi.int/press/pressreleases/114.html [accessed: 9 December 2008].

70 Hovil, L. and Lomo, Z. February 2005. Whose Justice? Perceptions of Uganda's Amnesty Act 2000: The Potential for Conflict Resolution and Long-Term Reconciliation.

of the Amnesty Act in 2003 brought the Amnesty Act into conformity with the ICC policy.[71] Here, it is important to notice that, in principle, those 'most responsible' may not be other than the leaders of the terrorist organizations or the commanders of the units (these are the only categories the Ugandan Amnesty Act precludes from amnesty).

The ICC remained silent on low-level perpetrators. The ICC seems to defer to the Ugandan authorities to deal with low-level perpetrators, whether through traditional justice, truth commissions or amnesties.

The OTP policy to prosecute those who bear the greatest responsibility while deferring low-level perpetrators to the Ugandan national system materializes the 'impunity gap'. The Prosecutor, in his *Paper on Some Policy Issues before the Office of the Prosecutor*, points to the possibility of such a 'gap'.[72] However, he identifies this gap as falling under the responsibility of national authorities. The Ugandan authorities have chosen restorative justice rather than a retributive or punitive form of justice. In terms of punitive justice, to end impunity as indicated in the Preamble of the Statute, the Amnesty Act creates an impunity gap on which the ICC chose to remain silent.

In this respect, the complementarity principle of the ICC was not able to encourage the national Ugandan system to prosecute low-level perpetrators of crimes falling under the jurisdiction of the Court.

Most probably here amnesties of low-level perpetrators will escape Article 17, and thus can render the case inadmissible under Article 17. Nevertheless, amnesties for those most responsible are admissible under the ambit of Article 17. The section *infra* will proceed to assess if amnesties fall under Article 53 or not.

Amnesty and Article 53   In order to initiate an investigation, Article 53 is taken into consideration. The Prosecutor is required to gather and analyse the information that comes to his attention and determine whether there is a reasonable basis to initiate an investigation. The Prosecutor will make the determination, according to Article 53(1), based on three factors: firstly, the 'factual legal basis' which indicates whether a crime within the jurisdiction of the Court has possibly occurred

---

Refugee Law Project Working Paper No. 15. Faculty of Law of Makerere University, 1-30, 6. Available at: www.refugeelawproject.org [accessed: 2 July 2009].

71   The Arrest Warrant of the five LRA leaders confirms that. See International Criminal Court. 14 October 2005. *Warrants of Arrest Unsealed Against Five LRA Commanders*. Press Release. The Hague. ICC20051410.056-En. Available at: www.icc-cpi.int/press/pressreleases/114.html [accessed: 9 December 2008].

72   International Criminal Court, Office of the Prosecutor. 2003. *Paper on Some Policy Issues before the Office of the Prosecutor*. ICC-OTP 2003, 1-9, 7. Available at: www.icc-cpi.int/library/organs/otp/030905_Policy_Paper.pdf [accessed: 20 February 2009].

or is occurring; secondly, the admissibility test under Article 17; and thirdly, the 'interest of justice' factor.[73]

In other words, Article 53(1) states a number of factors that are taken into consideration in determining if there is reasonable basis to initiate an investigation.[74] These factors are: the presence of reasonable basis to believe that a crime within the jurisdiction of the Court has been or is being committed;[75] the gravity of the crime; the interest of justice; and the interest of the victims.[76] This section will study these factors as part of an analysis of the Prosecutor's discretion towards amnesties. These factors are in most cases of domestic or local nature. Such an analysis will help to focus on how the aforementioned factors affect the Prosecutor's decision in particular and the path of international justice in general.

The 'interest of justice' criterion is not explicitly defined in the Statute. Article 21 indicates that the Court shall apply first the Statute, Elements of Crime and its Rules of Procedure and Evidence. Then, the Court shall implement applicable treaties and principles of international law, including international human rights law. Finally, the Court will apply general principles of law derived from national laws provided that these laws are consistent with the Statute and international law. The three sources of law must be consistent with internationally recognized human rights.[77] When the Statute does not provide a clear definition, the Court is to turn to secondary and tertiary sources.

The 'interest of justice' is one criterion for a 'reasonable basis' to proceed. As the term is left undefined, the Prosecutor has a broad degree of discretion in interpreting it.[78] Despite the absence of a primary source defining 'interest of justice', the obligation of the Prosecutor to apply secondary and tertiary sources does not eliminate his power of discretion on the matter.[79]

---

73   International Criminal Court, Office of the Prosecutor. 2003. *Paper on Some Policy Issues before the Office of the Prosecutor.* ICC-OTP 2003, 1-9, 3. Available at: www.icc-cpi.int/library/organs/otp/030905_Policy_Paper.pdf [accessed: 20 February 2009].

74   International Criminal Court, Office of The Prosecutor. 29 June 2005. *Report of The Prosecutor of The International Criminal Court, Mr Luis Ocampo-Moreno to the UN Security Council Pursuant to UNSC 1593.* The Hague, ICC-OTP-0629-105-En, 1-11, 2.

75   Article 53(1)(a) of the Rome Statute of the International Criminal Court, UN Doc. A/CONF.183/9.

76   Article 53(1)(c) and 53(2)(c) of the Rome Statute of the International Criminal Court, UN Doc. A/CONF.183/9. Admissibility under Article 17 is also a basic factor, but this section will refrain from discussing Article 17 as it has been discussed *supra*. Also, the 'gravity of the crime' has been analysed under Article 17.

77   Article 21 of the Rome Statute of the International Criminal Court, UN Doc. A/CONF.183/9.

78   Brubacher, Matthew R. 2004. Prosecutorial Discretion within the International Criminal Court. *Journal of International Criminal Justice,* 2, 1, 71-95, 79.

79   Various human rights treaties as well general principles of law do not have a clear definition of what constitutes 'interest of justice'.

Defining 'justice' and 'interest of justice' is not simple. As the term justice is a subjective term, there are different interpretations depending on various philosophical, cultural, political, economic and social values. What is 'just' in one society may not be just in another. *Black's Law Dictionary* defines justice as 'the proper management of laws. In jurisprudence, it is the constant and perpetual disposition of legal matters or disputes to render every man his dues'.[80] The *Juris Dictionary* describes it otherwise: 'justice is both a metaphysical and a political concept'.[81] Defining the term 'interest of justice' is just as difficult, leaving the Prosecutor of the ICC with considerable margin of discretion in approaching such terms.

The ambiguity inherent in interpreting 'interest of justice' raises fundamental questions of whether this notion is confined to retributive justice or whether it could include other non-prosecutorial programmes. The 'interest of justice' notion seems liable to inclusion into a broader interpretation for what is 'justice'. In the opinion of this author, this interpretation is confirmed if juxtaposed alongside Article 53(1)(c). Article 53(1)(c) correlates criminal justice considerations such as the gravity of the crime and the interests of the victim, with the broader concept of 'interest of justice'.[82] Some jurists indicate that the 'interest of justice' is interpretable according to three main alternatives. According to the first one, 'interest of justice' requires the prosecution of those most responsible. According to the second, the ICC must prosecute international crimes. The third alternative covers emergency situations whereby the Prosecutor could tolerate non-prosecutorial alternatives.[83] In two of these alternatives, amnesty could be tolerated within the Prosecutor's discretion. By the first alternative, the Prosecutor could decide not to proceed on low-level perpetrators under Article 53(1)(c).[84]

The OTP policy paper and the Prosecutor's practice adopt the first alternative in the argument *supra* in which only those 'most responsible' are to be prosecuted.[85] Yet, such an argument is not sufficient for understanding the 'interest of justice' and thus falls short of resolving its ambiguity.

---

80   Henry Campbell, B. 1979. *Black's Law Dictionary*. St Paul: West, fifth edition, 776.

81   *Juris Dictionary*, definition of 'justice'. Available at: www.jurisdictionary.com/dictionary/J.asp [accessed: 23 January 2008].

82   Robinson, D. June 2003. Serving the Interest of Justice: Amnesties, Truth Commissions and the International Criminal Court. *The European Journal of International Law*, 14, 481-509, 486.

83   Robinson, D. June 2003. Serving the Interest of Justice: Amnesties, Truth Commissions and the International Criminal Court. *The European Journal of International Law*, 14, 481-509, 489.

84   This is subject to the revision of the Pre-Trial Chamber. See Article 53(3)(b).

85   International Criminal Court. 14 October 2005. *Warrants of Arrest Unsealed Against Five LRA Commanders*. Press Release. The Hague. ICC20051410.056-En. Available at: www.icc-cpi.int/press/pressreleases/114.html [accessed: 9 December 2008].

'Interest of justice' as set out in Article 53 is quite elastic. The Rome Statute does not state explicitly how to evaluate it,[86] and so a further and more precise analysis of the 'interest of justice' requires a juxtapositional study of this notion, contrasting it with the gravity of the crime, interest of the victim, the effect of the investigation, and the feasibility of the investigation. These four factors are delineated in the Office of the Prosecutor policy.[87] It highlights four points that should be considered by the Prosecutor in deciding whether the investigation serves the 'interest of justice'. These points are: the gravity of the situation, the interests of the victims, the effect of an investigation, and the feasibility of the investigation. These factors are not exhaustive.[88] This section will refrain from delving deeply into the 'gravity of the crime' factor, the effect of an investigation, and the feasibility of such investigation, as any assessment of amnesty falls mostly – but not completely – beyond the scope of these factors. The effect of the 'gravity' factor in assessing a supposed amnesty is not crucial for this study; it is only substantial when amnesty covers crimes of low gravity. Yet, here the gravity of the crime and not the nature or the scope of amnesty is the determinant factor. The other two factors – the effect and feasibility of the investigation – also fall mostly outside the scope of amnesty, as they are constituencies of retributive justice, where investigation and prosecution are important stages of the process. However, these two factors could still have an impact on the Prosecutor's decision towards amnesty. The Prosecutor could still consider the possible effect of an investigation, through weighing the positive and negative consequences of this investigation. It will not be in the 'interest of justice' if the effect of an investigation could affect the stability of the situation. In addition, it is against the 'interest of justice' if the investigation has negative consequences for the victims' security and well-being. The victims' stand in relation to alternative justice mechanisms is taken into consideration.

However, if the interpretation of 'interest of justice' is broader in scope, other factors need to be taken into consideration, such as the interests of the international community,[89] the political effect of any investigation, the effect of the Prosecutor's intervention on ongoing disputes or the post-conflict reconciliation process, the

---

86 Danner, A.M. July 2003. Enhancing the Legitimacy and Accountability of Prosecutorial Discretion at the International Court. *The American Journal of International Law*, 510-572, 535.

87 International Criminal Court, Office of the Prosecutor. April 2004. Prosecution Guidelines Not to Initiate an Investigation 'in the Interest of Justice' pursuant to Article 53(1)(c), 16 April 2004, 1-14.

88 International Criminal Court, Office of the Prosecutor. May 2004. Interpretation and Scope of 'interest of Justice' in Article 53 of the Rome Statute, 7 May 2004. MoI 19-040507-1, 1-21, 2.

89 La Fraper Du Hellen, B. 1999. Round Table: Prospects for The Functioning of The International Criminal Court, in *The Rome Statute of the International Criminal Court: A Challenge to Impunity, Proceedings of the Trento Conference on the ICC*, edited by M. Politi and G. Nesi. 2001. Aldershot: Ashgate, 300.

effect of the conflict on the local community and the peace and security of the affected society, and the impact of the conflict on international community and the peace and security of the world.[90]

The 'interests of victims' notion is an important element in the Prosecutor's assessment concerning whether or not to proceed with the case. The 'interests of victims' is a fundamental factor in defining 'interest of justice.' The Statute does not include an explicit definition of the notion of 'interests of victims'. In this case, Article 21 of the Statute is invoked.[91]

Before delving into legal arguments concerning the 'interest of victims', a simple question should be addressed concerning scope. Is the interest of the victim respected through criminal prosecution or through non-prosecutorial programmes? Will retributive justice achieve justice for the victim or can restorative justice be a more favourable option? In the opinion of this author, it is through this loophole – if it is to be considered so – that amnesty could fall under the ambit of 'interest of justice', and thus under prosecutorial discretion within Article 53.

There are a number of decisive factors for determining the interest of victims. The first factor is the victims' attitudes towards any prosecutorial programme of the crimes alleged in that situation. The position of the victims is an important factor that cannot be ignored in deciding to proceed with the prosecution. An investigation may not serve the interest of the victims if the victims express their opposition to an investigation.[92] In addition, the Rome Statute guarantees that the views of the victims are heard during the proceedings.[93]

The second factor is the victims' position in relation to alternative justice mechanisms. Victims may consider other non-prosecutorial mechanisms. The victims may prefer achieving peace by other means, such as amnesty or by receiving compensation. Moreover, the victims may be interested in achieving

---

90   Brubacher, Matthew R. 2004. Prosecutorial Discretion within the International Criminal Court. *Journal of International Criminal Justice*, 2, 1, 71-95, 81.

91   Article 21 of the Rome Statute of the International Criminal Court, UN Doc. A/CONF.183/9. Article 21 includes the sources of law, which the Court will take into consideration, including the Rome Statute, Laws of Rules and Procedures, International Treaties and General Principles of Law (including domestic laws of major legal systems in the world).

92   In a number of national systems, the attitude of the victims is taken into consideration, such as in Australia, paragraph 2.10(O), Belgium, paragraph 2.25, Canada, paragraph 15.3(n). Also China: in that regard, see Chan, E. 2003. One Country, Two Systems. The Decision To Investigate and Prosecute in China and Special Administrative Region of Hong Kong. Paper submitted to the Seventh Conference of the International Society for the Reform of Criminal Law held in The Hague, the Netherlands, 24-28 August 2003. Available at: www.isrcl.org [accessed: 25 January 2009].

93   Articles 19(3), 68(3), 75(3), 82(1), 82(4) of the Rome Statute of the International Criminal Court, UN Doc. A/CONF.183/9.

justice through traditional or customary systems. Such options are not to be discarded.[94]

The Declaration of Basic Principles of Justice to Victims of Crime and Abuse of Power considers procedures of redress, including restorative, customary and traditional justice as options agreeing with the interest of the victims.[95] *The United Nations Handbook on Justice for Victims* confirms this argument.[96]

A third factor is the possible impact of an investigation on the victims' safety, physical or psychological well-being, dignity or privacy. Any investigation and prosecution with a negative effect on the interest of the victims, in terms of his or her physical or psychological well-being, may not serve the interest of justice.[97] Article 63(1) of the ICC Statute imposes an obligation on the Prosecutor to ensure the safety, physical and psychological well-being of victims and witnesses.[98] One can conclude that the safety of the victim is a factor that the Prosecutor has to take into consideration in all stages, starting from the decision to initiate an investigation to the investigation and prosecution. The Declaration of Basic Principles of Justice to Victims of Crime and Abuse of Power calls for measures to ensure the safety of the victims from intimidation and retaliation.[99]

Other factors affecting an investigation will not be analysed as they are of no relevance to the amnesty issue, which is the aim of this section.[100]

The factors indicated *supra* are guidelines that the Prosecutor takes into consideration in determining if there is a reasonable basis to proceed. However, the guidelines do not eradicate the discretionary power of the Prosecutor, which he or she enjoys within these guidelines. The determination of the impact of these

---

94   Hovil, L. and Lomo, Z. February 2005. Whose Justice? Perceptions of Uganda's Amnesty Act 2000: The Potential for Conflict Resolution and Long-Term Reconciliation. Refugee Law Project Working Paper No. 15. Faculty of Law of Makerere University, 1-30, 6. Available at: www.refugeelawproject.org [accessed: 2 July 2009].

95   Declaration of Basic Principles of Justice for Victims of Crime and Abuse of Power. Adopted by the General Assembly in the 96th plenary meeting on 29 November 1985. A/RES/40/34.

96   *The United Nations Handbook on Justice for Victims.* 1999. New York, 1-133, 34. Available at: www.uncjin.org/Standards/9857854.pdf [accessed: 12 December 2008].

97   International Criminal Court, Office of the Prosecutor. May 2004. Interpretation and Scope of 'interest of Justice' in Article 53 of the Rome Statute, 7 May 2004. Mol 19-040507-1, 1-21, 15.

98   Article 63(1) of the Rome Statute of the International Criminal Court, UN Doc. A/CONF.183/9.

99   Principle 6(d) of The Declaration of Basic Principles of Justice for Victims of Crime and Abuse of Power. Adopted by the General Assembly in the 96th plenary meeting on 29 November 1985. A/RES/40/34.

100   These factors are: the impact of investigation on the perception of the Court, eventual deterrence, promotion of the authority of law, contribution to the collecting and preservation of evidences.

factors on the victims is for the Prosecutor to assess in determining whether or the required threshold is met.

Amnesty could be addressed by the Prosecutor within the notion of 'interest of justice'. Under the 'interest of justice', the 'interests of victims' is a pivotal factor. Amnesty could be addressed under all factors that contributed to the interest of the victim. Although these factors indicated *supra* are not exhaustive, they constitute suitable guidelines through which the Prosecutor can address amnesty issues.

The Prosecutor's Power of Discretion and Amnesties

The argument *supra* requires analysis of the prosecutorial discretion under the Statute in brief. 'Discretion', according to the *Oxford Companion to Law*, is 'the faculty of deciding or determining in accordance with circumstances and what seems just, right, equitable, and reasonable in those circumstances'.[101] Discretion allows for choosing among two or more permissible courses of action.[102]

Prosecutorial discretion's limits and scope differ from one legal system to another. However, prosecutorial discretion is divisible among two broad approaches: the legalist approach and the opportunistic approach.[103] Under the legalist approach, the Prosecutor is bound to prosecute as long as there is enough evidence to justify prosecution. The German model provides a clear example based on the principle of legality, *legalitäetsprinzip*, as indicated in section 152(2) of the German Code of Criminal Procedure.[104] Under the opportunistic approach, the prosecutorial authority exercises discretionary power within certain defined guidelines as to whether or not to prosecute. Such a system operates mostly under English or Roman-Dutch common law.[105] The latter approach reflects the known principle of 'l'opportunité des poursuites', while the former approach reflects the principle of 'la legalité des poursuites'.[106]

---

101   See in Ntanda Nsereko, D.D. 2003. *Prosecutorial Discretion before National Courts and International Tribunals*. Guest Lecture Series of The Office of the Prosecutor. ICC-OTP and Individual Authors 2003, 1-15, 3.

102   Danner, A.M. July 2003. Enhancing the Legitimacy and Accountability of Prosecutorial Discretion at the International Court. *The American Journal of International Law*, 510-572, 518.

103   Brubacher, Matthew R. 2004. Prosecutorial Discretion within the International Criminal Court. *Journal of International Criminal Justice*, 2, 1, 71-95, 74.

104   Ntanda Nsereko, D.D. 2003. *Prosecutorial Discretion before National Courts and International Tribunals*. Guest Lecture Series of The Office of the Prosecutor. ICC-OTP and Individual Authors 2003, 1-15, 3.

105   Ntanda Nsereko, D.D. 2003. *Prosecutorial Discretion before National Courts and International Tribunals*. Guest Lecture Series of The Office of the Prosecutor. ICC-OTP and Individual Authors 2003, 1-15, 4.

106   Cote, L. March 2005. Reflections on the Exercise of Prosecutorial Discretion in International Criminal Law. *Journal of International Criminal Justice*, 162-185, 165.

National systems are divided between these two main approaches. However, the division is not clear. Either states' prosecutorial policies adopt one of these approaches, or they tend to combine characteristics from both.

The prosecutorial discretion before the International Criminal Court in particular and in international criminal law in general has been 'subsequently strengthened' by the *ad hoc* Tribunals ICTY and ICTR.[107] The practices and jurisprudences of the ICTY and ICTR reflect a prosecutorial discretion in which the prosecutors were able to launch investigation *ex officio* and decide whether to indict or not.[108] The prosecutors before these international courts enjoyed relative independence within certain limitations, such as the existence of ground that warrants an investigation,[109] and a *prima facie* case.[110] The Prosecutor of the Special Court for Sierra Leone (SCSL) also enjoyed quite considerable discretion in choosing cases for prosecution, again within defined limitations. The Prosecutor weighs a number of factors when deciding whether to proceed with an indictment or not. Open-ended terms such as peace and justice are also taken into consideration. Hence, the border between politics and law becomes blurred. In fact, it is difficult to determine if the political aspect (including stability and peace) affects the Prosecutor's decision or vice versa. The indictment of Charles Taylor by the SCSL Prosecutor David Crane,[111] and the case of the NATO,[112] are two clear examples.

The elaborated discretionary power which international criminal law witnessed with ICTY and ICTR jurisprudence, generated concern among many states which, of course, tend to be cautious towards any threat to their exercise of jurisdiction on their territories and citizens. Many states were not ready to accept a Prosecutor for the International Criminal Court with wide discretionary powers. That was reflected clearly in the Rome Conference.[113] States were also afraid that a Prosecutor with

---

107   Brubacher, Matthew R. 2004. Prosecutorial Discretion within the International Criminal Court. *Journal of International Criminal Justice*, 2, 1, 71-95, 75.

108   Article 18(1) of ICTY Statute and Article 17(1) of ICTR Statute.

109   Ntanda Nsereko, D.D. 2003. *Prosecutorial Discretion before National Courts and International Tribunals*. Guest Lecture Series of The Office of the Prosecutor. ICC-OTP and Individual Authors 2003, 1-15, 10.

110   Article 18(4) of ICTY Statute and Article 17 of ICTR Statute.

111   Cote, L. March 2005. Reflections on the Exercise of Prosecutorial Discretion in International Criminal Law. *Journal of International Criminal Justice*, 162-185, 172.

112   Statement by Justice Louis Arbour, Prosecutor of the ICTY and ICTR (1999) Press Release, The Hague, 13 May 1999, JL/PIU/401-E, as quoted in Kovacs, P. 1999. Intervention Armee des Forces de l'OTAN au Kosovo. *International Review of the Red Cross*, 103-128. Available at: www.icrc.org/web/fre/sitefre0.nsf/html/5FZEXP [accessed: 2 January 2009].

113   Fernández de Gurmendi, S.A. 1999. The Role of The International Prosecutor, in *The International Criminal Court: The Making of the Rome Statute: Issues, Negotiations and Results*, edited by R. Lee. The Hague: Kluwer, 175.

wide discretionary power would be a 'loose cannon' and could initiate politically motivated prosecutions.[114]

In the Preparatory Committee delegates suggested that the Prosecutor should have *proprio motu* powers, since the first draft of the ICC Statute created by the International Law Commission did not give the Prosecutor any power to initiate a *proprio motu* case.[115] The NGOs' role was pivotal here as they fought for the Prosecutor's independence in the Rome Statute.[116] Participants were strongly divided on this issue. The United States, for example, stood firmly against *proprio motu* powers for the ICC prosecutor. Other delegates rejected the US stand. In the end, a compromise solution was introduced by Germany and Argentina.[117] Their proposal preserved the Prosecutor's *proprio motu* powers, but limited such power to the supervision of the Pre-Trial Chamber.[118]

Article 53 indicates that the Prosecutor is under a duty to initiate investigation unless he or she determines that there is 'no reasonable basis to proceed'.[119] The use of 'shall' in Article 53 is diluted by allowing the Prosecutor to determine if there is reasonable ground to proceed or not. Here, 'shall' is more close to 'may', as 'unless' gives the Prosecutor the power to determine if there is reasonable ground to proceed. Moreover, 'reasonable basis' is not defined and it is for the Prosecutor to make her or his conclusion on the matter taking into consideration a number of factors. Among these, Article 53 indicates that the Prosecutor is to take into account the gravity of the crime, the interests of the victims, and in general the interest of justice. As mentioned *supra* in this chapter, where the measure of the gravity of the crime could be measured quantitatively,[120] the other factors are terms for which there is no explicit definition either within the Statute or in international criminal

---

114   Hiatt, F. July 1998. The Trouble with The War Crime Court, *The Washington Post*, 26 July 1998, 7, cited in Ntanda Nsereko, D.D. 2003. *Prosecutorial Discretion before National Courts and International Tribunals*. Guest Lecture Series of The Office of the Prosecutor. ICC-OTP and Individual Authors 2003, 1-15, 11.

115   Fernández de Gurmendi, S.A. 1999. The Role of The International Prosecutor, in *The International Criminal Court: The Making of the Rome Statute: Issues, Negotiations and Results*, edited by R. Lee. The Hague: Kluwer, 175, 177.

116   Fernández de Gurmendi, S.A. 1999. The Role of The International Prosecutor, in *The International Criminal Court: The Making of the Rome Statute: Issues, Negotiations and Results*, edited by R. Lee. The Hague: Kluwer, 177.

117   Bergsmo, M. and Pejic, J. 1999. Article 15, in *Commentary on the Rome Statute of the International Criminal Court: Observer's Note, Article by Article*, edited by O. Trifterer. Baden-Baden: Nomos Verlagsgesellschaft, 359, 363.

118   Scheffer, D. The US Ambassador at Large For War Crimes. 1998. Is an UN International Criminal Court in the Interest of the United States National? *Hearing before the Subcommittee on International Foreign Relations*. Tenth Congress.

119   Article 53(1) of the Rome Statute of the International Criminal Court, UN Doc. A/CONF.183/9.

120   Although an argument could be raised stating that the 'gravity of the crime' could be of qualitative nature also.

law.[121] This provides the Prosecutor with considerable power of discretion. Article 53(2) stipulates that the Prosecutor should conclude on the matter after evaluating these factors. Furthermore, Article 54 includes the use of 'may' when conducting investigation by the Prosecutor.[122] 'May' is also used referring to the procedural matters related to conducting investigations.[123] A number of experts confirm this analysis.[124]

This power of discretion in tackling values of the 'interest of victims' and 'interest of justice' leaves a considerable margin for the Prosecutor to address amnesties within the guideline of his or her prosecutorial policy.

On the other hand, this prosecutorial discretion is not without limits. The major restriction is the oversight of the Pre-Trial Chamber on the Prosecutor's discretionary powers. That was included in the Rome Statute to allay the fears expressed by the states of a Prosecutor with wide discretionary power.[125]

Article 53(1)(c) indicates that if the Prosecutor finds no reasonable basis to proceed in subparagraph c, he or she is to inform the Pre-Trial Chamber. In addition, at the investigation level, the Prosecutor's decision not to proceed is evaluated by the Pre-Trial Chamber.[126] Our analysis will focus solely on the decision not to proceed, precisely under paragraphs 53(1)(c) and 53(2)(c), since under such a decision the Prosecutor could defer to non-prosecutorial programmes such as amnesties. The decision of the Prosecutor to proceed with the Pre-Trial Chamber approval falls outside the scope of this study, as amnesty will not be covered in that case.

The prosecutorial discretion reflected in paragraphs 53(1)(c) and 53(2)(c) is under the supervision of the Pre-Trial Chamber.[127] The Prosecutor, as an

---

121   See *supra* argument on Article 53 and amnesty.

122   Article 54 of the Rome Statute of the International Criminal Court, UN Doc. A/CONF.183/9.

123   Article 54 of the Rome Statute of the International Criminal Court, UN Doc. A/CONF.183/9.

124   Gavron, J. 2002. Amnesties in the Light of Developments in International Law and the Establishment of the International Criminal Court. *International and Comparative Law Quarterly*, 51, 91-126, 105. Also, Brubacher, M.R. 2004. Prosecutorial Discretion within the International Criminal Court. *Journal of International Criminal Justice*, 2, 1, 71-95. Also, Ntanda Nsereko, D.D. 2003. *Prosecutorial Discretion before National Courts and International Tribunals*. Guest Lecture Series of The Office of the Prosecutor. ICC-OTP and Individual Authors 2003, 1-15, 10. Also, Cote, L. March 2005. Reflections on the Exercise of Prosecutorial Discretion in International Criminal Law. *Journal of International Criminal Justice*, 162-185.

125   Ntanda Nsereko, D.D. 2003. *Prosecutorial Discretion before National Courts and International Tribunals*. Guest Lecture Series of The Office of the Prosecutor. ICC-OTP and Individual Authors 2003, 1-15, 11.

126   Article 53(2) of the Rome Statute of the International Criminal Court, UN Doc. A/CONF.183/9.

127   Article 39(2)(iii) of the Rome Statute of the International Criminal Court, UN Doc. A/CONF.183/9.

independent body, is checked by the judicial body of the ICC. The function of the Pre-Trial Chamber, pertaining to Articles 53, is exercised by a single judge belonging to the Pre-Trial Chamber.[128] The Prosecutor's independence is limited through this mechanism. It is clear that the discretionary power of the Prosecutor of the ICC is much more restricted than that of his or her counterparts at the ICTY and ICTR.[129]

The judicial review of the Prosecutor's decision is likely to be evaluated with reference to Article 53(1)(c), 53(2)(c) or Article 15(3). Victims under Article 15(3) could testify before the Pre-Trial Chamber. The *proprio motu* power of the Prosecutor is under decisive judicial scrutiny by the Pre-Trial Chamber.[130]

Another factor that limits the Prosecutor's power of discretion is the Security Council.[131] Under Article 16 of the Statute, the Security Council can defer an investigation for a renewable 12 months by adopting a resolution under Chapter VII of the UN Charter.[132] Through this decision, the Security Council can block the Prosecutor's decision to investigate. A Security Council deferral would affect the decision of the Prosecutor to proceed based on the finding of a 'reasonable basis' to proceed, but it cannot affect the decision of the Prosecutor not to proceed under Article 53(1)(c), which cannot be overturned by the Security Council deferral. The Prosecutor's discretion pertaining to the possible amnesty will fall largely under Article 53(1)(c) where he or she could decide not to proceed because no reasonable basis to proceed exists, taking into consideration the gravity of the crime, the interest of the victims and the interest of justice.

A third important limitation is the control of the Assembly of State Parties (ASP) to the ICC Statute. The Prosecutor generally remains accountable to the Assembly of State Parties, which can remove him from office for misconduct.[133] The ASP does not exercise a direct control on the Prosecutor's power, but exercises something describable as 'pragmatic accountability'.[134] The Prosecutor

---

128   Article 57(2) of the Rome Statute of the International Criminal Court, UN Doc. A/CONF.183/9.

129   Ntanda Nsereko, D.D. 2003. *Prosecutorial Discretion before National Courts and International Tribunals.* Guest Lecture Series of The Office of the Prosecutor. ICC-OTP and Individual Authors 2003, 1-15, 11.

130   Brubacher, M.R. 2004. Prosecutorial Discretion within the International Criminal Court. *Journal of International Criminal Justice*, 2, 1, 71-95, 81.

131   Brubacher, M.R. 2004. Prosecutorial Discretion within the International Criminal Court. *Journal of International Criminal Justice*, 2, 1, 71-95, 82.

132   Tutrone, G. 2002. Powers and Duties of The Prosecutor, in *The Rome Statute of The International Criminal Court: A Commentary*, edited by A. Cassese, P. Gaeta and J.R.W.D. Jones. Oxford: Oxford University Press, 2, 1141.

133   Articles 46.1, 46.2(b) and 47 of the Rome Statute of the International Criminal Court, UN Doc. A/CONF.183/9.

134   Danner, A.M. July 2003. Enhancing the Legitimacy and Accountability of Prosecutorial Discretion at the International Court. *The American Journal of International Law*, 510-572, 524.

cannot ignore the states' positions on various political, economic and legal issues. The ASP represents more than 111 states resembling the bulk of the international community, and thus the Prosecutor's policy cannot be in contradiction with the desires of these states in particular and the international community in general.

Furthermore, the ASP has the potential to control the Prosecutor's power through the funding allocated to the Court in general and the Office of the Prosecutor in particular.[135] The ASP can decide what role the Prosecutor should play through the resources allocated to his office. The *Paper on Some Policy Issues before the Office of the Prosecutor* confirms this fact, as financial burden is a crucial element in deciding the number of cases in which the Prosecutor could initiate investigations.[136] Financial restrictions also affect the number of indictments that can be issued by the Prosecutor in one case. One of the reasons, therefore, that compelled the Prosecutor to focus his prosecutions on 'those most responsible' is the limited capabilities of the Court in terms of financial resources.[137]

The 'opportunistic model' of prosecutions, which the ICC Statute adopted, is more limited. A system of checks-and-balances is created between the Prosecutor's discretionary power, on one hand, and various legal and political restrictions on the other. One author says about the Prosecutor's discretion in international criminal law that 'like the hole in the doughnut, [it] does not exist except as an area left open by a surrounding belt of restriction'.[138] This much applies to the ICC's prosecutorial discretion.

Conclusion

In this section, this author aimed at highlighting how amnesties will hardly fall under Article 17, which addresses the prosecutorial process and the criminal investigation. The findings above highlight that an amnesty may not render the case inadmissible and the complementarity principle will remain functional. The case will be admissible as the non-prosecution of the state can be considered a status of 'unwilling' or 'inability' to investigate. This holds on the basis that an amnesty blocking prosecution is 'inconsistent with intent to bring the person

---

135   Danner, A.M. July 2003. Enhancing the Legitimacy and Accountability of Prosecutorial Discretion at the International Court. *The American Journal of International Law*, 510-572, Prosecutorial Discretion at the International Court. *The American Journal of International Law*, 510-572, 524.

136   International Criminal Court, Office of the Prosecutor. 2003. *Paper on Some Policy Issues before the Office of the Prosecutor*. ICC-OTP 2003, 1-9, 3. Available at: www.icc-cpi.int/library/organs/otp/030905_Policy_Paper.pdf [accessed: 20 February 2009].

137   International Criminal Court, Office of the Prosecutor. December 2005. *Informal Meeting of Legal Advisors of Ministries of Foreign Affairs in New York, 24 October 2005*; Statement by Luis Moreno-Ocampo, Prosecutor of the International Criminal Court. ICC-02/04-01/05-67, 1-31, 8.

138   Dworkin, R. 1977. *Taking Rights Seriously*. Cambridge, MA: Harvard University Press, 31.

concerned to justice',[139] it can be the result of the inability of the national system to carry prosecutions,[140] or it can be 'for the purpose of shielding the person concerned from criminal responsibility'.[141] Yet, amnesty is covered substantially under Article 53(1)(c), where the Prosecutor takes into consideration values such as the 'interests of victims' and the 'interest of justice' to evaluate whether to defer to national non-prosecutorial programmes, such as amnesty. The Prosecutor's decision is scrutinized by the Pre-Trial Chamber *stricto sensu*.

Practice shows that the ICC can refrain from prosecuting in case of two models of amnesties. The first refrain applies to amnesty granted for low-level perpetrators, since the prosecution policy of the ICC is to target those 'most responsible'. The ICC will not act on such amnesties, leaving the national systems to choose between prosecutorial and non-prosecutorial programmes. The Ugandan Amnesty Act is a clear example, as the unsealing of the arrest warrant by the ICC targeted those most responsible among the Lord's Resistance Army (LRA) leaders while leaving the Ugandan amnesty law intact for low-level perpetrators.[142] Yet, this materialized the 'impunity gap' which the OTP feared, as indicated in the *Paper on Some Policy Issues before the Office of the Prosecutor*. This example is a setback to the Court's capability to contribute to the national judicial system to prosecute international crimes.

The second type of amnesty, which the ICC could refrain from prosecuting, concerns the 'interest of the victims' and 'interest of justice'. Under these two notions, various factors are taken into consideration, covered above. It is at the Prosecutor's discretion – within certain checks and balances – to determine if there is 'reasonable grounds' to prosecute or defer to non-prosecutorial national programmes. From this, one can conclude that this type of amnesty will not hamper the complementarity principle, and the case will remain admissible before the ICC, given that the other factors for admissibility are fulfilled.

Pardons as a Possible Hurdle to Complementarity

Pardons that will be covered by this section are those granted after trial and conviction. It may seem at first that pardons do not directly affect the complementarity principle and the admissibility criteria of the ICC, however, for delving into the

---

139   Article 17(2) of the Rome Statute of the International Criminal Court, UN Doc. A/CONF.183/9.

140   Article 17(2) of the Rome Statute of the International Criminal Court, UN Doc. A/CONF.183/9.

141   Article 17(2)(a) of the Rome Statute of the International Criminal Court, UN Doc. A/CONF.183/9.

142   International Criminal Court. 14 October 2005. *Warrants of Arrest Unsealed Against Five LRA Commanders*. Press Release. The Hague. ICC20051410.056-En. Available at: www.icc-cpi.int/press/pressreleases/114.html [accessed: 9 December 2008].

ICC–national judicial systems relation (through complementarity), it is vital to focus on the impact of the ICC on the effectiveness of national prosecutions. To analyse the complementarity principle and its relation with national judicial systems entails analysing any potential hindrance to the ICC concerning the 'effectiveness of the national prosecutions', including the serving of the sentences of criminals convicted of committing international crimes.

The analysis of pardons is therefore indispensable for detecting where pardons fall within the admissibility test of the ICC. This includes the role of complementarity in the case of national pardons, as well as the effect of pardons on the complementarity principle itself. If pardons block the complementarity principle, this constitutes a negative effect on the ICC's ability to contribute to national judicial systems prosecuting international crimes.

The practice of pardons, similar to amnesties, goes back to a long time. During the times of Hammurabi, harsh penalties were balanced by rules to limit vengeance, mitigating the effect of these penalties.[143] In addition, pardons were used for reasons other than mercy, for example, to raise money or for raising armies, as pardoned persons often paid money for their pardon or promised to join the military.[144]

Historically, pardon power was vested in the king or chief executive's prerogatives. The English pardon power was one of the broad royal fiats.[145] Gradually, parliaments in many national systems eventually restricted the king's pardoning power.[146] The French Revolution went to the extreme to abolish the executive clemency altogether, considering it an executive interference in the work of the judiciary.[147] The legitimacy of pardons became even more problematic as states became democratic. Historically, crimes were considered offences against the person of the king, and thus granting a pardon is one of the king's rights.[148] In a democracy, since crimes are against the people, it is according to democratic principles for the representative of the people to grant. In reality, such authority is not solely vested in parliaments and legislatures. In general, pardons are granted by various bodies according to different systems. Pardoning power in modern times

---

143   King, L. 2000. *Hammurabi Code of Laws*. Available at: http://eqwc.evansville. edu/anthology/hammurabi.htm [accessed: 8 May 2009].

144   Duker, W.F. 1977. The Presidents Power to Pardon: A Constitutional History. *WM and Mary Law Review*, 18, 475, 478-749.

145   Kait, B. December 1996. Pardon Me? The Constitutional Case Against Presidential Self-Pardons! *Yale Law Journal*, 106, 3, 778-809, 782.

146   Kait, B. December 1996. Pardon Me? The Constitutional Case Against Presidential Self-Pardons! *Yale Law Journal*, 106, 3, 778-809, 782.

147   Tait, D. 2002. Pardons in Perspective: The Role of Forgiveness in Criminal Justice. *Vera Institute of Justice, Inc. Federal Sentencing Reporter*, 134-143, 136.

148   Slye, R. Winter 2004. The Cambodian Amnesties: Beneficiaries and the Temporal Reach of Amnesties For Gross Violations of Human Rights. *Wisconsin International Law Journal*, 99-117, 102.

can be vested in the chief executive, a board, the legislature or some combination of these bodies.[149]

There are various definitions of pardons, reflecting the lack of consensus on what precisely the term pardon means. *Black's Law Dictionary* defines pardon as an 'act or an instance of officially nullifying punishment or other legal consequences of a crime'.[150] Some other definitions confuse pardons with amnesties. Some jurists define pardon to refer to instances 'when a suspect is declared immune from prosecution for certain offences before guilt was established'.[151] One author defines pardons differently. He indicates that pardons are issued after an individual has been found liable for a wrongful act. Sometimes a pardon is issued after an individual has begun to serve a criminal sentence.[152] Another author defines pardons more restrictively as 'an executive intervention to thwart justice'.[153] Such a general definition excludes other branches of the state, such as the legislature, from any pardoning power. Bassiouni notes that pardons are usually granted after establishment of guilt.[154] Hence, at the very least pardons occur after conviction or sentencing.[155]

This study will address pardons issued after trial and conviction, or after a portion of an incarceration sentence is served. The analysis of pardons here will not cover pardoning before conviction or sentencing, as that will be an amnesty or a type of suspension of law.

Pardons in State Practice

Pardons have been used extensively throughout the world. Such power is allocated to defined branches of the government. The US system grants wide pardoning power to the president through the constitution.[156] Successive American presidents have used such power extensively. One of the famous examples is Gerald Ford's

---

149   Barnett, James D. February 1927. The Grounds of Pardon. *Journal of American Institute of Criminal Law and Criminology*, 17, 4, 490-530, 490.

150   Gamer, B.A. (ed.). 1999. *Black Law Dictionary*. St Paul: West, seventh edition, 1137.

151   See Sirica, J. 1979. *To Set the Record Straight: The Break-in, The Tapes, The Conspirators, The Pardon*. New York: Norton.

152   Slye, R. Fall 2002. The Legitimacy of Amnesties under International Law and General Principles of Anglo-American Law: Is a Legitimate Amnesty Possible? *Virginia Journal of International Law*, 173-241, 201.

153   Tait, D. 2002. Pardons in Perspective: The Role of Forgiveness in Criminal Justice. *Vera Institute of Justice, Inc. Federal Sentencing Reporter*, 134-143, 136.

154   Bassiouni, M.Ch. 1996. *International Extradition: United States Law and Practice*. United States: Oceana Publications, 629-630.

155   Kait, B. December 1996. Pardon Me? The Constitutional Case Against Presidential Self-Pardons! *Yale Law Journal*, 106, 3, 778-809, 780.

156   Kait, B. December 1996. Pardon Me? The Constitutional Case Against Presidential Self-Pardons! *Yale Law Journal*, 106, 3, 778-809, 780.

pardon of his predecessor Richard Nixon, although the pardon here was granted before any indictment, which does not fall under the type of pardon this section discusses. In terms of international crimes, the US practice does not prohibit pardons. The Calley case, in which President Nixon granted Captain Calley partial pardon for the My Lai war crime[157] in the context of Vietnam War,[158] demonstrates this.

State practice in terms of granting pardons is widespread. Monarchs and chief executives continue to grant pardons (usually for ordinary crimes). In Islamic states often kings and presidents granted pardons on certain feasts or ceremonies.[159] Others provide pardons for improving relations between states.[160]

In terms of international crimes, Algeria pardoned thousands of prisoners 'to promote and strengthen the values of solidarity, assistance and forgiveness'.[161] The significance of these pardons is that they covered several convicted persons who were involved in violent attacks that amounted to possible war crimes, terrorism and other international crimes. Lithuania, after declaring independence in 1991, pardoned more than 50,000 Lithuanians who were convicted as war criminals by Soviet courts. Among the pardoned persons, there were many war criminals that assisted the Nazis in persecuting Jews.[162] Macedonia pardoned 11 guerrillas, eight of which were convicted for plotting or carrying out terrorist attacks during the Macedonian conflict.[163] Some have also criticized Israel for pardoning Palestinian

---

157   See Eckhardt, W.G. Summer 2000. Essay on the Trials of the Century: My Lai: An American Tragedy. *University of Missouri at Kansas City Law Review*, 671-708.

158   President Richard Nixon allowed the 'disgraced' Lieutenant to serve his sentence under house arrest. A series of appeals reduced Calley from life down to 20 years, and then 10 years. On 10 September 1975, Calley was paroled serving only three-and-a-half years. Available at: www.courttv.com/archive/greatesttrials/mylai/aftermath.html [accessed: 26 October 2008].

159   For example, the Moroccan Monarch pardoned or reduced prison sentences for 1,111 people to mark the Eid Al-fitr feast. Available at: www.newkerala.com/news.php?action=fullnews&aid=47768 [accessed: 27 February 2009].

160   The Tunisian President pardoned 26 French prisoners who were sentenced in Tunisia for drug crimes. That was done to improve relations with France. Available at: www.arabicnews.com/ansub/daily/day/991108/1999110821.html [accessed: 27 February 2008].

161   The Presidential Office of Algeria. Available at: www.news24com/news24/Africa/news/0,,2-11-1447_1827264,00.html [accessed: 20 March 2009].

162   *Jewish News Weekly*. Available at: www.jewishsf.com/content/2-0-/module/displaystory/story_id/6056/edition_id/131/format/html/displaystory.html [accessed: 27 February 2009].

163   Heinrich, M. December 2001. Macedonia Pardons 11 Guerrillas to Launch Amnesty. Available at: www.alb.net.com/amcc/cgi-bin/viewsnews.cgi?newsid100758367 9,97020 [accessed: 19 March 2009].

militants who were convicted of 'terrorist crimes' and violations of international humanitarian law.[164]

Pardons and Various Human Rights and International Human Law Instruments

In terms of various human rights and international humanitarian law instruments, the situation is also not clear. There is no explicit prohibition of pardons for international crimes. Yet, related treaties and instruments show that pardons for international crimes most probably will not be tolerated.

Article 5 of the Genocide Convention imposes an obligation on states to 'provide effective penalties for persons guilty of genocide'.[165] The term 'effective penalties' refers to detention sentences in the retributive sense of justice. Hence, pardon may be considered as inconsistent with the obligation imposed on member states to enforce effective penalties. Amnesty International supports this argument, as it considers national amnesties and pardons inconsistent with the duty to punish persons who have committed the crime of genocide.[166]

With respect to war crimes, the four Geneva Conventions of 1949 impose a duty on member states to 'enact any legislation necessary to provide effective penal sanctions for persons committing, or ordering to be committed any of the grave breaches'.[167] This phrase may not explicitly prohibit pardons, but the term 'effective penal sanctions' arguably excludes pardons. Pardons waive the sentence of the accused, and thus render the penalty ineffective. Hence, the Geneva Conventions implicitly do not tolerate pardons as they render the penal sanction ineffective. Yet, here the situation becomes complex when pardons mitigate the sentence or terminate the sentence after serving a considerable duration of it.

With the exception of torture and apartheid, most offences within crimes against humanity rely on customary bases. The stand of customary law towards pardons

---

164   Beres, L.R. 1998. Israel's Freeing of Terrorists Violates International Law. Available at: www.gamla.org.il/english/Article/1998/dec/1002.htm [accessed: 19 March 2009].

165   Article 5 of the Genocide Convention on the Prevention and Suppression of the Crime of Genocide (1948) 78, U.N.T.S 277.

166   Amnesty International. November 1997. The International Criminal Court: Making the Right Choices- Part III. Ensuring Effective State Cooperation, AI Index: IOR40/13/97.

167   Article 49 of Convention for Amelioration of the Conditions of the Wounded and the Sick in Armed Forces in the Field. 1949. 75U.N.T.S 31. Also see Article 50 of the Convention for Amelioration of the Conditions of the Wounded, Sick and Shipwrecked Members of the Armed Forces at Sea. 1949. 75U.N.T.S 85. Also, see Article 129 of Convention (III) relative to the Treatment of Prisoners of War. Article 146, paragraph 1, of Fourth Geneva Convention Relative To the Protection of Civilian persons in Time of War. Geneva (1949) Diplomatic Conference of Geneva of 1949. Entry into Force October 21, 1950. The Geneva Conventions of 12 August 1949, International Committee of the Red Cross, Geneva, 75-152.

is blurred. For treaty-based crimes, Article 4(2) of the Convention against Torture indicates that each 'state party shall make these offences punishable by appropriate penalties which take into account their grave nature'.[168] Here 'appropriate penalties' stipulates the necessity to impose penal sanctions on the offenders. The spirit of the Convention against Torture is to prosecute and punish criminals who commit torture. If pardons eliminate 'appropriate penalties', then they can be prohibited under the Convention. The International Convention on the Suppression and Punishment of the Crime of Apartheid imposes an obligation on state parties to 'adopt legislative, judicial and administration measures to prosecute, bring to trial and punish'[169] persons responsible for the crime of apartheid. The Convention does not elaborate on the nature or duration of the punishment. Nevertheless, here again a pardon that eliminates punishment is incompatible with the stipulations of Article IV of the Convention. Simultaneously, a pardon that could end a sentence of which a portion has been served is potentially more complex and unclear with respect to whether or not it breaches the Apartheid Convention.

As for other customary crimes against humanity, the situation is more complex. State practice and *opinio juris* does not support the existence of prohibition of pardons in customary international law.[170]

Other international human rights treaties do not explicitly address the issue of pardons for international crimes. The International Covenant of Civil and Political Rights (ICCPR) includes general articles on the protection of human rights, including fair trial provisions. However, the Covenant's articles do not directly cover pardons specifically. They implicitly preserve the right of persons who are sentenced to death to seek pardon or commutation of the sentence.[171] This reflects an encouragement for the abolition or restriction of the adoption of the death penalty, rather than encouraging pardons. It cannot be considered recognition of pardons for international crimes.

The United Nation's General Assembly has opposed national amnesties and pardons for crimes against humanity and war crimes. This was stated in Resolution 3074, which stressed on the punishment of persons for whom there is evidence of having committed war crimes or crimes against humanity.[172] It explicitly prohibits

---

168   Article 4(2) of The United Nations Convention against Torture and Other Cruel, Inhuman or Degrading Treatment or Punishment. 1984. G.A. res. 39/46, annex, 39 U.N. GAOR Supp. (no. 51) at 197, UN Doc. A/39/51, entered into force 26 June 1987.

169   Article IV(b) of The International Convention on the Suppression and Punishment of the Crime of Apartheid. 1973. Adopted and opened for signature, ratification by G.A. Resolution 3068 (XXVIII) of 30 November 1973. Entry into force 18 July 1976. Available at: www.unhchr.ch/html/menu3/b/11.htm [accessed: 9 May 2009].

170   See *supra* argument on state practice pertaining for international crimes.

171   Article 4(6) of International Covenant on Civil and Political Rights (1996), G.A. res. 2200A (XXI), 21 U.N. GAOR Supp. (no. 16) at 52, UN Doc. A/6316 (1966), 999 U.N.T.S. 171, entered into force 23 March 1976.

172   General Assembly GA 3074 (xxviii). Principles of International Cooperation in the Detection, Arrest, Extradition and Punishment of persons Guilty of War Crimes and

states from taking any legislative measure that could prejudice the international obligation of the state to detect, arrest, extradite and punish persons guilty of war crimes and crimes against humanity. This can be interpreted as prohibiting pardons for crimes against humanity and war crimes, as pardon is practically the elimination of punishment for these crimes. The UN Human Rights Committee in its 1995 Report on Argentina expressed concern over the state's use of pardons. It indicates that 'the presidential pardon of top military personnel is inconsistent with the requirements of the Covenant (International Covenant for Civil and Political Rights)'.[173] The Committee recommended that the use of pardons should not foster an atmosphere of impunity and denial of effective remedies.[174] The Committee, in its Observations on Ecuador of 1998, welcomed the constitutional prohibition of granting pardons for human rights violations.[175]

Furthermore, Amnesty International,[176] among others, considers amnesties, pardons for war crimes, crimes against humanity, genocide, torture, extra-judicial executions and enforced disappearances – as stipulated in Article IX of the Sierra Leone Peace Accord signed at Lomé in July 1999 – inconsistent with international law.[177]

Despite this, international treaties and instruments do not include an explicit prohibition of pardons for the core crimes of the ICC. Some treaties, such as the Genocide Convention, Geneva Conventions, Convention against Torture, and the Apartheid Convention, include a duty to punish perpetrators of international crimes by applying effective penalties. Under such duty, one could argue that pardons for international crimes are prohibited as they eliminate punishment and penalties.

Pardons in the Rome Statute

Pardons in the drafting process of the Rome Statute   The International Law Commission's Draft for an ICC Statute included an explicit reference to pardons – mainly pardons pertaining to ICC served sentences in states of imprisonment. Article 60 organizes pardons, paroles and commutation of Court's sentences served in state of imprisonment. It indicates that states shall notify the Court of any pardon, parole or commutation of sentences, and grants the Court the power

---

Crimes against Humanity, adopted on 3 December 1973.

173   Human Rights Committee. 1995. Comments on Argentina, UN Doc. CCPR/C/79/Add.46 (1995), para. 3

174   Human Rights Committee. 1995. Comments on Argentina, UN Doc. CCPR/C/79/Add.46 (1995), para. 10 and 15.

175   Human Rights Committee. 1998. Concluding Observations of the Human Rights Committee: Ecuador. 18/08/98. CCPR/C/79/Add.92, para. 7.

176   Amnesty International. November 2003. *Sierra Leone Special Court for Sierra Leone: Denial of Right to Appeal and Prohibition of Amnesties for Crimes under International Law*. Available at: http://web.amnesty.org/library/index/engafr510122003 [accessed: 5 July 2008].

177   Sierra Leone Peace Accord, Lomé, July 1999, UN Doc. S/1999/777, Art. IX.

to decide on the benefit of any possible pardon that could be granted by any state of imprisonment.[178]

Paragraph 4 of Article 60 is of particular interest, as it requests the Court's chamber to stipulate whether the sentence is served according to specific laws of the state of imprisonment. The consent of the Court is not required on subsequent action by the state of imprisonment in conformity with existing laws. The Court is to be notified before 45 days of any decision that could materially affect the terms or extend imprisonment. Furthermore, Article 60(5) prohibits any reduction of the sentence, except for restriction under Article 60(3) and 60(4).[179]

As for possible pardons for national sentences, the complementarity article in the draft statute does not explicitly address the issue of pardons or amnesties. Yet, Article 42, to the extent that it recognizes some exceptions to the *ne bis in idem*, states under paragraph 3 that in considering the penalty to be imposed on a person convicted under this statute, the Court shall take into account to what extent a penalty imposed by another court for the same act has been served.[180] Under this Article, any pardon could cause the Court to retry the convicted person as such a pardon is an exemption to the *ne bis in idem* principle.

The report of the Preparatory Committee on the establishment of an International Criminal Court of March-August 1996 included a number of opinions related to pardons under Article 60.[181] Some stated that pardons for ICC sentences should be left to the Court. Another view supported paragraph 4 of Article 60. In addition, some indicated that the Court, as a judicial body, should not look into extra-legal matters, but rather that a separate entity should be created to deal with such pardons.[182]

With respect to sentences from national courts and the *ne bis in idem* principle, the Report argued that the 'exception' to the principle of *ne bis in idem* within

---

178   Article 60 of International Law Commission Draft of an International Criminal Court. 1994. Available at: http://untreaty.un.org/ilc/texts/instruments/english/drafts%20Articles/7_4_1994.pdf [accessed: 5 March 2009].

179   Article 60(5) of International Law Commission Draft of an International Criminal Court. 1994. Available at: http://untreaty.un.org/ilc/texts/instruments/english/drafts%20Articles/7_4_1994.pdf [accessed: 5 March 2009].

180   Article 42(3) of International Law Commission Draft of an International Criminal Court. 1994. Available at: http://untreaty.un.org/ilc/texts/instruments/english/drafts%20Articles/7_4_1994.pdf [accessed: 5 March 2009].

181   Report of the Preparatory Committee on the Establishment of an International Criminal Court. *Proceedings of the Preparatory Committee during March, April and August 1996.* Available at: www.npwj.org/netrep/cdrpm/prepcom/prepcom.pdf [accessed: 15 May 2009].

182   Discussion over Article 60, Report of the Preparatory Committee on the Establishment of an International Criminal Court. *Proceedings of the Preparatory Committee during March, April and August 1996*, 74. Available at: www.npwj.org/netrep/cdrpm/prepcom/prepcom.pdf [accessed: 15 May 2009].

Article 42(b) should extend to include parole, pardons and amnesties.[183] This is in conformity with the ICC draft of 1994.

The Report of the Preparatory Committee to the Rome Conference moved the pardon issue for the Court sentences to Article 100. It includes two options. The first option preserves the right for the prisoner to apply to the ICC for pardons if national laws allow such application for similar crimes. The second option includes an absolute prohibition on any release by the state of enforcement. Article 100 includes a footnote showing concern for any possible politicization of pardons, and thus suggests that the power of granting pardons should go to the Assembly of State Parties.[184]

Also, the *ne bis in idem* principle was moved to Article 18 in the draft of the Preparatory Committee to the Rome Convention. It included a bracketed Article 19 that explicitly prohibited a manifestly unfounded decision on pardoning or suspending the enforcement of sentences.[185] In the discussion of the Committee of the Whole, there was a general desire among delegates to delete Article 19.[186] Even the sympathizers of the retention of Article 19 admitted that it could complicate and impose further delay on reaching a comprehensive agreement on the adoption of the Statute by the end of the conference.[187]

The omission of any article on pardons reflects many delegations' objection to the interference of the Court in the administration or political decision-making process of the states.[188] The consultation pertaining pardons was generally

---

183   Article 42, Report of the Preparatory Committee on the Establishment of an International Criminal Court. *Proceedings of the Preparatory Committee during March, April and August 1996*, 39. Available at: www.npwj.org/netrep/cdrpm/prepcom/prepcom. pdf [accessed: 15 May 2009].

184   UN Diplomatic Conference on the establishment of an International Criminal Court, Volume II.B. Report of the Preparatory Committee on the Establishment of an international Criminal Court. Available at: www.un.org/law/icc/rome/proceedings/E/ Rome%20Proceedings_v3_e.pdf [accessed: 15 June 2009].

185   Article 19, UN Diplomatic Conference on the establishment of an International Criminal Court, Volume II.B. Report of the Preparatory Committee on the Establishment of an International Criminal Court, 29. Available at: www.un.org/law/icc/rome/proceedings/ E/Rome%20Proceedings_v3_e.pdf [accessed: 15 June 2009].

186   The majority of states were in favour of the deletion of Article 19. These states included United Kingdom, Senegal, Afghanistan, Turkey, Israel, Venezuela, Poland, France, Indonesia, Pakistan, China, India. Malawi, Algeria, Switzerland, Jordan, Singapore, Brazil, Peru, Norway, Nigeria, Egypt, Sudan, Morocco, Botswana, Vietnam, Uruguay, Oman and Iran. See 'the summary records of the meeting of the Committee of the Whole' during the Rome conference. Available at: www.un.org/law/icc/rome/proceedings/E/ rome%20proceedings_v2_e.pdf [accessed: 15 June 2009].

187   See the position of Japan, Switzerland, Japan, Brazil, Italy, Botswana, Austria, New Zealand and Kuwait. Available at: www.un.org/law/icc/rome/proceedings/E/ rome%20proceedings_v2_e.pdf [accessed: 15 June 2009].

188   El-Zeidy, M. Summer 2002. The Principle of Complementarity: A Machinery to Implement International Criminal Law. *Michigan Journal of International Law*, 23, 4,

unsuccessful. The Rome Statute, in the end, remained silent on pardons that could be granted by states to national sentences. Article 103 of the ICC Statute alone deals with possible pardons for ICC sentences and not national sentences.[189] The silence of the Statute on pardons is a serious loophole.

Pardons and Article 17   Article 17 was formulated to organize the jurisdictional relation between the ICC and national courts. Article 17(1) renders the case inadmissible when the case 'is investigated or prosecuted by a state that has jurisdiction over it, unless the state is unwilling or unable to carry out genuinely the investigation or prosecution'.[190] Pardons will not fall under the ambit of this Article, as this Article is drafted to deal with ongoing investigations or prosecutions, while pardons are granted after the end of this stage and when a sentence has been imposed. The 'present' verb tense of Article 17(1)(a) confirms this.

Article 17(1)(b) deals with an investigated case and a decision not to prosecute is taken by the state that has jurisdiction over the case. The Court will render the case inadmissible in such a scenario. Again, the pardon in this case does not fall under the ambit of this paragraph, as granting a pardon in general requires the previous existence of conviction. Pardon cannot be granted if no punishment has been already ruled.[191] Under this paragraph, there is no possibility for conviction and thus no room for subsequent pardons.

Article 17(1)(c) considers the case admissible when the trial has already been conducted in a manner inconsistent with the intention to bring the person concerned to justice, or the trial was not conducted independently or impartially in accordance with the norms of due process recognized by international law.[192] This is the juxtapositional reading of Articles 17(1)(b) and 20(3). Clearly, Article 17(1)(c) is silent on the issue of pardons. One could argue that pardons granted as part of a trial that lacks the intention to bring the person concerned to justice, and thus aims to shield the accused (and later the convicted person), are to be caught by Article 17(1)(c). This argument can consider the proceedings, including prosecution, conviction and then pardons, disingenuous. This will render the case admissible before the ICC. This view, to a certain extent, is in conformity with John Holmes' views expressed in his article on complementarity.[193]

869-978, 904.

189   Article 103 of the Rome Statute of the International Criminal Court, UN Doc. A/CONF.183/9.

190   Article 17 of the Rome Statute of the International Criminal Court, UN Doc. A/CONF.183/9.

191   This book has already adopted a definition for pardons, which covers only pardons granted after conviction, and not before.

192   Article 17(1)(c) of the Rome Statute of the International Criminal Court, UN Doc. A/CONF.183/9.

193   Holmes, J. 1999. The Principle of Complementarity, in *The International Criminal Court: The Making of the Rome Statute, Issues, Negotiations, Results*, edited by R. Lee. The Hague: Kluwer, 77.

Yet Article 17(1)(c) and the previous argument fall short of covering pardons granted after a *bona fide* trial. This Article fails to tackle a scenario similar to the William Calley case, where he was properly tried, but received a pardon from President Nixon.[194] 'Unwillingness' is thus not reflected in the judicial system, and one cannot argue that the proceedings followed through in a matter 'inconsistent with the intent to bring the person concerned to justice'.[195] According to William Schabas, a case in which the individual is properly tried, but then is subsequently pardoned, may bar the Court from intervention, rendering the case inadmissible.[196]

Since Article 17 is silent on pardons – unless pardons are granted as part of a process reflecting state unwillingness to prosecute – this section will now proceed to analyse whether pardons fall under the ambit of Article 20. The correlation between the complementarity principle under Article 17 and Article 20 is already established, via Article 17(1)(c). The study of the status of national pardons under Article 20 is indispensable here.

Pardons and Article 20   Article 20 includes the *ne bis in idem* principle. The same person cannot be tried and punished more than once for the same conduct or crime.[197]

Article 20(3)(a) indicates that the ICC can try a person more than once if the 'proceedings' were conducted for the purpose of shielding the person concerned from criminal responsibility.[198] Article 20(3)(b) also authorizes the ICC to try a person more than once who has been convicted or acquitted if the 'proceedings' were not conducted independently or impartially in accordance with the norms of due process recognized by international law, and were conducted in a manner inconsistent with an intent to bring the person concerned to justice.[199]

If pardons fall under one of the situations specified in Article 20(3), then the ICC could render the case admissible under Article 17, and a retrial will allow the Court to disregard such pardons.[200] If the pardon renders the national proceedings inconsistent with the Statute's stipulation of independence or impartiality, stated under Article 20(3), then the case will be admissible. Here our analysis needs to

---

194   Eckhardt, W.G. Summer 2000. Essay on the Trials of the Century: My Lai: An American Tragedy. *University of Missouri at Kansas City Law Review*, 671-708, 671.

195   Article 17(2)(c) of the Rome Statute of the International Criminal Court, UN Doc. A/CONF.183/9.

196   Schabas, W. 2001. *An Introduction to the International Criminal Court.* Cambridge: Cambridge University Press, 70.

197   Van Den Wyngart, Ch. and Ongena, T. 2002. Ne bis in idem Principle, Including the Issue of Amnesty, in *The Rome Statute of The International Criminal Court: A Commentary*, edited by A. Cassese, P. Gaeta and J.R.W.D. Jones. Oxford: Oxford University Press, I, 706.

198   Article 20(3)(a) of the Rome Statute of the International Criminal Court, UN Doc. A/CONF.183/9.

199   Article 20(3)(b) of the Rome Statute of the International Criminal Court, UN Doc. A/CONF.183/9.

200   Article 20(3) is connected to Article 17.

focus on how the term 'proceedings' needs to be interpreted broadly[201] to include the serving of the sentence. If the Court interprets the term 'proceedings' to include all stages at the national level, starting with investigation, prosecution, conviction, acquittal and the serving of the sentence, then an argument could be made that a pardon after conviction could be considered as either an interference in the course of justice – and that will affect the impartiality and the independence of 'proceedings' in its broad sense – or it could be inconsistent with the intention to bring a person concerned to justice. The Commentary of the International Law Commission on Article 12 of the ILC draft code of crimes of 1996 indicated that the failure to impose or enforce a punishment that is proportional to the committed crime, may indicate an element of fraud in the administration of justice.[202] Article 12 of the ILC draft on crimes against peace and security of mankind considers, in paragraph 3, the serving of the sentence as a criterion, *inter alia*, to fulfil the *ne bis in idem* principle.[203]

This argument overlaps with John Holmes' analysis, which views the *ne bis in idem* principle under Article 20(3) as a possible solution. He presumes that offering pardons after conviction could lead to the proceedings being other than genuine.[204]

The 'and' in Article 20(3), according to some jurists, supports the above argument. 'And' is a keyword as it is a conjunction between the manner in which the proceedings were conducted and the intention of the administration to administer justice in a manner consistent with the intention to bring the person concerned to justice.[205] Thus if issued from an authority in an intention inconsistent with bringing the concerned person to justice a pardon could be admissible under Article 20(3)(b).

The above reasoning is valid if the pardoning authority is the same as the prosecuting and the convicting one, in which case there is lack of intention to pursue justice. However, there are other scenarios that are more complex, and do

---

201   Van Den Wyngart, Ch. and Ongena, T. 2002. Ne bis in idem Principle, Including the Issue of Amnesty, in *The Rome Statute of The International Criminal Court: A Commentary*, edited by A. Cassese, P. Gaeta and J.R.W.D. Jones. Oxford: Oxford University Press, I, 727.

202   International Law Commission Report. 1996. *Draft Code of Crimes against the Peace and Security of Mankind*, Chapter II. Available at: www.un.org [accessed: 15 June 2009].

203   International Law Commission. 1996. *Draft Code of Crimes against the Peace and Security of Mankind*. Text adopted by the International Law Commission on its forty-eighth session in 1996. Available at: http://untreaty.un.org/ilc/texts/instruments/english/draft%20Articles/7_4_1996.pdf [accessed: 15 June 2009].

204   Holmes, J. 1999. The Principle of Complementarity, in *The International Criminal Court: The Making of the Rome Statute, Issues, Negotiations, Results*, edited by R. Lee. The Hague: Kluwer, 1-54.

205   El-Zeidy, M. Summer 2002. The Principle of Complementarity: A Machinery to Implement International Criminal Law. *Michigan Journal of International Law*, 23, 4, 869-978, 904.

not coincide with the above. Confusion may arise if, for example, a *bona fide* trial has taken place and a proportionate sentence was given to the convicted person, reflecting the intention of the judicial system to conduct a fair trial, but a subsequent executive authority decides to pardon the convicted individual. In such an instance, the 'proceedings' that led to conviction and sentencing cannot be considered 'not genuine', or lacking the intention to bring the person concerned to justice. The case of William Calley reflects such a scenario. The judiciary convicted Calley properly, but when Nixon became president, he pardoned him. The Rome Statute is silent in such cases, and the language of Articles 20 and 17 is unable to cope with such pardons. Furthermore, if a restricted interpretation of 'proceedings' with respect to Article 20(3) is adopted, then pardons may fall outside the ambit of this Article, as well as that of Article 17.

The states' stand in the discussion of the Preparatory Committee on the establishment of the ICC and the Committee of the Whole in the Rome Conference show that states did not aim to prohibit themselves from granting pardons.[206] They did not want the Court to interfere further in the political decision-making process (including pardons) of sovereign states.[207] The Court cannot ignore the states' will in that regard. Hence, a restricted interpretation of the term 'proceeding' in Articles 20 and 17 could prevail. If this is juxtaposed with the *travaux préparatoire*, then the Court may refrain from exercising jurisdiction over pardons granted after the case has already been tried at the national level. This is disappointing for whoever hoped that the ICC could be empowered to overcome states' sovereignties to end impunity and deliver justice.

Pardons and ICC sentences   Part 10 of the Statute organizes the enforcement mechanism of the ICC sentences. The issue of pardons or reduction of ICC sentences is discussed here. Before analysing the articles, it is important to note that possible pardons or reductions of ICC sentences do not fall under the complementarity principle of Article 17 or the *ne bis in idem* principle under Article 20. In fact, such pardons fall under the enforcement power of the ICC for its own sentences.

Article 103(1) states that the ICC sentences are to be served in those states designated by the Court among a list of states that have indicated their willingness

---

206   UN Diplomatic Conference on the establishment of an International Criminal Court, Volume II.B. Report of the Preparatory Committee on the Establishment of an International Criminal Court. Also, see the summary records of the meeting of the Committee of the Whole during the Rome conference. Available at: www.un.org/law/icc/rome/proceedings/E/rome%20proceedings_v2_e.pdf [accessed: 15 June 2009].

207   Holmes, J. 1999. The Principle of Complementarity, in *The International Criminal Court: The Making of the Rome Statute, Issues, Negotiations, Results*, edited by R. Lee. The Hague: Kluwer, 59-60. Also, Holmes, J. 2002. Complementarity: National Courts versus the International Criminal Court, in *The Rome Statute of The International Criminal Court: A Commentary*, edited by A. Cassese, P. Gaeta and J.R.W.D. Jones. Oxford: Oxford University Press, I, 678.

to the Court.[208] The state of imprisonment may set some conditions on imprisonment sentences subject to the approval of the Court. The acceptance of the ICC is crucial, and in the case of refusal, the Court could transfer the sentenced person to a prison in another state.[209]

Article 105 indicates that only the Court shall have the authority over any application of appeal or revision. Article 106 follows by stipulating that the enforcement of sentences of imprisonment is solely subject to the supervision of the Court.

However, sections relevant to possible pardons fall under Articles 103(2)(a) and Article 110.[210] Under the ILC draft, pardons for ICC sentences were covered by Article 60(4), which grants the Court the power to stipulate any application of possible pardons, parole or commutation of sentences.[211] Under provisions of Article 60(3) of the ILC draft or Articles 103(2)(a) and 110 of the ICC, the two instruments grant the Court the exclusive authority of supervision and approval over any commutation or pardoning of sentences.[212]

Under Article 103(2)(a), the enforcing state is under an obligation to notify the Court of any measure that could materially affect the term of imprisonment.[213] A 45-day notice should be respected by the state of imprisonment during which no release of the sentenced person should take place, pursuant to Article 110.

With respect to the possible release or pardoning of the sentenced person by the state of enforcement, Article 110 is the *lex specialis*. It explicitly prohibits any release of prisoners before the expiration of the sentence date. In paragraph 2 of Article 110, the Statute grants the Court the exclusive authority to determine a reduction of the sentence, including the possibility for pardons. In addition, paragraph 4 of this Article indicates a number of factors that could be a basis for the reduction of sentences. The final decision is in the hands of the Court, which can exercise broad discretion.

Clearly, the authority to pardon ICC sentences, as they require the Court's approval, is not an obstacle or a loophole to the complementarity principle. Such a

---

208   Article 103(1)(a) of the Rome Statute of the International Criminal Court, UN Doc. A/CONF.183/9.

209   Article 104 of the Rome Statute of the International Criminal Court, UN Doc. A/CONF.183/9.

210   Articles 103(2) and 110 of the Rome Statute of the International Criminal Court, UN Doc. A/CONF.183/9.

211   Article 60(4) of the International Law Commission Draft of an International Criminal Court (1994). Available at: http://untreaty.un.org/ilc/texts/instruments/english/drafts%20Articles/7_4_1994.pdf [accessed: 15 June 2009].

212   Kress, C. and Sluiter, G. 2002. Imprisonment, in *The Rome Statute of The International Criminal Court: A Commentary*, edited by A. Cassese, P. Gaeta and J.R.W.D. Jones. Oxford: Oxford University Press, II, 1791.

213   Article 103(2)(a) of the Rome Statute of the International Criminal Court, UN Doc. A/CONF.183/9.

process falls under 'enforcement' as stipulated by the Statute, which is not related to Article 17 or Article 20.

However, from the above one can gather that, vis-à-vis the enforcement mechanism of the Court sentences, if the Statute leaves room for pardons and reductions of sentences, then the Statute does not prohibit pardons in general. By analogy, if a national authority grants a subsequent pardon on grounds recognized by the ICC in order to commute a sentence under Article 110 after a *bona fide* national trial, then the Court would likely find it difficult to reject such a national measure. Based on a rational analysis rather than a legal one, it will be illogical to recognize such a 'legitimate' practice for the Court while denying it for national authorities.

Conclusion

Article 17 is silent on pardons, as is the rest of the Statute, presenting a serious lacuna.[214] However, it is for the Court to decide on the matter as the Statute reserves the Court's right to decide on the matter. The Statute appropriates power to the Court to decide its own competence on a case-by-case basis.[215] On the other hand, the *travaux préparatoire*, as stated earlier, confirms that states intended to delete any prohibition on granting pardons by member states.[216] During the formation of the Statue, many states feared establishing a Court with strong intrusive power able to affect state sovereignty and the administration of justice by member states.[217] The Court has to consider this when exercising its jurisdiction. The traditional concepts of international law, such as state sovereignty, continue to be predominant vis-à-vis an international court that could contribute to a new world order that is based on accountability for human rights violations, and exercise such a role independently from states' stand on cooperation with the Court.

The Statute's silence engendered a debate on whether the language in Article 17 and Article 20 is capable of dealing with pardons. A creative and broad interpretation of the term 'proceedings' under Articles 17 and 20(3) could expand the Court's jurisdiction to cover pardons, but only when pardons reflect unwillingness and lack of intention to bring the person concerned to justice. However, this remains subject to the Court's policy on the matter, as the Court

---

214   Van Den Wyngart, Ch. and Ongena, T. 2002. Ne bis in idem Principle, Including the Issue of Amnesty, in *The Rome Statute of The International Criminal Court: A Commentary*, edited by A. Cassese, P. Gaeta and J.R.W.D. Jones. Oxford: Oxford University Press, I, 727.

215   Van Den Wyngart, Ch. and Ongena, T. 2002. Ne bis in idem Principle, Including the Issue of Amnesty, in *The Rome Statute of The International Criminal Court: A Commentary*, edited by A. Cassese, P. Gaeta and J.R.W.D. Jones. Oxford: Oxford University Press, I, 725.

216   The deletion of untitled Article 19 is an evidence of that.

217   See the argument in the Report of the Committee of the Whole.

is its own arbiter in conformity with the principle *Kompetenz-Kompetenz*.[218] Yet, even interpreted broadly, pardons not reflecting an intention to shield the convicted will escape Articles 17 and 20(3). Furthermore, it becomes more complex when pardons are given after a *bona fide* trial. A pardon, for instance, given by a newly elected executive for a sentenced person who was properly tried before may lead to such a scenario. The ICC may be paralysed when faced with such a situation.

A restrictive analysis of the legal language of the Statute indicates that its Articles – mainly Articles 17 and 20 – were not drafted to cover pardons. Pardons escape the complementarity principle of the Court, and will not be admissible before the Court. The interpretation of the legal language of the Statute must be conducted in a manner reflecting the intention of the drafters, and in the case of ambiguity of the treaty Articles, one has to turn to the *travaux préparatoires* to deduce the intention of the member states.[219] Relevant discussions in the Preparatory Committee and the Committee of the Whole clearly indicate that states were in favour of not allowing the Court to meddle in the administrative powers of the state. Therefore, the intention of the states was not to include pardons within the jurisdiction of the ICC. The deletion of the untitled Article 19 from the draft statute clearly reflects this,[220] and leaves pardons outside the scope of the complementarity principle. Any pardon subsequent to a proper trial will not trigger the complementarity principle under Article 17.

Given these two approaches, the author aggresses with the more restrictive approach. This restrictive analysis conforms better with the intention of the drafters in the Statute in particular and international treaty law in general. Drafters explicitly rejected a role for the Court in the administrative power of the state regarding pardons, and the Court should not try to circumvent this intention. The Rome Statute's silence on pardons was deliberate, and if states wanted to prohibit pardons before the ICC, they would have indicated this explicitly. This is unfortunate as it shows that states remain cautious towards having an international court that can transcend the traditional limitations of international law to create a new dynamic on the international level. This fear is vivid in some articles of the Statute, including pardons. Pardons are a serious loophole for the admissibility mechanism of the ICC, which should be solved in the Review Conference of the Rome Statute in 2010.

218　Van Den Wyngart, Ch. and Ongena, T. 2002. Ne bis in idem Principle, including the Issue of Amnesty, in *The Rome Statute of The International Criminal Court: A Commentary*, edited by A. Cassese, P. Gaeta and J.R.W.D. Jones. Oxford: Oxford University Press, I, 726.

219　Article 32 of the Vienna Convention on the law of Treaties, signed at Vienna 23 May 1969, entry into force 27 January 1980, 1155U.N.T.S.331, 8I.L.M.679.

220　Dugard, J. 2002. Possible Conflicts of Jurisdiction with Truth Commissions, in *The Rome Statute of The International Criminal Court: A Commentary*, edited by A. Cassese, P. Gaeta and J.R.W.D. Jones. Oxford: Oxford University Press, I, 700.

Security Council as a Possible *de Facto* and *de Jure* Obstacle to Complementarity

The relation between the International Criminal Court and the Security Council is a contentious issue in the Rome Statute. If one is to analyse the powers granted to the Security Council, under the Statute and in relation to the ICC jurisdiction, then there are a number of *de jure* or *de facto* obstacles that can block the application of the complementarity principle. In principle, Article 16 blocks the jurisdiction of the ICC, but does not affect the substantive requirements of the complementarity mechanism.

Before discussing the Article specifying the relation between the Court and the Council, one must enumerate the possible overlaps between the Court (a judicial body) and the Security Council (a political body) pertaining to situations of a threat to the peace and security in the world.

The Statute empowers the Court to exercise jurisdiction over four core crimes: war crimes, crimes against humanity, genocide and aggression (the latter is suspended until a definition is agreed upon). However, these crimes often occur during a conflict that might constitute a threat to international peace and security. Scenarios such as this bring the jurisdiction of the Court in conflict with the mandate of the Security Council.[221] The situation becomes even more complex when the ICC exercises jurisdiction over the crime of aggression; tension between the Security Council and the ICC will always be a possibility. Taking the above into consideration, the author *infra* will analyse the relation between the ICC and the Council with a focus on the Security Council's mandate under the Statute and its possible obstruction of the complementarity principle. Therefore, the following analysis will be limited to cases of deferrals by the Security Council rather than referrals.

This section's scope is limited to dealing with Article 16, which establishes the relation of the Security Council and the International Criminal Court in relation to deferring the ICC jurisdiction through a Security Council resolution adopted under Chapter VII. The Security Council referral under Article 13 will be discussed in the coming chapters. Article 13 does not constitute any possible obstacle to complementarity, as it organizes referrals to the ICC rather than deferrals. Article 13 will be analysed later while discussing the complementarity principle through Security Council referral.

---

221   Schabas, W. September 2004. United States Hostility to the International Criminal Court: it's all about the Security Council. *The European Journal of International Law*, 15, 701-721, 710.

Drafting History of Article 16

Article 16 has an extraordinary drafting history.[222] It is arguably one of the most important and sensitive provisions of the Rome Statute, due to the tension the article subsumes between the political and the legal dimensions.

Initially, the International Law Commission's Draft indicated in Article 23(3) that a prosecution arising from a situation which is 'being dealt with' by the Security Council under Chapter VII of the United Nations Charter may not be initiated unless the Security Council provides its authorization.[223] Through this initial formula the Security Council in general and the permanent members in particular had broad reaching powers to limit the ICC's jurisdiction, to the extent that listing the situation under the agenda of the Security Council under Chapter VII would block the ICC jurisdiction.[224] Article 23(3) of the ILC draft has been heavily criticized due to the broad authority that was granted to both the Security Council and to the permanent members. It would be sufficient for a permanent member to veto the resolution that grants the ICC jurisdiction over a situation that is 'being dealt with', to obstruct the ICC jurisdiction. The Preparatory Committee heavily criticized the loose term 'being dealt with', as the term allows the Council to bar the exercise of jurisdiction of the ICC by merely listing the situation on its agenda.[225]

This proposal was reversed by a proposal submitted by Singapore in the August 1997 session of the Preparatory Committee.[226] The Singapore proposal was a compromise with the intention to limit the suspension of the jurisdiction of the ICC to cases in which the Council requests that the ICC not initiate or continue proceedings.[227] The Singapore proposal states that 'no investigation or prosecution may be commenced or proceeded with under this Statute where the

222   Pejic, J. Winter 2001. The United States and the International Criminal Court: One Loophole Too Many. *University of Detroit Mercy Law Review*, 78, 267-297, 273.

223   International Law Commission. 1994. *Draft Statute for An International Criminal Court*, prepared by the International Law Commission, in report of the International Law Commission on the work of its forty-sixth session, U.N. GAOR, 49th session supp. no. 10, at 84, UN Doc. A/49/10.

224   International Law Commission. 1994. *Draft Statute for An International Criminal Court*, prepared by the International Law Commission, in Report of the International Law Commission on the work of its forty-sixth session, U.N GAOR, 49th session supp. no. 10, at 84, UN Doc. A/49/10.

225   Bergsmo, M. and Pejic, J. 2000. On Article 16, in *Commentary on the Rome Statute of the International Criminal Court: Observer's Note, Article by Article*, edited by Otto Triffterer. Baden-Baden: Nomos Verlagsgesellschaft, 377, para. 9.

226   El-Zeidy, M. Summer 2002. The Principle of Complementarity: A Machinery to Implement International Criminal Law. *Michigan Journal of International Law*, 23, 4, 869-978, 913.

227   Zimmermann, A. 1998. The Creation of a Permanent International Criminal Court. *Max Planck Yearbook of United Nations Law*, 12, 169, 218.

Security Council has, acting under chapter VII of the UN Charter, given a direction to that effect'.[228]

The proposal was later amended by a Costa Rican proposal and then by a British one. The Costa Rican proposal required a 'formal and specific decision' by the Security Council.[229] The British proposal replaced the word 'direction' with 'request'.[230] The proposal and the amendments were practically a reversal of the original version of the ILC Draft Statute on the Security Council–ICC relationship.[231] These proposals became the grounds for Article 16 in the Rome Statute.

The significance of the reversal is that it required a positive decision by the Security Council for a deferral. It allows the Court to proceed if only one permanent Security Council member vetoes the adoption of a resolution under Chapter VII.

Article 16 of the Rome Statute developed from this compromise. It was the outcome of extensive political negotiations and bargaining between two contradicting views. One represented by the 'like-minded' group, and the other represented by the permanent Security Council members (except the UK).[232]

Article 16 of the Rome Statute

Article 16 states that 'no investigation or prosecution may be commenced under this Statute for a period of twelve months after the Security Council, in a resolution adopted under chapter VII of the Charter of the United Nations, has requested the Court to the effect; that request may be renewed by the Council under the same conditions'.[233]

---

228 Bergsmo, M. and Pejic, J. 2000. On Article 16, in *Commentary on the Rome Statute of the International Criminal Court: Observer's Note, Article by Article*, edited by Otto Triffterer. Baden-Baden: Nomos Verlagsgesellschaft, 375, para. 4.

229 The proposal of Costa Rica states that: 'No investigation or prosecution may be commenced or proceeded with under this Statute, where the Security Council has, acting under Chapter VII of the Charter of the United Nations, taken a formal and specific decision and limited for certain period of time to that effect', see Bergsmo, M. and Pejic, J. 2000. On Article 16, in *Commentary on the Rome Statute of the International Criminal Court: Observer's Note, Article by Article*, edited by Otto Triffterer. Baden-Baden: Nomos Verlagsgesellschaft, 376.

230 The British proposal reads: 'No investigation or prosecution may be commenced or proceeded with under this Statute for a period of twelve months after the Security Council'.

231 Pejic, J. Winter 2001. The United States and the International Criminal Court: One Loophole Too Many. *University of Detroit Mercy Law Review*, 78, 267-297, 277.

232 Kirsch, P. and Holmes, J. January 1999. The Rome Conference on an International Criminal Court Negotiating Process. *The American Journal of International Law*, 93, 1, 2-12, 4.

233 Article 16 of the Rome Statute of the International Criminal Court, UN Doc. A/CONF.183/9.

Under Article 16 of the Rome Statute, when a requisite majority of the Council members conclude that the ICC jurisdiction could hamper or damage the Council's effort to maintain international peace and security the Security Council may halt an ICC investigation or proceedings.[234] An affirmative decision by the majority of the members of the Council can defer the ICC jurisdiction for a period of 12 months. Such a decision requires the support of nine members of the Council and no veto from any of the five permanent members. Any veto would block a Security Council resolution.[235] This changes the initial formula under Article 23(3) of the ILC Draft, which stated that it was enough for any permanent member to veto the withdrawal of a situation from the Council's agenda to prevent the ICC from exercising jurisdiction.

Invoking Article 16 requires certain conditions be fulfilled. Firstly, there should be a threat to international peace and security – the Security Council must be acting act under Chapter VII. Secondly, the Security Council is passing the deferral via a resolution. Thirdly, the deferral is not immediately permanent, but for a renewable period of 12 months. Fourthly, the deferral could cover a situation or a case.[236]

Firstly, acting under Chapter VII   Article 16 requires that the situation be a threat to peace and security, and that raises a valid question concerning what constitutes a threat to peace and security in the world. The drafting history of the UN Charter indicates that the delegates failed to adequately qualify what constitutes a threat to world peace and security.[237] The UN Charter, as well as the Security Council practice itself,[238] indicates that the Council enjoys wide discretionary powers in defining what constitutes a threat to international peace and security.[239] Once the Security Council determines a situation as a threat to international peace and security under Article 39 of the UN Charter, the Council can act under Chapter

---

234   El-Zeidy, M. Summer 2002. The Principle of Complementarity: A Machinery to Implement International Criminal Law. *Michigan Journal of International Law*, 23, 4, 869-978, 914.

235   MacPherson, B. July 2002. Authority of the Security Council Exempt Peace Keepers from International Criminal Court Proceedings. *ASIL Insights*. Available at: www. asil.org/insights.htm [accessed: 11 April 2009].

236   El-Zeidy, M. November 2002. The United Nations Dropped the Atomic Bomb of Article 16 of the ICC Statute: Security Council Power of Deferrals and Resolution 1422. *Vanderbilt Journal of Trans National Law*, 35, 1503-1548, 1514.

237   Russel, R.B. 1958. *A History of the United Nations Charter 1940-1945*. Washington, DC: Brookings Institution, 637.

238   The Security Council on various occasions has defined the threat to peace and security broadly. See, for example, Resolution 731(1991) where the failure of Libya to renounce terror was considered a threat to peace and security in the world. Security Council Resolution 713(1991). UN Doc. S/Res/731(1991).

239   Zappalà, S. 2003. The Reaction of the US to the Entry into Force of the ICC Statute: Comments on UN SC Resolution 1422 (2002) and Article 98 Agreements. *Journal of International Criminal Justice*, 1, 114-134, 119.

VII. In spite of this, such discretionary power is still limited by the Charter of the UN, and the Council is bound not to act beyond the objective of the Charter. Otherwise, the Security Council will overstep the bounds of the treaty and then the Security Council may be acting *legibus solutus* (not bounded by law),[240] rendering its actions to be invalid. Yet, there is no body, whether of judicial or political character, to monitor the Security Council's actions, and the Security Council is the judge of its own powers under the Charter.[241] The International Court of Justice itself declined from using its provisional powers when the Security Council acted under Chapter VII.[242]

With respect to the relation between the ICC and the Security Council under Article 16, the Court is to decide whether the Security Council validly acted under Chapter VII, and whether or not there was a threat to international peace and security. Hence, the ICC will monitor the conformity of Security Council deferrals with the Rome Statute, and decide whether or not the Security Council has acted *ultra vires*. It is unlikely that the ICC will tolerate a deferral by a Security Council resolution under Chapter VII, which is unconstrained by the norms of international law in general, and the UN Charter in particular.[243] The ICC will then decide if the deferral has been issued in accordance with Article 16 or not.[244]

Secondly, an affirmative decision requirement   As mentioned earlier, this requires a majority vote of at least nine out of 15 of the Council's permanent and non-permanent members, without any veto. Article 16 is the reverse of Article 23(3) of the ILC Draft Statute,[245] and the ICC is no longer subordinated to the Security Council.[246] Many experts agree that the final language of Article 16 limited the Security Council's capability to impede the Court's jurisdiction, as now Article 16 requires a majority agreement within the Council – an agreement that is usually not easily reached.[247]

---

240   See the case of *Prosecutor* v. *Tadic*, case no. IT-94-1-AR72, at paragraph 28.

241   ICJ Report. 1962. 'Certain Expenses of the United Nations', 151, 168.

242   ICJ Reports. 1992. Provisional Measures, *Libya* v. *UK*; *Libya* v. *US*, 3, 114. Orders of 14 April 1992.

243   Neha, J. April 2005. A Separate Law for Peace Keepers: The Clash between the Security Council and the Court. *The European Journal of International Law*, 16, 239-255, 243.

244   Lee, R. March 2002. How the World Will Relate to the Court: An Assessment of the ICC Statute. *Fordham International Law Journal*, 25, 750-763, 758.

245   See argument *supra*.

246   Kirsch, P. August 2001. Negotiating On Institution for Twenty-First Century: Multilateral Diplomacy and International Criminal Court. *McGill Law Journal*, 46, 1141-1161, 1148.

247   Article 27(3) of the UN Charter indicates that matters treated by the Security Council as falling under the category of 'other matters' related to the discharge of the Council responsibility for the maintenance of international peace and security require nine votes.

Thirdly, Article 16 and the 12-month limitation   The 12-month limitation in Article 16 was recommended by Canada.[248] This limitation intended to further decrease the power of the Security Council vis-à-vis the ICC. The 12-month period further limits the Security Council powers to obstruct the ICC jurisdiction. As Philip Kirsch describes, Article 16 can delay ICC proceedings, but cannot block the ICC jurisdiction permanently.[249] Security Council Resolutions 1422 and 1487,[250] which invoked Article 16 of the Rome Statute, respect the 12-month period. However, Security Council Resolution 1497,[251] which obstructs the ICC jurisdiction permanently for non-state parties participating in peacekeeping forces in Liberia, did not invoke Article 16 and did not respect the 12-month period. The inclusion of the 12-month period is significant because it requires a majority vote and the presence of similar conditions for its renewal. In two years' time, a number of Security Council members will be changed, and the majority may not be easily secured again.

Fourthly, Security Council's deferral of a situation or a case   One important point concerns whether a deferral by the Security Council is on a case-by-case basis or if it is a deferral for a situation in itself; i.e. it is unclear when the deferral is to be requested. This means that the request could be made before an investigation or prosecution starts or during an investigation or prosecution. However, Article 16 does not indicate for when a deferral is – whether for a situation in itself or on a case-by-case scenario. The legal language of Article 16 does not give an explicit answer to this issue. Some jurists argue that the Security Council under Article 16 could defer a 'matter' from the ICC's jurisdiction.[252] However, the argument raised *infra* is that the Security Council has the power to defer the ICC jurisdiction under Article 16 on both a case-by-case basis, as well in general situations.

With respect to the legal language, Article 16 discusses an investigation or a prosecution; that is, the Security Council resolution may request the blocking of an ongoing investigation or prosecution or the blocking of an investigation or prosecution that is in the process of commencing. Usually, defined cases and not general situations are subjects of prosecutions. An investigation can be

---

248   Gargiulo, P. 1999. The Controversial Relationship between the International Criminal Court and Security Council, in *Essays on the Rome Statute of the International Criminal Court*, edited by W. Schabas and F. Lattanzi. Ripa Fagnano Alto: Editrice il Sirente, 1, 67-103, 88.

249   Kirsch, P. August 2001. Negotiating On Institution for Twenty-First Century: Multilateral Diplomacy and International Criminal Court. *McGill Law Journal*, 46, 1141-1161, 1148.

250   Resolution 1422 (1192), Security Council, UN Doc. S/Res1422 (2002). Also, Resolution 1487 (2003), Security Council, UN Doc. S/Res1487 (2003).

251   Resolution 1497 (2004), Security Council, UN Doc. S/Res1497 (2004).

252   Abbas, A. Winter 2005. The Competence of the Security Council to Terminate Jurisdiction of The International Criminal Court. *Texas International Law Journal*, 4, 263-309, 271.

more general, including specific cases and situations.[253] One could argue that an investigation, especially before prosecution, could cover more than one case, and more than one defined case will lead to a general situation.

The initial Article 23 of the ILC Draft talks about a 'situation' which is being dealt with by the Security Council. Yet, this was criticized in the Preparatory Committee.[254] The drafting history of Article 16 shows that the intention of some of the drafters of the ICC Statute was to limit the Security Council's use of deferrals to a case-by-case intervention.[255] A consensus was not reached and the final version of Article 16 included the term 'investigation', which could include an investigation of a situation or an investigation of a precise case. Hence, while the Security Council could defer a specific case from the ICC jurisdiction for a renewable period of time under Chapter VII, it can also defer a situation itself. Arguments from Mathew Brubacher, Mohamed El Zeidy and Ademola Abbas support such a standpoint.[256]

Other jurists attempted to interpret Article 16 more restrictively.[257] Article 16, they argue, tolerates deferrals for specific cases and not situations. Such an analysis is incongruous with the intention behind inserting Article 16 in the Rome Statute. The logic behind drafting Article 16 is to prevent a conflict between the jurisdiction of the ICC and the powers of the Security Council in instances presenting a threat to peace and security in the world. Experience shows that the intervention of international justice in an ongoing conflict situation could sometimes destabilize

---

253   El-Zeidy, M. Summer 2002. The Principle of Complementarity: A Machinery to Implement International Criminal Law. *Michigan Journal of International Law*, 23, 4, 869-978, 914.

254   Bergsmo, M. and Pejic, J. 2000. On Article 16, in *Commentary on the Rome Statute of the International Criminal Court: Observer's Note, Article by Article*, edited by Otto Triffterer. Baden-Baden: Nomos Verlagsgesellschaft, 377.

255   That was mentioned by New Zealand and Canada at the hearing of 10 July 2002 in the Security Council pertaining to the adoption of Resolution 1422. Also, Germany's representative to the UN indicated that the Security Council could not exceed the case-by-case power. See in Stahn, C. February 2003. The Ambiguities of Security Council Resolution 1422. *The European Journal of International Law*, 14, 1, 85-104. Human Rights Watch supports this stand. See Human Rights Watch News: The ICC and The Security Council Resolution 1422 and Policy Analysis. Available at: www.hrw.org [accessed: 11 June 2009].

256   See Brubacher, M.R. 2004. Prosecutorial Discretion within the International Criminal Court. *Journal of International Criminal Justice*, 2, 1, 71-95, 84. Also, El-Zeidy, M. November 2002. The United Nations Dropped the Atomic Bomb of Article 16 of the ICC Statute: Security Council Power of Deferrals and Resolution 1422. *Vanderbilt Journal of Trans National Law*, 35, 1503-1548, 1514.

257   See MacPherson, B. July 2002. Authority of the Security Council Exempt Peace Keepers from International Criminal Court Proceedings. *ASIL Insights*. Available at: www.asil.org/insights.htm [accessed: 11 April 2009].

peace negotiations.[258] One can cite the indictment of Charles Taylor by the Special Court for Sierra Leone's Prosecutor Goldstone and the indictment of the Bosnian Serb leaders Karadzic and Mladic, which eventually prevented their participation in the Dayton peace talks.[259] In the latter case, the international community dealt with the whole situation in Bosnia and Herzegovina, and a deferral to the Security Council for a specific case would not have solved the problem. The Security Council must address whole situation to find a comprehensive peaceful settlement. Therefore, if Article 16 is limited to a case-by-case scope, it will not serve the purpose for which the Article was drafted.

On the other hand, the Security Council's deferral for a situation or a case must be done on a case-by-case scenario.[260] In other words, the deferral should be applied to a defined situation or case, and not a general one. Otherwise, the deferral will act as a measure of impunity for international crimes, and hence be inconsistent with the Rome Statute in particular and international law in general.[261]

The final decision on the argument above is theoretical. According to the Statute, it is for the ICC to determine whether the Security Council has abided by Article 16 in its deferral or acted *ultra vires* under the Rome Statute.[262]

Article 16 stipulates a delay or obstruction of an investigation or prosecution that has commenced or proceeded.[263] Under this Article, the Council delays the investigation or prosecution of the ICC for a (renewable) 12-month period, but does not render the case inadmissible. The case will remain admissible if it already fulfils the admissibility criteria (including Article 17). The investigation or prosecution will 'freeze' until the expiration of the 12-month period, but legally and technically the case will remain admissible (if the requirements of admissibility remain fulfilled).

The Security Council deferral does not fall under any of the admissibility criteria under Article 17. It cannot be considered either reflecting 'unwillingness' or 'inability' on behalf of national authorities who have jurisdiction over the case. The Security Council deferral under Article 16 is not correlated to the admissibility of the case under Article 17, but rather delays or obstructs the Court's jurisdiction for a period of time, although theoretically Article 16 does not affect the admissibility

---

258   Stahn, C. February 2003. The Ambiguities of Security Council Resolution 1422. *The European Journal of International Law*, 14, 1, 85-104, 91.

259   Schabas, W. September 2004. United States Hostility to the International Criminal Court: It is all about the Security Council. *The European Journal of International Law*, 15, 701-721, 711.

260   Stahn, C. February 2003. The Ambiguities of Security Council Resolution 1422. *The European Journal of International Law*, 14, 1, 85-104. 9.

261   The core crimes of the ICC are considered by now *jus cogens* crimes, and actions preventing prosecution could be considered void under international law.

262   Brubacher, Matthew R. 2004. Prosecutorial Discretion within the International Criminal Court. *Journal of International Criminal Justice*, 2, 1, 71-95, 83.

263   Article 17 of the Rome Statute of the International Criminal Court, UN Doc. A/CONF.183/9.

of the case under Article 17, it *de facto* blocks the complementarity principle for a (renewable) 12-month period. Article 16 allows the Security Council to defer an ongoing prosecution for a case that could have already been admissible under Article 17. Hence, such a deferral discards the Court's jurisdiction for a period of time, and *de facto* 'suspends' the admissibility of the case.

The Security Council and the ICC in Practice

The relation between the Security Council and the ICC in practice will be analysed by addressing the three main resolutions relevant to the ICC jurisdiction: Resolutions 1422,[264] 1487[265] and 1497.[266] The aim here is again to test extent to which the Security Council can obstruct the complementarity principle of the ICC. Resolutions 1422 and 1487 invoked Article 16 of the Rome Statute, while Resolution 1497 is broader and does not invoke Article 16. This study will not delve into the motives behind the adoption of these resolutions by the Security Council, but rather into whether or not the Security Council acted in conformity with Article 16.

Resolution 1422 was adopted on 12 July 2002.[267] Based on Article 16 of the Rome Statute, the resolution exempted current or former peacekeeping personnel of non-state parties to the Rome Statute from the jurisdiction of the ICC for a period of 12 months beginning 1 July 2002. Resolution 1422 blocked the ICC from commencing or continuing an investigation or prosecuting troops for possible perpetration of war crimes, crimes against humanity and genocide. This was the result of pressure from US delegates, which aimed at discarding the ICC jurisdiction to protect US troops in peacekeeping missions.[268] Resolution 1422 claimed to be consistent with Article 16 of the Rome Statute. It was adopted under Chapter VII and purportedly consistent on the grounds that the resolution was in the interest of peace and security as it enabled member states to contribute to peacekeeping operations.[269] It also expressed the intention to renew the request under the same conditions each 1 July for a 12-month period for as long as necessary.[270] Although the Resolution received unanimous support in the Council due to the US pressure, a number of states showed,[271] formally or informally, concern and criticism to a

---

264   Resolution 1422 (2002), Security Council, UN Doc. S/Res1422(2002).
265   Resolution 1487 (2003), Security Council, UN Doc. S/Res1487(2003).
266   Resolution 1497 (2004), Security Council, UN Doc. S/Res1497(2004).
267   Resolution 1422 (2002), Security Council, UN Doc. S/Res1422(2002).
268   Stahn, C. February 2003. The Ambiguities of Security Council Resolution 1422. *The European Journal of International Law*, 14, 1, 85-104, 85.
269   Resolution 1422 (2002), Security Council, UN Doc. S/Res1422(2002).
270   Resolution 1422 (2002), para. 2, Security Council, UN Doc. S/Res1422(2002).
271   Representatives of the following states, among others, raised concerns: France, China, Ireland, Mexico, Colombia, Syrian Arab Republic, Cameroon, Guinea, Mauritius, Samoa, Malaysia, Germany, Argentina, Cuba, New Zealand, South Africa, Costa Rica, Islamic Republic of Iran, Jordan, Liechtenstein, Brazil, Switzerland and Venezuela. All

number of issues in the Resolution.[272] Canada expressed deep concern for granting sweeping exemption for peacekeepers, since this is broader than the scope of the relation with the ICC.[273] The United Kingdom also showed serious concern about discussions that took place prior to adopting the Resolution and about restricting the ICC.[274]

Furthermore, Resolution 1422 was criticized for exceeding the powers granted to the Security Council by the ICC under Article 16, as well as for violating the UN Charter in particular and international law in general. The section here will focus mainly on whether the Security Council acted *ultra vires* with respect to powers granted under Article 16, allowing us to analyse whether the Resolution blocks the ICC jurisdiction. It will refrain from delving into the conformity of Resolution 1422 with the UN Charter or international law.

Amnesty International argued that Resolution 1422 was contrary to the Rome Statute,[275] as it was written in conflict with the initial intention of the drafters of Article 16, whose aim was to enable the Security Council to undertake delicate peace negotiations for a period of time in exceptional circumstances.[276] Moreover, Human Rights Watch criticized Resolution 1422 for making general exceptions to the jurisdiction of the ICC.[277] For both NGOs the intention to renew the Resolution indefinitely, as indicated in the Resolution, was inconsistent with Article 16.[278]

These criticisms have valid grounds. A legal analysis of Resolution 1422 in correlation with Article 16 of the Rome Statute uncovers a number of deficiencies as correlated to Article 16. Article 16, as mentioned before, requires certain conditions to be fulfilled. The first requirement is that there should be a threat to peace and security, which is a prerequisite for action under Chapter VII. However, it is unclear how exempting peacekeepers of non-state parties from the jurisdiction

---

documented in El-Zeidy, M. November 2002. The United Nations Dropped the Atomic Bomb of Article 16 of the ICC Statute: Security Council Power of Deferrals and Resolution 1422. *Vanderbilt Journal of Trans National Law*, 35, 1503-1548, 1503-1548.

272   El-Zeidy, M. November 2002. The United Nations Dropped the Atomic Bomb of Article 16 of the ICC Statute: Security Council Power of Deferrals and Resolution 1422. *Vanderbilt Journal of Trans National Law*, 35, 1503-1548, 1511.

273   Statement by the representative of Canada, UN SCOR, 57th session, 4568th mtg, UN Doc. S/pv4568(2002). Available at: www.un.org [accessed: 22 June 2009].

274   UN SCOR, 57th Session, 4568th mtg, UN Doc. S/pv4568(2002).

275   Amnesty International. May 2003. International Criminal Court: Security Council Must Refuse to Renew Resolution 1422, AI index: IOP 40/008/2003, 1-8, 2.

276   Amnesty International. May 2003. International Criminal Court: Security Council Must Refuse to Renew Resolution 1422, AI index: IOP 40/008/2003, 1-8, 3.

277   Human Rights Watch. The ICC and Security Council: Resolution 1422, Legal and Policy Analysis, 2.5. Available at: www.hrw.org [accessed: 11 June 2009].

278   Amnesty International. May 2003. International Criminal Court: Security Council Must Refuse to Renew Resolution 1422, AI index: IOP 40/008/2003, 1-8, 4.

of the Court could be linked to a threat to international peace and security.[279] The determination of situations constituting threats to peace and security should be made on a case-by-case base.[280] Resolution 1422 provides blanket immunity for peacekeeping forces in various areas and situations in the world. Some of these conflicts are a threat to international peace and security, while others are not. The general character of Resolution 1422 is in contradiction with the requirements of Article 16. Secondly, the inclusion of the intention to renew Resolution 1422 indefinitely after a year's time is also inconsistent with Article 16, since this eradicates the previous requirement to re-confirm the existence of threat to international peace. The determination of a threat to international peace and security cannot be hypothetical (12 months in advance). The last point to be highlighted is that the aim behind Resolution 1422 is contrary to the purpose of establishing the ICC as indicated in the Preamble of the Rome Statute. Resolution 1422 grants immunity (from accountability) for international crimes for a category of individuals (peacekeepers), while the Statute stresses that the establishment of the ICC is to end impunity for perpetrators of international crimes.[281] In this sense, Resolution 1422 also contradicts Article 27.[282]

Based on the above, Resolution 1422 does not conform to the requirements of Article 16, despite its claims to the contrary. The ICC has so far remained silent on the issue, and one has to wait for possible cases involving peacekeepers of non-state parties to see whether or not the ICC will respect Resolution 1422. This analysis remains hypothetical, as Resolution 1422 and its successor, Resolution 1487, have both expired.

However, this raises the question of possible conflict between Security Council resolution and the ICC jurisdiction. In other words, if the ICC declares Resolutions 1422 and 1487 in conflict with the Rome Statute, will the resolutions of the Security Council under Chapter VII prevail or the competence of the ICC to decide on its jurisdiction supersede Security Council resolutions?

Some argued that the Security Council acted *ultra vires* in adopting Resolution 1422.[283] Yet, this point might be irrelevant as there is no higher authority in the

---

279   Stahn, C. February 2003. The Ambiguities of Security Council Resolution 1422. *The European Journal of International Law*, 14, 1, 85-104. 87.

280   El-Zeidy, M. November 2002. The United Nations Dropped the Atomic Bomb of Article 16 of the ICC Statute: Security Council Power of Deferrals and Resolution 1422. *Vanderbilt Journal of Trans National Law*, 35, 1503-1548, 1503-1514. See also HRW Report on Resolution 1422.

281   Article 27 disregards any immunity that bars the Court from exercising its jurisdiction.

282   Neha, J. April 2005. A Separate Law for Peace Keepers: The Clash between the Security Council and the Court. *The European Journal of International Law*, 16, 239-255, 245.

283   MacPherson, B. July 2002. Authority of the Security Council Exempt Peace Keepers from International Criminal Court Proceedings. *ASIL Insights*. Available at: www.asil.org/insights.htm [accessed: 11 April 2009].

UN to determine whether Security Council resolutions are consistent with the UN Charter or not. The International Court of Justice in the Lockerbie case refrained from delving into the competence of the Security Council.[284] The Security Council, as a *sui generis* political body, acts as a judicial organ that decides its competence and its discretionary powers towards threats to world peace and security. Since the Security Council determines for itself the consistency of its actions, there is no other body that could invalidate the UN Security Council's resolutions. The conflict between Security Council resolutions and the ICC jurisdiction are ruled by Article 103 of the UN Charter, which states that 'in the event of a conflict between the obligations of the members of the United Nations under the present Charter and their obligations under any other international agreement, their obligations under the present Charter prevail'.[285] Security Council resolutions thus supersede the obligations of state parties to the Rome Statute in case of conflict. Hence, even if in conflict with the Article 16, Security Council resolutions nonetheless bind state parties to the Rome Statute, as state parties to the UN Charter. The argument above finds support in the Lockerbie case before the International Court of Justice, where the ICJ held that Libya's responsibilities under the UN Charter override its obligations towards the Convention for the Suppression of Unlawful Acts against the Safety of Civil Aviation 1971.[286]

Resolution 1487 is the renewal of Resolution 1422. Some of the paragraphs of Resolution 1487 are taken from Resolution 1422 *verbatim*. In terms of substance, Resolution 1487 is a renewal of Resolution 1422 without modification.[287] However, the renewal faced stronger disapproval and a number of Security Council members abstained from voting in favour.[288] The automatic renewal of Resolution 1422 through Resolution 1487 was criticized by the then UN Secretary-General Kofi Annan as sending the wrong signal that the Council 'wishes to claim absolute and permanent immunity for people serving in the operations it establishes or authorizes'.[289] The same argument and criticism can be voiced against Resolution 1487.

---

284   ICJ, *Libya* v. *United Kingdom*. 1994. Case Concerning the Interpretation and Application of the 1971 Montreal Convention Arising from the Aerial Incident at Lockerbie, Provisional Measures, 94 ILR 478.

285   Article 103, Charter of the United Nations. Available at: www.un.org/aboutun/Charter/intod.htm [accessed: 19 June 2009].

286   ICJ, *Libya* v. *United Kingdom*. 1994. Case Concerning the Interpretation and Application of the 1971 Montreal Convention Arising from the Aerial Incident at Lockerbie, Provisional Measures, 94 ILR 478.

287   Pestojova, K. Fall 2004. Was The United States Justified In Renewing Resolution 1487 In Light of Abu Ghraib Prison Abuse Scandal? *ILSA Journal of International and Comparative Law*, 11, 195-216, 203.

288   France, Germany and Syria abstained from the vote. See Citizens For Global Solutions, US Policy On The ICC. 30 June 2004. Available at: http://globalsolutions.org/programs/lawjustice/icc/resources/uspolicy.html [accessed: 11 July 2009].

289   UNSCOR, 58th session, 4772nd mtg, UN Doc. S/PV.4772(2003).

However, the failure of the United States to renew Resolution 1487[290] had some implications on peacekeeping resolutions. The vote on the renewal was scheduled for 21 May 2004, but was then postponed indefinitely, as the United States could not secure the necessary support for the resolution at that time.[291]

This failure was replaced by a new policy for exempting peacekeeping forces of non-state parties from the ICC jurisdiction. This was reflected in Resolution 1497,[292] a much more dangerous and general resolution if compared with Resolutions 1422 and 1487.

The difference between Resolution 1497 and previous Resolutions 1422 and 1487 is fundamental. Although all three exclude the jurisdiction of the ICC vis-à-vis peacekeeping forces of non-state parties, the implications of Resolution 1497 differ. Resolutions 1422 and 1487 are 'deferral' resolutions while Resolution 1497 is a 'terminating' resolution.[293] Resolutions 1422 and 1487 were adopted under the umbrella of Article 16 (at least that was claimed in the resolutions themselves), while Resolution 1497 does not invoke Article 16 and has a broader scope in terms of blocking the ICC's jurisdiction.

Resolution 1497 is also different in terms of circumstances; it is tied to a specific situation: Liberia. However, the significance of this Resolution is that it was not adopted under Article 16 of the Rome Statute, and it excluded the ICC jurisdiction over 'current or former officials or personnel from a contributing State, which is not a party to the Rome Statute of the International Criminal Court'.[294] The United Nations Stabilization Forces in Liberia's personnel of non-state parties are hence subject to the jurisdiction of that contributing state.[295]

A number of remarks could be made on Resolution 1497 in relation to the ICC in general and Article 16 in particular. Firstly, Resolutions 1422, 1487 and 1497 are all adopted under Chapter VII. Secondly, the Security Council managed to establish the existence of a threat to international peace and security, while it failed to do so under Resolutions 1422 and 1487. Thirdly, the Resolution covers a specific situation – Liberia – and is not of a general character as Resolutions 1422 and 1487. Fourthly, Resolution 1497 provides immunity permanently to current or former personnel of contributing non-state parties, and not for a 12-month period.

---

290   Citizens for Global Solutions. 23 June 2004. US Withdrew It Demands for Peacekeeping Exemption Renewal. Available at: http://globalsolutions.org/programs/lawjustice/news/nounscrenewal.html [accessed: 14 June 2009].

291   Pestojova, K. Fall 2004. Was The United States Justified In Renewing Resolution 1487 In Light of Abu Ghraib Prison Abuse Scandal? *ILSA Journal of International and Comparative Law*, 11, 195-216, 197.

292   Resolution 1497. 2004. Security Council. UN Doc. S/Res1497(2004).

293   Abbas, A. Winter 2005. The Competence of the Security Council to Terminate Jurisdiction of The International Criminal Court. *Texas International Law Journal*, 4, 263-309, 265.

294   Resolution 1497, para. 7. 2004. Security Council. UN Doc. S/Res1497(2004).

295   Resolution 1497, para. 7. 2004. Security Council. UN Doc. S/Res1497(2004).

Fifthly, the Resolution is not adopted under Article 16 of the Rome Statute;[296] and as a result it has a much broader scope.

Despite not invoking Article 16 of the Rome Statute, Resolution 1497 fulfils some of its requirements. The Resolution managed to establish the existence of peace and security.[297] In addition, it dealt with a specific existing case and not a general hypothetical situation (as was the case with Resolutions 1422 and 1487).

On the other hand, the Resolution violates Article 16 by not respecting the 12-month period.[298] In that respect, Resolution 1497 terminates the ICC jurisdiction permanently over peacekeepers for non-state parties in Liberia. That gives it a broader scope in terms of its legal and temporal effect, but still of limited scope when compared to Resolutions 1422 and 1487 in terms of *ratione loci*. The Resolution is restricted to Liberia, while the former resolutions are of global scope. The last point highlighted is that Resolution 1497 does not mention Article 16 in any of its paragraphs. Hence, the Security Council deliberately did not adopt Resolution 1497 under Article 16.

Article 16 did not succeed to solve fully the contentious relation between the ICC and the Security Council. The Security Council can expansively use its powers vis-à-vis the ICC. The Security Council has the ability, not only to defer the ICC jurisdiction under Article 16, but also to terminate the Court's jurisdiction on a broader scope than what is invested in the Rome Statute.[299]

This again raises the question of whether the Security Council has acted *ultra vires* according to the Statute. The simple answer seems to be affirmative, as Article 16 is breached.

However, in this respect a number of questions arise. Firstly, is the ICC bound by the Security Council Resolution 1497? Secondly, are state parties of the Rome Statute bound to respect the resolution or their obligation under the Rome Statute in case of conflict?

With respect to the first question, the drafters of the Rome Statute described the relation with the Security Council in Articles 13 and 16. The former Article is related to referrals, while the latter is the sole article on deferring cases from the ICC jurisdiction for a defined period of time.[300] Under Article 16, it is for the Court, as its own arbiter, to decide whether or not the Security Council has

---

296   Neha, J. April 2005. A Separate Law For Peace Keepers: The Clash between the Security Council and the Court. *The European Journal of International Law*, 16, 239-255, 245.

297   Resolution 1497, para. 7. 2004. Security Council. UN Doc. S/Res1497(2004).

298   Abbas, A. Winter 2005. The Competence of the Security Council to Terminate Jurisdiction of The International Criminal Court. *Texas International Law Journal*, 4, 263-309, 266.

299   Abbas, A. Winter 2005. The Competence of the Security Council to Terminate Jurisdiction of The International Criminal Court. *Texas International Law Journal*, 4, 263-309, 265.

300   Schabas, W. 2001. *An Introduction to the International Criminal Court.* Cambridge: Cambridge University Press, 66.

respected Article 16. Hence, if Security Council acts exceed the limit of the Article, the Court may consider the Security Council as acting *ultra vires* with respect to Article 16, and thus not consider itself bound by the resolution. Resolution 1497 arguably exceeded the ambit of Article 16,[301] and could thus be considered *ultra vires* according to the Rome Statute.

The case becomes more complex when answering the second question, i.e. whether state parties are under an international obligation to respect Resolution 1497 and their obligations under the Rome Statute. Since Security Council Resolution 1497 was not adopted in correlation with Article 16 of the Rome Statute, this could be considered an independent action by an international organization having legal restrictions on another international organization (the ICC). The United Nations is a treaty-based organization bound by stipulations of the UN Charter. The ICC, on the other hand, is also a treaty-based organization for which its Statute has been ratified by 111 member states in March 2010.[302] However, the UN Charter is considered a *sui generis* treaty, as Article 103 of the Charter grants the UN treaty supremacy over other international treaties. It states that in case of contradiction between the obligation of member states under the Charter and their obligations towards other international treaties, the obligation under the UN Charter prevails.[303]

In addition, the obligation to abide by Security Council Resolutions under Chapter VII supersedes the obligations of state parties according to Article 98 of the Rome Statute.[304] It is important to note that the 111 members of the Rome Statute are also members of the United Nations. Thus Security Council resolutions, under Chapter VII, are granted primacy over the obligations of these states towards other treaties. Yet, a small loophole exists that could reverse this primacy, and that is when measures taken by the Security Council are *ultra vires* and inconsistent with the UN Charter. The Security Council is the creation of a treaty and must not overstep the limits of that treaty.[305]

---

301   Abbas, A. Winter 2005. The Competence of the Security Council to Terminate Jurisdiction of The International Criminal Court. *Texas International Law Journal*, 4, 263-309, 271.

302   Coalition for the ICC. Available at: www.iccnow.org [accessed: 16 March 2010].

303   Article 103, Charter of the United Nations. Available at: www.un.org/aboutun/Charter/intod.htm [accessed: 4 May 2009].

304   Article 98 respects the international obligations of member states that are previous to their obligations to the Rome Statute. Article 98 of the Rome Statute of the International Criminal Court, UN Doc. A/CONF.183/9.

305   Neha, J. April 2005. A Separate Law For Peace Keepers: The Clash between the Security Council and the Court. *The European Journal of International Law*, 16, 239-255, 242.

Security Council resolutions granting immunity for peacekeepers have provoked strong criticism from the international community.[306] Some consider granting immunity to peacekeepers from the ICC jurisdiction outside the maintenance of peace and security.[307] The Security Council enjoys broad discretionary power to decide what constitutes a threat to international peace and security.[308] Article 39 of the UN Charter grants the Security Council the power to 'determine the existence of any threat to peace, breach of peace ... and [it] shall make recommendations or decide what measures shall be taken'.[309] The Charter does not define what a threat to peace is, or what contributes to maintaining peace, leaving the Security Council with broad discretionary power to do so. These powers could be limited by Article 24, which stipulates that the Security Council shall act in accordance with the purposes and principles of the United Nations.[310] In adopting Resolution 1497, the Security Council claims that the aim behind it (including operative paragraph 7) is to encourage contributions to peacekeeping operations in Liberia, which would contribute to a peaceful settlement in accordance with the purposes of the United Nations. There is no other body to monitor the legality of the Security Council actions.

Given the above, states will most likely meet their primary obligations to the Security Council resolutions under Chapter VII before fulfilling their obligations to the Rome Statute; this will probably be the case for Resolution 1497, despite intense criticism. Future state practices will of course confirm or invalidate this conclusion.

Conclusion

The aim of the above section is not to analyse Security Council resolutions, but to analyse the extent to which the Security Council could upset the complementarity principle in theory and practice.

---

306   Criticism was raised by Canada, France, China, Ireland, Mexico, Colombia, Syrian Arab Republic, Cameroon, Guinea, Mauritius, Samoa, Malaysia, Germany, Argentina, Cuba, New Zealand, South Africa, Costa Rica, Islamic Republic of Iran, Jordan, Liechtenstein, Brazil, Switzerland and Venezuela. UN Doc. s/pv.4568.

307   Stahn, C. February 2003. The Ambiguities of Security Council Resolution 1422. *The European Journal of International Law*, 14, 1, 85-104. 87. Also, Amnesty International. June 2004. Open Letter to The Security Council Regarding Renewal of Security Council Resolution 1487. Available at: http://web.amnesty.org/library/index/ENGIOR400092004 [accessed: 11 June 2009].

308   *Libya* v. *United Kingdom*. 1994. Case Concerning the Interpretation and Application of the 1971 Montreal Convention Arising from the Aerial Incident at Lockerbie, Provisional Measures, International Court of Justice, 94 ILR 478.

309   Article 39, Charter of the United Nations. Available at: www.un.org/aboutun/Charter/intod.htm [accessed: 12 July 2009].

310   Article 24, Charter of the United Nations. Available at: www.un.org/aboutun/Charter/intod.htm [accessed: 12 June 2009].

In theory, Article 16 can delay the commencement of an investigation or prosecution for a period of 12 months. The admissibility criteria in Article 17 indicate that the Court will exercise jurisdiction if the national courts are unwilling or unable.[311] However, Security Council deferrals are not correlated to a condition of 'inaction' or 'unwillingness' or 'inability'. Article 16 can only delay the ICC jurisdiction by suspending an investigation or prosecution for a period of time (12 months). If the period is renewed continuously, and the conditions for a new resolution are met, then the ICC jurisdiction can be excluded for as long as it is necessary. Based on the above, the complementarity principle is *de facto* upset, although the admissibility criteria can still be fulfilled.

The practice of the Security Council towards deferring the ICC jurisdiction is different. In Resolutions 1422 and 1487, the Security Council invoked Article 16 to discard the ICC jurisdiction, although the Council overstepped the limits of this Article. Through these deferrals, the ICC jurisdiction was excluded for peacekeeping forces of non-state parties for two consecutive years. That temporarily upset the complementarity principle in the case of 'unwilling' or 'inability' of national courts to prosecute possible perpetrators who served as peacekeepers.

Some experts argue that Resolution 1422 (and later Resolutions 1487 and 1497) did not upset the complementarity principle as it is related to citizens of non-state parties to the Rome Statute,[312] and the ICC legal effect, as a treaty-based organization, should be limited to its member states. This argument can be refuted, as the Rome Statute in this case is only applying the principle of territoriality,[313] which is an established principle for states to exercise jurisdiction.[314] Through the complementarity principle, member states have granted the ICC the power to exercise jurisdiction on their territories and on all possible perpetrators of international crimes who are present on their territories. This indicates that the automatic renewal of Resolution 1422 and then 1487, without respecting the requirements of Article 16, have led to a *de facto* paralysis of the Court's jurisdiction and its complementarity principle.

Resolution 1497 is even more dangerous and problematic, as it permanently excludes the ICC jurisdiction on non-state parties' peacekeeping forces in Liberia. The Resolution does not invoke Article 16. It places the Security Council and the

---

311   Article 17 of the Rome Statute of the International Criminal Court, UN Doc. A/CONF.183/9.

312   Abbas, A. Winter 2005. The Competence of the Security Council to Terminate Jurisdiction of The International Criminal Court. *Texas International Law Journal*, 4, 263-309, 272.

313   Akande, D. December 2003. The Jurisdiction of the International Criminal Court Over Nationals of Non-Parties: Legal Basis and Limits. *Journal of International Criminal Justice*, 618-656, 622, 623.

314   S.S. 'Lotus' Case. September 1927. Permanent Court of International Justice, Judgment no. 9, 12th Session, Series A – no. 10 Collection of Judgments A.W. Sijthoff's Publishing Company, Leiden.

ICC in direct confrontation, as the Resolution under the Rome Statute is clearly *ultra vires*. The ICC could label the Resolution *ultra vires* under the Statute, and thus consider it non-binding for the Court. However, the argument raised before indicates that the obligation of the state parties under the UN Charter to respect Resolution 1497 under Chapter VII supersedes their obligation under the Rome Statute.

Resolution 1497 can permanently prevent the jurisdiction of the Court from prosecuting this category of individuals when their national judicial system is 'unwilling' or 'unable' to adjudicate them for possible perpetration of core crimes under the Statute. However, the problem may not materialize if national courts genuinely exercise their primary jurisdiction.

In this author's opinion, Resolution 1497 shows that the Rome Statute's attempt to define the authority of the Security Council vis-à-vis the ICC was not successful. The Security Council in reality can impede the ICC's jurisdiction more than what was envisioned for the Council within Article 16 and that upsets the complementarity principle of the Court when cases are rendered admissible.

Chapter 5

Complementarity and State Referral:
The North Uganda Situation[1]

In December 2003, Uganda referred the situation in north Uganda to the ICC. The north Ugandan situation is the first state referral to the ICC. Although the primary focus of the Office of the Prosecutor was on the Democratic Republic of Congo (DRC), the Ugandan referral superseded the DRC.

The Ugandan referral is of interest here since this has been the first application of the complementarity principle at practice in a state referral scenario. Internal, external, legal and political factors combine to affect the assessment of the situation and the organization of the jurisdictional relation between the referring state and the ICC through the complementarity principle.

Background on the Conflict

For the past three decades, northern Uganda has been the scene of a brutal civil war between a number of factions and Yoweri Museveni's government.[2] The armed conflict in northern Uganda is one of the longest sustained armed conflicts not of an international character.[3] Jan Egeland, the then UN's Emergency Relief Coordinator (ERC), has described the environment in northern Uganda as the 'world's largest forgotten emergency'.[4]

---

1 A substantial part of this chapter has been published by this author in an article in the *International Criminal Law Review*, January 2010. See Jurdi, N.N. 2010. The Prosecutorial Interpretation of the Complementarity Principle: Does It Really Contribute to Ending Impunity on the National Level? *International Criminal Law Review*, 10, 73-96. President of Uganda Refers Situation Concerning The Lord's Resistance Army (LRA) To The ICC. 29 January 2004. The Hague, ICC-20040129-44-En.

2 See The Refugee Law Project. 28 July 2004. *The Refugee Law Project's Position Paper on The Announcement of Formal Investigations of The Lord's Resistance Army: The Chief Prosecutor of The International Criminal Court And Its Implications on The Search For Peaceful Solutions To The War In Northern Uganda*. Faculty of Law, Makerere University, 1-12.

3 Ssenyonjo, M. November 2005. Accountability of Non-State Actors in Uganda for War Crimes and Human Rights Violations: Between Amnesty and the International Criminal Court. *Journal of Conflict and Security Law*, 10, 405-433, 405.

4 *The Monitor*. 11 November 2003. Statement made by Jan Egeland during his Mission to Uganda on 7-10 November 2003, 4.

Uganda has a lengthy history of successive insurgencies. There are verbose explanations as to the main causes of the various rebellions in northern Uganda. In the past, the north was seen as a reservoir of labour for army recruiters. The British colonizers deliberately reserved the introduction of industry and cash crops to the south, keeping the north as a reservoir of manual labour.[5] Post-independence Uganda continued to depend heavily on army recruitment from the north, while the south enjoying relative economic prosperity. During the last 25 years, the political and military power belonged to northern ethnic groups. However, the victory of Yoweri Museveni's National Resistance Army (NRA) shifted power and patronage to south-western Uganda.[6] For many, therefore, the Lord's Resistance Army rebellion is merely a continuation of the ethnic competition that has characterized Ugandan politics.[7]

The last 25 years have witnessed a number of insurgencies, the longest lasting being that of the Lord's Resistance Army (LRA), a rebel group led by a self-proclaimed 'prophet' Joseph Kony, a leader who purportedly seeks to overthrow Museveni's government and install a system based on the Biblical Ten Commandments.[8]

Since 1986, there have been four rebellions in Acholiland. One critical and new Acholi grievance began when the short-lived military government of General Tito Okello agreed to an interim peace pact with the National Resistance Army of Yoweri Museveni at the end of 1985. The National Resistance Army broke the agreement, as it invaded Kampala and took over the government in January 1986. Many Acholis have never forgiven this betrayal of the peace agreement. Moreover, when the NRA took power, the pacification activities of the NRA in the north and east resulted in a number of human rights abuses and killings. The direct cause of the rebellion against the Museveni government can be traced back to the way the National Resistance Army soldiers behaved when they reached the northern region of Uganda. While it can be argued that the underlying cause of the LRA insurgency is an attempt by the defeated northern forces to regain power, the immediate cause of the rebellion was the abusive and undisciplined behaviour of the National Resistance Army deployed in the north.[9]

---

5   International Crisis Group. 14 April 2004. *Northern Uganda: Understanding and Solving the Conflict*, ICG Africa Report No. 77.

6   Ruaudel, H. and Timpson, A. 12 December 2005. *Situation Report; Northern Uganda from a Forgotten War to an Unforgivable Crisis – The War against Children*. Institute for Security Studies, 1-16.

7   Apuuli, K.Ph. 1 March 2006. The ICC Arrest Warrants for the Lord's Resistance Army Leaders and Peace Prospects for Northern Uganda. *Journal of International Criminal Justice*, 49, 179-187, 181.

8   The American Non-Governmental Organizations Coalition for the International Criminal Court; a Program of the United Nations Association of the United States of America. 16 February 2006. The Current Investigation by the ICC of the Situation in Northern Uganda. Available at: www.amicc.org [accessed: 14 June 2009].

9   Apuuli, K.Ph. 1 March 2006. The ICC Arrest Warrants for the Lord's Resistance Army Leaders and Peace Prospects for Northern Uganda. *Journal of International Criminal*

In response to these NRA military campaigns, soldiers of the former national army, the Uganda National Liberation Army (UNLA), fled to Sudan in July 1986 and then returned to northern Uganda to mount the first rebellion against the Museveni government. The rebels named themselves the Uganda People's Democratic Army (UPDA). The remnants of the former army then joined with senior Acholi politicians to establish the Uganda People's Democratic Movement (UPDM).[10] A peace agreement signed in Gulu in 1988 brought most of the fighters out of the bush. However, Acholi combatants did not trust Museveni's government, and vestigial forces of the UPDA refused to be part of any peace negotiations. In 1987, they joined Alice Auma 'Lakwena' and her 'Holy Spirit Movement' (HSM). Lakwena became a virtual 'priestess', claiming spiritual powers. Although defeated by the government in Jinja 1988, Lakwena succeeded to gather a large number of followers inside and outside the Acholi region. The government seriously underestimated the effectiveness of the Holy Spirit rebellion (as it has with the LRA), and allowed Alice Lakwena's guerrillas to occupy, albeit temporarily, large areas of central Uganda.

The HSM was an Acholi millennial movement with a syncretic mixture of Christian and traditional eschatology. The priestess Lakwena saw her leadership leading to a cathartic revival of Acholi social discipline and martial strength. Lakwena was defeated near Jinja, and fled into exile in Kenya where she has remained ever since as a refugee, although the Ugandan government continues to negotiate her return with an offer of a house and cash. Her father, Severino Lukoya, continued the rebellion for nearly six months, until Joseph Kony, in 1987, became the new leader of what was initially known as the 'Lord's Salvation Army', and later the Lord's Resistance Army. The UPDA and HSM were similar in that they both articulated reasons for rebellion with which most Acholi sympathized at the time. The Acholi had deep objections against the new government for depriving the Acholi of their political, military and economic power.[11]

Ugandan Peace Process

The Ugandan conflict witnessed numerous peace initiatives trying to end the brutal conflict, yet these initiatives failed in stopping the ongoing conflict that has caused the death and suffering of thousands of civilians. In the past 25 years, there have been several initiatives, starting with 'Goodwill Peace Mission'[12] and

Justice, 49, 179-187, 181.

   10   Refugee Law Project. February 2004. *Behind the Violence: Causes, Consequences and the Search for Solutions to the War in Northern Uganda.* Working Paper No. 11, 5.

   11   Ruaudel, H. and Timpson, A. 12 December 2005. *Situation Report; Northern Uganda from a Forgotten War to an Unforgivable Crisis – The War against Children.* Institute for Security Studies, 1-16, 4.

   12   Lucima, O. (ed.) 2002. *Protracted Conflict, Elusive Peace: Initiatives To End The Violence In Northern Uganda.* Accord No. 11.

followed by a series of other initiatives: the Bigombe Peace Initiative[13] (November 1993-February 1994), Kacoke Madit,[14] the Community of Sant'Egidio peace initiative, Equatoria Civic Fund Peace Initiative[15] (1997-1998), Carter Centre Process[16] (1998-2002), Acholi Religious Leaders Peace Initiative (ARLPI)[17] and the Northern Ugandan Peace Initiative. All of these failed to create a breakthrough in the ongoing conflict. Other initiatives, including the initiative of Winnipeg Conference[18] (September 2000), the Awoo Nyim Ceasefire (June 2001),[19] Civil

---

13   Human Rights and Peace Centre and Liu Institute for Global Issues. 30 October 2003. The Hidden War: The Forgotten People – War In Acholiland and Its Ramifications for Peace and Security in Uganda. Kampala/Uganda; Lucima, O. (ed.) 2002. *Protracted Conflict, Elusive Peace: Initiatives to End the Violence in Northern Uganda.* Accord No. 11.

14   Lucima, O. (ed.) 2002. *Protracted Conflict, Elusive Peace: Initiatives to End the Violence in Northern Uganda.* Accord No. 11. Also, Liu Institute for Global Issues. February 2003. *Update on the Human Security Situation in Northern Uganda – Report of the Liu Institute Mission to Northern Uganda 7-27 January 2003.* Vancouver: Liu Institute for Global Issues.

15   Lucima, O. (ed.) 2002. *Protracted Conflict, Elusive Peace: Initiatives to End the Violence in Northern Uganda.* Accord No. 11. Also, Liu Institute for Global Issues. February 2003. *Update on the Human Security Situation in Northern Uganda – Report of the Liu Institute Mission to Northern Uganda 7-27 January 2003.* Vancouver: Liu Institute for Global Issues.

16   Lucima, O. (ed.) 2002. *Protracted Conflict, Elusive Peace: Initiatives to End the Violence in Northern Uganda.* Accord No. 11. Also, Liu Institute for Global Issues. February 2003. *Update on the Human Security Situation in Northern Uganda – Report of the Liu Institute Mission to Northern Uganda 7-27 January 2003.* Vancouver: Liu Institute for Global Issues. See also The Carter Centre. 14 February 2000. New Reports on Sudan-Uganda Peace Process. Emory Report, 52, 21, 14. Available at: www.cartercentre.org [accessed: 18 May 2004].

17   Human Rights and Peace Centre and Liu Institute for Global Issues. 30 October 2003. The Hidden War: The Forgotten People – War in Acholiland and Its Ramifications for Peace and Security in Uganda. Kampala, Uganda; Lucima, O. (ed.) 2002. *Protracted Conflict, Elusive Peace: Initiatives to End the Violence in Northern Uganda.* Accord No. 11. Also, Liu Institute for Global Issues. February 2003. *Update on the Human Security Situation in Northern Uganda – Report of the Liu Institute Mission to Northern Uganda 7-27 January 2003.* Vancouver: Liu Institute for Global Issues; Gilbert, M. March 2001. The Role of the Acholi Religious Leaders Peace Initiative (ARLPI) in Peace Building in Northern Uganda, in *The Effectiveness of Civil Society Initiatives in Controlling Violent Conflicts and Building Peace – A Study of Three Approaches in the Greater Horn of Africa.* USAID/Management Systems International.

18   Lucima, O. (ed.) 2002. *Protracted Conflict, Elusive Peace: Initiatives To End The Violence In Northern Uganda.* Accord No. 11. Also, Liu Institute for Global Issues. February 2003. *Update on the Human Security Situation in Northern Uganda – Report of the Liu Institute Mission to Northern Uganda 7-27 January 2003.* Vancouver: Liu Institute for Global Issues.

19   Refugee Law Project. February 2004. *Behind the Violence – Causes, Consequences and the Search for Solutions to the War in Northern Uganda.* Refugee Law Project Working Paper No. 11.

Society Organizations for Peace in Northern Uganda (CSOPNU)[20] and Oduru Kuc (2003),[21] failed to end the conflict.

Recent Situation

Until recently, fighting has occurred continuously between UPDF forces and the LRA. There are a number of indicators that soldiers on both sides have committed atrocities. No doubt, the LRA has been weakened due to pressure from the UPDF, the effects of Sudan's withdrawal of assistance and Uganda's Amnesty Commission.[22] The signature of the Sudan Peace Accord on 9 January 2005 and the Security Council's referral of the situation in Darfur to the ICC may have positively influenced the conflict. John Garang, the late first Vice-President of Sudan and leader of the Sudan People's Liberation Army (SPLM), was a staunch opponent of the LRA's activities in Sudan. He stated on various occasions that the LRA is unwelcome in southern Sudan and will be 'treated as enemies of United Sudan'.[23] This resulted in the creation of a hostile environment for the LRA in Sudan.[24]

Negotiations were restored in the last years between the LRA and the Ugandan government in an attempt to end the conflict. The negotiation led to the signature of the Agreement of Accountability and Reconciliation between the Government of the Republic of Uganda and the Lord's Resistance Army/Movement signed on 29 June 2007.[25] Furthermore, in February 2008, the LRA and the Ugandan government agreed to establish a special court to deal with international crimes committed during

---

20   Human Rights and Peace Centre and Liu Institute for Global Issues. 30 October 2003. The Hidden War: The Forgotten People – War in Acholiland and Its Ramifications for Peace and Security in Uganda. Kampala, Uganda.

21   Human Rights and Peace Centre and Liu Institute for Global Issues. 30 October 2003. The Hidden War: The Forgotten People – War in Acholiland and Its Ramifications for Peace and Security in Uganda. Kampala, Uganda; Lucima, O. (ed.) 2002. *Protracted Conflict, Elusive Peace: Initiatives to End the Violence in Northern Uganda.* Accord No. 11.

22   Conciliation Resources, *Accord,* Issue 11: Key Texts and Agreements, *The Amnesty Act, 2000.* Available at: www.c-r.org/our-work/accord/northern-uganda/documents/2000_Jan_The_Amnesty_Act.doc [accessed: 14 September 2008].

23   IRIN News. 11 January 2005. *OCHA: Uganda, Optimism That Sudanese Peace Deal Could Help Pacify Northern Uganda.* IRINnews.org. Available at: www.irinnews.org/report.asp?ReportID=45000&SelectRegion=East_Africa&SelectCountry=UGANDA-SUDAN [accessed: 10 September 2008].

24   The American Non-Governmental Organizations Coalition for the International Criminal Court; a Program of the United Nations Association of the United States of America. 16 February 2006. The Current Investigation by the ICC of the Situation in Northern Uganda, 1-10, 6. Available at: www.amicc.org [accessed: 14 September 2008].

25   Agreement On Accountability and Reconciliation; Between The Government of the Republic of Uganda and The Lord's Resistance Army/Movement, Juba Sudan. 29 June 2007.

the conflict.[26] However, LRA leadership has kept insisting since 2008 that it will not come out of the bush to sign the final draft peace agreement without the withdrawal of the ICC arrest warrants. Since then, the final draft has never been signed.

Parties to the Conflict and Perpetration of International Crimes

The Lord's Resistance Army

The LRA initially emerged as a guerrilla rebel group. The increasing difficulties in attacking government troops led the LRA to resort to terror tactics as opposed to the control of territory, i.e. attacking 'softer' targets, such as civilian women and children, and civilian targets.[27] The LRA's strategy focused on gruesome tactics, such as the abduction, maiming and mutilating of children. The LRA has been notorious for abducting children wantonly and systematically. These abductions were largely means for other ends, namely the forcible recruitment of boys and girls in the LRA as child soldiers and sex slaves.[28] The LRA's campaign against children during this war can be marked as one of the most ferocious assaults on children in modern times.

The LRA has not revealed any coherent ideology or rational political agenda. Reports by UN agencies, NGOs and the media provide a consistent account of a brutal insurgency focused on the use of terrorist tactics. The LRA's frequent attempts to mobilize the Acholi people of northern Uganda against the government have failed, not the least because the LRA derived most of its membership from forcibly conscripted Acholi child soldiers, and because the Acholi population has been the primary victim of LRA atrocities. From the early days of Kony's assumption of leadership in 1991, the LRA began to target civilians. When peace negotiations with Uganda collapsed in 1994, the LRA escalated its violence against civilians, reflected by the increase of the frequency and ferocity of its attacks.[29]

---

26   BBC News. 19 February 2008. Ugandan Rebels and the Government Have Agreed to Set Up a Special Court to Deal With Alleged War Crimes – One of the Obstacles to a Final Peace Deal. Available at: http://news.bbc.co.uk/2/hi/africa/7252774.stm [accessed: 22 March 2008].

27   *The Economist*. 20 April 2002. The Lord's Army Resists, 44.

28   Apuuli, K.Ph. 1 March 2006. The ICC Arrest Warrants for the Lord's Resistance Army Leaders and Peace Prospects for Northern Uganda. *Journal of International Criminal Justice*, 49, 179-187, 181.

29   UN High Commissioner for Human Rights. 2003. *Report on the Mission Undertaken by Her Office, Pursuant to Commission Resolution 2000/60, to Assess the Situation on the Ground with Regard to the Abduction of Children from Northern Uganda*. UN Doc. E/CN.4/2002/86 (2001), paragraphs 12-13. Available at: www.ohchr.org/english [accessed: 16 September 2008]; see also Human Rights Watch, Stolen Children: Abduction and Recruitment in Northern Uganda, 4; Human Rights First, Background on the Conflict in Northern Uganda (n.d.). Available at: www.humanrightsfirst.org/International_ justice/regions/uganda/uganda.htm [accessed: 16 September 2008].

The exclusive reliance of the LRA on children is a strong indicator of its lack of popularity among the population in northern Uganda. Almost 85 per cent of its forces are abducted or forcibly conscripted village children.[30] With a lack of access to volunteers among the Acholi, coercion was the only means for the LRA to maintain its force levels.[31] The UN Office for the Coordination of Humanitarian Affairs (OCHA) figures showed that the LRA rebels have abducted more than 20,000 children to serve as fighters, porters, and sex slaves, and killed tens of thousands of civilians in the northern and eastern regions of Uganda.[32] This is a tragic dilemma, where the perpetrator is itself the victim. The war in northern Uganda has had tragic effects with thousands dead and over one million people displaced.[33]

The Lord's Resistance Army and International Crimes

There are numerous signs that LRA rebels have breached international law applicable to non-international armed conflicts.[34] Additionally, the alleged crimes committed in the region, such as conscription or enlistment of children under 15 years of age into the army, wilful killing, rape, sexual slavery, forced pregnancy and forced displacement of civilians, may constitute crimes against humanity (under Article 7 of the Rome Statute) or war crimes (under Article 8 of the Rome Statute).

Common Article 3 of Geneva Conventions, which applies to any case of 'armed conflict not of an international character' requires, 'as a minimum', that persons taking no active part in hostilities be 'treated humanely'.[35] It also explicitly

---

30   International Criminal Court. 29 January 2004. *Background Information on the Situation in Uganda.*

31   UNHCHR Report on Uganda; The UN High Commissioner for Human Rights stated in a November 2001 report to the Human Rights Commission: 'the LRA is devouring the lives of children in Northern Uganda in order to sustain itself, given that it cannot attract young men to the rebel movement as volunteers', paragraph 16.

32   IRIN News. 9 June 2005. *Uganda: Waiting For Elusive Peace in the War-Ravaged North.* Available at: www.irinnews.org/report.asp?ReportID=47568&SelectRegion=East_ Africa [accessed: 16 September 2008].

33   International Crisis Group. 22 September 2004. *Reports: Uganda, Conflict History.* Available at: www.crisisgroup.org/home/index.cfm?action=conflict_search&l=1&t=1&c_ country=111 [accessed: 16 September 2008].

34   Moir, L. 2002. *The Law of Internal Armed Conflict.* Cambridge: Cambridge University Press; Provost, R. 30 September 2005. *International Human Rights and Humanitarian Law.* Cambridge: Cambridge University Press; and Renteln, A. 1999. The Child Soldier: The Challenge of Enforcing International Standards. *Whittier Law Review,* 21, 191-205.

35   That could include, 'namely, any of the following acts committed against persons taking no active part in the hostilities, including members of armed forces who have laid down their arms and those placed hors de combat by sickness, wounds, detention or any other cause: (i) Violence to life and person, in particular murder of all kinds, mutilation, cruel treatment and torture; (ii) Committing outrages upon personal dignity, in particular

forbids intentionally directing attacks against the civilian population or individual civilians not taking part directly in hostilities, and intentionally directing attacks against buildings, material, medical units and transport, and personnel using the distinctive emblems of the Geneva Conventions. It also proscribes committing rape, sexual slavery, enforced prostitution, forced pregnancy, enforced sterilization, and conscripting or enlisting children under the age of 15 years into armed forces or groups or using them to participate actively in hostilities.[36]

As shown above, it seems that the LRA rebels have often committed several war crimes. In particular, they have intentionally directed attacks against civilians not taking direct part in hostilities; attacked civilian objects; committed sexual violence and conscripted children under the age of 15 into rebel armed forces. These are some of the most serious crimes of concern to the international community, over which the ICC has jurisdiction.[37]

Ugandan Peoples' Defence Forces

The Ugandan military, called the Uganda Peoples' Defence Forces (UPDF), originated from the National Resistance Army, a guerrilla force recruited and trained by Yoweri Museveni to overthrow the government of Milton Obote in the middle of the 1980s. The UPDF has significant influence in the decision-making process, although its role in politics has decreased with the development of civilian institutions and the enactment of the 1995 Constitution that provides the parliament with the power to regulate the composition of the UPDF.[38]

---

humiliating and degrading treatment; (iii) Taking of hostages; (iv) The passing of sentences and the carrying out of executions without previous judgement pronounced by a regularly constituted court, affording all judicial guarantees, which are generally recognised as indispensable'. Article 8(2)(c) of the Rome Statute of the International Criminal Court, UN Doc. A/CONF.183/9.

36   See Convention (IV) relative to the Protection of Civilian Persons in Time of War. 12 August 1949. Geneva. Available at: www.icrc.org/ihl.nsf/7c4d08d9b287a42141256 739003e636b/6756482d86146898c125641e004aa3c5 [accessed: 16 March 2009].

37   Article 5(1) of the Rome Statute of the International Criminal Court, UN Doc. A/CONF.183/9.

38   Article 209 of the Constitution of the Republic of Uganda stipulates that: 'The functions of the Uganda Peoples' Defence Forces are – (a) to preserve and defend the sovereignty and territorial integrity of Uganda; (b) to co-operate with the civilian authority in emergency situations and in cases of natural disasters; (c) to foster harmony and understanding between the Defence Forces and civilians; and (d) to engage in productive activities for the development of Uganda.' Article 210 of the Constitution stipulates that the: 'Parliament shall make laws regulating the Uganda Peoples' Defence Forces, and in particular, providing for – (a) the organs and structures of the Uganda Peoples' Defence Forces (b) recruitment, appointment, promotion, discipline and removal of members of the Uganda Peoples' Defence Forces and ensuring that members of the Uganda Peoples' Defence Forces are recruited from every district of Uganda; (c)

Having been successful in armed resistance against the government in 1981-1986, President Museveni's government quickly resorted to military means to solve emergent political problems.[39] The UPDF military strategy towards the LRA was to deprive it of new abductees and food supplies by protecting the civilian population in protected IDP camps. The UPDF has also begun to invest more resources in creating local defence units to protect camps and roads so that the UPDF resources can be used for offensive measures against the LRA.

In March 2002, the UPDF launched an aggressive offensive against the LRA dubbed 'Operation Iron Fist'.[40] Ironically, instead of making the region safer for civilians, the military operation led to large numbers of the LRA returning to northern Uganda, with accompanying intensive retaliatory violence and committing human rights violations.[41] This has left the civilian population in the so-called 'protected camps' inadequately protected against attacks by the LRA. It is, therefore, less surprising that in one attack at the IDP camp (Barlonyo) in north-eastern Uganda, the LRA was able to massacre more than 200 people,[42] in what the UN Secretary-General condemned as a 'senseless massacre'.[43] The UN Human Rights Committee (HRC) expressed regret, as the conflict was ongoing, that the Ugandan government had not taken sufficient steps to ensure the rights to life, liberty and security of persons affected by the armed conflict in northern Uganda, particularly internally displaced persons.

President Museveni regards the LRA commanders as 'empty-headed criminals' and thus prefers a military solution to end the conflict.[44] However, in a speech to members of parliament in September 2003, he noted that 'I have been fighting wars for the last 33 years non-stop. Therefore, there is no way you can change

---

terms and conditions of service of members of the Uganda Peoples' Defence Forces; and (d) the deployment of troops outside Uganda'. Constitution of the Republic of Uganda. Available at: www.government.go.ug/constitution/chapt4.htm on 8/14/01 [accessed: 16 March 2009].

39   Aliro, O. 23-30 July 2003. Why Museveni and Byanyima Divorced, Interview with the former Director at the Movement Secretariat, Winnie Byanyima, *The Monitor*.

40   Apuuli, K.Ph. 1 March 2006. The ICC Arrest Warrants for the Lord's Resistance Army Leaders and Peace Prospects for Northern Uganda. *Journal of International Criminal Justice*, 49, 179-187, 182.

41   Article 209(a) of The Constitution of the Republic of Uganda. Available at: www.government.go.ug/constitution/chapt4.htm on 8/14/01 [accessed: 16 March 2009].

42   IRIN News. 23 February 2003. *Uganda: Rebels Massacre More than 200 in Lira IDPs Camp*; and IRIN News. 25 February 2004. *Uganda: Focus on LRA Attack on Barlonyo IDPs Camp*.

43   UN News Service. 23 February 2004. Annan Condemns Rebel Massacre of Nearly 200 Civilians in Northern Uganda. Available at: www.un.org [accessed: 16 March 2009].

44   *The Monitor*, 10 October 2003.

the political direction of Uganda by forceful means'.[45] This change towards a peaceful settlement to the protracted conflict has lead to the re-initiation of the peace process that ended in a draft final agreement by 27 March 2008, but Kony refused to sign before the quashing of the ICC arrest warrants.[46]

Alleged Crimes Committed by the UPDF

There are several allegations of UPDF crimes, including torture, rape, recruitment of children, indiscriminate targeting, forced displacement of civilians and failure to protect civilians.

According to Human Rights Watch, in 2001 the government established a system of covert 'safe houses' where persons suspected of supporting opposition politicians or rebels, are held. With no real oversight by the Ugandan judiciary and no access given to Ugandan government human rights officials, these places of detention facilitated torture and other abuses by shielding abusers from scrutiny.[47] Reports by Amnesty International and Uganda Human Rights Activists (UHRA) have accused the Ugandan security forces, particularly the Violent Crime Crack Unit (VCCU) and Chieftaincy of Military Intelligence (CMI), of using torture.[48] The Uganda Human Rights Commission reported the use of torture in prisons and on persons in police custody.[49] The Foundation for Human Rights Initiative has also formed a coalition of eight NGOs to counter the use of torture in Uganda.[50] Human Rights Watch reports that the UPDF has developed a policy of detaining and torturing all political opposition, not just the LRA.[51] The Committee against Torture (CAT) called on the Ugandan government in June 2005 to take all necessary legislative, administrative and judicial measures to prevent acts of torture and ill-treatment in its territory, and in particular to act 'without delay to protect the civilian population in areas of armed conflict in northern Uganda from violations by the Lord's Resistance Army and members of the security forces'.[52]

---

45   *The New Vision*. 10 September 2003. Museveni Rules Out Forceful Takeover, Vision Reporters.

46   *Sudan Tribune*. 1 April 2008. Ugandan Rebel Leader Postpones Peace Deal Signing. Available at: www.sudantribune.com/spip.php?article26584 [accessed: 14 June 2009].

47   Human Rights Watch. 29 March 2004. State of Pain: Torture in Uganda, 16.

48   *The Monitor*. 24 April 2004. Rights Activists Accuse State Organs of Torture.

49   Ugandan Parliament. 7 April 2004. Prisons Service Blames Violation of Prisoners' Human Rights on Inadequate Funding, Ugandan Parliament.

50   *New Vision*. 5 May 2004. Anti-Torture Body Formed.

51   The American Non-Governmental Organizations Coalition for the International Criminal Court; a Program of the United Nations Association of the United States of America. 16 February 2006. The Current Investigation by the ICC of the Situation in Northern Uganda. Available at: www.amicc.org [accessed: 14 June 2009].

52   Convention against Torture, Concluding Observations: Uganda, CAT/C/CR/34/UGA (21/06/2005), para. 10 (n).

In terms of indiscriminate targeting, various actors have accused the UPDF of using indiscriminate force in targeting the LRA. The UNICEF executive director has asked the government to protect the lives of the abducted children during helicopter attacks.[53] Amnesty International has also reportedly criticized the UPDF for killing civilians during helicopter attacks.[54] However, no known charges or national proceedings have been brought concerning allegations of indiscriminate targeting.

Furthermore, Human Rights Watch has reported incidents of rape in IDP camps by UPDF soldiers.[55] The ARLPI also reported that more than 27 women and girls were raped by UPDF soldiers in Kitgum and Pader districts between June and December 2002.[56] Human Rights Watch reported that the UPDF acted with virtual impunity and the victims had little recourse to redress. The Uganda Human Rights Commission reportedly had no presence in the camps. Victims' access to police was difficult, and those making complaints against the UPDF could be subject to harassment, torture or execution. When a complaint was made against a soldier, the UPDF commanding officer must detain the suspect, yet if the officer refuses to cooperate, there is no appeal. It is common for accused soldiers either to flee to other barracks or to be transferred out of the district to avoid prosecution.[57]

There are scattered reports of soldiers being arrested for the crime of defilement.[58] In April 2004, the High Court in Gulu sentenced a UPDF soldier to 10 years' imprisonment for raping a 56-year-old woman. The woman was also given financial compensation for treatment in case she suspected she had contracted any sexually transmitted diseases.[59]

With respect to recruitment of children, there are reports that the UPDF has recruited and used children as guides both in Uganda and Sudan to help locate the LRA.[60] The rate of child recruitment is reportedly higher in the UPDF-

---

53   *New Vision.* 27 May 2004. UNICEF Warns On Air Strikes.

54   *New Vision.* 9 June 2004. Government to Probe Amnesty File.

55   Human Rights Watch. 29 March 2004. State of Pain: Torture in Uganda. Section VI. Available at: http://hrw.org/reports/2004/uganda0404/ [accessed: 14 June 2009].

56   See chronology of LRA abuses documented by the ARLPI. Available at: www. acholipeace.org [accessed: 16 December 2005]

57   Forced Displacement in Northern Uganda, written statement submitted by International Educational Development to the UN Sub-Commission on the Promotion and Protection of Human Rights. Available at: www.webcom.com/hrin/parker/sub01wsu.html [accessed: 16 September 2006].

58   *The Monitor.* 5 June 2004. 23 Soldiers for Trial on Murder. These cases are still pending. Soldiers not satisfied with the decisions of the Division Court Martial can appeal to the General Court Martial sitting at Makindye, Kampala.

59   *New Vision.* 23 April 2004. Soldier Gets 10 Years for Rape.

60   Human Rights Watch. 29 March 2004. State of Pain: Torture in Uganda, section VI. Available at: http://hrw.org/reports/2004/uganda0404/ [accessed: 16 March 2006].

controlled Local Defence Units (LDU).[61] The UNICEF and the Coalition to Stop the Use of Child Soldiers reported that the UPDF was training child soldiers in eastern DRC.[62] Ugandan officials have denied that there are child soldiers within the UPDF,[63] although they have admitted that child soldiers are often recruited into LDUs. The 1995 Ugandan Constitution stipulates, in Article 34(3) and (4), that children (persons under the age of 16 for this specific provision) 'shall not be employed in, or required to perform work that is likely to be hazardous or to interfere with their education or to be harmful to their health or physical, mental, spiritual, moral or social development'.[64] The National Resistance Army (NRA) Statute 3/92, the Conditions of Service Men Regulations 1993 and the Conditions of Services (Officers) Regulations 1993 all require that any recruit who is between 18 and 30 years needs a recommendation from a guardian.

Regarding forced displacement, at the beginning of the conflict in 1996, the UPDF ordered civilians living in Gulu to move to protected IDP camps. Although the UPDF continues to maintain that the approximately 350,000 to 400,000 persons moved voluntarily to these camps, many assert that they were forced to move into the camps[65] by bombing and burning villages and murdering, beating and threatening those who would not comply.[66]

---

61   Coalition to Stop the Use of Child Soldiers. 25 June 2003. *Child Soldiers Coalition Reports Alarming Levels of Abductions and Recruitment of Children by LRA and UPDF in Northern Uganda.*

62   Coalition to Stop the Use of Child Soldiers. 21 February 2001. *UN Finds Congo Child Soldiers.* Child Soldiers 1379 Report. Available at: www.childsoldiers.org/cs/ childsoldiers.nsf/0/c560bb92d962c64c80256c69004b0797?OpenDocument [accessed: 16 September 2008].

63   UN Security Council. 31 January 2003. *Child Soldiers: Letter from Uganda to the UN President of the Security Council.*

64   Article 34 of the Constitution of the Republic of Uganda. Available at: www. government.go.ug/constitution/chapt4.htm on 8/14/01 [accessed: 16 March 2009].

65   Under Article 17 of Additional Protocol II to the Geneva Conventions of 12 August 1949, 'The displacement of the civilian population shall not be ordered for reasons related to the conflict unless the security of the civilians involved or imperative military reasons so demand. Should such displacements have to be carried out, all possible measures shall be taken in order that the civilian population may be received under satisfactory conditions of shelter, hygiene, health, safety and nutrition', Protocol Additional to the Geneva Conventions of 12 August 1949, and Relating to the Protection of Victims of Non-International Armed Conflicts (Protocol II), Adopted on June 1977 by the Diplomatic Conference on the Reaffirmation and Development of International Humanitarian Law applicable in Armed Conflicts. Entry into force, 7 December 1978. Available at: www.unhchr.ch/html/menu3/b/94.htm [accessed: 16 March 2009].

66   International Educational Development to the UN Sub-Commission on the Promotion and Protection of Human Rights. July-August 2001. Forced Displacement in Northern Uganda, written statement submitted by International Educational Development to the UN Sub-Commission on the Promotion and Protection of Human Rights. Fifty-

On 2 October 2002, the UPDF issued an oral order to civilians living in Gulu, Pader and Kitgum to move to internally displaced camps:

> This announcement goes to all law-abiding citizens in the abandoned villages of Gulu, Pader and Kitgum districts to vacate with immediate effect ... This is because we have discovered that the LRA terrorists when pursued by the UPDF hide in huts located in these villages ... Get out of these villages in order not to get caught in cross fire.[67]

Forty-eight hours after this order was issued, the UPDF began shelling, bombing and using helicopter gun ships to attack the areas around the camps. This may be justified if the order suggests that the displacement was related to 'imperative military reasons' or the security of the population. According to the UN Guiding Principles on Internal Displacement, 'prior to any decision requiring the displacement of persons, the authorities concerned shall ensure that all feasible alternatives are explored in order to avoid displacement altogether'.[68] In addition, the UPDF has been criticized for the prolonged period of forced displacement, which has affected nearly 70 per cent of the northern Uganda population since 1996.[69]

Further criticism of the government of Uganda has been raised on the bases of lack of protection of civilians and internally displaced persons during armed conflict and, in particular, civilians who were displaced by their orders. However, IDP camps frequently remained subject to LRA attacks. Museveni and the UPDF have often defended the inability of the UPDF to provide protection by stating that the designated IDP camps are not officially recognized, and that the UPDF cannot provide protection for people outside the camp. They claimed that there was a lack of communication between units, that the LRA used multiple simultaneous attacks to divert the UPDF, and that the donors have placed too many restrictions on defence spending.

The UPDF has been accused of committing crimes that fall under the jurisdiction of the ICC, in particular crimes of torture, rape, murder and forcible transfer of a population. While there is evidence that not all alleged crimes have been investigated, some of the allegations have been investigated at the national level. To analyse these investigations, the complementarity test and the gravity criterion has to be applied.

---

third session, agenda item 2. Available at: www.webcom.com/hrin/parker/sub01wsu. html [accessed: 16 March 2009].

67   Global IDP Project. July 2003. Army Displaced 300,000 People. Available at: www.db.idpproject.org/Sites/IdpProjectDb/idpSurvey.nsf/wViewCountries/BCA796EFE6 FE85C2C1256DDE0034984A [accessed: 19 March 2009].

68   Principle 7 of the Guiding Principles on Internal Displacement. Available at: www. unhchr.ch/html/menu2/7/b/principles.htm [accessed: 14 September 2008].

69   Human Rights Watch. 29 March 2004. State of Pain: Torture in Uganda, section VI. Available at: http://hrw.org/reports/2004/uganda0404/ [accessed: 15 March 2009].

Uganda's Referral to the ICC

Political Background

In December 2003, the Ugandan President Yoweri Museveni decided to refer the LRA crimes to the ICC. Museveni met in London with ICC Prosecutor Moreno-Ocampo to announce the referral.[70] The meeting was also meant to establish a basis for future cooperation between Uganda and the International Criminal Court.[71]

   The Ugandan referral is the first application of Articles 13(a) and 14 by a state party under the Statute.[72] One should analyse the possible political reasons behind such a referral. Uganda had an important political aim – engaging the international community to capture and prosecute the LRA.[73] The conflict has been 'long forgotten',[74] and Uganda's resort to international justice, through the referral to the ICC, was a means for pushing this long-forgotten conflict back on the international agenda.[75] It was an attempt to lighten the burden on Uganda's shoulders to find a settlement for the ferocious insurgency. In addition, through surrendering prosecutorial authority to an international jurisdiction, Uganda aimed to ensure that justice would be achieved without politicization of any trials involving the LRA,[76] which would relieve Uganda from any accusation of not holding impartial trials.

Uganda's Referral and the Statute

At the legal level, there are no prerequisites for a state referral, but as the complementarity principle is applied, the national system should at least be either

---

70   President of Uganda Refers Situation Concerning The Lord's Resistance Army (LRA) To The ICC. 29 January 2004. The Hague, ICC-20040129-44-En.

71   President of Uganda Refers Situation Concerning The Lord's Resistance Army (LRA) To The ICC. 29 January 2004. The Hague, ICC-20040129-44-En.

72   Articles 13(a) and 14 of the Rome Statute of the International Criminal Court, UN Doc. A/CONF.183/9.

73   Akhavan, P. April 2005. Developments at the International Criminal Court: The Lord's Resistance Army Case: Uganda's Submission of the First State Referral to the International Criminal Court. *The American Journal of International Law*, 99, 403-429, 405.

74   *The Monitor.* 11 November 2003. Statement made by Jan Egeland during his Mission to Uganda on 7-10 November 2003, 4.

75   Akhavan, P. April 2005. Developments at the International Criminal Court: The Lord's Resistance Army Case: Uganda's Submission of the First State Referral to the International Criminal Court. *The American Journal of International Law*, 99, 403-429, 405.

76   Akhavan, P. April 2005. Developments at the International Criminal Court: The Lord's Resistance Army Case: Uganda's Submission of the First State Referral to the International Criminal Court. *The American Journal of International Law*, 99, 403-429, 405.

unable or unwilling to initiate proceedings, or there must be absence of any action on behalf of the national system.[77] The Ugandan referral does not seem to fulfil the inability or unwillingness test under Article 17, which raises the question of whether a state having a judicial system that is both willing and able to prosecute can voluntarily defer jurisdiction to the ICC.[78] The Uganda judicial system falls under the 'no action' category. However, to secure the validity of this designation, some light should be shed on the Ugandan judicial system, which entails inspecting the availability and effectiveness of the judiciary, including the structure of the judicial system and its functions. It also requires highlighting any investigations into or prosecutions of the LRA rebels or the UPDF soldiers, including discussing the genuineness of the national proceedings and the impact of the recent Amnesty Act on prosecuting international crimes.

The Ugandan judicial system's availability and effectiveness   The Ugandan court system consists of a tier of formal court, called the Courts of Judicature, and a tier of informal courts, the latter at the local level.[79] The Courts of Judicature consist of the following courts in hierarchical order: the Supreme Court, the Court of Appeal/Constitutional Court, the High Court; and Subordinate Courts, including the Magistrates' Courts and the Qadhi Courts.[80]

The Supreme Court is the final court of appeal for constitutional matters and for matters provided by the Law.[81] The head of the Supreme Court – the Chief Justice – is responsible for the administration and supervision of all courts in Uganda. The Court of Appeal functions as an appellate court for decisions of the High Court and, as the first instance constitutional court for resolving constitutional issues. The High Court has broad original jurisdiction in all civil and criminal matters, as well as appellate jurisdiction in matters decided by the Subordinate Courts. The headquarters of the High Court are in Kampala, but seven circuits exist in the following districts: Masaka, Mbale, Nakawa, Fort Portal, Mbarara, Gulu and Jinja. The Magistrate Courts, headed by the Chief Magistrates, have the power of to supervise all magisterial courts within their area of jurisdiction. Under the

---

77   The International Criminal Court, Office of the Prosecutor. 2003. *Paper on Some Policy Issues before the Office of the Prosecutor*. ICC-OTP 2003, 1-9, 4. Available at: www.icc-cpi.int/library/organs/otp/030905_Policy_Paper.pdf [accessed: 20 February 2009].

78   Akhavan, P. April 2005. Developments at the International Criminal Court: The Lord's Resistance Army Case: Uganda's Submission of the First State Referral to the International Criminal Court. *The American Journal of International Law*, 99, 403-429, 405.

79   Republic of Uganda, Courts of Judicature. Available at: www.judicature.go.ug [accessed: 16 March 2009].

80   Republic of Uganda, Courts of Judicature. Available at: www.judicature.go.ug [accessed: 16 March 2009].

81   Republic of Uganda, the Supreme Courts of Uganda. Available at: www.judicature.go.ug/index.php?option=com_content&task=view&id=35&Itemid=50   [accessed: 16 March 2009].

Chief Magistrate, Magistrates Grade I and Grade II exercise judicial functions over matters provided by the law. The special Family and Children's Courts deal with matters concerning children and are presided over by Magistrates Grade II. The Qadhi Courts have competence over the application of Islamic law in certain issues of family law such as inheritance and marriage.[82]

At the informal level, Local Council Courts have competence to adjudicate certain matters of law, with the exception of most criminal matters. Local Council Courts, now known as Executive Committee Courts, are structured hierarchically starting from the village (Executive Committee Village Courts/LC I Courts), and then moving upward to the parish (Executive Committee Parish Courts/LC II Courts), and then to the sub-county level (Executive Committee Sub-County Courts/LC III Courts). They are monitored by the Chief Magistrates, who can adjudicate over appeals of decisions of the Executive Committee Sub-County Court.[83]

The Military Court System is independent from the Courts of Judicature. The US Department of State Report on Human Rights Practices in Uganda states that a sentence by a military court can only be appealed before the senior leadership in the UPDF, while sentences by a Field Court Martial cannot be appealed.[84]

a. *Administration of the Courts of Judicature*

With respect to Public Prosecution (PP), the Directorate of Public Prosecutions (DPP) is an independent body headed by the Director of Public Prosecutions. The Director of the PP is appointed by the President on the recommendation of the Public Service Commission and with approval of parliament. The Director of Public Prosecutions is the head of prosecutions in the Uganda criminal system. The Criminal Investigation Department (CID) of the Police Force conducts criminal investigations. In addition, the Anti-Terrorism Act of 2002 requires the consent of the DPP to prosecute for crimes of terrorism.[85] Moreover, the consent of the Attorney General is required under the International Criminal Court Bill of 2004 before proceedings may be started with regard to the crimes proscribed

---

82 Chapter 8 of the Constitution of the Republic of Uganda. Available at: www. government.go.ug/constitution/chapt4.htm on 8/14/01 [accessed: 16 March 2009].

83 Regan, F. 1994. Legal Resources Development in Uganda. *International Journal of Sociology of Law*, 22, 203.

84 US Department of State. 25 February 2004. *Bureau of Democracy, Human Rights, and Labour, Country Reports on Human Rights Practices – Uganda 2003 Section 1(e)*. Available at: www.state.gov/g/drl/rls/hrrpt/2003/27758.htm [accessed: 16 March 2009].

85 See Section 3 of the Ugandan Anti-Terrorism Act. 2002. Assented to by the President on 21 May 2002 and came into force on 7 June 2002.

under the Bill. This consent does not hinder the lawfulness of an arrest or custody of a person accused of a crime under the Bill.[86]

b. *Quality of Ugandan National Justice System*
The UN Special Rapporteur on the Independence of Judges and Lawyers, in his December 2003 report, outlined a number of criteria or factors that are important in determining the independence of the judiciary.[87] Some of these factors are taken into account in order to assess the overall quality of the Ugandan justice system. Where applicable, the focus will be on the quality of the justice system in northern Uganda. This assessment does not aim to give a comprehensive judgment on the Ugandan Justice system, but rather to see to what extend the Ugandan courts are capable of conducting trials according to international standards taking into consideration a number of non-exhaustive examples on certain practices. A number of criteria will be analysed: the jurisprudence of the Supreme Court, the Ugandan Human Rights Commission decisions, access to the Courts, delay in justice, and the jurisdiction of Martial Courts.

i. *The Supreme Court Jurisprudence*
The judiciary seems relatively independent although the president has broad powers to nominate judges. One can cite the Supreme Court's important decision that sidelined the parliament's Constitutional Amendment of 2000.[88] The decision can be viewed as an indication of an effective separation of powers and of the independence of the judiciary.[89]

ii. *The Uganda Human Rights Commission (UHRC) decisions*
Despite various obstacles, the Commission managed to render a number of governmental measures and decisions that included violations of human rights and rights of the individual. In these decisions, the UHRC requested that the government pay compensation to the victims of human rights abuses. The UHRC has investigated cases involving torture and other human rights abuses

---

86   See Section 17 of the International Criminal Court Bill. 2004, Draft of 19 April 2004. Uganda eventually adopted the ICC law on 9 March 2010. More information is available at: www.reviewconference.or.ug/index.php?option=com_content&view=article &id=64&Itemid=64 [accessed: 10 April 2010].

87   Despouy, L. 30 December 2003. Report of the Special Rapporteur on the Independence of Judges and Lawyers: Civil and Political Rights, Including the Questions of: Independence of the Judiciary, Administration of Justice, Impunity. E/CN.4/2004/60.

88   Articles 258 to 262 of the Constitution of the Republic of Uganda. Available at: www.government.go.ug/constitution/chapt4.htm on 8/14/01 [accessed: 16 March 2009].

89   Despouy, L. 30 December 2003. Report of the Special Rapporteur on the Independence of Judges and Lawyers: Civil and Political Rights, Including the Questions of: Independence of the Judiciary, Administration of Justice, Impunity. E/CN.4/2004/60.

by the UPDF, the Chieftaincy of Military Intelligence (CMI), and has awarded compensation to the victims.[90] Facts show, however, that the UHRC is unable to supervise UPDF actions,[91] although UHRC representatives claim that the Commission maintains a high level of cooperation with the UPDF and the authorities. The problem ultimately lies at the level of the Attorney General, whose responsibility it is to take action in cases referred to it by the UHRC. Although these investigations reflect some independent overview of government actions, which strengthens the rule of law,[92] they are not conducted for establishing the criminal responsibility of perpetrators in accordance with Article 17 of the ICC Statute (read in conjunction with Article 21(3) of the ICC Statute). The UHRC has forwarded some complaints to the Department of Public Prosecutions and recommended that criminal investigations be commenced. The DPP has complied with some of these recommendations.[93]

iii. Lack of access to courts in the north

In Kitgum and Pader, effective access to justice does not seem to be available to all civilians due to lack of funding and limited facilities, including the unavailability of lawyers.[94] This lack of access to judicial services and courts presents a structural impediment to the proper functioning and independence of the judiciary.[95]

The judicial system suffers from inequality in terms of access. In rural areas, the population's main access to justice is through

---

90   See, for example, UHRC Gulu, *Walter* v. *Attorney General*, Complaint no. UHRC/ G/91/2001: UHRC Gulu, *Abugkoji* v. *Attorney General*, Complaint no. G/326/1999; UHRC Kampala, *Bagole* v. *Attorney General*, Complaint no. 519 of 2001; UHRC Kampala, *Stephen* v. *Attorney General*, Complaint no. 357/2000.

91   Uganda Human Rights Commission. 9 April 2003. *UHRC Annual Report Jan 2002-Sept 2002: 2002 Highlights*. Kampala, 9. Available at: www.uhrc.org/archive.php [accessed: 13 September 2008].

92   Despouy, L. 30 December 2003. Report of the Special Rapporteur on the Independence of Judges and Lawyers: Civil and Political Rights, Including the Questions of: Independence of the Judiciary, Administration of Justice, Impunity. E/CN.4/2004/60, para. 29.

93   Uganda Human Rights Commission. 18 April 2003. *UHRC Annual Report January 2001 – September 2002*. Kampala, 7, 10. Available at: www.uhrc.org/archive.php [accessed: 11 December 2008].

94   Northern Uganda Peace and Dialogue Initiative, 15.

95   Despouy, L. 30 December 2003. Report of the Special Rapporteur on the Independence of Judges and Lawyers: Civil and Political Rights, Including the Questions of: Independence of the Judiciary, Administration of Justice, Impunity. E/CN.4/2004/60, para. 33.

the local council courts.[96] Reports have highlighted briberies and discrimination against women within this judicial process. This violates the principle of equal access to justice, constituting an infringement of the independence and impartiality of the judiciary.[97]

iv. Delay in justice

The Ugandan judicial system suffers generally from delays in proceedings. The lack of resources and an ineffective judicial administration have resulted in a serious backlog of cases. This holds especially true for the High Court. There are also allegations that lower courts are severely understaffed, weak and inefficient.[98] Delay in justice may result in a denial of justice and even impunity, which severely hampers the effective functioning of the judiciary.[99] In addition, lengthy detention periods are common and, according to the Ugandan Constitution, suspects charged with a capital offence may be held in pre-trial detention for up to a year before trial, although the legal period is often surpassed.[100] Human Rights Watch found that adjournments were routinely given by the High Court due to 'pending investigations', and that the majority of the prison population (70 per cent) consisted of pre-trial detainees.[101] The average time of pre-trial detention is between 24 and 36 months. Many observers and experts have raised their concern that this extensive delay in the court system violates the due process rights of the accused.[102]

---

96   Despouy, L. 30 December 2003. Report of the Special Rapporteur on the Independence of Judges and Lawyers: Civil and Political Rights, Including the Questions of: Independence of the Judiciary, Administration of Justice, Impunity. E/CN.4/2004/60, para. 35, Section 1(e).

97   Despouy, L. 30 December 2003. Report of the Special Rapporteur on the Independence of Judges and Lawyers: Civil and Political Rights, Including the Questions of: Independence of the Judiciary, Administration of Justice, Impunity. E/CN.4/2004/60, para. 50.

98   US Department of State. 25 February 2004. *Bureau of Democracy, Human Rights, and Labour, Country Reports on Human Rights Practices – Uganda 2003 Section 1(e).* Available at: www.state.gov/g/drl/rls/hrrpt/2003/27758.htm [accessed: 16 March 2009].

99   Despouy, L. 30 December 2003. Report of the Special Rapporteur on the Independence of Judges and Lawyers: Civil and Political Rights, Including the Questions of: Independence of the Judiciary, Administration of Justice, Impunity. E/CN.4/2004/60, para. 35.

100   Article 23(6)(c) of the Constitution of the Republic of Uganda. Available at: www.government.go.ug/constitution/chapt4.htm on 8/14/01 [accessed: 16 March 2009].

101   Human Rights Watch. 29 March 2004. State of Pain: Torture in Uganda, section VI. Available at: http://hrw.org/reports/2004/uganda0404/ [accessed: 16 March 2009].

102   Uganda Law Society. 2003. *Review of Military Justice under the UPDF Bill,* Larkin Reynolds, Section 6.

v. *Extensive jurisdiction of martial courts*

In June 2002, 'Operation Wembley' established a special joint security team from members of the intelligence services police, and the army, for the purposes of addressing violent crimes in Kampala. This system was replaced by the Violent Crime Crack Unit (VCCU), which also had the power to arrest and try civilians before a court martial in cases of possession of military weapons.[103] The jurisprudence of Human Rights Committee, the European Court of Human Rights, the Inter-American Court of Human Rights, and the African Commission of Human and People's Rights clearly assert that bringing civilians before military courts is a breach of to the right to due process and the principle of 'lawful judge'.[104] Therefore, 'Operation Wembley' did not support the independence and impartiality of the Ugandan judiciary, but rather was a threat to it.[105]

National Proceedings in the Context of the LRA–UPDF Conflict

Investigations

a. *Investigation against UPDF crimes*

On the judicial level, some actions were taken against certain violations of human rights by the UPDF. For instance, in one incident, UPDF soldiers raided the Gulu Central Prison in order to prevent the absconding of 21 prisoners. During this operation, the opposition activist Peter Oloya was killed in a suspected extra-judicial killing.[106] In February 2003, the High Court declared the army's actions illegal and awarded damages against the State.[107]

However, a number of violations of human rights and humanitarian law by the UPDF have taken place without any investigation or judicial remedy. For example, the killing of a civilian by a UPDF soldier on 14 February 2003 at an army detachment in Alwal has not been investigated.

---

103   US Department of State. 25 February 2004. *Bureau of Democracy, Human Rights, and Labour, Country Reports on Human Rights Practices – Uganda 2003 Section 1(e).* Available at: www.state.gov/g/drl/rls/hrrpt/2003/27758.htm [accessed: 16 March 2009].

104   Human Rights Committee, Press Release. 7 April 1997. *Human Rights Committee Concludes Consideration of Lebanon's Report.* HR/CT/492. Available at: www.un.org/News/Press/docs/1997/19970407.hrct492.html [accessed: 16 March 2009].

105   Despouy, L. 30 December 2003. Report of the Special Rapporteur on the Independence of Judges and Lawyers: Civil and Political Rights, Including the Questions of: Independence of the Judiciary, Administration of Justice, Impunity. E/CN.4/2004/60, para. 60.

106   Amnesty International Report. 2003. Available at: http://web.amnesty.org/report2003/Uga-summary-eng [accessed: 16 March 2009].

107   Northern Uganda Peace and Dialogue Initiative, 15.

On 1 May 2003, UPDF soldiers killed Esther Angeyo, reportedly in an accidental shooting, outside the Pabbo Internally Displaced Persons (IDP) camp. In May 2003, the government announced that it would compensate her husband Mzee Nyero Santo Akol, for the death of his wife. Yet, a year later no compensation was paid. On 11 July 2003, the police killed a student at Kitgum High School while trying to disperse a riot, and no measures were taken against the police officers who were responsible for the killing. In February 2003, UPDF soldiers reportedly shot and killed a Sudanese national in an ambush intended for LRA rebels at the Pabbo IDP camp. The incident did not bring any measure against the soldiers responsible for the killing.[108]

No actions were taken against UPDF soldiers for a number of crimes or violations. The following are non-exhaustive examples of some of these incidents; the killing of two civilians by a helicopter gunship in Lira district in August 2002; the killing of Emmanuel Onencan who was mistaken for a rebel in September 2002; the killing of a village official in Omoro County of the Gulu district in October 2002 during combat with LRA forces; and the killing of one person in the crossfire between UPDF troops and Allied Democratic Front (ADF) rebels in May 2002.[109]

Furthermore, there have been allegations of violations of human rights by the Ugandan official authorities in the application of the Anti-Terrorism Act. There have been claims that security forces used 'safe houses' to detain persons suspected of terrorist acts. These unofficial detentions, if proven, contravene the Ugandan Constitution.[110]

b. Investigation against LRA crimes

Under the Anti-Terrorism Act, some of the LRA members, who received amnesty, have been subsequently rearrested under this Act in 2002.[111] For instance, in August 2004, eight people were arrested by a joint army and police operation in Gulu on accusations of allegedly collaborating with the

---

108   Northern Uganda Peace and Dialogue Initiative, 15; US Department of State. 25 February 2004. *Bureau of Democracy, Human Rights, and Labour, Country Reports on Human Rights Practices – Uganda 2003 Section 1(a)*. Available at: www.state.gov/g/drl/rls/hrrpt/2003/27758.htm [accessed: 16 March 2009].

109   Northern Uganda Peace and Dialogue Initiative, 15; US Department of State. 25 February 2004. *Bureau of Democracy, Human Rights, and Labour, Country Reports on Human Rights Practices – Uganda 2003 Section 1(a)*. Available at: www.state.gov/g/drl/rls/hrrpt/2003/27758.htm [accessed: 16 March 2009].

110   See *UHRC Annual Report Jan 2002-Sept 2002*, delivered in Kampala on 9 April 2003, 9. Available at: www.uhrc.org/reports.php?y=2002&subCatId=1 [accessed: 16 March 2009].

111   Amnesty International Report. 2003. Available at: http://web.amnesty.org/report2003/Uga-summary-eng [accessed: 16 March 2009].

Lord's Resistance Army.[112] In addition, a bodyguard to LRA leader Joseph Kony was captured in September 2004 by UPDF forces. The nature of judicial actions taken against this person has not been specified.[113]

Prosecutions
  a. *Prosecutions against UPDF crimes before Ugandan courts*
  In terms of trials in civilian courts, there are a number of indications that UPDF prosecutions for non-combat related crimes against civilians have taken place. There have been a number of national proceedings for alleged murders by UPDF soldiers. The Uganda Human Rights Commission ordered the government to pay compensation to the family of George Onencan who the army shot dead in Odek sub-county, Gulu district on 31 January 2003.[114]

  In terms of military trials, the Field Court Martial sitting in Lira-Palwoi in the Pader district under the chair of Lieutenant Colonel George Etyang brought UPDF soldiers to trial. The charges brought against these soldiers included a variety of crimes that have allegedly been committed during military operations. Only one accused was named as of that time; Captain Fred Kavuma, who was charged with failure to protect 13 civilians killed in an IDP camp in Pader in March 2004.[115]

  Moreover, three soldiers were tried and found guilty by a Military Court Martial; Private Richard Wigiri was found guilty of murdering Monica Achiro in December 2002 and a Military Court Martial near Kitgum found the two other soldiers, Privates Kambacho Ssenyonjo and Alfred Okech, guilty of killing three civilians on 4 January 2003. The rights of the defendants were not fully respected though, as the defendants reportedly lacked access to legal representation, and as the execution was carried out approximately one hour after the sentences were passed.[116]

  In another case, an Emergency Field Court Martial tried on 25 March 2002 two soldiers for killing a parish priest and his driver. The trial allegedly lasted only two hours and 26 minutes. The soldiers were subsequently executed. The short duration of the trial is a strong indication that it did not meet the international standards of a fair trial, and therefore did not meet the requirements set forth in Article 17 and Article 21(3) of the ICC Statute.

---

112   *New Vision*. 4 August 2004. Eight LRA Agents Arrested.

113   *New Vision*. 14 September 2004. Army Catches Kony Guard.

114   *New Vision*. 28 May 2004. Uganda Human Rights Commission Tells Govt to Pay Family 25m.

115   *The Monitor*. 9 May 2004. Military Courts get Underway in Pader.

116   Northern Uganda Peace and Dialogue Initiative, 15; US Department of State. 25 February 2004. *Bureau of Democracy, Human Rights, and Labour, Country Reports on Human Rights Practices – Uganda 2003 Section 1(a)*. Available at: www.state.gov/g/drl/rls/hrrpt/2003/27758.htm [accessed: 16 March 2009].

The execution of soldiers was reported as an accepted disciplinary measure that is applied by senior military officials within the UPDF.[117] In an attempt to prevent unlawful executions and disrespect to due process in this trial, the UPDF conducted an internal investigation regarding the execution of these two soldiers following accusations of unconstitutionality, and found that the executions were lawful.[118]

Although some proceedings against errant UPDF soldiers did occur, as mentioned above, many open sources indicate that numerous abuses committed by the UPDF against civilians were not in fact prosecuted. Investigations of summary executions, torture, rape and substandard conditions of detention, if they occurred, were kept internal and thereby adopted the impression of impunity.[119] Certain reports point out that the measures taken against errant soldiers were in general mild, or lacked clear criteria. These measures may range from the violation being left unpunished to the rare court martial without a thorough investigation. The appropriate punishment was often left at the discretion of the field commander in charge.[120] Even when punishment was imposed, it has often targeted low-ranking officers.

In terms of its inability to provide protection for internally displaced persons, the UPDF has blamed mainly low and middle ranking officers, and arrested and tried several on charges of 'negligence of duty' and 'causing death of civilians'.[121] For instance, in an LRA attack on the Lukodi camp, the UPDF arrested the local army commander, accusing him of running away and leaving the camp unprotected.[122] On another occasion, two battalion commanders were arrested for failing to pass on information to units that could have provided protection.[123] Those arrested were tried before a court martial.

---

117   Amnesty International Report. 2003. Available at: http://web.amnesty.org/report2003/Uga-summary-eng [accessed: 16 March 2009].

118   US Department of State. 25 February 2004. *Bureau of Democracy, Human Rights, and Labour, Country Reports on Human Rights Practices – Uganda 2003 Section 1(a)*. Available at: www.state.gov/g/drl/rls/hrrpt/2003/27758.htm [accessed: 16 March 2009].

119   Human Rights Watch. July 2003. *Uganda, Abducted and Abused: Renewed Conflict in Northern Uganda*, 15, 12 (A). Available at: www.hrw.org/reports/2003/uganda0703/ [accessed: 16 March 2009].

120   Human Rights Watch. July 2003. *Uganda, Abducted and Abused: Renewed Conflict in Northern Uganda*, 15, 12 (A). Available at: www.hrw.org/reports/2003/uganda0703/ [accessed: 16 March 2009].

121   IRIN News. 25 May 2004. *Uganda: Army Arrests Officers after Second Rebel Attack On an IDP Camp in Days*.

122   Deutsche Presse Agentur. 9 June 2004. Ugandan Government Says 19 Die in Rebel Attack on Refugee Camp.

123   IRIN News. 25 May 2004. *Uganda: Army Arrests Officers after Second Rebel Attack On an IDP Camp in Days*.

More importantly, according to Ugandan Justice Akiki-Akiiza, the War Crimes Division of the Ugandan High Court that was established along the lines of the unsigned Juba Agreement on Accountability in 2008, would not prosecute members of the UPDF. The War Crime Division would only prosecute those covered by the Agreement without including perpetrators from the UPDF.[124] It seems that the Division was established to solve the 'problem' of the ICC indictments rather than ending impunity for the atrocities and crimes committed during the long-lasting conflict.

b. *Prosecutions against LRA crimes before Ugandan courts*

The data indicated *infra* shows a number of judicial measures taken against collaborators or individuals attached to the LRA. Most of the measures were carried out on grounds of treason. The UPDF in the Pader district arrested 26 people during the first week of October 2004. They were accused of collaborating with the LRA, which included monitoring the movements of the army and supplying mobile phones and food to the rebels.[125] Another 19 individuals were arrested on allegations of collaboration. The army announced that the suspects pleaded guilty to spying and providing relief aid to the rebels.[126] They were later remanded to the High Court. In September 2004, two employees at the Entebbe Airport were charged with treason for allegedly spying on a military base on behalf of the LRA.[127] Moreover, a Catholic priest was arrested in November 2004 for collaborating with the LRA.[128] In September 2003, four detainees were executed after being accused of collaborating with a rebel group without indicating the name of the group. They were arrested by the Joint Anti-Terrorism Task Force (JATF).[129] In late 2002, a remarkable legal incident occurred as two boys, who were LRA abductees, were subsequently granted amnesty after being charged with treason. After a petition to the government by Human Rights Watch, the boys were granted amnesty and charges were dropped.[130] In addition, in November 2002, an individual was accused of financing the

---

124 Amoru, P. 18 September 2008. Uganda: Local War Crimes Court Excludes UPDF From Trial. *The Monitor*. Available at: http://allafrica.com/stories/200809180042.html [accessed: 21 February 2010].

125 *The Monitor*. 8 October 2004. UPDF Arrests 26 Over LRA Links; *New Vision*. 8 October 2004. Suspected LRA Rebel Partners Detained.

126 *New Vision*. 15 October 2004. Army Nets 19 LRA Spies.

127 *New Vision*. 7 September 2004. Airport Personnel Linked to LRA Rebels.

128 *The Monitor*. 3 November 2004. Priest held over LRA Links; *The Monitor*. 5 November 2004. Catholic Priest to be Prosecuted.

129 Human Rights Watch. 3 October 2003. *Uganda: Security Force Executions Reported*. Available at: http://hrw.org/english/docs/2003/10/03/uganda6428.htm [accessed: 10 March 2009].

130 Human Rights Watch. July 2003. *Uganda, Abducted and Abused: Renewed Conflict in Northern Uganda*, 15,12 (A). Available at: www.hrw.org/reports/2003/

LRA following agents tapping his telephone,[131] charged with treason, and then sent to Luzira prison.

Genuineness of national proceedings and the amnesty law   After years of conflict, a military solution seemed incapable of ending the war in northern Uganda. In 1998, the government faced internal and external pressure to end the rebellion. The failure of the military and the political process in ending the conflict created room for the use of a legislative measure that could weaken the LRA and end the conflict. The government introduced an amnesty law pardoning any rebel that lay down his/her weapon. The amnesty Bill was introduced to the parliament in 1998. The Bill was finally passed as the Amnesty Act 2000. The Act offered pardon to all Ugandans who have been engaged in acts of rebellion against the government of Uganda since 26 January 1986.[132] It offered blanket immunity to rebels who voluntarily disarmed. The supporters of the amnesty law have argued that the Acholi people, who were the victims of the LRA crimes and the families of the LRA's mostly abducted soldiers, should be allowed to end the LRA insurgency by using local traditional dispute resolution institutions. The majority of the population in Acholiland seemed in favour of pardoning the rebels to end the insurgency.[133] The Act itself staked its legitimacy in what its preamble termed 'the expressed desire of the people of Uganda to end armed hostilities, reconcile with those who have caused suffering and rebuild their communities' and 'the desire and determination of the government to genuinely implement its policy of reconciliation'.[134]

The Act created the Amnesty Commission, which has been the body responsible for granting amnesty under this law. It also established the Demobilization and Resettlement Team, which assisted in the disarmament and decommissioning processes. The Act has required continuous three-month renewals.[135]

By June 2005, more than 15,000 former combatants and abductees of the LRA had taken advantage of the Amnesty Act.[136] The government has also made efforts

---

uganda0703/ [accessed: 16 March 2009]. Also, *New Vision*. 5 April 2003. Treason Suspects Apply for Amnesty.

131   *New Vision*. 22 November 2002. LRA Man on Treason.

132   Apuuli, K.Ph. 1 March 2006. The ICC Arrest Warrants for the Lord's Resistance Army Leaders and Peace Prospects for Northern Uganda. *Journal of International Criminal Justice*, 49, 179-187, 183.

133   *The East African*, 16 February 2004.

134   Ssenyonjo, M. November 2005. Accountability of Non-State Actors in Uganda for War Crimes and Human Rights Violations: Between Amnesty and the International Criminal Court. *Journal of Conflict and Security Law*, 10, 405-433, 413.

135   The American Non-Governmental Organizations Coalition for the International Criminal Court; a Program of the United Nations Association of the United States of America. 16 February 2006. The Current Investigation by the ICC of the Situation in Northern Uganda, 1-10, 6. Available at: www.amicc.org [accessed: 13 September 2008].

136   IRIN News. 9 June 2005. *Uganda: Forgiveness as an Instrument of Peace.*

to reintegrate former LRA rebels into the army.[137] The outcome of the Amnesty Act was successful, and the number of LRA fighters dropped drastically. Nonetheless, debate continued over the validity of this act with regard to the state's duty to prosecute international crimes, and the extent of conformity of the amnesty with international standards.

Although the Amnesty Act has provided a blanket amnesty to LRA rebels who gave up fighting, there has been an exemption for the top commanders.[138] In addition, there has not been complete impunity for captured LRA members. Accused LRA soldiers and collaborators, including children, arrested by the authorities have primarily been detained on charges of treason, a crime that may warrant the death penalty. Treason has been defined in the Penal Code as levying war against Uganda, including plotting to overthrow the government and causing or attempting to cause the death of or injury to the president.[139] The Suppression of Terrorism Act of 2002 has counted collaboration with the rebels as treason or misprision to treason. The Act has referred to 'opponents of the state' making members of the LRA susceptible to suspicion of treason. The Act has clearly designated the LRA as a terrorist organization, and parties and groups attempting to establish dialogue with the LRA were accused of collaborating with a terrorist organization. The Acholi Religious Leaders Peace Initiative, for instance, was under scrutiny for this reason.[140]

High Courts have exercised jurisdiction over cases of treason or terrorism. Operation Iron Fist led to increased arrests of suspected LRA-collaborators, but reportedly no more than five cases of treason were transferred to the jurisdiction of the Gulu High Court in the last six months of 2002 and in all of 2003.[141] There has been a considerable delay in the process of arresting and then referring to

---

137   *New Vision*. 1 December 2004. UPDF Absorbs 932 LRA Rebels and LDUs.

138   According to an ICC Press Release, President Museveni has indicated his intention to amend this amnesty to exclude the leadership of the LRA, ensuring that those bearing the greatest responsibility for the crimes against humanity committed in Northern Uganda are brought to justice. Press Release. 29 January 2004. *President of Uganda Refers Situation Concerning the Lord's Resistance Army (LRA) to the ICC*. Available at: www.icc-cpi.int/pressrelease_details&id=16.html [accessed: 16 March 2009]. See also, Asia Africa Intelligence Wire. 16 December 2003. *Uganda: New Amnesty Act to Exclude Rebel LRA Leaders*. Available at: www.accessmylibrary.com/comsite5/bin/pdinventory.pl?pdlanding= 1&referid=2930&purchase_type=ITM&item_id=0286-19714599 [accessed: 16 September 2009]. Also, *The Monitor*. 6 July 2006. Museveni Amnesty to Kony Illegal – ICC.

139   Republic of Uganda. 1970. The Penal Code Act, sections 25, 27.

140   Internal Displacement Monitoring Centre. May 2004. *Anti-terrorism Laws Undermine Amnesty Act of 2000*. Available at: www.internal-displacement.org/8025708F004CE90B/ (httpEnvelopes)/88FA701937E475A9802570B8005AAD12?OpenDocument [accessed: 21 October 2008].

141   Human Rights Watch. July 2003. *Uganda, Abducted and Abused: Renewed Conflict in Northern Uganda*, 15,12 (A). Available at: www.hrw.org/reports/2003/ uganda0703 [accessed: 16 March 2009].

the courts, and the fate of most suspects of treason and terrorism charges has been a prolonged detention in military custody without trial.[142] In treason and anti-terrorist cases before the High Court, the suspect may be detained for up to a year while an investigation is conducted, without the possibility of bail and without being charged with an offence before an impartial tribunal.[143] Arbitrary arrests, particularly mass arrests of people under the Anti-Terrorism Act have been criticized as a major problem.[144] Reports indicated that various human rights abuses have been committed by the Ugandan authorities in connection with the treason cases, such as political detention, detention without charges, use of undisclosed locations for detention, and mistreatment during detention.[145] By the end of 2003, around 160 individuals were detained on charges of treason.[146] As reports showed that former rebels who have been pardoned under the Amnesty Act were rearrested under the Suppression of Terrorism Act of 2002,[147] there has been a conflict between granting amnesties to LRA soldiers and arresting collaborators on grounds of treason.

Concluding Remarks

The data highlighted *supra* shows the Ugandan judicial system is not in a full or partial state of failure. The data included *supra* clearly indicates that the Ugandan judicial system is available and functioning. However, the judicial process suffers from a number of malfunctions and obstacles that may prevent the impartial and efficient delivery of justice. Some of the cases indicated *supra* shed light on excessive delays in detaining suspects in violation of their rights. Some detainees were never brought before a judicial body, and some detentions took place in unmonitored prisons. These deficiencies, whether in the law enforcement mechanism or in the judicial process, are violations of human rights and the principle of fair trial. The decisions of the Ugandan Human Rights Commission (UHRC) confirm the

---

142   Human Rights Watch. July 2003. *Uganda, Abducted and Abused: Renewed Conflict in Northern Uganda*, 15,12 (A). Available at: www.hrw.org/reports/2003/uganda0703 [accessed: 16 March 2008].

143   Human Rights Watch. July 2003. *Uganda, Abducted and Abused: Renewed Conflict in Northern Uganda*, 15,12 (A). Available at: www.hrw.org/reports/2003/uganda0703 [accessed: 16 March 2008].

144   Politinfo US. 11 November 2004. Country Reports on Human Rights Practices; Human Rights in Uganda, Released on 31 March 2003, 9.

145   Politinfo US. 11 November 2004. Country Reports on Human Rights Practices; Human Rights in Uganda, Released on 31 March 2003, 12

146   US Department of State. 25 February 2004. *Bureau of Democracy, Human Rights, and Labour, Country Reports on Human Rights Practices – Uganda 2003 Section 1(e)*. Available at: www.state.gov/g/drl/rls/hrrpt/2003/27758.htm [accessed: 16 March 2009].

147   Amnesty International. January – December 2003. *Uganda Annual Report 2004*. Available at: http://web.amnesty.org/report2004/uga-summary-eng [accessed: 16 March 2009].

occurrence of many of these violations. In a number of decisions, the UHRC has ordered the government to pay compensation to the victims of these violations.[148]

However, the structure of courts martial has been criticized for not respecting the due process rights of the accused soldiers, arguably to protect national interests.[149] This is evident in the willingness of military officials to execute soldiers as a disciplinary measure to protect state security, evidenced by executions of UPDF soldiers in both 2002 and 2003 for killings.[150] In both cases, the accused were denied access to legal counsel and the trials lasted for only a few hours, and were immediately followed by execution. In 2002, it was announced that the accused would be executed even before the court heard the case. The legal expertise during such trials is limited. The rules of evidence are more lenient in the court martial and are at the discretion of the judges. Consequently, confessions obtained through alleged misconduct or torture can still be admitted in the court martial system.[151] The appeal process in the court martial system is restricted mainly to the death penalty, while the list of offences that may incur the death sentence is broad and extensive.[152] Moreover, the right to appeal or seek pardon or reduction of sentence is denied if convicted before a Field Court Martial, not to mention that bail is rarely granted. Based on that, one can say that Uganda's criminal justice system is available and functions relatively well, however, it suffers from lack of full independence and impartiality in trying crimes committed by the LRA or the UPDF.[153]

---

148   The UHRC awarded compensation to a number of individuals for abuses by the police or UPDF-soldiers. These non-exhaustive examples show the following: the Tribunal also awarded compensation to Christopher Nsereko for the torture he was subjected to after being arrested for unknown reasons in 1997. In June, British citizen Hassouna was awarded damages for repeated occasions of arrest and beatings by security agents. See Politinfo US. 11 November 2004. Country Reports on Human Rights Practices; Human Rights in Uganda, Released on 31 March 2003. For example, in February 2003 the Tribunal awarded 59 million shillings to Stephen Gidudu as compensation for three months of torture after being wrongfully arrested by UPDF soldiers. The UPDF in April subsequently initiated an investigation into the actions of the soldiers. See *New Vision*. 9 April 2003. UPDF Probes Torture Case.

149   Politinfo US. 11 November 2004. Country Reports on Human Rights Practices; Human Rights in Uganda, Released on 31 March 2003, 2, 12.

150   Amnesty International. January-December 2003. *Uganda Annual Report 2004*. Available at: http://web.amnesty.org/report2004/uga-summary-eng [accessed: 16 March 2009].

151   Human Rights Watch. 29 March 2004. State of Pain: Torture in Uganda, section VI. Available at: http://hrw.org/reports/2004/uganda0404/ [accessed: 16 March 2009].

152   Politinfo US. 11 November 2004. Country Reports on Human Rights Practices; Human Rights in Uganda, Released on 31 March 2003, 12.

153   Pena, M. and Kocabayoglu, S. 13 October 2005. *The ICC And Alternative Justice Mechanisms in Africa Introduction*. The American Non-Governmental Organizations Coalition for the International Criminal Court; a Program of the United Nations Association

The Application of Complementarity on Uganda's Referral

Complementarity under State Referral in Abstract

According to Article 14, 'a state party may refer to the prosecutor a situation in which one or more crimes within the jurisdiction of the Court appear to have been committed'.[154] Under the Statute, this triggering mechanism will be scrutinized – when the jurisdictional requirements are fulfilled – in accordance with the requirements of the complementarity principle under Article 17.[155]

The triggering mechanism under Articles 13(a) and 14 empowers the Court to exercise its jurisdiction if other jurisdictional parameters are fulfilled. However, the admissibility test remains applicable, and the Court has to satisfy itself whether or not the referral is admissible under the complementarity principle.[156]

In applying the complementarity test to a state referral *in abstracto*, one could ask if the requirements of Article 17 are fulfilled. The answer is not simple, and state referrals could raise complex issues when applying Article 17. Among others, it is ambiguous whether the admissibility of the referral will be considered an indication of 'inaction' by the state or an indication of 'unwillingness' or 'inability' of the national system. On the other hand, some argue that referrals will always pass the complementarity test, and that cases should be rendered admissible.[157] According to the latter view, the complementarity principle was invoked in the Statute to preserve the rights of the states to prosecute core crimes. The states' referrals resemble a waiver of such right, at which point the application of complementarity becomes unnecessary.[158] This view does not find grounds in the *Ad Hoc* Committee negotiations, where the opinion of some states to restrict

---

of the United States of America, 1-10, 2. Available at: www.amicc.org/docs/ICC%20Alter native%20Justice%20Africa.pdf [accessed: 16 March 2009].

154   Article 14 of the Rome Statute of the International Criminal Court, UN Doc. A/CONF.183/9.

155   Southwick, K. Fall 2005. Investigating War in Northern Uganda: Dilemmas for the International Criminal Court. *Yale Journal of International Affairs*, 105-119, 108.

156   Article 53 of the Rome Statute of the International Criminal Court, UN Doc. A/ CONF.183/9. See also, Akhavan, P. April 2005. Developments at the International Criminal Court: The Lord's Resistance Army Case: Uganda's Submission of the First State Referral to the International Criminal Court. *The American Journal of International Law*, 99, 403-429, 413.

157   Benzing, M. 2003. The Complementarity Regime of the International Criminal Court: International Criminal Justice between State Sovereignty and the Fight against Impunity. *Max Planck Yearbook of United Nations Law*, 7, 591-632, 630.

158   The argument is that it is primary uncontested role of the state to prosecute international crime, and thus the state referral is a transfer of this right to the ICC, and that will render the case admissible. See Benzing, M. 2003. The Complementarity Regime of the International Criminal Court: International Criminal Justice between State Sovereignty and the Fight against Impunity. *Max Planck Yearbook of United Nations Law*, 7, 591-632, 630.

state referrals to those states on whose territory the crimes were committed, whose nationals were involved, as victims or perpetrators, or the states having the alleged perpetrators in custody was not upheld.[159] The drafters of the Rome Statute chose to allow 'all' state parties to refer situations to the Court. This was put forward in the Preparatory Committee in 1996, and received the support of the majority of states in the Rome Conference.[160] The final formula preserved the applicability of the complementarity principle regarding state referrals.[161]

Initially, there were two views of complementarity among jurists. Some writers argued that complementarity could imply two competing interpretations: a negative interpretation, and a positive interpretation.[162] The 'negative interpretation' implies that 'the ICC should be a substitute for national trials only when there is a failure to prosecute by the relevant national judicial system'.[163] Thus, under the negative interpretation, Article 17 restricts the ICC jurisdiction to cases in which states are unwilling or unable to prosecute. Referrals, then, that do not meet the admissibility criteria either listed under 'unwillingness' or under 'inability' as indicated in Articles 17(2) and 17(3) will be rendered inadmissible.[164] A referral by state parties, under Articles 13(a) and 14 that have judicial systems that are not in total or partial collapse and that are willing to prosecute will be declared inadmissible. This interpretation of the complementarity principle adopts a rigid approach that restricts open-ended possibilities for rendering referrals admissible.

The positive interpretation of the complementarity principle states that 'Article 17 limits ICC jurisdiction through the criterion of unwillingness or inability only when there is a conflict between the ICC and a national criminal jurisdiction'.[165]

---

159   Kirsch, Ph. and Robinson, D. 2002. Referral by State Parties, in *The Rome Statute of The International Criminal Court: A Commentary*, edited by A. Cassese, P. Gaeta and J.R.W.D. Jones. Oxford: Oxford University Press, volume I, 622.

160   Wilmshurst, E. 1999. Jurisdiction of the Court, in *The International Criminal Court: The Making of the Rome Statute, Issues, Negotiations, Results*, edited by R. Lee. The Hague: Kluwer, 134.

161   Holmes, J. 1999. The Principle of Complementarity, in *The International Criminal Court: The Making of the Rome Statute, Issues, Negotiations, Results*, edited by R. Lee. The Hague: Kluwer, 78.

162   Akhavan, P. April 2005. Developments at the International Criminal Court: The Lord's Resistance Army Case: Uganda's Submission of the First State Referral to the International Criminal Court. *The American Journal of International Law*, 99, 403-429, 413.

163   Akhavan, P. April 2005. Developments at the International Criminal Court: The Lord's Resistance Army Case: Uganda's Submission of the First State Referral to the International Criminal Court. *The American Journal of International Law*, 99, 403-429, 413.

164   Akhavan, P. April 2005. Developments at the International Criminal Court: The Lord's Resistance Army Case: Uganda's Submission of the First State Referral to the International Criminal Court. *The American Journal of International Law*, 99, 403-429, 413.

165   Akhavan, P. April 2005. Developments at the International Criminal Court: The Lord's Resistance Army Case: Uganda's Submission of the First State Referral to the International Criminal Court. *The American Journal of International Law*, 99, 403-429, 413.

In other words, the test of unwillingness or inability applies when there is an intention by both the ICC and the national states to prosecute. It is only in cases of jurisdictional competition between state parties and the Court that the complementarity principle applies. According to the positive interpretation of complementarity, Articles 17(2) and 17(3) will not apply if there is no conflict of jurisdiction between states and the Court.[166] Hence, voluntary state referral, according to this view, will be always admissible, if other requirements are fulfilled, and hence the application of the complementarity test is not necessary. In this author's opinion, the positive interpretation could be criticized as it may encourage states to be lazy in prosecuting international crimes, and that will prevent the ICC from contributing to the indirect enforcement mechanism of international criminal law.

In the first practice of state referral – the Ugandan referral of the northern Ugandan situation – the ICC adopted the negative interpretation of complementarity,[167] rendering the Ugandan judicial system 'unable'. Even before the referral, the *Informal Expert Paper: The Principle of Complementarity in Practice* shows that the complementarity principle remains applicable for uncontested admissibility.[168] Even if states do not contest the ICC for their primary jurisdiction, the ICC has to justify admissibility under Article 17. In the case of absence of initiation of investigation, Article 17(1)(a)-(c) is to be applied, and if its criteria are not satisfied, the case will be admissible.[169] The argument *supra* finds explicit support in Article 19(1), which stipulates that '[t]he Court shall satisfy itself that it has jurisdiction in any case brought before it. The Court may, on its own motion, determine the admissibility of a case in accordance with Article 17'.[170]

Article 19(2)(a) permits an accused or a person to challenge the admissibility 'of a case on the grounds referred to in Article 17'.[171] Similar privilege is entrusted to the state that has jurisdiction, or according to Article 12 and to the Prosecutor.[172]

---

166 Akhavan, P. April 2005. Developments at the International Criminal Court: The Lord's Resistance Army Case: Uganda's Submission of the First State Referral to the International Criminal Court. *The American Journal of International Law*, 99, 403-429, 414.

167 Moreno-Ocampo, L. March 2005. *The International Criminal Court: Hopes and Fears*, Coca-Cola World Fund at Yale Lecture, New Haven, 2.

168 The International Criminal Court, Office of the Prosecutor. 2003. *Informal Expert Paper: The Principle of Complementarity in Practice*. ICC-OTP 2003, 1-38, 17. Available at: www.icc-cpi.int/library/organs/otp/complementarity.pdf [accessed: 11 August 2009].

169 The International Criminal Court, Office of the Prosecutor. 2003. *Informal Expert Paper: The Principle of Complementarity in Practice*. ICC-OTP 2003, 1-38, 17. Available at: www.icc-cpi.int/library/organs/otp/complementarity.pdf [accessed: 11 August 2009].

170 Article 19(1) of the Rome Statute of the International Criminal Court, UN Doc. A/CONF.183/9.

171 Article 19(2)(a) of the Rome Statute of the International Criminal Court, UN Doc. A/CONF.183/9.

172 Article 19(2) of the Rome Statute of the International Criminal Court, UN Doc. A/CONF.183/9.

State referrals apply both Articles 14 and 17 simultaneously. Yet, for the situation to be admissible before the ICC there must be no investigation by the national judicial system or the system must be 'unable' or 'unwilling' to investigate and prosecute.

With respect to 'no action', as mentioned in the previous chapter on complementarity, the ICC can exercise its jurisdiction if national courts have not taken any action.[173] The Office of the Prosecutor's Policy Paper stipulates that 'there is no impediment to the admissibility of a case before the Court where no State has initiated any investigation. There may be cases where inaction by states is the appropriate course of action'.[174] Hence, when states refer a situation without any action of investigation or prosecution, the Court can render the case admissible since the exercise of the ICC jurisdiction is activated primarily by the lack of action by the national courts of the relevant states, those qualifying as either the territorial state, the state of nationality of the alleged perpetrators or the state of nationality of the victims.[175] This type of referral falls under the so-called 'uncontested jurisdiction'.[176] However, this study will show that state referrals are more complex than this.

Further complexity stems from the fact that a state referral demonstrates a clear willingness to prosecute by the referring state;[177] yet if the judicial system is 'able', then the referral must fall under the 'unwillingness' category for it to be admissible before the ICC. This leads to a contradiction: how can 'inaction' fall under 'unwillingness' while the state referral itself is a sign of a state's willingness to prosecute? The answer is not simple, and in certain extreme and complex scenarios, the state may have one organ that is willing while another is not. Such an approach will create a contradiction, and could lead to results opposite to those intended by the ICC pertaining to encouraging national systems to prosecute. This will be elaborated later in this chapter.

---

173   Olasolo, H. 26 March 2004. *The Triggering Procedure of the International Criminal Court, Procedural Treatment of the Principle of Complementarity, and the Role of Office of the Prosecutor*. Guest Lecture Series of the Office of the Prosecutor, The Hague, 1-22, 14.

174   The International Criminal Court, Office of the Prosecutor. 2003. *Paper on Some Policy Issues before the Office of the Prosecutor*. ICC-OTP 2003, 1-9, 5. Available at: www.icc-cpi.int/library/organs/otp/030905_Policy_Paper.pdf [accessed: 20 February 2009].

175   Olasolo, H. 26 March 2004. *The Triggering Procedure of the International Criminal Court, Procedural Treatment of the Principle of Complementarity, and the Role of Office of the Prosecutor*. Guest Lecture Series of the Office of the Prosecutor, The Hague, 1-22, 15.

176   The International Criminal Court, Office of the Prosecutor. Internal Memorandum, Report on the Referral of the Situation involving the Lord's Resistance Army, Ug/Anlys/Phase1.

177   Southwick, K. Fall 2005. Investigating War in Northern Uganda: Dilemmas for the International Criminal Court. *Yale Journal of International Affairs*, 105-119, 109.

Some jurists argue that 'unwillingness' is not abstract, as a state may be unwilling to prosecute at the domestic level, but willing to do so before the ICC.[178] The OTP states that 'groups bitterly divided by conflict may oppose prosecutions at each others' hands and yet agree to a prosecution by a Court perceived as neutral and impartial'.[179] Examples from East Timor, Sierra Leone and, recently, Lebanon support such reasoning. This interpretation, however, could be contradictory with the requirement of 'unwillingness' as set out in Article 17. Article 17(2) requires a 'special intention', on behalf of the judicial authority, aimed at shielding the person concerned, or an intention not to bring the person concerned to justice, or unjustified delay that presumes bad faith.[180] In the scenario *supra*, 'unwillingness' to prosecute before a national court in favour of the ICC does not fulfil the 'special intention' requirement of 'unwillingness' under Article 17(2), as the intention of the state initially is not to shield, but to choose a different forum for prosecution.

To solve this dilemma, states may resort to 'self-referrals', which entails not taking any action. This is initially a situation in which the case is neither 'being investigated or prosecuted' (Article 17(1)(a) of the ICC Statute) nor 'has been investigated' (Article 17(1)(b) of the ICC Statute).[181] Thus, such a referral (accompanied by a lack of action at the national level) does not fall under 'unwillingness' or 'inability' under Article 17. This leads to a practical waiver of complementarity. The deliberate abstention from initiating a national investigation renders the international proceedings admissible vis-à-vis the (passive) referring state.[182] This practice is gaining grounds in law and legal policy.[183] The Democratic Republic of Congo (DRC) referral confirms this practice.[184] Furthermore, the *travaux préparatoires* do not demonstrate, or even suggest, that Article 17 prohibits voluntary relinquishment of national criminal jurisdiction to the ICC.[185]

---

178 Akhavan, P. April 2005. Developments at the International Criminal Court: The Lord's Resistance Army Case: Uganda's Submission of the First State Referral to the International Criminal Court. *The American Journal of International Law*, 99, 403-429, 415.

179 The International Criminal Court, Office of the Prosecutor. 2003. *Paper on Some Policy Issues before the Office of the Prosecutor*. ICC-OTP 2003, 1-9, 5. Available at: www.icc-cpi.int/library/organs/otp/030905_Policy_Paper.pdf [accessed: 20 February 2009].

180 Article 17(2) of the Rome Statute of the International Criminal Court, UN Doc. A/CONF.183/9.

181 Claus, K. December 2004. Self-Referrals and Waivers of Complementarity. *Journal of International Criminal Justice*, 2, 4, 944-950, 944.

182 Claus, K. December 2004. Self-Referrals and Waivers of Complementarity. *Journal of International Criminal Justice*, 2, 4, 944-950, 944-945.

183 Claus, K. December 2004. Self-Referrals and Waivers of Complementarity. *Journal of International Criminal Justice*, 2, 4, 944-950, 944.

184 Decision on the Prosecutor's Application for a Warrant of Arrest, Article 58, *Prosecutor* v. *Thomas Lubanga Dyilo*, Pre-Trial Chamber, ICC-01/04-01/06. 10 February 2006, para. 29-32.

185 Report of the Ad Hoc Committee on the Establishment of an International Criminal Court, UN GAOR, 50th Session, Supp. no. 22, para. 47, UN Doc. A/50/22 (1995).

Yet, this book argues that such prosecutorial interpretation is inconsistent with the purpose of the ICC, and the intention of the drafters, which is primarily to encourage national systems to prosecute when they are willing and able.

With respect to instances of 'unwillingness', voluntary state referrals are unlikely to be rendered admissible solely based on 'unwillingness' to carry out the investigation or prosecution.[186] This argument finds support in a number of aspects. Firstly, as mentioned earlier, the referral in itself is a sign of good intention,[187] and thus it is unlikely to find a state that voluntarily relinquishes its national jurisdiction to the ICC through self-referral while at the same time aims to shield the perpetrators, or applies justice in bad faith. Secondly, for a referral to be rendered admissible on the grounds of the unwillingness of a national judicial system, there should be an investigation taking place. Referrals, however, are typically intended for cases in which no judicial actions have been initiated.[188]

With respect to 'inability', under the complementarity principle a referral could be admissible due to inability of the state to carry out the investigation or prosecution. In other words, a state that is unable to obtain the accused or the necessary evidence and testimony or is otherwise unable to carry out its proceedings due to the total or substantial collapse or unavailability of the national judicial system can refer the situation to the ICC. This referral will be admissible under Article 17.[189] The DRC referral falls initially under this category. In the early days of the DRC referral, it was clearly that the collapsed judicial system in the Ituri region was in a state of disarray.[190]

Ugandan Referral and Admissibility Requirements

On 16 December 2003, the Republic of Uganda submitted the Referral of the Situation Concerning the Lord's Resistance Army to the ICC-OTP pursuant to Articles 13(a) and 14 of the Statute.[191] Paragraph 40 of the Ugandan referral reads:

---

186   Article 17(2) of the Rome Statute of the International Criminal Court, UN Doc. A/CONF.183/9.

187   Southwick, K. Fall 2005. Investigating War in Northern Uganda: Dilemmas for the International Criminal Court. *Yale Journal of International Affairs*, 105-119, 108.

188   Still there could be some exceptions to that. In the Ugandan case, the Ugandan authorities have conducted some form of investigations, at least in relation to some (lower-level) members of the LRA using treason and anti-terrorism legislation before referral.

189   Article 17(1)(b) and 17.3 of the Rome Statute of the International Criminal Court, UN Doc. A/CONF.183/9. Also, see in Moreno-Ocampo, L. March 2005. *The International Criminal Court: Hopes and Fears*, Coca-Cola World Fund at Yale Lecture, New Haven, 2.

190   Human Rights Watch. January 2004. *Democratic Republic of the Congo: Confronting Impunity*, 1-11, 4. Available at: http://hrw.org/english/docs/2004/02/02/congo7230_txt.htm [accessed: 22 May 2008].

191   ICC Press Release. 29 January 2004. *President of Uganda Refers Situation Concerning the Lord's Resistance Army (LRA) to the ICC*. Available at: www.icc-cpi.int

> Pursuant to Article 14(1) of ICC Statute, Uganda requested the prosecutor to investigate the situation concerning the LRA for the purpose of determining whether one or more specific persons should be charged with the commission of crimes against humanity for acts committed on or after 1st of July 2002.[192]

In the referral, the Republic of Uganda indicated that the ICC was the most appropriate and effective forum for the investigation into and prosecution of those bearing the greatest responsibility for the crimes within the referred situation, given the gravity of the crimes, the interests of the victims and the need to further national reconciliation and rehabilitation.

On 29 July 2004, the Prosecutor determined that there was a reasonable basis to initiate an investigation,[193] considering the available information – in light of the referral – a sufficient basis upon which to continue the analysis of the situation concerning the LRA and to determine whether to initiate an investigation.

In applying Article 17 to the Uganda referral, a number of contentious issues need to be discussed in order to analyse the conformity of the referral with the complementarity principle.

Ugandan judicial system and 'unwillingness'   Firstly, in terms of 'unwillingness', Uganda has shown on a number of occasions its willingness to prosecute UPDF soldiers for possible perpetration of international crimes. President Museveni stated the willingness of Uganda to prosecute any crimes committed by the UPDF: 'if cases (involving Ugandan military personnel) are brought to our attention, we will try them ourselves'.[194] This seems to be a 'selective' willingness. Nevertheless, the Ugandan position did not affect the ICC interpretation, as the Court considered the referral applicable to the whole situation in northern Uganda, including crimes committed by the LRA and the UPDF. The ICC Prosecutor considered himself mandated impartially to investigate all grave crimes in northern Uganda.[195] Jurists

---

[accessed: 22 May 2009].

    192   Uganda Referral, Unofficial Copy, ICC Document, Referral para. 40.

    193   The American Non-Governmental Organizations Coalition for the International Criminal Court; a Program of the United Nations Association of the United States of America. 16 February 2006. The Current Investigation by the ICC of the Situation in Northern Uganda, 1-10, 1. Available at: www.amicc.org [accessed: 16 March 2009].

    194   Agence France-Presse. 25 February 2004. Museveni Pledges to Cooperate with ICC to Probe Uganda War Crimes. Available at: www.spacewar.com/2004/040225143401.8peoxfh1.html [accessed: 25 March 2009].

    195   The American Non-Governmental Organizations Coalition for the International Criminal Court; a Program of the United Nations Association of the United States of America. 18 October 2005. The Current Investigation by the ICC of the Situation in Northern Uganda, 5. Available at: www.amicc.org [accessed: 11 December 2009].

such as Payam Akhavan,[196] Mahnoush H. Arsanjani and W. Michael Reisman[197] count Uganda as the first time of a referral for a state bearing 'willingness'.

In assessing 'unwillingness' under Article 17 and in the instance of the Ugandan referral, two important aspects need to be taken into consideration. Firstly, 'unwillingness', as elaborated in previous chapters, requires certain material and mental elements. According to the Office of the Prosecutor:

> [a] State is unwilling if the national decision has been made and proceedings are or were being undertaken for the purpose of shielding the person concerned from criminal responsibility; there has been an unjustified delay which is inconsistent with an intent to bring the person concerned to justice; or the proceedings were not or are not being conducted independently or impartially.[198]

The analysis of the actions of the Ugandan national system shows that there are no signs that Uganda is prosecuting LRA or UPDF war crimes or crimes against humanity for those most responsible, but the Ugandan authorities appear to have conducted some form of investigation, at least in relation to some (lower-level) members of the LRA using treason and anti-terrorism legislation.[199] These investigations are limited and target only a few low-level perpetrators. The Ugandan referral is a vivid indicator of Uganda's good intentions in terms of pursuing prosecution (at least with respect to LRA crimes). The Uganda instance then constitutes a case of 'no action' – no proceedings were held for those most responsible – but at the same time we cannot consider this lack of action an instance of shielding the persons concerned from criminal responsibility.

In a general assessment of Uganda's position with respect to 'unwillingness', one can deduce that the referral does not fall under the legal ambit of the 'unwillingness' test under Article 17. On the contrary, the Ugandan referral is a crucial indicator of the state's good faith. The actions taken against a few low-level perpetrators show that the proceedings did not aim to shield them, and were not accompanied by unjustified delay, which is inconsistent with an intent to bring them to justice.[200] Nonetheless, the OTP found the referral admissible as no action, until then, was taken against those most responsible by Uganda. The Ugandan

---

196   Akhavan, P. April 2005. Developments at the International Criminal Court: The Lord's Resistance Army Case: Uganda's Submission of the First State Referral to the International Criminal Court. *The American Journal of International Law*, 99, 403-429, 415.

197   Arsanjani, M.H. and Reisman, W.M. April 2005. The Law-in-Action of the International Criminal Court. *The American Journal of International Law*, 99, 2, 385-403, 397.

198   The International Criminal Court, Office of the Prosecutor. 2003. *Paper on Some Policy Issues before the Office of the Prosecutor*. ICC-OTP 2003, 1-9, 4. Available at: www.icc-cpi.int/library/organs/otp/030905_Policy_Paper.pdf [accessed: 20 February 2009].

199   See p. 155.

200   See pp. 155-8.

referral was thus not admissible on the ground of 'unwillingness', but rather on other grounds.

Ugandan judicial system and 'inability'   In terms of 'inability', Article 17(3) includes three criteria that the Court will take into consideration in determining whether the national system is able or not. The first two criteria are total or substantial collapse of the national judicial system, or unavailability of its national judicial system. The third criterion is the state's inability to obtain the accused or the necessary evidence and testimony or is otherwise unable to carry out its proceedings. Some states in the Rome Conference believed that requiring the two criteria could limit the Court's ability to act.[201] This necessitated the addition of the phrase 'or otherwise unable to carry out its proceedings'.[202] Hence, the ICC will render the referral admissible if the national judicial system is unable according to the requirements delineated *supra* according to Article 17(3) of the Statute.

The wording of this provision divides the criteria between two cumulative sets. The first two criteria constitute the first set, while the third criterion constitutes the second set. Hence, to fulfil the requirements of provision 17(3), the national system should be, firstly, either 'unavailable' or 'collapsed' *and*, secondly, the state must be unable to obtain the accused or the evidence and testimony, or otherwise unable to carry out proceedings.[203]

a.   *Total or substantial collapse, or unavailability*
With respect to the first set, the Ugandan judicial system does not suffer from substantial or total collapse. Despite the conflict in the north, the Ugandan judicial system remains functional.[204] The Ugandan referral itself confirms this in paragraphs 24 and 25 of the referral, which stipulate that 'there is no doubt that Ugandan courts have the capacity to give captured LRA leaders a fair and impartial trial'.[205] As for the term 'unavailability', as mentioned in the previous chapter, it is not defined in the Rome Statute, but rather left as an open-ended term that could have multiple interpretations. At the extreme, the system will very likely be designated 'unavailable' if

---

201   Holmes, J. 1999. The Principle of Complementarity, in *The International Criminal Court: The Making of the Rome Statute, Issues, Negotiations, Results*, edited by R. Lee. The Hague: Kluwer, 49.

202   El-Zeidy, M. Summer 2002. The Principle of Complementarity: A Machinery to Implement International Criminal Law. *Michigan Journal of International Law*, 23, 4, 869-978, 884.

203   The International Criminal Court, Office of the Prosecutor. 2003. *Informal Expert Paper: The Principle of Complementarity in Practice*. ICC-OTP 2003, 1-38, 14. Available at: www.icc-cpi.int/library/organs/otp/complementarity.pdf [accessed: 11 August 2009].

204   U.S. Department of State. January 2005. *Background Note on Uganda*. Available at: www.State.Gov/R/Pa/Ei/Bgn/2963.htm [accessed: 16 March 2009].

205   Uganda Referral, Unofficial Copy, ICC Document, Referral paragraphs 24 and 25.

the judicial system is simply non-existent.[206] Unlike the case of the DRC, where the judicial system in the Ituri region was destroyed at the time of the referral, this was not the case for Uganda.[207] Moreover, *the Informal Expert Paper: The Principle of Complementarity in Practice* indicated that:

> the following facts and evidences that may be relevant to the first set of considerations in the inability test (total or substantial collapse or unavailability of national judicial system):
> - Lack of necessary personnel, judges, investigators, and prosecutors;
> - Lack of judicial infrastructure;
> - Lack of substantive or procedural penal legislation rendering system 'unavailable';
> - Lack of access rendering system 'unavailable';
> - Obstruction by uncontrolled elements rendering system 'unavailable'; and
> - Amnesties, immunities rendering system 'unavailable'.[208]

In the analysis of this non-exhaustive list, one can conclude that the Ugandan judicial system does not lack the necessary personnel, judges, investigators, or prosecutors.[209] Moreover, the Ugandan system enjoys a well-structured judicial infrastructure.[210]

In addition, some jurists point out the wide acceptance of the reasoning that the defects of domestic codes and laws can render a national system

---

206   Cárdenas, C. 25-26 June 2004. The Admissibility Test Before The International Criminal Court Under Special Consideration of Amnesties And Truth Commissions, in *Complementary Views on Complementarity Proceedings of the International Roundtable on the Complementary Nature of the International Criminal Court, Amsterdam 25-26 June 2006*, edited by J. Kleffner and G. Kor. May 2006. Cambridge: Cambridge University Press, 8.

207   Citizens for Global Solutions. June 2004. In Uncharted Waters: Seeking Justice before the Atrocities Have Stopped, The International Criminal Court in Uganda and the Democratic of the Congo, 1-43, 20.

208   The International Criminal Court, Office of the Prosecutor. 2003. *Informal Expert Paper: The Principle of Complementarity in Practice.* ICC-OTP 2003, 1-38, 29. Available at: www.icc-cpi.int/library/organs/otp/complementarity.pdf [accessed: 11 August 2009].

209   Moy, H.A. Spring 2006. Recent Development: The International Criminal Court's Arrest Warrants and Uganda's Lord's Resistance Army: Renewing the Debate over Amnesty and Complementarity. *The Harvard Environmental Law Review*, 19, 267-277, 272.

210   The section *supra* on the Ugandan judicial system confirms that the system is functional and its structure was not affected by the conflict in the North. See also Moy, H.A. Spring 2006. Recent Development: The International Criminal Court's Arrest Warrants and Uganda's Lord's Resistance Army: Renewing the Debate over Amnesty and Complementarity. *The Harvard Environmental Law Review*, 19, 267-277, 272.

unavailable. However, Uganda can still prosecute ICC core crimes as ordinary crimes without violating Article 20 of the Statute.

One aspect of 'obstruction by uncontrolled elements rendering the system unavailable'[211] is worth further analysis. The scope of the terms 'obstruction' and 'uncontrolled' is questionable. This clause gains crucial importance, since it is on this basis that Uganda considered its system 'unavailable'.

Uganda's referral to the ICC reads, 'the referral concludes that any case involving LRA crimes would be admissible due to the fact that the Ugandan justice system is "unavailable" because of the inability to arrest the accused'.[212] The justification for their referral is the Ugandan judiciary's inability to arrest the suspects, rather than any inability or unwillingness to investigate and prosecute. Prosecutor Moreno-Ocampo himself has justified rendering the case admissible because the Ugandan government is unable to prosecute the LRA 'because [the rebels] are in Sudan' and it is difficult for Uganda to capture them.[213]

As shown above,[214] the Ugandan judicial system is not in a full or partial state of failure. The Ugandan judicial system is available and functioning, albeit it suffers from some malfunctions and obstacles.

In fact, this may be more the case in the DRC referral where the state of partial failure of the Congolese judicial system was initially materialized. Firstly, the Ituri region suffered from the absence of the necessary personnel, judges, investigators and prosecutors.[215] Secondly, there was a lack of judicial infrastructure; most courts were not functioning in Bunia, the personnel were not paid for years, the magistrates were badly trained, and there was mismanagement and corruption.[216] The ICC Prosecutor confirmed this in 'The Prosecution Submission of Further Information and Material' before the Pre-Trial Chamber.[217] Thirdly, the DRC arguably

---

211   The International Criminal Court, Office of the Prosecutor. 2003. *Informal Expert Paper: The Principle of Complementarity in Practice*. ICC-OTP 2003, 1-38, 29. Available at: www.icc-cpi.int/library/organs/otp/complementarity.pdf [accessed: 11 August 2009].

212   Uganda Referral, Unofficial Copy, ICC Document, Referral para. 30.

213   Moreno-Ocampo, L. March 2005. *The International Criminal Court: Hopes and Fears*, Coca-Cola World Fund at Yale Lecture, New Haven, 2.

214   See pp. 171-2.

215   Human Rights Watch. September 2004. A Human Rights Watch Briefing Paper: *Making Justice Work: Restoration of the Legal System in Ituri, DRC*. Available at: www. hrw.org/backgrounder/africa/drc0904/index.htm [accessed: 11 August 2009].

216   Human Rights Watch. January 2004. *Democratic Republic of the Congo: Confronting Impunity*, 1-11, 4. Available at: http://hrw.org/english/docs/2004/02/02/congo7230_txt.htm [accessed: 11 August 2009].

217   Prosecution's Submission of Further Information and Materials, *Prosecutor* v. *Thomas Lubanga Dyilo*, Pre-Trial Chamber I, ICC-01/04-01/06. 25 January 2006, para. 11-12.

continued to lack a substantive or a procedural penal legislation that incorporates the crimes of the Rome Statute in the national system. In the *Thomas Lubanga Diyalo* case, the ICC cited the DRC for not prosecuting Lubanga for the crime of conscripting and enlisting children under the age of 15 in armed conflict.[218] Also, vis-à-vis the lack of access to the judicial system, victims and witnesses were terrified to come before national courts to testify against possible perpetrators.[219] This put the judicial system in the Ituri region during the time of referral in a state of inability.[220]

The Ugandan government claimed in its referral that 'without international cooperation and assistance, it cannot succeed in arresting those members of the LRA leadership and others most responsible for the above mentioned crimes'.[221] One author argues that:

> This inability has nothing to do with the collapse or unavailability of the Ugandan judicial system as envisioned under Article 17, however. Uganda is unable to adjudicate the case because of the limited capabilities of its army, the tactical advantages of the insurgent group, and the complex role of Sudan, which has supported the LRA but permits the Ugandan army to cross its border to root out the rebels.[222]

The Court more likely relied on the requirement for an 'obstruction by uncontrolled elements rendering system unavailable', which was included in the *Informal Expert Paper: The Principle of Complementarity in Practice*,[223] in order to consider the Ugandan judicial system 'unavailable'. This move is dubious, as it was based on the lack of capability to capture the LRA commanders. This shortage is due to the deficiency in the law enforcement organs (police and army) to arrest the LRA perpetrators and not because of the unavailability of the judicial system. Mahnoush H. Arsanjani and W. Michael Reisman consider the Ugandan judicial system operational with no indication that is 'unavailable'.

---

218   Human Rights Watch. March 2007. *A Summary of the Case Law of the International Criminal Court*, 1-11, 2.

219   Global Rights. August 2005. S.O.S Justice, What Justice is there for Vulnerable Groups in Eastern DRC? 1-12, 6.

220   Global Rights. August 2005. S.O.S Justice, What Justice is there for Vulnerable Groups in Eastern DRC? 1-12, 6.

221   Uganda Referral, Unofficial Copy, ICC Document, Referral para. 24 and 25.

222   Southwick, K. Fall 2005. Investigating War in Northern Uganda: Dilemmas for the International Criminal Court. *Yale Journal of International Affairs*, 105-119, 108.

223   The International Criminal Court, Office of the Prosecutor. 2003. *Informal Expert Paper: The Principle of Complementarity in Practice*. ICC-OTP 2003, 1-38, 29. Available at: www.icc-cpi.int/library/organs/otp/complementarity.pdf [accessed: 11 August 2009].

In order to consider the judicial system 'unable', the system should first be either totally or substantially collapsed or unavailable, and then the system should be unable to obtain the accused or the necessary evidence and testimony or to carry out its proceedings.

b.   *'Inability to obtain the accused or the necessary evidence and testimony or otherwise unable to carry out its proceedings'*
The first and second sets are both required to establish 'inability'. The national authority must meet both the criteria of a total or substantial collapse or unavailability *and* the inability to obtain the accused or the necessary evidence and testimony or the inability to carry out its proceedings.[224] The Ugandan referral was rendered admissible because the rebels were difficult to capture.[225] There is no doubt that the Ugandan authorities are not able to capture LRA suspects, which falls under the inability of the Uganda authorities 'to obtain the accused'.[226] Uganda's referral thus meets this requirement, but even with respect to this criterion, an important question must be raised: if senior members of the LRA are arrested, what will be the status of this requirement? When those most responsible are arrested, the Ugandan authorities will become indirectly or directly 'able to obtain the accused'. Furthermore, the ICC is a court that lacks enforcement power, and rather depends on states' cooperation.[227] Therefore, if Uganda itself cannot obtain the accused, the DRC, Sudan must be called upon for assistance.[228] Sudan has already been uncooperative with the Court in the Darfur Security Council referral. Thus in practical terms, the inability to obtain the accused will be a problem for the ICC as well as Uganda. However, in the DRC case, the ICC enjoyed, in addition to the cooperation of the DRC, the support and cooperation of the UN mission MONUC. This advantage assisted in the

---

224   Holmes, J. 1999. The Principle of Complementarity, in *The International Criminal Court: The Making of the Rome Statute, Issues, Negotiations, Results*, edited by R. Lee. The Hague: Kluwer, 49.

225   Moreno-Ocampo, L. March 2005. *The International Criminal Court: Hopes and Fears*, Coca-Cola World Fund at Yale Lecture, New Haven, 2.

226   Article 17(3) of the Rome Statute of the International Criminal Court, UN Doc. A/CONF.183/9.

227   The International Criminal Court, Office of the Prosecutor. 2003. *Paper on Some Policy Issues before the Office of the Prosecutor*. ICC-OTP 2003, 1-9, 5. Available at: www.icc-cpi.int/library/organs/otp/030905_Policy_Paper.pdf [accessed: 20 February 2009].

228   In fact, the ICC has requested Uganda, Sudan and the Democratic Republic of Congo (DRC) to execute the warrants against the indicted LRA leadership. See Apuuli, K.Ph. 1 March 2006. The ICC Arrest Warrants for the Lord's Resistance Army Leaders and Peace Prospects for Northern Uganda. *Journal of International Criminal Justice*, 49, 179-187, 184.

initiation of the first trial against the accused Lubanga after being captured post the Ndoki attack against MONUC.[229]

If the accused LRA commanders are arrested and surrendered to the ICC, Uganda, among others (Sudan, DRC, or the LRA accused commanders), can challenge the jurisdiction of the Court once in non-exceptional circumstances: LRA suspects when arrested may challenge the admissibility of the ICC on the ground that Uganda is not anymore unable to obtain the accused. The challenge may take place prior to or at the commencement of the trial.[230] Such a challenge, if it occurs, will have an important and complex impact on understanding the Court's interpretation of the complementarity principle on this aspect.

The discussion above on the Ugandan referral and on 'inability' can be summarized as the following: while Uganda is unable to obtain the accused, this does not entail that the Ugandan judicial system is unavailable. The failure of Uganda to capture the suspects is not due to the inability of the judicial system, but because its law enforcement body 'could not succeed in arresting those members of the LRA leadership and others most responsible for the above mentioned crimes'.[231] This is inadequate for designating the Ugandan judiciary unavailable.[232] Furthermore, if we accept this reasoning, then national judicial systems unable to obtain the accused because a foreign hosting state refuses to extradite, can be considered 'unavailable', hence rendering the case admissible before the ICC.[233] Such a scenario could create undesired complexities, needless to say that it is inconsistent with the aim of the

---

229   Prosecution's Submission of Further Information and Materials, *Prosecutor v. Thomas Lubanga Dyilo*, Pre-Trial Chamber I, ICC-01/04-01/06. 25 January 2006. Paragraph 8.

230   Article 19(4) of the Rome Statute of the International Criminal Court, UN Doc. A/CONF.183/9.

231   Uganda Referral, Unofficial Copy, ICC Document, Referral para. 24 and 25.

232   'Certain NGOs consider that Uganda has a relatively well functioning criminal justice system'. See The American Non-Governmental Organizations Coalition For The International Criminal Court: A Program of the United Nations Association of the United States of American. 18 October 2005. ICC: The Current Investigation by the ICC of the Situation in Northern Uganda. Available at: www.amicc.org [accessed: 10 October 2009].

233   The Informal Paper on the Principle of Complementarity includes a list of factors that would render the system 'unavailable'. The list does not include the reason stipulated in the Ugandan Referral to render the Ugandan judicial system 'unavailable'. See The International Criminal Court, Office of the Prosecutor. 2003. *Informal Expert Paper: The Principle of Complementarity in Practice*. ICC-OTP 2003, 1-38, 29. Available at: www.icc-cpi.int/library/organs/otp/complementarity.pdf [accessed: 11 August 2009].

drafters of the statute to preserve the primary jurisdiction of state parties under the complementarity principle.[234]

Moreover, the inability of the Ugandan judicial system is attributed to factors other than a total or substantial collapsed judicial system, which raises the question of whether a state party's referral would unnecessarily entangle the ICC in political complexities.[235]

'Inaction' According to Article 17, cases may be deemed inadmissible in circumstances where the relevant state is taking action, or has taken action, in relation to a case. According to the Office of the Prosecutor, in cases where the relevant state is neither investigating nor prosecuting, the case will be admissible before the ICC.[236]

Accordingly, in relation to those bearing the greatest responsibility for crimes committed in northern Uganda, the Ugandan authorities have not conducted national proceedings,[237] preferring instead that the cases be dealt with by the ICC. Hence, no action has been taken or was intended to be taken by the Ugandan judicial system to investigate or prosecute those most responsible for international crimes within the northern Uganda situation. In strict legal terms, referral within these parameters will be rendered admissible as long as the ICC is adopting such an interpretation.[238]

It seems that there is nothing in law or policy to indicate that states cannot voluntarily relinquish their jurisdiction to the ICC.[239] Yet, bearing in mind the primary duty of states to exercise its criminal jurisdiction over international

---

234   Preamble of the Rome Statute of the International Criminal Court, UN Doc. A/CONF.183. Also, The International Criminal Court, Office of the Prosecutor. 2003. *Paper on Some Policy Issues before the Office of the Prosecutor.* ICC-OTP 2003, 1-9. Available at: www.icc-cpi.int/library/organs/otp/030905_Policy_Paper.pdf [accessed: 20 February 2009].

235   Southwick, K. Fall 2005. Investigating War in Northern Uganda: Dilemmas for the International Criminal Court. *Yale Journal of International Affairs*, 105-119, 108. See also Arsanjani, M.H. and Reisman, W.M. April 2005. The Law-in-Action of the International Criminal Court. *The American Journal of International Law*, 99, 2, 385-403, 395.

236   International Criminal Court, Office of the Prosecutor, JCCD. *Internal Memorandum: Report on the Referral of the Situation involving the Lord's Resistance Army.* Ug/Anlys/Phase1, 1-12, 6.

237   The Ugandan Referral implies this reality. ICC Referral. 29 January 2004. *President of Uganda Refers Situation Concerning the Lord's Resistance Army (LRA) to the ICC.* The Hague. Available at: www.icc-cpi.int/php/index.php [accessed: 21 March 2009].

238   The International Criminal Court, Office of the Prosecutor. 2003. *Paper on Some Policy Issues before the Office of the Prosecutor.* ICC-OTP 2003, 1-9. Available at: www. icc-cpi.int/library/organs/otp/030905_Policy_Paper.pdf [accessed: 20 February 2009].

239   Akhavan, P. April 2005. Developments at the International Criminal Court: The Lord's Resistance Army Case: Uganda's Submission of the First State Referral to the International Criminal Court. *The American Journal of International Law*, 99, 403-429, 414.

crimes,[240] such policy can have a negative impact on the ICC's image and efficiency, as 'willing and able' states can 'throw the load' to the ICC to prosecute international crimes for various reasons without fulfilling their primary duty to prosecute. Such a situation will not encourage national systems to prosecute international crimes, but rather the opposite, as states may choose to relinquish their jurisdiction for political, financial and other domestic reasons.

Although the Ugandan judiciary took no action against the top leaders of the LRA, the ICC Prosecutor did not choose to render the referral admissible on these grounds. In theory, there is nothing preventing the Prosecutor from rendering the referral admissible on the grounds of 'no action' taken by Uganda against those most responsible. Later, the ICC relied heavily on the 'inaction' scenario to render the case of the senior leadership of the LRA admissible.

On the other hand, in the DRC referral the ICC Prosecutor, and then the Pre-Trial Chamber adopted a pragmatic position, considering the DRC as not having taken action regarding the crimes the Court has been investigating. The DRC authorities arrested Lubanga and accused him of crimes allegedly committed by the FPLC in or after military attacks from May 2003 onward. The ICC Prosecutor stated that he has not focused on these crimes during this period.[241] The DRC authorities issued an arrest warrant on 19 March 2005 against Thomas Lubanga charging him with the crime of genocide (Article 164 of the DRC Military Criminal Code) and crimes against humanity (Articles 166-169 of the DRC Military Criminal Code), in addition to the ordinary crimes of murder and illegal detention.[242] However, the definitions of some of these crimes are different from internationally recognized definitions. For instance, crimes against humanity in Article 166 of the Military Criminal Code are within Article 8 of the Rome Statute subsumed under war crimes.[243] The Prosecutor issued an arrest warrant against Thomas Lubanga Diyalo for enlisting and conscripting children under 15 in armed conflict (Article 8 of the Rome Statute). The pragmatic stand is vivid in the Pre-Trial Chamber decision when it considered that it is a condition *sine qua non* for a case, within the investigation of a situation, to be inadmissible that national proceedings encompass both the

---

240　The Preamble of The Statute delineates the primary duty of states to exercise its criminal jurisdiction over international crimes, and the Court's jurisdiction is to complement national jurisdiction. See Preamble, paragraphs 6 and 10 of the Rome Statute of the International Criminal Court, UN Doc. A/CONF.183/9.

241　Prosecution's Submission of Further Information and Materials, *Prosecutor* v. *Thomas Lubanga Dyilo*, Pre-Trial Chamber I, ICC-01/04-01/06. 25 January 2009. Paras 18 and 20.

242　Decision on the Prosecutor's Application for a Warrant of Arrest, Article 58, *Prosecutor* v. *Thomas Lubanga Dyilo*, Pre-Trial Chamber, ICC-01/04-01/06. 10 February 2006. Para. 33.

243　Wetsh'okondo Kosos, M. February 2005. *Human Rights and Justice Sector Reform in Africa: Why Congo Need the ICC?*, Open Society Justice Initiative, 58-62, 60-61. Available at: www.justiceinitiative.org/db/resource2/fs?..&rand=0.849487244243 [accessed: 5 June 2009].

conduct and the person subject of the case.[244] The ICC invoked the same grounds for admissibility in *Mathieu Ngudjolo Chui* case. In fact, the same legal language on admissibility in Lubanga's case is repeated *verbatim* in the Pre-Trial Chamber I decision concerning the evidence and information provided by the Prosecutor for the issuance of a warrant of arrest.[245]

The Prosecutor's application before the Pre-Trial Chamber was for charges of child conscripting and enlisting. The Pre-Trial Chamber adopted a pragmatic position, qualifying the case as a set of 'specific incidents during which one or more specific crimes within the jurisdiction of the Court seem to have been committed by one or more identified suspects'.[246] Based on this, the Pre-Trial Chamber found that the DRC arrest warrants contained no reference to Thomas Lubanga's alleged criminal responsibility in enlisting and using children under 15 years old to actively participate in hostilities as part of the UPC/FPLC's policy and practice.[247] The Office of the Prosecutor has delineated in its policy paper that 'there is no impediment to the admissibility of a case before the Court where no State has initiated any investigation. There may be cases where inaction by States is the appropriate course of action'.[248] In a strict reading of the above, the interpretation adopted by the Pre-Trial Chamber does not contravene Article 17 of the Statute nor is it inconsistent with the Prosecutor's policy paper. However, this author considers the Court's stand is pragmatic in the sense that the accused was already arrested and indicted for crimes against humanity and genocide, and the Statute of the ICC stressed positive cooperation between the Court and the state parties. Since the ICC signed a cooperation agreement with the DRC, the ICC could have cooperated with the DRC to amend the national indictment that is being investigated by the local authorities to include the incidents of interest to the ICC, i.e. crimes within the jurisdiction of the Court. The drafters of the Rome Statute aimed to establish a court that can exercise jurisdiction when the states do

---

244 Decision on the Prosecutor's Application for a Warrant of Arrest, Article 58, *Prosecutor* v. *Thomas Lubanga Dyilo*, Pre-Trial Chamber, ICC-01/04-01/06. 10 February 2006. 1-65, para. 20.

245 Decision on the Evidence and Information Provided By the Prosecution For The Issuance of a Warrant of Arrest for Mathieu Ngudjolo Chui Situation in the Democratic Republic of the Congo, Pre-Trial Chamber I, the Case of The *Prosecutor* v. *Mathieu Ngudjolo Chui*, unsealed on 12 February 2008, ICC-01/04-02/07 (6 July 2007), paragraph 21.

246 Decision on the Prosecutor's Application for a Warrant of Arrest, Article 58, *Prosecutor* v. *Thomas Lubanga Dyilo*, Pre-Trial Chamber, ICC-01/04-01/06. 10 February 2006. 1-65, para. 21.

247 Decision on the Prosecutor's Application for a Warrant of Arrest, Article 58, *Prosecutor* v. *Thomas Lubanga Dyilo*, Pre-Trial Chamber, ICC-01/04-01/06. 10 February 2006. 1-65, para. 38.

248 The International Criminal Court, Office of the Prosecutor. 2003. *Paper on Some Policy Issues before the Office of the Prosecutor.* ICC-OTP 2003, 1-9, 5. Available at: www.icc-cpi.int/library/organs/otp/030905_Policy_Paper.pdf [accessed: 20 February 2009].

not execute their primary role in this regard.[249] However, in the *Lubanga case*, the DRC was exercising its primary role of prosecuting international crimes alleged to Thomas Lubanga (yet not precisely the same conduct).

This same argument is applicable to the *Katanga* case, where Germain Katanga was also already under the custody of the Congolese authorities in Kinshasa long before the Pre-Trial Chamber issued his arrest warrant on 2 July 2007.[250] In fact, according to William Schabas, the DRC's justice system was doing a better job, because it was addressing crimes of greater gravity.[251] If the ICC Prosecutor aims to maximize the impact of his investigations, one can raise the question about the benefits of considering the DRC in a status of 'inaction' when the DRC is willing and already detained the accused Lubanga. The answer is negative, and the application of complementarity in this sense does not seem to contribute to the national DRC system.

Back to the Ugandan case, the admissibility of the Ugandan 'inaction' referral remains in conformity with the prosecutorial policy of the ICC.[252] However, this study indicates that such a policy of admissibility can create political and practical complexities that could hamper the Court's initial role aimed to encourage national systems to fulfil their duties under the Statute, and to prosecute international crimes. A pattern of rendering all 'inaction' referrals admissible could lead to contradictory results within the prosecutorial policy of the OTP itself. For instance, on the one hand, the *Paper on Some Policy Issues before the Office of the Prosecutor* stresses the importance of encouraging national systems to exercise their primary duty to prosecute crimes that fall under the ambit of the Statute,[253] while, on the other hand, since the ICC's policy will render admissible all referrals where no action was taken by national authorities, there is a danger that such a policy will encourage 'laziness' on the part of state parties to investigate and prosecute. States in many instances may prefer to refer the cases to the Court despite having an able and willing judicial system. The referral will transfer the burden from the states to the ICC along with the attached political, financial and social complexities.

---

249   Preamble of the Rome Statute of the International Criminal Court, UN Doc. A/CONF.183/9.

250   The International Criminal Court, Office of the Prosecutor. 18 October 2007. *Background Information Sheet Situation in the Democratic Republic of the Congo – Case of Germain Katanga.* Available at: www.icc-cpi.int/library/cases/ICC-01-04-01-07-BckInfo-ENG.pdf [accessed: 25 March 2009].

251   Schabas, W. 23 June 2007. *Complementarity in Practice: Some Uncomplimentary Thoughts,* Presentation at the 20th Anniversary Conference of the International Society for the Reform of Criminal Law, Vancouver, 1-28, 20.

252   The International Criminal Court, Office of the Prosecutor. 2003. *Paper on Some Policy Issues before the Office of the Prosecutor.* ICC-OTP 2003, 1-9. Available at: www.icc-cpi.int/library/organs/otp/030905_Policy_Paper.pdf [accessed: 20 February 2009].

253   The International Criminal Court, Office of the Prosecutor. 2003. *Paper on Some Policy Issues before the Office of the Prosecutor.* ICC-OTP 2003, 1-9. Available at: www.icc-cpi.int/library/organs/otp/030905_Policy_Paper.pdf [accessed: 20 February 2009].

There exists a real concern that instead of stimulating national judicial systems to take positive actions to prosecute these crimes, such a policy will encourage states to pass their duties onto the ICC. In addition, states benefit from referring the situation to the ICC by avoiding the financial costs of such prosecutions. If this becomes a trend, the ICC may become overburdened and end up being a judicial shopping forum for able and willing states that prefer to use the Court instead of their national judicial systems.[254]

Furthermore, the ICC's interpretation of inaction, as was shown in the DRC case, was restrictive. The ICC was probably able to cooperate with the DRC to amend its arrest warrants to include crimes included in the case investigated by the ICC. One may argue that the DRC did not adopt the ICC Bill at that time,[255] and thus some of the core crimes of the ICC were not yet incorporated in the national criminal law. However, Article 20 of the Statute does not prevent states from prosecuting ICC crimes as ordinary ones, and the DRC can still prosecute through such means.

Conclusion on Uganda's referral (accolades and criticism)   There are number of positive and negative aspects that have evolved during this short practice of the ICC. On one hand, the policy of encouraging state referrals had a positive impact since it has allowed the Court to function in a cooperative setting that could assist in facilitating a supportive environment. In such an atmosphere, the Prosecutor would be guaranteed the assistance of the national authorities in his investigations, and in providing the necessary level of protection to investigators and witnesses.[256] Such a cooperation allows for the division of labour between the ICC and the national judicial system in which a burden-sharing arrangement is reached, whereby the cases of those most responsible are dealt with by the ICC, whilst cases of low-level perpetrators are processed through the national justice system.[257]

---

254   Arsanjani, M.H. and Reisman, W.M. April 2005. The Law-in-Action of the International Criminal Court. *The American Journal of International Law*, 99, 2, 385-403, 392.

255   Amnesty International. 3 February 2006. *Democratic Republic of Congo: Parliament must Reform and Enact International Criminal Court Bill*, AI Index: AFR 62/002/2006. Available at: http://web.amnesty.org/library/Index/ENGAFR620022006?ope n&of=ENG-COD [accessed: 24 June 2009].

256   Based on the Annex of the Prosecutor Policy Paper on Some Policy Issues before the Office of the Prosecutor, 'under the Statute, the Prosecutor relies on co-operation to carry out his investigation, the Prosecutor will in general seek where possible to make this support explicit through a referral'. See The International Criminal Court, Office of the Prosecutor. 2003. *Paper on Some Policy Issues before the Office of the Prosecutor*. ICC-OTP 2003, 1-9, 4. Available at: www.icc-cpi.int/library/organs/otp/030905_Policy_Paper. pdf [accessed: 20 February 2009].

257   The International Criminal Court, Office of the Prosecutor. 2003. *Paper on Some Policy Issues before the Office of the Prosecutor*. ICC-OTP 2003, 1-9, 5. Available at: www.

On the other hand, the Ugandan referral displays a number of negative aspects of the ICC in practice. Firstly, according to a number of reports, Uganda does not seem to fulfil the 'inability' criterion as stipulated in Article 17:[258] the Ugandan system is unable to arrest the suspects, rather than being unable or unwilling to investigate and prosecute.

Secondly, the Ugandan referral was initially a 'selective or asymmetrical self-referral', that is Uganda only referred the LRA crimes in northern Uganda.[259] The Prosecutor was aware of that, and construed the referral as entailing the referral of the whole situation in northern Uganda.[260] Moreno-Ocampo interpreted the reference to the 'situation concerning the Lord's Resistance Army' as covering 'crimes within the situation of northern Uganda by whomever committed'.[261] This interpretation is in conformity with the requirements of the ICC Statute, specifically Article 14 and Rule 44(2) of the Rules of Procedure and Evidence (RPE).[262]

Thirdly, the policy of encouraging and seeking state referrals[263] might lead to certain negative outcomes vis-à-vis fulfilling the purposes of the Statute to end impunity and to affirm state duties to prosecute international crimes.[264] One author considers that '[a] policy of actively seeking self-referrals is more problematic in that it may inadvertently give rise to expectations of a *quid pro quo* while the prosecutor can promise no more than to do international justice objectively, and in a fair and efficient manner'.[265]

---

icc-cpi.int/library/organs/otp/030905_Policy_Paper.pdf [accessed: 20 February 2009].

258   Southwick, K. Fall 2005. Investigating War in Northern Uganda: Dilemmas for the International Criminal Court. *Yale Journal of International Affairs*, 105-119, 109. See also, Arsanjani, M.H. and Reisman, W.M. April 2005. The Law-in-Action of the International Criminal Court. *The American Journal of International Law*, 99, 2, 385-403, 397.

259   International Criminal Court. 29 January 2004. *Press Release; President of Uganda Refers Situation Concerning The Lord's Resistance Army (LRA) To The ICC*. The Hague, ICC-20040129-44-En.

260   Claus, K. December 2004. Self-Referrals and Waivers of Complementarity. *Journal of International Criminal Justice*, 2, 4, 944-950, 946.

261   Letter by the Chief Prosecutor of 17 June 2004 addressed to the President of the ICC as attached to the decisions of the Presidency of ICC; The Decision of the Presidency Assigning the Situation in Uganda to Pre-Trial Chamber II, 5 July 2004, ICC-02/04.

262   On that provision, see Lindenmann, J. 2001. The Rules of Procedure and Evidence on Jurisdiction and Admissibility, in *International and National Prosecution of Crimes under International Law*, edited by H. Fischer, C. Kress and S.R. Lueder. Berlin: Berlin Verlag Arno Spitz GmbH/Berliner Wissenschaftsverlag, 181-182.

263   The International Criminal Court, Office of the Prosecutor. 2003. *Paper on Some Policy Issues before the Office of the Prosecutor*. ICC-OTP 2003, 1-9, 4. Available at: www.icc-cpi.int/library/organs/otp/030905_Policy_Paper.pdf [accessed: 20 February 2009].

264   Preamble of the Rome Statute of the International Criminal Court, UN Doc. A/CONF.183/9.

265   Claus, K. December 2004. Self-Referrals and Waivers of Complementarity. *Journal of International Criminal Justice*, 2, 4, 944-950, 947.

In simple words, 'inaction' will render the case admissible. In such a scenario, an enormous range of cases could be potentially admissible, and a *de facto* waiver of complementarity is most probable.[266] The complementarity principle was the result of a compromise reached within the negotiating process for the Rome Statute. The mechanism was thereby shaped to recognize and respect the primary duty of states to prosecute these core crimes over which they have jurisdiction. It is only when states do not exercise this right and duty that the ICC will exercise jurisdiction. According to the ICC prosecutorial policy, when states wilfully refer a situation, they consciously defer their jurisdictional right to the ICC, and the complementarity principle becomes substantially unnecessary, as the states themselves have waived their uncontested right to prosecute in favour of the ICC. However, following the analysis above, this could lead to undesirable results, as states may become more and more reluctant to prosecute, leaving the responsibility to the ICC. Referring to the ICC may in various cases be favoured for political motives since states may prefer to ease certain pressures by passing on the burden of international justice.[267] Moreover, the referral will always be the least expensive, as the financial burden will fall on the ICC, and the state will be relieved from the expenses entailed by national prosecutions.[268] The prosecutorial policy of the ICC should be aware of such realities and prevent the Court from becoming a judicial shopping forum for states able and willing to prosecute, but reluctant to exercise their duties under the Statute. Unrestricted referrals will weaken the Court's potential to encourage states to investigate and prosecute international crimes, and might overburden the limited resources of the Court.

---

266   According to El-Zeidy, such a possibility was not completely ruled out in the discussions of the 1995 Ad hoc Committee. See El-Zeidy, M. 2005. The Ugandan Government Triggers the First Test of the Complementarity Principle: An Assessment of the First State's Party Referral to the ICC. *International Criminal Law Review*, 5, 83-119, 100.

267   The Refugee Law Project's indicates that the Ugandan referral served, among others, two political interests for the Ugandan government; the referral 'shifted public and international discourse from the plight of the people affected by the war and the need to end it through peaceful means to discourses on justice and punishing perpetrators of crimes against humanity and war crimes', and the referral represented 'a trump card to re-assert democratic credentials at the International level, ones which had been damaged by the failure of *Operation Iron Fist*'. See The Refugee Law Project. 28 July 2004. *The Refugee Law Project's Position Paper on the Announcement of Formal Investigations of the Lord's Resistance Army by the Chief Prosecutor of the International Criminal Court and its Implications on the Search for Peaceful Solutions to the War in Northern Uganda*, 1-12. Available at: www.refugeelawproject.org/resources/papers/archive/2004/RLP.ICC. investig.pdf [accessed: 18 September 2008].

268   Practically the burden will fall on all state parties cumulatively through their contribution to the budget of the ICC.

Gravity as an Admissibility Criterion

Article 17(1)(d) speaks about the gravity of the 'case' as an admissibility criterion different from the gravity of the crime criterion stipulated under Article 53(1)(c). The use of the term 'case' in the Statute is complicating and confusing. Within the admissibility criteria, the Statute refers to 'cases', but its meaning is applicable to both situations and cases.[269] One author states that:

> It is also necessary to point out that the content of the expression 'case' in the Statute is, in our view, quite confusing. Article 17, for example, in defining the concepts of admissibility or inadmissibility, refers exclusively to 'cases'. However, these concepts are applicable both in the context of situations of crisis in the framework of the triggering procedure and in the context of 'cases' in the framework of the criminal proceedings.[270]

This is due to a number of factors: firstly, Article 17 was drafted before the distinction between situations and cases was introduced.[271] Secondly, many changes and amendments were included in the final package, and time constraints prevented the drafters from adjusting the definition of the concepts of admissibility in light of the distinction between 'situations' and 'cases'.[272]

In practice, to assess 'the gravity of the case', the ICC must assess both the 'gravity of the crimes' and 'those bearing the greatest responsibility' for those crimes within its assessment of the admissibility factor of 'sufficient gravity of the case' under Article 17, paragraph 1(d). The *Paper on Some Policy Issues before the Office of the Prosecutor* stipulates that 'the concept of gravity should not be exclusively attached to the act that constituted the crime but also to the degree of participation in its commission'.[273] In terms of crimes, the prosecutorial policy of the ICC has indicated its intention to adopt a sequenced selection process while

---

269   Olasolo, H. 2005. The Triggering Procedure of the International Criminal Court, Procedural Treatment of the Principle of Complementarity, and the Role of Office of The Prosecutor. *International Criminal Law Review*, 5, 121–146, 129.

270   Olasolo, H. 2005. The Triggering Procedure of the International Criminal Court, Procedural Treatment of the Principle of Complementarity, and the Role of Office of The Prosecutor. *International Criminal Law Review*, 5, 121–146, 129.

271   Olasolo, H. 2005. The Triggering Procedure of the International Criminal Court, Procedural Treatment of the Principle of Complementarity, and the Role of Office of The Prosecutor. *International Criminal Law Review*, 5, 121–146, 129.

272   Williams, Sh.A. 1999. Article 17: Issues of Admissibility, in *Commentary on the Rome Statute of the International Criminal Court: Observer's Note, Article by Article*, edited by O. Triffterer. Baden-Baden: Nomos Verlagsgesellschaft, 383-394, 387-388.

273   The International Criminal Court, Office of the Prosecutor. 2003. *Paper on Some Policy Issues before the Office of the Prosecutor*. ICC-OTP 2003, 1-9, 6. Available at: www.icc-cpi.int/library/organs/otp/030905_Policy_Paper.pdf [accessed: 20 February 2009].

assessing the 'gravity' of the situation.[274] In other words, the ICC will prioritize situations according to gravity. Moreno-Ocampo argued that the DRC and Darfur situations were the most grave, and ranked the Ugandan case as the third gravest situation the ICC was looking into at the time.[275] The Pre-Trial Chamber confirmed this in the *Prosecutor* v. *Lubanga* case, where it adopted a gravity-driven selection of the crimes within which the conduct presented particular features rendering the case especially grave.[276] That becomes realized by the systematic pattern of incidence or large-scale occurrence, and by causing social alarm in the international community.[277]

Furthermore, the Prosecutor indicated that the factors required to assess the 'gravity' threshold include 'the nature of the crimes, the scale of the crimes, the manner in which the crimes were committed, the impact of the crimes',[278] and the number of victims, particularly of the most serious crimes.[279] The Office of the Prosecutor elaborated further criteria that need to be taken into consideration as indicative of 'gravity'. These criteria are: the number of persons apparently involved in the crime; the level of perpetration of the persons involved; and the availability of national proceedings, at least in respect of some of the alleged perpetrators.[280]

In the assessment of the Ugandan case, the ICC Prosecutor indicated that one of the factors he took into consideration was the number of victims,[281] particularly in the most serious crimes such as killings, because killings are normally reported.

---

274 Moreno-Ocampo, L. 2006. Symposium: International Criminal Tribunals in the 21st Century: Keynote Address: Integrating the Work of the ICC into Local Justice Initiatives. *American University International Law Review*, 21, 497-503, 499.

275 Moreno-Ocampo, L. 2006. Symposium: International Criminal Tribunals in the 21st Century: Keynote Address: Integrating the Work of the ICC into Local Justice Initiatives. *American University International Law Review*, 21, 497-503, 499.

276 Decision on the Prosecutor's Application for a Warrant of Arrest, Article 58, *Prosecutor* v. *Thomas Lubanga Dyilo*, Pre-Trial Chamber, ICC-01/04-01/06. 10 February 2006, para. 45.

277 Decision on the Prosecutor's Application for a Warrant of Arrest, Article 58, *Prosecutor* v. *Thomas Lubanga Dyilo*, Pre-Trial Chamber, ICC-01/04-01/06. 10 February 2006, para. 46.

278 The International Criminal Court, Office of the Prosecutor. 2003. *Paper on Some Policy Issues before the Office of the Prosecutor*. ICC-OTP 2003, 1-9, 5. Available at: www.icc-cpi.int/library/organs/otp/030905_Policy_Paper.pdf [accessed: 20 February 2009].

279 Moreno-Ocampo, L. 2006. Symposium: International Criminal Tribunals in the 21st Century: Keynote Address: Integrating the Work of the ICC into Local Justice Initiatives. *American University International Law Review*, 21, 497-503, 499.

280 The International Criminal Court, Office of the Prosecutor. 17 February 2005. *Revised Discussion Paper on ICC-OTP Case Selection Criteria*, 11.

281 Moreno-Ocampo, L. 2006. Symposium: International Criminal Tribunals in the 21st Century: Keynote Address: Integrating the Work of the ICC into Local Justice Initiatives. *American University International Law Review*, 21, 497-503.

However, the OTP considered that there appeared to have been serious crimes committed within the territory of Uganda (state party) or within the territory of Sudan (non-state party) by nationals of a state party (Ugandans). The crimes include murder, enslavement, torture, rape and other forms of sexual violence, enforced disappearance, and other inhumane acts, committed as part of a widespread and systematic attack against a civilian population.[282] In term of the number of victims, various human rights groups and witnesses accused the LRA rebels of such crimes.[283] The LRA rebels were also accused of abducting, indoctrinating and physically and sexually abusing young children. They abducted more than 20,000 children and forced them to become child soldiers.[284] This is clearly a war crime committed on a wide scale.[285] The outcome of this war has been thousands of deaths and the displacement of over 1.4 million people in northern Uganda and Acholiland.[286]

Another factor the Prosecutor has taken into account is the impact of crimes.[287] No doubt, the impact of the crimes on the Ugandan civilians in the north was massive. Thousands have suffered and more than a million displaced.

It was not difficult for the ICC Prosecutor to conclude that the elements of gravity were fulfilled in the Ugandan case. The Prosecutor initially invoked a quantitative view towards 'sufficient gravity', but Moreno-Ocampo left the door open for a qualitative interpretation of 'gravity'. He himself raises the question of whether gravity is simply the number of killings, or if it is constituted by

---

282   International Criminal Court. 14 October 2005. *Warrants of Arrest Unsealed Against Five LRA Commanders*. Press Release. The Hague. ICC20051410.056-En. Available at: www.icc-cpi.int/press/pressreleases/114.html [accessed: 9 December 2008]. Also, Amnesty International. 4 August 2006. *Public Statement: Uganda: Amnesty International Calls for an Effective Alternative to Impunity*. AI Index: AFR 59/004/2006, News Service No. 203. Available at: www.amnestyusa.org/regions/africa/document. do?id=ENGAFR590042006 [accessed: 9 December 2008].

283   The American Non-Governmental Organizations Coalition For The International Criminal Court: A Program of the United Nations Association of the United States of America. 16 February 2006. First Arrest Warrants Issued for Lord's Resistance Army, 1-8, 2. Available at: www.amicc.org [accessed: 9 March 2009].

284   IRIN News. 9 June 2005. *The UN Office for the Coordination of Humanitarian Affairs (OCHA); Uganda, Waiting for Elusive Peace in the War-Ravaged North*. Available at: www.irinnews.org/report.asp?ReportID=47568&SelectRegion=East_Africa [accessed: 9 December 2008].

285   Article 8 of the Rome Statute of the International Criminal Court, UN Doc. A/CONF.183/9.

286   IRIN News. 9 June 2005. *The UN Office for the Coordination of Humanitarian Affairs (OCHA); Uganda, Waiting for Elusive Peace in the War-Ravaged North*. Available at: www.irinnews.org/report.asp?ReportID=47568&SelectRegion=East_Africa [accessed: 9 December 2007].

287   Moreno-Ocampo, L. 2006. Symposium: International Criminal Tribunals in the 21st Century: Keynote Address: Integrating the Work of the ICC into Local Justice Initiatives. *American University International Law Review*, 21, 497-503, 499.

other factors, with wider-scale implications.[288] The inclusion of the 'impact of the crime' as one of the factors in determining the gravity adds a qualitative criterion to the assessment of 'gravity'.

Despite the OTP's attempt to establish a defined objective policy and strategy regarding, *inter alia*, 'sufficient gravity', the term remains somewhat open-ended. For instance, at what level should the Prosecutor draw the line to determine the number of victims that will make the crime be of sufficient gravity? For example, would 100 deaths be enough, and 98 insufficient?

Although the ICC Prosecutor stated that he would apply impartiality when addressing the 'gravity' criterion,[289] criticism was raised against the one-sided investigation of the LRA (the UPDF's alleged crimes were excluded from any investigation). Human Rights Watch and the Refugee Law Project (RLP) of Makerere University criticized the ICC for ignoring numerous documented instances in which UPDF soldiers committed war crimes that could fall under the jurisdiction of the ICC, such as rapes, torture, killings, and arbitrary arrests and detentions of the civilian population in northern Uganda.[290] The Prosecutor's answer to these criticisms was logical but no less pragmatic. He indicated that impartiality itself requires equal application of the 'gravity' criterion on both parties to the conflict, and since, according to Moreno-Ocampo, the LRA crimes were much graver than those of the UPDF, the OTP decided to initiate investigation of the crimes committed by the LRA. The ICC Prosecutor stated that 'the crimes committed by the LRA were [found to be] much more numerous and of much higher gravity than crimes allegedly committed by the UPDF'.[291] That, however, does not mean that the ICC will not later look into possible crimes committed by the UPDF.[292] The modification of the Prosecutor of Uganda's

---

288   Moreno-Ocampo, L. 2006. Symposium: International Criminal Tribunals in the 21st Century: Keynote Address: Integrating the Work of the ICC into Local Justice Initiatives. *American University International Law Review*, 21, 497-503, 499.

289   Moreno-Ocampo, L. 2006. Symposium: International Criminal Tribunals in the 21st Century: Keynote Address: Integrating the Work of the ICC into Local Justice Initiatives. *American University International Law Review*, 21, 497-503, 501.

290   Human Rights Watch. 14 October 2005. *ICC Takes Decisive Step for Justice in Uganda*. Available at: http://hrw.org/english/docs/2005/10/14/uganda11880.htm [accessed: 19 December 2008]. See also, Human Rights Watch. September 2005. *Uprooted and Forgotten: Impunity and Human Rights Abuses in Northern Uganda*, 17, 12(A). Available at: www.hrw.org/reports/2005/uganda0905/index.htm [accessed: 16 December 2008]. See also Apuuli, K.Ph. 1 March 2006. The ICC Arrest Warrants for the Lord's Resistance Army Leaders and Peace Prospects for Northern Uganda. *Journal of International Criminal Justice*, 49, 179-187, 184.

291   Statement by Chief Prosecutor Luis Moreno-Ocampo. 14 October 2005. Available at: www.icc-cpi.int/library/organs/otp/Uganda-LMOSpeech14102005.pdf [accessed: 9 December 2006].

292   Moy, H.A. Spring 2006. Recent Development: The International Criminal Court's Arrest Warrants and Uganda's Lord's Resistance Army: Renewing the Debate over Amnesty

referral to include the whole situation in northern Uganda and not only LRA crimes[293] is a clear indicator of the ICC's rejection of one-sided referrals, as it contradicts the purposes of the Statute and the principle of impartiality.

The 'grave' situation in northern Uganda was not contested, and hence the fulfilment of this criterion did not become a controversial issue. However, although the Prosecutor's delay or freeze of investigation against the Ugandan authorities and the UPDF could have some grounds in law and policy, it is unclear how the ICC could initiate such an investigation while at the same time securing the continuous cooperation of Uganda.

Political and Practical Challenges

The ICC's jurisdiction and realpolitik   Aside from the legal analysis of the Statute and its articles, one cannot neglect the medium in which the ICC is functioning and the various political actors that interact and affect the ICC's judicial role. It would be short-sighted to restrict research on the complementarity principle in particular, and the international-national jurisdictional relation in general, to the legal interpretation of the articles of the Statute and its rules of evidence and procedure.

Initiating an investigation for a case while securing political support from major stakeholders is an important element that cannot be ignored. It seems that the ICC Prosecutor took into consideration the lessons of the *ad hoc* Tribunals in this regard. The ICTY and ICTR, although established under Chapter VII of the UN Charter, remained dependent on state cooperation.[294] The practice of the ICTY and ICTR showed that the statutory advantages of the UN Prosecutor are outweighed by the weak enforcement mechanism, which these courts faced in general.[295]

A comparison between the ICC, on one hand, and the ICTY and ICTR, on the other hand, clearly shows that the ICC Prosecutor's statutory authority is more limited than that of the ICTY and ICTR.[296] Relying solely on statutory powers for the functions of the ICC does not seem enough to secure state cooperation.[297]

---

and Complementarity. *The Harvard Environmental Law Review*, 19, 267-277, 270.

293   Claus, K. December 2004. Self-Referrals and Waivers of Complementarity. *Journal of International Criminal Justice*, 2, 4, 944-950, 946.

294   Williams, P.R. and Waller, K.M. 2002. Coercive Appeasement: The Flawed International Response to the Serbian Rogue Regime. *New England Law Review*, 36, 825-898.

295   Wartanian, A. Summer 2005. The ICC Prosecutor's Battlefield: Combating Atrocities While Fighting For States' Cooperation Lessons from the U.N. Tribunals Applied To the Case of Uganda. *Georgetown Journal of International Law*, 36, 1289-1314, 1292.

296   Wartanian, A. Summer 2005. The ICC Prosecutor's Battlefield: Combating Atrocities While Fighting For States' Cooperation Lessons from the U.N. Tribunals Applied To the Case of Uganda. *Georgetown Journal of International Law*, 36, 1289-1314, 1292.

297   Wartanian, A. Summer 2005. The ICC Prosecutor's Battlefield: Combating Atrocities While Fighting For States' Cooperation Lessons from the U.N. Tribunals Applied

The ICC Prosecutor, whether relying on the Statute or through a pragmatic policy, cannot ignore certain political realities in initiating an investigation under Article 53. The Prosecutor, when making a decision under Article 53(2) on whether or not to commence a criminal prosecution, does not depend solely on legal criteria. In fact, while assessing 'interests of justice' perspective, he is to also assess the political convenience of doing so.[298] The Prosecutor has the necessary political discretion 'to evaluate the convenience of starting a criminal prosecution in order to achieve a certain political goal identified as the "interests of justice"'.[299] The application of Article 53 subsumes the application of Article 17.

Some experts argue that the ICC chose the first investigation as an ideal referral in which the cooperation of the concerned state (Uganda) is guaranteed.[300] The case of the conflict in northern Uganda is less politically contentious among the major international and regional powers. Over the years, the LRA even lost regional support, and is now facing various difficulties in finding a refuge for its rebels after Sudan – the alleged supporter of the LRA – indicated on a number of occasions that their presence is unwelcome in southern Sudan.[301] The LRA's request for DRC approval to move to DRC territories has also been declined.[302] The United States itself has labelled the LRA as a terrorist organization.[303] It seems, hence, that the Prosecutor must have taken into consideration the political context of the conflict, and the possible political support for the ICC investigation, as the ICC depends fully on state cooperation, which is a political decision on behalf of the concerned states. Prosecutor Moreno-Ocampo has

To the Case of Uganda. *Georgetown Journal of International Law*, 36, 1289-1314, 1292.

298   Olasolo, H. 2003. The Prosecutor of the ICC before the Initiation of Investigations: A Quasi-Judicial or a Political Body? *International Criminal Law Review*, 3, 87–150, 110.

299   Olasolo, H. 2003. The Prosecutor of the ICC before the Initiation of Investigations: A Quasi-Judicial or a Political Body? *International Criminal Law Review*, 3, 87–150, 110.

300   Wartanian, A. Summer 2005. The ICC Prosecutor's Battlefield: Combating Atrocities While Fighting For States' Cooperation Lessons from the U.N. Tribunals Applied To the Case of Uganda. *Georgetown Journal of International Law*, 36, 1289-1314, 1302.

301   Cocks, Tim. 16 January 2007. Sudanese President Omar Hassan al-Bashir vowed to 'get rid of the LRA from Sudan', in Reuters: Uganda LRA to Go Home, Army Says Would Be 'War'. Available at: http://sg.news.yahoo.com/070115/3/45zeg.html [accessed: 6 March 2009].

302   Apuuli, K.Ph. 1 March 2006. The ICC Arrest Warrants for the Lord's Resistance Army Leaders and Peace Prospects for Northern Uganda. *Journal of International Criminal Justice*, 49, 179-187, 179.

303   Reeker Ph.T., Deputy Spokesman. 6 December 2001. US State Department, Press Statement: Terrorist Exclusion List Published by US State Department. Available at: www.immigrationlinks.com/news/news1204.htm [accessed: 10 December 2008].

stated on a number of occasions that he is 'a stateless prosecutor'[304] who depends on state and international actors for enforcing ICC decisions.

The ICC Prosecutor favoured for a first case a state referral by a state highly interested in prosecuting and punishing the LRA rebels.[305] The referral was encouraging to many supporters of the Court, but later developments frustrated this optimistic view.[306]

In November 2004, Uganda proposed an amnesty for the LRA rebels on the condition that rebels end the insurgency and engage in internal reconciliation mechanisms. The amnesty law was seen as an alternative to any future investigations and prosecutions by the ICC. According to Bassiouni, 'this was tantamount to a withdrawal of the referral, and it engendered much concern since the Rome Statute does not contemplate the retraction of a referral to the Court'.[307] Furthermore, Museveni 'pledged total amnesty to Joseph Kony despite his indictment by the ICC, on the condition that he respond positively to peace being mediated by the southern Sudan government'.[308] The ICC refused the offer, and reminded Uganda of its obligations before the Statute. The Court pointed out that such an offer contravenes the Rome Statute.[309] If the offer stands, it will likely have drastic effects on Uganda's cooperation with the ICC, a cooperation that is vital for the ICC's ability to execute the arrest warrants against LRA commanders.[310] The recent peace negotiation concluded by February 2008 a draft peace deal that includes the establishment of a special national court to deal with alleged war crimes. This came as an attempt to

---

304   Moreno-Ocampo, L. 2006. Symposium: International Criminal Tribunals in the 21st Century: Keynote Address: Integrating the Work of the ICC into Local Justice Initiatives. *American University International Law Review*, 21, 497-503.

305   Ms. Olivia Swaak-Goldman stated, 'The Prosecutor adopted the policy of inviting voluntary referrals by territorial States as a first step in triggering the jurisdiction of the Court in order to increase cooperation'. Swaak-Goldman, Olivia. 25 September 2006. Second Public Hearing of the Office of the Prosecutor; Outlining the Three-Year Report. The Hague. Available at: www.icc-cpi.int/organs/otp/otp_public_hearing/otp_ph2/otp_ph2_HGstates.html [accessed: 9 March 2007].

306   Bassiouni, M.Ch. 1 July 2006. The ICC – Quo Vadis? *Journal of International Criminal Justice*, 4, 421-428, 425.

307   Bassiouni, M.Ch. 1 July 2006. The ICC – Quo Vadis? *Journal of International Criminal Justice*, 4, 421-428, 425.

308   *New Vision*. 19 December 2006. Uganda: Museveni Offers LRA's Kony Way Out, Kampala. Available at: http://allafrica.com/stories/200612190045.html [accessed: 9 March 2008].

309   Blogger News Network. 5 July 2006. International Court Wants Uganda Rebel Leader Despite Amnesty Offer. Available at: www.bloggernews.net/2006/07/International-court-wants-uganda-rebel.html [accessed: 9 March 2008].

310   International Criminal Court. 14 October 2005. *Warrants of Arrest Unsealed Against Five LRA Commanders*. Press Release. The Hague. ICC20051410.056-En. Available at: www.icc-cpi.int/press/pressreleases/114.html [accessed: 9 December 2008].

drop the ICC arrest warrants, since the Lord's Resistance Army rebels have refused to disarm, while three of the LRA leaders are still wanted by the ICC.[311] It remained unclear whether this was a serious national step by the Ugandan government and the LRA to prosecute perpetrators of international crimes or it was just a means to avoid ICC prosecutions. This argument remains hypothetic as the LRA did not sign the agreement, and it was never implemented.

The argument here is that in spite of the uncontested legal obligation of Uganda to cooperate with the Court, and despite the fact that Uganda has voluntarily referred the situation to the ICC, its cooperation cannot be guaranteed.[312] Various political and practical factors have become entangled with the legal aspect to affect the complementarity relation and cooperation between the Court and the state.

Cooperation with the ICC   The Statute grants the Court the power to enter into agreements and arrangements as it deems necessary to facilitate cooperation.[313] The requirement for such agreements, and their content, is to be determined by the state or concerned NGOs and the OTP. The ICC prosecutorial policy on cooperation seems to develop along the lines of securing and maintaining the continuous and sustainable support and cooperation of states and organizations, as that will help to organize and ease the requests for cooperation between the OTP and states and organizations. The OTP has emphasized officially that one of its goals is to develop a network of relationships with national authorities, multilateral institutions, NGOs and other entities and bodies.[314] These relations with concerned state parties are to be transformed into cooperation agreements. The goal is to ensure that assistance and practical resources to mount an investigation are available in any type of situation.[315]

In the case of Uganda's referral, the situation seems ideal as the referring state and the Court's interest are aligned. According to one author, 'the prosecutor

---

311   BBC News. 19 February 2008. Ugandans Reach War Crimes Accord.

312   Wartanian, A. Summer 2005. The ICC Prosecutor's Battlefield: Combating Atrocities While Fighting For States' Cooperation Lessons from the U.N. Tribunals Applied To the Case of Uganda. *Georgetown Journal of International Law*, 36, 1289-1314, 1302.

313   Article 4 of the Rome Statute of the International Criminal Court, UN Doc. A/Conf.183/9.

314   The International Criminal Court, Office of the Prosecutor. 14 September 2006. *The Office of the Prosecutor Report on Prosecutorial Strategy*. The Hague, 1-11, 3. Available at: www.icc-cpi.int/library/organs/otp/OTP_Prosecutorial-Strategy-20060914_English.pdf [accessed: 2 June 2009].

315   The International Criminal Court, Office of the Prosecutor. 2003. *Paper on Some Policy Issues before the Office of the Prosecutor*. ICC-OTP 2003, 1-9, 5. Available at: www.icc-cpi.int/library/organs/otp/030905_Policy_Paper.pdf [accessed: 20 February 2009].

should be able to rely on the Ugandan government to facilitate his investigation, to help arrest indicted war criminals, and to enforce the tribunal's orders'.[316]

However, the argument *supra* points out that the Prosecutor should not rely solely on this 'cooperation', as Uganda political interests may change. For instance, as the ICC Prosecutor did not eliminate the possibility of prosecuting UPDF personnel later, one cannot predict the subsequent attitude of Uganda, and whether their current cooperation could be altered later. One should keep in mind that in all scenarios Uganda is under an obligation to cooperate with the ICC under Part 9 of the Statute.[317] As mentioned before, the Prosecutor has stated that he is not ignoring any UPDF crimes, but simply decided to start with the LRA crimes, as they are graver.[318] This implies that UPDF crimes could be subsequently prosecuted, which may cause Uganda to stop cooperating with the Court. In such a case, jurisdictional tension between the Court and the Uganda could prevail over the current agreement and harmony.

Hence, cooperation throughout the entire process cannot be guaranteed. If problems of cooperation appear, the ICC Prosecutor has to turn to alternative methods of enforcement. The experience of the ICTY may be of help,[319] although the ICTY Prosecutor's authority is wider than the ICC. In the case of northern Uganda, the ICC Prosecutor may have to turn to one of the potential actors that can affect the prosecution. The list includes:

a. States that have alternative possible jurisdiction, such as Sudan or the DRC, and major powers.
b. The UN Security Council can also be a great source for the OTP if there is political consensus among members of the Council. The Security Council can pass 'resolutions providing for aid, condemning actions of a non-cooperative state, instituting economic and diplomatic sanctions, and authorizing the use of military'.[320] The role of the Security Council is crucial especially in the Council's own referrals under Article 13(b) of

---

316   Wartanian, A. Summer 2005. The ICC Prosecutor's Battlefield: Combating Atrocities While Fighting For States' Cooperation Lessons from the U.N. Tribunals Applied To the Case of Uganda. *Georgetown Journal of International Law*, 36, 1289-1314, 1303.

317   Part 9 on International Cooperation and Judicial Assistance, the Rome Statute of the International Criminal Court, UN Doc. A/Conf.183/9.

318   Moreno-Ocampo, L. 2006. Symposium: International Criminal Tribunals in the 21st Century: Keynote Address: Integrating the Work of the ICC into Local Justice Initiatives. *American University International Law Review*, 21, 497-503.

319   Williams, P.R. and Waller, K.M. 2002. Coercive Appeasement: The Flawed International Response to the Serbian Rogue Regime. *New England Law Review*, 36, 825-898, 888.

320   Wartanian, A. Summer 2005. The ICC Prosecutor's Battlefield: Combating Atrocities While Fighting For States' Cooperation Lessons from the U.N. Tribunals Applied To the Case of Uganda. *Georgetown Journal of International Law*, 36, 1289-1314, 1303.

the ICC Statute.[321]

c. The Prosecutor can turn to the Assembly of State Parties in case of future lack of cooperation on behalf of Uganda. However, state parties may deny assistance to the Prosecutor of the Court by declining to provide documents or evidence that could threaten 'national security' according to Article 72 of the Statute.[322]

d. International and regional organizations: for instance, economic international organizations can successfully push unwilling states to cooperate by conditioning monetary aid on their cooperation. The success in getting Croatia to surrender a number of high-ranking officials to the ICTY is an encouraging example in that regard.[323] Similar tactics could be used in the case of Uganda if the latter became uncooperative.

e. Non-governmental organizations (NGOs):[324] international NGOs are the ones out in the field every day, recording events, reporting them, and lobbying for international assistance.[325] Practice showed that their role was important in supporting international courts in areas of evidence gathering[326] and gaining access to witnesses, whether in the Balkans or in Africa.

---

321   Article 13(b) of the Rome Statute of the International Criminal Court, UN Doc. A/CONF.183/9.

322   Article 72 of the Rome Statute of the International Criminal Court, UN Doc. A/ CONF.183/9. Wedgwood, R. 1998. International Criminal Tribunals and State Sources of Proof: The Case of Tihomir Blaškic. *Leiden Journal of International Law*, 11, 635-654.

323   Wartanian, A. Summer 2005. The ICC Prosecutor's Battlefield: Combating Atrocities While Fighting For States' Cooperation Lessons from the U.N. Tribunals Applied To the Case of Uganda. *Georgetown Journal of International Law*, 36, 1289-1314, 1304.

324   Wartanian, A. Summer 2005. The ICC Prosecutor's Battlefield: Combating Atrocities While Fighting For States' Cooperation Lessons from the U.N. Tribunals Applied To the Case of Uganda. *Georgetown Journal of International Law*, 36, 1289-1314, 1302.

325   Human Rights Watch. September 2004. *The International Criminal Court: How Nongovernmental Organizations Can Contribute To the Prosecution of War Criminals*. 1-17, 14-24. Available at: www.hrw.org/backgrounder/africa/icc0904/icc0904.pdf [accessed: 9 March 2009].

326   Efforts and reports of Amnesty International for example remain crucial to shed light on the atrocities and crimes occurring in various places of the world such as Darfur or Northern Uganda, and that with other factors assist in exerting pressure on the UN to take further actions. See for example Amnesty International Press Release pertaining Human Rights Council Decision to send Fact Finding Mission to Darfur, Amnesty International. 13 December 2008. UN: Human Rights Council Resolution a Lukewarm Response to Deepening Crisis in Darfur. Available at: http://news.amnesty.org/index/ ENGIOR410292006 [accessed: 21 March 2009].

If Uganda becomes unwilling to cooperate, these actors may play a decisive role in supporting measures that the Prosecutor could invoke to resolve the issue, such as freezing the assets of individual criminals,[327] providing military forces, or using cash rewards to help arrest indicted persons.[328] However, the cooperation of these actors is not automatically secured. There are various political variables that affect these actors' decision to cooperate and it is possible for there to be a situation where full cooperation is not secured.

To recap, in practice the complementarity principle can face more challenges from without than from within, i.e. from states rather than from within the articles of the Statute. In the case of a lack of cooperation on behalf of the referring states, the Court remains in vital need of cooperation from political and economic players who could influence the situation. This positions the Court, as a judicial body, in a dependent position regarding these political entities. The complementarity principle in practice requires certain non-legal factors to exist for the Court to meet the goals of the Statute to end impunity and punish perpetrators of international crimes. With such a weak enforcement system, the efficiency of the ICC depends in practice on states and other political actors. In a scenario where the cooperation of these factors is not secured, the ICC will be powerless and ineffective regarding national systems. A weak enforcement system[329] will hardly deter states to take steps to meet their obligations under the Statute to reform the national system.[330]

Conclusion

In July 2005, the ICC issued its first arrest warrants under seal by the Pre-Trial Chamber. This was to ensure the safety and well-being of victims, potential witnesses,

---

327   Kalinauskas, M. 2002. The Use of International Military Force in Arresting War Criminals: The Lessons of the International Criminal Tribunal for the Former Yugoslavia. *The University of Kansas Law Review*, 50, 383-429, 402.

328   These measures were used by the ICTY regarding non-cooperative states and accused persons. See Scharf, M. Spring 1999. Clear and Present Danger: Enforcing the International Ban on Biological and Chemical Weapons Through Sanctions, Use of Force, and Criminalization. *Michigan Journal of International Law*, 20, 477-521, 496.

329   Annie Wartanian considers that the enforcement mechanism for non-compliance under the ICC is relatively weak. Wartanian, A. Summer 2005. The ICC Prosecutor's Battlefield: Combating Atrocities While Fighting For States' Cooperation Lessons from the U.N. Tribunals Applied To the Case of Uganda. *Georgetown Journal of International Law*, 36, 1289-1314, 1294.

330   The Preamble of the ICC delineates the duty of every state to punish perpetrators of international crimes to end impunity. Preamble of the Rome Statute of the International Criminal Court, UN Doc. A/CONF.183/9.

and their families. On 13 October 2005, the ICC unsealed these arrest warrants.[331] The Chamber's decision to unseal the arrest warrants came after ensuring that security and protection for the victims and witnesses have been secured in Uganda.[332] The arrest warrants were for those most responsible for the crimes committed by the LRA. Human Rights activists and NGOs expect the ICC investigation to later cover crimes committed by the Ugandan army.

The Ugandan referral does not fulfil the 'inability' criteria as stipulated in Article 17.[333] The Ugandan judicial system is unable to arrest suspects, rather than being unable or unwilling to investigate and prosecute. The LRA leadership was based in northern Uganda, and the Ugandan system has remained functional, able and willing to prosecute.

Furthermore, the above arguments indicate that the policy of encouraging and seeking state referrals[334] could have negative outcomes for fulfilling the purposes of the Statute to end impunity and to affirm state duties to prosecute international crimes.[335] The presumption that state referrals could guarantee state cooperation is inaccurate.

Moreover, according to the OTP, 'inaction' by national authorities might render the case admissible before the ICC. In such scenario, every state self-referral could be admissible, and a *de facto* waiver of complementarity occurs. It is when states do not exercise their right and duty to prosecute these core crimes, that the ICC will exercise jurisdiction. Based on this formula, some argued that when states wilfully refer a situation on their territories or involving their nationals, they consciously defer this right to the ICC, and the complementarity principle is obviated, as the states themselves have waived their right to prosecute in favour of the ICC.[336]

---

331   International Criminal Court. 14 October 2005. *Warrants of Arrest Unsealed Against Five LRA Commanders*. Press Release. The Hague. ICC20051410.056-En. Available at: www.icc-cpi.int/press/pressreleases/114.html [accessed: 9 December 2008].

332   Ahmedani, M. et al. Fall 2005. Updates from the International Criminal Courts. *Human Rights Brief*, 13, 37-52, 47.

333   Southwick, K. Fall 2005. Investigating War in Northern Uganda: Dilemmas for the International Criminal Court. *Yale Journal of International Affairs*, 105-119, 109. See also, Arsanjani, M.H. and Reisman, W.M. April 2005. The Law-in-Action of the International Criminal Court. *The American Journal of International Law*, 99, 2, 385-403, 397.

334   Based on the Annex of the Prosecutor Policy Paper on Some Policy Issues before the Office of the Prosecutor, 'under the Statute, the prosecutor relies on co-operation to carry out his investigation; the prosecutor will in general seek where possible to make this support explicit through a referral'. See The International Criminal Court, Office of the Prosecutor. 2003. *Paper on Some Policy Issues before the Office of the Prosecutor*. ICC-OTP 2003, 1-9, 4. Available at: www.icc-cpi.int/library/organs/otp/030905_Policy_Paper. pdf [accessed: 20 February 2009].

335   Preamble of the Rome Statute of the International Criminal Court, UN Doc. A/CONF.183/9.

336   Benzing, M. 2003. The Complementarity Regime of the International Criminal Court: International Criminal Justice between State Sovereignty and the Fight against

However, such an interpretation will lead to undesired results, as states may become more and more reluctant to prosecute by themselves, instead placing the burden on the ICC. Referring to the ICC may in various cases be favoured for political motives, as states may prefer to ease certain pressures by instead burdening the international court.[337] Moreover, the referral will always be financially less exhausting, since the financial burden will fall on the ICC, and the state will be relieved of the expenses of prosecutions.[338] Unrestricted referrals will weaken any possible contribution of the Court to the national judicial systems to prosecute international crimes. It will also overburden the limited resources of the Court with numerous referrals.

Finally, the ICC enforcement system suffers from certain structural flaws. With such weaknesses, in cases of non-cooperation, it is hard to imagine how the complementarity principle could encourage states to take national steps to meet their obligations under the Statute to reform the national systems.[339]

On the opposite, when there is support to the ICC, its contribution becomes tangible. The previous negotiations between the LRA and the Ugandan government in 2007 and 2008 highlight the impact the ICC can have at the national level when the international and regional systems are supportive of the ICC role. The Agreement of Accountability and Reconciliation between the Government of the Republic of Uganda and the Lord's Resistance Army/Movement signed on 29 June 2007[340] is significant on various levels. The Agreement refers to the complementarity principle in setting out the obligations accepted in the Agreement, and the parties to the Agreement are clearly aware of Uganda's obligations before the ICC despite the attempt to incorporate alternative justice mechanisms, such as traditional reconciliation methods practised by local communities in northern Uganda.[341] Paragraph three of the Preamble to the Agreement makes specific reference to Uganda's international obligations; it states that Uganda is 'committed to preventing impunity and promoting redress in accordance with the Constitution

---

Impunity. *Max Planck Yearbook of United Nations Law*, 7, 591-632, 630.

337 One of the reasons behind Uganda's referral; see The Refugee Law Project. 28 July 2004. The Refugee Law Project's Position Paper on the Announcement of Formal Investigations of the Lord's Resistance Army by the Chief Prosecutor of the International Criminal Court and its Implications on the Search for Peaceful Solutions to the War in Northern Uganda, 1-12. Available at: www.refugeelawproject.org/resources/papers/archive/2004/RLP.ICC.investig.pdf [accessed: 9 November 2005].

338 Practically the burden will fall on all state parties cumulatively through their contribution to the budget of the ICC.

339 The Preamble of the ICC delineates the duty of every state to punish perpetrators of international crimes to end impunity. Preamble of the Rome Statute of the International Criminal Court, UN Doc. A/CONF.183/9.

340 Agreement on Accountability and Reconciliation; Between the Government of the Republic of Uganda and The Lord's Resistance Army/Movement, Juba Sudan. 29 June 2007.

341 Preamble, Agreement on Accountability and Reconciliation; Between the Government of the Republic of Uganda and The Lord's Resistance Army/Movement, Juba Sudan. 29 June 2007.

and international obligations and recalling in this connection, the requirement of the Rome Statute of the International Criminal Court (ICC) and in particular the principle of complementarity'.[342] Although the Agreement tries to retain the primary role of the national system to achieve justice (by focusing on non-criminal proceedings), it also emphasizes the complementarity principle. This reflects the significant impact the complementarity principle had on promoting accountability at the national level. It is too early to determine if these national quasi- or non-criminal proceedings (alternative justice mechanisms) will fulfil the *ne bis in idem* principle under Article 20 to defer the ICC jurisdiction in favour of Uganda's proceedings.

An important question concerns the impact that the complementarity principle had on the parties to the conflict. This is evident in the inclusion of accountability mechanisms in the Annexure to the Agreement,[343] in spite of the long culture of impunity in Uganda. Furthermore, in February 2008, the LRA and the Ugandan government agreed to establish a special court to deal with international crimes committed during the conflict.[344] Although the jurisdiction of this court remains unclear, such a step could be interpreted as an impact of the ICC arrest warrants, along with the complementarity principle. These are important developments,[345] and support the arguments made previously as to the potential of the ICC to contribute to the indirect enforcement mechanism of international criminal law when stakeholders' support is secured, i.e. whether it succeeded in imposing accountability for individuals who allegedly bear 'particular responsibility for the most serious crimes especially international crimes'.[346]

It would have been a golden chance to analyse how complementarity could have been applied if the agreement had been implemented. Unfortunately, the LRA did not sign the final agreement, and the issue remains an unsettled matter.

---

342   Paragraph 4 of the Preamble, Agreement on Accountability and Reconciliation; Between the Government of the Republic of Uganda and The Lord's Resistance Army/Movement, Juba Sudan. 29 June 2007.

343   Annexure to the Agreement on Accountability and Reconciliation. Agreement on Accountability and Reconciliation; Between the Government of the Republic of Uganda and The Lord's Resistance Army/Movement, Juba Sudan. 29 June 2007.

344   BBC News. 19 February 2008. Ugandan Rebels and the Government Have Agreed to Set Up a Special Court to Deal With Alleged War Crimes – One of the Obstacles to a Final Peace Deal. Available at: http://news.bbc.co.uk/2/hi/africa/7252774.stm [accessed: 22 March 2009].

345   According to Human Rights Watch, the Agreement and its Annex are of significant importance, as they include trials for most serious crimes. The success of such accountability efforts will fully depend on serious commitments of the LRA and the Ugandan government leadership for prosecuting those most responsible for international crimes. See Human Rights Watch. February 2008. Analysis of the Annex to the June 29 Agreement on Accountability and Reconciliation.

346   Paragraph 6.1, Agreement on Accountability and Reconciliation; Between the Government of the Republic of Uganda and The Lord's Resistance Army/Movement, Juba Sudan. 29 June 2007, 6.

Chapter 6

Complementarity and Security Council Referral: The Darfur Situation

In February 2003, the conflict in Darfur had erupted and created what the United Nations labelled as one of the world's worst humanitarian disasters.[1] The then UN Secretary-General Kofi Annan has described the Darfur crisis as 'little short of hell on earth'.[2] The death tolls and the gravity of the crimes committed within this conflict attracted the attention of the world, including the Security Council.

The conflict in Darfur situation is the first Security Council (SC) referral to the ICC under Article 13 of the Statute. The Darfur referral is of importance because it is different from other situations, as it is a Security Council referral for a non-state party under Article 13, while other situations are state referrals. The chapter will shed light on the application of the complementarity principle in a SC referral if compared to other kinds of referrals.

Background on the Conflict

The conflict began when two African rebel movements, the Sudan Liberation Movement/Army (SLM/A) and the Justice and Equality Movement (JEM), revolted against the government, claiming a chronic neglect of Darfur and its people. The government retaliated by calling upon the local tribes to assist in fighting the rebels adopting an old political trick by exploiting existing tribal tensions in Darfur. The government's counter-insurgency campaign has been led by an Arab militia, frequently referred to as 'Janjaweed'.[3] The conflict has resulted in the displacement of between 1.45 and 1.6 million people, among whom 200,000 have moved into neighbouring Chad, and more than 300,000 people among these

---

1   Andersson, H. 2004. Screams of Sudan's Starving Refugees. BBC News. 26 June. Available at: http://www.bbc.co.uk/2/hi/programmes/from our correspondent/3840 427.stm [accessed: 16 May 2009]. See also, Amanpour, Ch. 2004. Sudan's Hellish Humanitarian Crisis. *CNN.* 12 May. Available at: http://edition.cnn.com/2004/WORLD/africa/05/12/sudan.crisis [accessed: 16 June 2009].

2   UN Press Release. 16 March 2005. *United Nations Human Rights Experts Call for Urgent, Effective Action on Darfur, Sudan,* AFR/1126 and HR/4822.

3   AMICC, A Program of the United Nations Association of the United States of America. 16 February 2006. The Current Investigation by the ICC of the Situation in Darfur. 1-14, 1, 2. Available at: www.amicc.org [accessed: 11 May 2009].

are believed to have lost their lives.[4] Thousands of women have been raped, and hundreds of thousands of villages have been looted, destroyed or bombarded by aerial raids.[5] The conflict witnessed various human rights and humanitarian law violations.[6]

The causes of the conflict in Darfur seem to be complex. Historically, tribal groups have come into conflict over land, water or livestock. Such disputes were settled through traditional tribal mechanisms. However, the smuggling of weapons further aggravated these inter-tribal conflicts, in particular through the borders with Chad and Libya.[7] As Darfur suffered an increasing scarcity of water and other resources, relations between herdsmen tribes (mainly Arabs) and farmers (mostly the African tribes Fur, Zaghawa and Massaleit) became increasingly tense. The intensity of conflicts increased significantly with the formation of village defence groups and militias, and the influx of small arms and light weapons into the region. Moreover, the people of Darfur have felt marginalized and discriminated by the central government in favour of the Arab tribes.[8] The 'Darfurians' suffered from a long-time lack of significant political voice in Khartoum. On the other hand, many governmental officials – including President al-Bashir[9] – have tried to distance the Sudanese government from the conflict, repeatedly claiming that the current crisis stems from local disputes between herdsmen and farmers over natural resources,

---

4   Quénivet, N. July-September 2006. The Report of the International Commission of Inquiry on Darfur: The Question of Genocide. *Human Rights Review*, 38-68, 40.

5   Amnesty International USA. 6 September 2005. *Sudan: Human Rights Concerns*. Available at: www.amnestyusa.org/countries/sudan/index.do [accessed: 19 May 2009].

6   International Criminal Court, Office of the Prosecutor. 5 June 2008. *Seventh Report of the Prosecutor of the International Criminal Court to the UN Security Council Pursuant to the UNSCR 1593(2005)*. Available at: www.icc-cpi.int/library/organs/otp/UNSC_2008_En.pdf [accessed: 7 July 2009]. See also United Nations Commission of Inquiry. 25 January 2005. Report of the International Commission of Inquiry on Darfur to the United Nations Secretary-General, Pursuant to Security Council Resolution 1564 of 18 September 2004, para. 3. Available at: www.un.org/News/dh/sudan/com_inq_darfur.pdf [accessed: 16 May 2009].

7   United Nations Commission of Inquiry. 25 January 2005. *Report of the International Commission of Inquiry on Darfur to the United Nations Secretary-General, Pursuant to Security Council Resolution 1564 of 18 September 2004*, para. 58. Available at: www.un.org/News/dh/sudan/com_inq_darfur.pdf [accessed: 16 May 2009].

8   'Those who considered themselves ethnically African were angered by the government's practice of awarding most of the top posts in the region to local Arabs, even though they were thought to be the minority there'. Power, S. 30 August 2004. Dying in Darfur. Can the Ethnic Cleansing in Sudan be Stopped? Available at: www.newyorker.com/archive/2004/08/30/040830fa_fact1 [accessed: 16 May 2009]. See also Udombana, N.J. Fall 2005. Pay Back Time in Sudan? Darfur in the International Criminal Court. *Tulsa Journal of Comparative and International Law*, 13, 1-57, 3, 4.

9   *Al-Anbaa Newspaper*. 14 August 2004. President Al-Bashir Gives Interview to Lebanese Al Mustaqbal Newspaper on Darfur.

and that the official efforts to address it have been successful and that the region is getting calmer.[10]

Main Parties to the Conflict

The main parties involved in the conflict are the Janjaweed militia, the Sudan Liberation Movement/Army(SLM/A), the Justice and Equality Movement (JEM), the National Movement for Reform and Development (NMRD), the Sudanese National Movement for the Eradication of Marginalization, and the Sudanese government forces.

Janjaweed   The term 'Janjaweed' stems from the Arabic word 'man on a horse'. It is somewhat shrouded in ambiguity as it may refer both to government-backed militias used in the government's military campaign, and opportunistic armed groups who have taken advantage of the collapse of the rule of law.[11] The government-backed militia has been recruited from the 'Abala', camel-herding nomads who migrated to the Darfur region in the 1970s from Chad and West Africa and from tribes from northern Darfur.[12] The militia has reportedly recruited troops primarily from groups such as the Beni Halba and certain sub-clans of the Rizeigat, Ma'aliya and Irayqat.[13] They have played a key role in recruiting militia members, as well as taken command responsibility during certain attacks. The tribal leader Mussa Hilal has played such a command role.[14] A second group of members consists of Chadian Arab ethnic groups, such as the Awlad Zeid, Awlad Rashid, Salamat and individuals from the Central African Republic.[15]

The highest level of the Sudanese government has been involved in supporting, recruiting and arming the Janjaweed with a complete impunity for activities that

---

10   SUNA. 22 September 2004. General Al-Dabi Affirms Stability of Security Situations In Darfur States. See also, *Akhbar Alyoum Daily*. 3 August 2004. Deputy Governor of Southern Darfur State Says the State is Stable.

11   Human Rights Watch. 11 August 2004. *Empty Promises? Continuing Abuses In Darfur, Sudan: A Human Rights Watch Briefing Paper*, 1-37. Available at: www.hrw.org/backgrounder/africa/sudan/2004/sudan0804.pdf [accessed: 16 May 2009].

12   Human Rights Watch. 20 July 2004. *Darfur Documents Confirm Government Policy of Militia Support; A Human Rights Watch Briefing Paper*. Available at: http://hrw.org/english/docs/2004/07/19/darfur9096.htm [accessed: 16 May 2009].

13   International Crisis Group. 25 March 2004. *Darfur Rising: Sudan's New Crisis*, ICG Africa Report. Nairobi/Brussels, 76, p.16.

14   Human Rights Watch. 11 August 2004. *Empty Promises? Continuing Abuses In Darfur, Sudan: A Human Rights Watch Briefing Paper*, 1-37. Available at: www.hrw.org/backgrounder/africa/sudan/2004/sudan0804.pdf [accessed: 16 May 2009].

15   International Crisis Group. 25 March 2004. *Darfur Rising: Sudan's New Crisis*, ICG Africa Report. Nairobi/Brussels, 76, 16.

may reach the level of crimes against humanity and war crimes.[16] The militia is said to be responsible for widespread assaults on civilians, including killings, rapes and the carrying out of a 'scorched-earth' tactic ordered by the Sudanese government. Some reports have accused the government of offering the Janjaweed a bounty for attacking certain communities.[17] The government, however, largely denies providing the militia with support. The Sudanese government reportedly has recruited 20,000 Janjaweed militia members.[18]

Although the structure and command of the Janjaweed is largely unknown, reports speak of three separate divisions set up by the government, they are the Strike Force, the Border Guard and the Hamina (traditional tribal leaders).[19]

Sudan Liberation Movement/Army (SLM/A)   The SLM/A is the largest rebel group and consists mainly of people from the Zaghawa, Fur, Masalit and several smaller Darfurian tribes. Formerly known as the Darfur Liberation Front, the SLM/A emerged in full force in February 2003 when it launched a number of attacks against police stations. It controls the largest territory, including the northern band of north Darfur along areas in west and south Darfur.[20] The SLM/A agenda claims to create a united democratic Sudan and works for the recognition of a more just distribution of wealth and development between the centre and peripheries of Sudan.[21]

Initially, the SLM/A Secretary-General was Minni Arkou Minnawi, but then the Movement witnessed a major split into two factions, one headed by Minnawi, and the other loyal to Abdelwahid Mohamed El Nur, an ethnic Fur.[22] Minnawi signed the May Agreement[23] with the Sudanese government in 2006 to be appointed the Senior Assistant to President al-Bashir and, at the same time, the chairperson of

---

16   Human Rights Watch. 20 July 2004. *Darfur Documents Confirm Government Policy of Militia Support; A Human Rights Watch Briefing Paper*. Available at: http://hrw.org/english/docs/2004/07/19/darfur9096.htm [accessed: 16 May 2009].

17   International Crisis Group. 23 August 2004. *Darfur Deadline: A New International Action Plan*, 83, 3. Available at: www.crisisgroup.org/home/index.cfm?id=2920&l=1 [accessed: 16 May 2009].

18   Human Rights Watch. April 2004. *Darfur in Flames: Atrocities in Western Sudan*, 16, 5, 23. Available at: http://hrw.org/reports/2004/sudan0404/ [accessed: 22 June 2009].

19   International Crisis Group. 25 March 2004. *Darfur Rising: Sudan's New Crisis*, ICG Africa Report. Nairobi/Brussels, 76, 16.

20   Human Rights Watch. November 2004. *If We Return, We Will Be Killed: Consolidation of Ethnic Cleansing in Darfur, Sudan*, 32. Available at: http://hrw.org/backgrounder/africa/darfur1104/darfur1104.pdf [accessed: 16 May 2009].

21   BBC News. 30 September 2004. *Who are Sudan's Darfur Rebels?* Available at: http://news.bbc.co.uk/2/hi/africa/3702242.stm [accessed: 16 May 2009].

22   BBC News. 30 September 2004. *Who are Sudan's Darfur Rebels?* Available at: http://news.bbc.co.uk/2/hi/africa/3702242.stm [accessed: 16 May 2009].

23   Darfur Peace Agreement. 5 May 2006. Available at: www.unmis.org/english/dpa. Htm [accessed: 14 February 2008].

the Transitional Darfur Regional Authority that was established in April 2007. Minnawi continues to show his discontent with the implementation of the Darfur Peace Agreement.[24] The Abdelwahid Mohamed El Nur faction opposes the Darfur Peace Agreement demanding more direct SLM/A participation in implementation of security arrangements and rejects the Darfur Peace Agreement's provisions on political representation and a victim's compensation fund.[25]

Justice and Equality Movement (JEM)   The Justice and Equality Movement (JEM) was formed in 2002 and has the strongest diplomatic impact despite its smaller army compared to SLM/A. It consists primarily of members from the Zaghawa group and several of its leaders were originally members in the Popular Congress, an Islamist political party.[26] Its leader Khalil Ibrahim Muhammad is a veteran Islamist. Other than their call for a united, federal Sudan based on equality and a fair distribution of resources, the JEM's political goals remain vague.[27] The group retains ties with Hassan al-Turabi, and that caused the government to fear that al-Turabi is using Darfur as a tool for returning to power in Khartoum.[28] In January 2006, the JEM merged with the Sudan Liberation Movement, headed by Minnawi, to form the Alliance of Revolutionary Forces of West Sudan, but then negotiated as single entities in Abuja peace talks.

The JEM rejects the Darfur Peace Agreement considering that the protocols on power and wealth sharing do not adequately address the conflict's root causes represented in the structural inequities between Sudan's centre and its periphery.[29] In February 2010, the JEM signed a peace agreement with the Sudanese government to end the conflict and to integrate JEM forces in the governmental structure.[30]

---

24   *The New Sudan Vision*. 11 March 2008. Sudan's Minni Arcua Minnawi Discontented with DPA Implementation, Wraps Up Visit to the US. Available at: www.newsudanvision. com/news/sudans-minni-arcua-minnawi-discontented-dpa-implementation-wraps-visit-us-855 [accessed: 25 March 2009].

25   International Crisis Group. 20 June 2006. Darfur's Fragile Peace Agreement Africa Briefing No. 39. Available at: www.crisisgroup.org/home/index.cfm?id=4179 [accessed: 25 March 2009].

26   Human Rights Watch. November 2004. *If We Return, We Will Be Killed; Consolidation of Ethnic Cleansing in Darfur, Sudan*, 32. Available at: http://hrw.org/backgrounder/africa/darfur1104/darfur1104.pdf [accessed: 16 May 2009].

27   International Crisis Group. 25 March 2004. *Darfur Rising: Sudan's New Crisis*, ICG Africa Report. Nairobi/Brussels, 76, 20.

28   International Crisis Group. 25 March 2004. *Darfur Rising: Sudan's New Crisis*, ICG Africa Report. Nairobi/Brussels, 76, 2.

29   *The New Sudan Vision*. 11 March 2008. Sudan's Minni Arcua Minnawi Discontented with DPA Implementation, Wraps Up Visit to the US. Available at: www.newsudanvision. com/news/sudans-minni-arcua-minnawi-discontented-dpa-implementation-wraps-visit-us-855 [accessed: 25 March 2009].

30   *Sudan Vision Daily Newspaper*. 24 February 2010. Government, JEM Sign Ceasefire Framework Agreement in Doha.

National Movement for Reform and Development (NMRD)   The National Movement for Reform and Development is another rebel group headed by former JEM Chief of Staff Gabril Abdel Kareem Badri, known as Tek. It broke away from the JEM in April 2004 due to disagreements over Hassan al-Turabi's influence over the movement.[31] Tek is on the UN sanctions list for alleged war crimes.[32]

Sudanese National Movement for the Eradication of Marginalization   Not much is known about this group. Certain reports indicate that the Movement could have been at a time a front organization for the SLM/A, facilitating its campaign without appearing to break the ceasefire.[33] The group claimed responsibility for an attack on the village of Ghubeish on 27 December 2004.

Crimes Committed in Darfur

The Darfur conflict has witnessed the occurrence of grave atrocities against the civilian population. Many of these crimes fall under the jurisdiction of the ICC. The Report of the United Nations Commission of Inquiry on Darfur indicated that 'some of these violations are very likely to amount to war crimes, and given the systematic and widespread pattern of many of the violations, they would also amount to crimes against humanity'.[34] With respect to the crime of genocide, the Commission found that some of the objective elements of genocide have materialized in Darfur,[35] but was unable to prove the existence of a policy of genocidal intention on the part of the Sudanese government.[36]

---

31   IRIN News. 13 January 2005. *How Credible is Darfur's Third Rebel Movement?* Available at: www.irinnews.org/report.aspx?reportid=52658 [accessed: 26 May 2009].

32   Security Council Resolution 1762. 25 April 2006. Available at: http://daccessdds. un.org/doc/UNDOC/GEN/N06/326/77/PDF/N0632677.pdf?OpenElement   [accessed: 2 October 2008]. See also, BBC News. 5 May 2006. *Who are Sudan's Darfur Rebels?* Available at: http://news.bbc.co.uk/2/hi/africa/7039360.stm [accessed 16 May 2009].

33   Reuters. 29 December 2005. Sudan says Darfur Rebel Groups Involved in Attack. Available at: www.sudantribune.com/spip.php?mot34&debut_affiche_news=10 [accessed: 26 May 2009].

34   United Nations Commission of Inquiry. 25 January 2005. *Report of the International Commission of Inquiry on Darfur to the United Nations Secretary-General, Pursuant to Security Council Resolution 1564 of 18 September 2004*, para. 630. Available at: www.un.org/News/dh/sudan/com_inq_darfur.pdf [accessed: 16 May 2009].

35   United Nations Commission of Inquiry. 25 January 2005. *Report of the International Commission of Inquiry on Darfur to the United Nations Secretary-General, Pursuant to Security Council Resolution 1564 of 18 September 2004*, para. 507. Available at: www.un.org/News/dh/sudan/com_inq_darfur.pdf [accessed: 16 May 2009].

36   United Nations Commission of Inquiry. 25 January 2005. *Report of the International Commission of Inquiry on Darfur to the United Nations Secretary-General, Pursuant to Security Council Resolution 1564 of 18 September 2004*, para. 515. Available at: www.un.org/News/dh/sudan/com_inq_darfur.pdf [accessed: 16 May 2009].

Prosecutor Moreno-Ocampo indicated to the Security Council that the OTP found 'evidence [that] provides reasonable grounds to believe that individuals identified have committed crimes against humanity and war crimes'.[37] The ICC Prosecutor found 'reasonable grounds to believe' that Omar al-Bashir has committed the crimes of genocide, and therefore genocide was committed in Darfur. The indictment of President al-Bashir added the crime of genocide.[38] The Prosecutor decision is awaiting Pre-Trial Chamber's consideration after the Appeal Chamber annulled the Pre-Trial Chamber's previous decision that denied issuing an arrest warrant for al-Bashir for the crime of genocide, and remanded the matter 'to the Pre-Trial Chamber for a new decision, using the correct standard of proof'.[39]

Crimes against humanity   There is a reasonable basis to believe that crimes against humanity, under Article 7 of the Statute, have occurred in Darfur.[40] These crimes include murder, extermination,[41] deportation or forcible transfer,[42] torture, rape, sexual slavery, forced pregnancy, conscription of child soldiers, and persecution on racial, ethnic and cultural grounds occurring on either widespread or systematic scale. The World Health Organization has estimated 70,000 deaths as of October 2004, and the UN Under-Secretary General for Humanitarian Affairs Jan Egeland estimated 180,000 deaths as of March 2005.[43] About 1.8 million civilians have

---

37   International Criminal Court, Office of the Prosecutor. 16 December 2006. Fourth Report of the Prosecutor of the International Criminal Court, Mr Luis Ocampo to the UN Security Council Pursuant to the UNSCR 1593(2005). Available at: www.icc-cpi.int/library/organs/otp/OTP_ReportUNSC4-Darfur_English.pdf [accessed: 25 June 2009].

38   International Criminal Court, Office of the Prosecutor. 14 July 2008. *Prosecutor's Application under Article 58, ICC-02/05-151*; Corrigendum to Prosecution's Application under Article 58 filed on 14 July 2008, ICC-02/05-151-US-Exp-Corr. A public redacted version was filed on 12 September 2009 under the number ICC-02/05-157-AnxA.

39   *Prosecutor* v. *Omar Hassan Ahmad Al Bashir*. 3 February 2010. Judgment on the Appeal of the Prosecutor against the 'Decision on the Prosecution's Application for a Warrant of Arrest against Omar Hassan Ahmad Al Bashir', ICC-02/05-01/09-OA.

40   International Criminal Court, Office of the Prosecutor. 16 December 2006. Fourth Report of the Prosecutor of the International Criminal Court, Mr Luis Ocampo to the UN Security Council Pursuant to the UNSCR 1593(2005). Available at: www.icc-cpi.int/library/organs/otp/OTP_ReportUNSC4-Darfur_English.pdf [accessed: 25 June 2009].

41   United Nations Commission of Inquiry. 25 January 2005. *Report of the International Commission of Inquiry on Darfur to the United Nations Secretary-General, Pursuant to Security Council Resolution 1564 of 18 September 2004*, para. 269-300. Available at: www.un.org/News/dh/sudan/com_inq_darfur.pdf [accessed: 16 May 2009].

42   United Nations Commission of Inquiry. 25 January 2005. *Report of the International Commission of Inquiry on Darfur to the United Nations Secretary-General, Pursuant to Security Council Resolution 1564 of 18 September 2004*, para. 322. Available at: www.un.org/News/dh/sudan/com_inq_darfur.pdf [accessed: 16 May 2009].

43   World Health Organization. 15 October 2004. *WHO Media Briefing: Mortality Projections for Darfur*. Available at: www.who.int/disasters/repo/14985.pdf [accessed: 6

been displaced, most often due to military attacks against their villages, and the systematic destruction and looting of their properties, as well as killing, rape, torture and other forms of violence. By June 2008, continuous violations have resulted in further displacing 100,000 individuals.[44] High rate of sexual violence and rape has continued in Darfur to add to the previous hundreds of cases that were documented in previous years.[45] For instance, by March 2005, reports managed to document 100 cases of rape committed mainly by alleged Sudanese government and Janjaweed forces. This appears to be a sample of a broader pattern;[46] the Sudanese government claims that in areas where such crimes took place there is a significant presence of enemy combatants.

The High-Level Mission on the Situation of Human Rights in Darfur, established by the Human Rights Council, stipulated in its report that crimes against humanity continue to occur in the region with gross and systematic violations of human rights and grave breaches of international humanitarian law.[47] Moreover, the OTP found reasonable grounds to believe that Ahmad Harun and Ali Kushayb bear criminal responsibility in relation to counts of crimes against humanity, including rape, murder, persecution, torture, forcible transfer, destruction of property,

---

June 2008]. See also BBC Report of 14 March 2005 quoting John Egeland: 'It could be just as well more than 200,000 [over 18 months] but I think 10,000 a month is a reasonable figure'. Available at: http://news.bbc.co.uk/2/hi/africa/4349063.stm [accessed: 16 June 2008].

44   International Criminal Court, Office of the Prosecutor. 5 June 2008. *Seventh Report of the Prosecutor of the International Criminal Court to the UN Security Council Pursuant to the UNSCR 1593(2005)*, para. 73. Available at: www.icc-cpi.int/library/organs/otp/UNSC_2008_En.pdf [accessed: 7 July 2009].

45   International Criminal Court, Office of the Prosecutor. 5 June 2008. *Seventh Report of the Prosecutor of the International Criminal Court to the UN Security Council Pursuant to the UNSCR 1593(2005)*, para. 75. Available at: www.icc-cpi.int/library/organs/otp/UNSC_2008_En.pdf [accessed: 7 July 2009].

46   Médecins Sans Frontières. 8 March 2005. *The Crushing Burden of Rape: Sexual Violence in Darfur*. Available at: www.doctorswithoutborders.org/publications/reports/2005/sudan03.pdf [accessed: 16 June 2009]. Between October 2004 and the first half of February 2005, doctors from Doctors Without Borders/Médecins Sans Frontières (MSF) on its own treated almost 500 rape victims in South and West Darfur. See also MSF-Netherlands. 7 December 2004. The People of Darfur have the Right to Ask Why. Available at: www.msf.org/msfInternational/invoke.cfm?objectid=27A81758-C4B6-4FD9-81EDE9D9266E3519&component=toolkit.Article&method=full_html&CFID=314357&CFTOKEN=73920792 [accessed: 16 May 2009]. See also United Nations Commission of Inquiry. 25 January 2005. *Report of the International Commission of Inquiry on Darfur to the United Nations Secretary-General, Pursuant to Security Council Resolution 1564 of 18 September 2004*. Available at: www.un.org/News/dh/sudan/com_inq_darfur.pdf [accessed: 16 May 2009].

47   Human Rights Council. 7 March 2007. Report of the High-Level Mission on the Situation of Human Rights in Darfur pursuant to Human Rights Council Decision S-4/101, Human Rights Council Fourth Session, A/HRC/4/80, para. 76, 24.

pillaging, inhumane acts, outrage upon personal dignity and attacks against the civilian population.[48]

War crimes   There are also reasons to believe that war crimes, as specified under Article 8(2)(c), have been committed in Darfur. A state of armed conflict of non-international character can be said to have been in existence in Darfur since at least February 2003, when sustained fighting began between the JEM and SLA against the Sudanese government and forces allied to it.[49] The UN Commission of Inquiry has documented numerous cases of pillaging on systematic as well as widespread bases, mainly against African non-Arab tribes.[50]

The ICC Prosecutor found evidences of numerous occurrences of war crimes in Darfur.[51] The Prosecutor found reasonable grounds to believe that Ahmad Harun and Ali Kushayb bear criminal responsibility in relation to counts of war crimes.[52]

Genocide   There is credible information that the conflict may have some racial and ethnic dimensions. Certain crimes committed reflect a 'persecutional' intention on racial and ethnic lines. The scale of the crimes committed meets the threshold required for cases of genocide, but other elements of the crime of genocide do not seem to be fulfilled.

The crime of genocide requires the existence of objective elements (*actus reus*) and subjective elements (*mens rea*). The objective element consists of two elements. Firstly, the offence must take the form of '(a) killing, or (b) causing serious bodily or mental harm, or (c) inflicting on a group conditions of life calculated to bring about

---

48   International Criminal Court. February-March 2007. *The Office of the Prosecutor and its Investigation in Darfur, Sudan*, ICC News Letter, 13. Available at: www.icc-cpi. int/library/about/newsletter/files/ICC-NL13-200702_En.pdf [accessed: 16 July 2009].

49   United Nations Commission of Inquiry. 25 January 2005. *Report of the International Commission of Inquiry on Darfur to the United Nations Secretary-General, Pursuant to Security Council Resolution 1564 of 18 September 2004*, para. 76. Available at: www.un.org/News/dh/sudan/com_inq_darfur.pdf [accessed: 16 May 2009].

50   United Nations Commission of Inquiry. 25 January 2005. *Report of the International Commission of Inquiry on Darfur to the United Nations Secretary-General, Pursuant to Security Council Resolution 1564 of 18 September 2004*, para. 393. Available at: www.un.org/News/dh/sudan/com_inq_darfur.pdf [accessed: 16 May 2009].

51   International Criminal Court, Office of the Prosecutor. 16 December 2006. Fourth Report of the Prosecutor of the International Criminal Court, Mr Luis Ocampo to the UN Security Council Pursuant to the UNSCR 1593(2005). Available at: www.icc-cpi.int/library/organs/otp/OTP_ReportUNSC4-Darfur_English.pdf [accessed: 25 June 2009].

52   International Criminal Court, Office of the Prosecutor. 16 December 2006. Fourth Report of the Prosecutor of the International Criminal Court, Mr Luis Ocampo to the UN Security Council Pursuant to the UNSCR 1593(2005). Available at: www.icc-cpi.int/library/organs/otp/OTP_ReportUNSC4-Darfur_English.pdf [accessed: 25 June 2009].

its physical destruction; or (d) imposing measures intended to prevent birth within the group, or (e) forcibly transferring children of the group to another group'.[53] The second objective element relates to the targeted group that must be defined along national, ethnical, racial or religious group lines.

The subjective element constitutes of two components: '(a) the criminal intent required for the underlying offence (killing, causing serious bodily or mental harm, etc.) and, (b) the intent to destroy, in whole or in part the group as such'. This second intent 'is an aggravated criminal intention or *dolus specialis*'.[54]

It is worth analysing the findings of the Commission of Inquiry – with a focus on the subjective element – in comparison to other legal opinions.[55] The Commission invoked a developed definition of the *mens rea* for the genocide. Some jurists criticized the Commission's interpretation of the *dolus specialis*.[56] The Commission invoked the jurisprudence of the ICTY, specifically that of the *Jelisic* case, where the Appeals Chamber noted that:

> [A]s to proof of specific intent, it may, in the absence of direct explicit evidence, be inferred from a number of facts and circumstances, such as the general context, the perpetration of other culpable acts systematically directed against the same group, the scale of atrocities committed, the systematic targeting of victims on account of their membership of a particular group, or the repetition of destructive and discriminatory acts.[57]

From the facts and circumstances, the Commission was unable to determine any genocidal intention (*dolus specialis*). It analysed some cases to conclude that elements of the genocide were not fulfilled. It identified, among others, the attack of 22 January 2004 on Wadi Saleh, where the attackers executed seven

---

53   United Nations Commission of Inquiry. 25 January 2005. *Report of the International Commission of Inquiry on Darfur to the United Nations Secretary-General, Pursuant to Security Council Resolution 1564 of 18 September 2004*, para. 490, 495. Available at: www.un.org/News/dh/sudan/com_inq_darfur.pdf [accessed: 16 May 2009].

54   United Nations Commission of Inquiry. 25 January 2005. *Report of the International Commission of Inquiry on Darfur to the United Nations Secretary-General, Pursuant to Security Council Resolution 1564 of 18 September 2004*, para. 490, 495. Available at: www.un.org/News/dh/sudan/com_inq_darfur.pdf [accessed: 16 May 2009].

55   Such as that of Claus Kress. See Kress, C. July 2005. The Darfur Report and Genocidal Intent. *Journal of International Criminal Justice*, 3, 562-577.

56   Kress, C. July 2005. The Darfur Report and Genocidal Intent. *Journal of International Criminal Justice*, 3, 562-577, 566.

57   *Prosecutor v. Goran Jelisic*. 5 July 2001. International Tribunal for the Prosecution of Persons Responsible for Serious Violations of International Humanitarian Law Committed in the Territory of the Former Yugoslavia since 1991, Case No. IT-95-10-A. Available at: www.un.org/icty/jelisic/appeal/judgement/jel-aj010705.pdf [accessed: 5 June 2009].

but spared the lives of the rest of the villagers (of the same ethnic background) after burning the village.[58]

Rejecting this methodology, Claus Kress challenged the purpose-based approach (adopted by the UN Commission) in favour of a knowledge-based approach.[59] Kress argues the requirements of genocidal intent should be satisfied if the perpetrator targeted members of a protected group with the knowledge that the goal or manifest effect of the campaign was the destruction of the group in whole or in part. In other words, the *dolus specialis*, identifying the intention 'to physically destroy a protected group' should be replaced by the view that such intent could be fulfilled by the individual's knowledge of a genocidal campaign; if not *dolus specialis*, at least *dolus eventualis* regarding, in the very least, the partial destruction of the protected group.[60] This position is supported by the opinions of US scholar, Alexander K.A. Greenawalt, Spanish scholar Alicia Gil Gil and the Swiss jurist Hans Vest.[61]

If the ICC Prosecutor adopts this empirical-oriented approach, then indicting for the crime of genocide becomes possible, especially since it is relatively easy to prove the objective element.[62] The ICC did recently indict President al-Bashir for the crime of genocide. The Prosecutor decision was not confirmed by the Trial Chamber, but then confirmed on appeal. The Appeal Chamber annulled the Pre-Trial Chamber's previous decision, and remanded the matter 'to the Pre-Trial Chamber for a new decision, using the correct standard of proof'.[63]

---

58   United Nations Commission of Inquiry. 25 January 2005. *Report of the International Commission of Inquiry on Darfur to the United Nations Secretary-General, Pursuant to Security Council Resolution 1564 of 18 September 2004*, para. 513. Available at: www.un.org/News/dh/sudan/com_inq_darfur.pdf [accessed: 16 May 2009].

59   The Knowledge-Based Approach was elaborated by the US scholar, Alexander K.A. Greenawalt. See Greenawalt, A.K.A. 1999. Rethinking Genocidal Intent: The Case For a Knowledge-Based Interpretation. *Columbia Law Review*, 99, 2259-2294, 2259, 2288.

60   Kress, C. July 2005. The Darfur Report and Genocidal Intent. *Journal of International Criminal Justice*, 3, 562-577, 562.

61   Gil Gil, A. 1999. *Derecho Penal Internacional: Especial consideracion del delito de genocidio*. Madrid: Editorial Tecnos, 259 et seq.; see also Gil Gil, A. 1999. Die Tatbestände der Verbrechen gegn die Menschlichkeit und des Völkermordes im Römischen Statut des Internationalen Strafgerichtshofs, *Zeitschrift für die gesamte Strafrechtswissenschaft*, 112, 381-397, 395. See Vest, H. 2002. *Genozid durch organisatorische Machtapparate*. Baden-Baden: Nomos Verlagsgesellschaft, 104.

62   Quénivet, N. July-September 2006. The Report of the International Commission of Inquiry on Darfur: The Question of Genocide. *Human Rights Review*, 38-67, 47.

63   *Prosecutor v. Omar Hassan Ahmad Al Bashir*. 3 February 2010. Judgment on the Appeal of the Prosecutor against the 'Decision on the Prosecution's Application for a Warrant of Arrest against Omar Hassan Ahmad Al Bashir', ICC-02/05-01/09-OA.

Security Council Referral (Negatives and Positives)

On 31 March 2005, the Security Council adopted Resolution 1593, which referred the situation in Darfur to the International Criminal Council under Article 13(b).[64] Many lauded the first referral, as it represented a further vote of confidence for the ICC from the major powers, and an important change in US policy. Unfortunately, a number of problems accompanied this historic step.[65] Before delving into Resolution 1593 and the referral, it is important to note that this study limits itself to analyse the referral's conformity with Article 13(b) of the Statute and not with respect to the UN Charter.

For the ICC, the referral has a number of positive implications. It is an opportunity to fight against impunity, and for accountability for international crimes, as Darfur has become 'a byword for impunity, a wilderness of atrocity and crime, and probably the world's worst humanitarian disaster'.[66] With the Sudanese government unwilling to protect its citizens in Darfur, the international community felt obligated to respond. The discussions prior to the adoption of the referring Resolution ranged from establishing a regional *ad hoc* tribunal[67] to extending the ICTR mandate,[68] but the Security Council chose instead to use the ICC with the aim of ending impunity in Darfur, by adopting the recommendation of the UN Commission of Inquiry.[69] The option of a regional *ad hoc* tribunal was rejected since experience proved that this was expensive and time consuming.[70] The option to extend the ICTR's mandate proved to be impractical, since the ICTR

---

64   United Nations Security Council Resolution 1593. 31 March 2005. UN Doc. S/RES/1593.

65   Happold, M. 1 January 2006. Darfur, the Security Council, and the International Criminal Court. *International and Comparative Law Quarterly*, 55, 226-238, 226.

66   Udombana, N.J. Fall 2005. Pay Back Time in Sudan? Darfur in the International Criminal Court. *Tulsa Journal of Comparative and International Law*, 13, 1-57, 3.

67   Africa News. 9 February 2005. Sudan; African Union Tribunal Proposed for War Crimes in Darfur, see also *Scotland on Sunday*. 30 January 2005. No Relief for Sudan's Agony as UN Quibbles over the Case for Genocide.

68   United Nations Commission of Inquiry. 25 January 2005. *Report of the International Commission of Inquiry on Darfur to the United Nations Secretary-General, Pursuant to Security Council Resolution 1564 of 18 September 2004*, para. 573-582. Available at: www.un.org/News/dh/sudan/com_inq_darfur.pdf [accessed: 16 May 2009].

69   United Nations Commission of Inquiry. 25 January 2005. *Report of the International Commission of Inquiry on Darfur to the United Nations Secretary-General, Pursuant to Security Council Resolution 1564 of 18 September 2004*, para. 678. Available at: www.un.org/News/dh/sudan/com_inq_darfur.pdf [accessed: 16 May 2009].

70   United Nations Commission of Inquiry. 25 January 2005. *Report of the International Commission of Inquiry on Darfur to the United Nations Secretary-General, Pursuant to Security Council Resolution 1564 of 18 September 2004*, para. 648. Available at: www.un.org/News/dh/sudan/com_inq_darfur.pdf [accessed: 16 May 2009].

was already struggling to cope with pending cases and meet the deadline for the 'completion strategy'.[71]

Thus, the ICC quickly became an available option, for relatively expedient and less costly trials for international crimes. The Darfur referral could be viewed, in a way, as a tacit recognition by certain major powers of the importance of the ICC as a vital institution that enjoys the necessary legitimacy to prosecute international crimes.[72] In addition, the referral is a major step towards restoring real peace in Sudan; for many, peace cannot be bought at the price of justice.[73]

On the other hand, the Security Council referral through Resolution 1593 subsumed a number of contentious points that do not conform with Article 13(b) of the ICC Statute.

Firstly, the Resolution exempts certain categories of civilians and persons from the jurisdiction of the Court in contradiction to the Rome Statute.[74] The Resolution invokes in its preamble Article 16. However, it interprets the Article incorrectly. Paragraph 6 of the Resolution stipulates that:

> [N]ationals, current or former officials or personnel from a contributing State outside Sudan which is not a party to the Rome Statute of the International Criminal Court shall be subject to the exclusive jurisdiction of that contributing State for all alleged acts or omissions arising out of or related to operations in Sudan established or authorized by the Council or the African Union.[75]

The immunity provided in this Resolution clearly exceeds the requirements and limits of Article 16,[76] and is close to the immunity provided in Security Council Resolution 1497. This book has shown above that the deferral of ICC jurisdiction, under Resolution 1497, does not fall under the ambit of Article 16. Resolution 1593 also has not been fully consistent with Article 16, as it has provided a blanket amnesty to specified potential offenders, namely nationals, current or former

---

71   United Nations Commission of Inquiry. 25 January 2005. *Report of the International Commission of Inquiry on Darfur to the United Nations Secretary-General, Pursuant to Security Council Resolution 1564 of 18 September 2004*, para. 575. Available at: www.un.org/News/dh/sudan/com_inq_darfur.pdf [accessed: 16 May 2009].

72   Udombana, N.J. Fall 2005. Pay Back Time in Sudan? Darfur in the International Criminal Court. *Tulsa Journal of Comparative and International Law*, 13, 1-57, 9.

73   Udombana, N.J. Fall 2005. Pay Back Time in Sudan? Darfur in the International Criminal Court. *Tulsa Journal of Comparative and International Law*, 13, 1-57, 10.

74   Happold, M. 1 January 2006. Darfur, the Security Council, and the International Criminal Court. *International and Comparative Law Quarterly*, 55, 226-238, 231.

75   United Nations Security Council Resolution 1593. 31 March 2005. UN Doc. S/RES/1593.

76   Heyder, C. 2006. The U.N. Security Council's Referral of the Crimes in Darfur to the International Criminal Court in Light of U.S. Opposition to the Court: Implications for the International Criminal Court's Functions and Status. *Berkeley Journal of International Law*, 24, 650-671, 657.

officials or personnel from contributing non-state parties who have exclusive jurisdiction over them.[77]

Secondly, the immunity provided does not respect the 12-month renewable period under Article 16; rather it grants unlimited temporal blanket amnesty from the ICC's jurisdiction.[78] This is unfortunate since Article 13(b) refers to 'situations', while the Council seems to have 'salami-sliced' the situation to exempt some parties or persons from the jurisdiction of the Court. Neither Article 13 nor 16 gives the Security Council the power to act in such a manner.[79] Again, Resolution 1593, in this respect, follows the path of Resolution 1497. Many experts saw the latter as an unlawful resolution in which the Security Council acted *ultra vires* vis-à-vis the Rome Statute. As a result, the same argument can be raised against paragraph 6 of Resolution 1593.[80]

Thirdly, the language of Resolution 1593 does not impose an equal obligation on all states to cooperate fully with the ICC. It rather uses ambiguous language that imposes different obligations for various parties and non-parties to the Rome Statute.[81] The Resolution mandates that the Sudanese government and the other parties to the conflict in Darfur cooperate fully with the Court, while it just 'urges' other 'states ... to cooperate fully'.[82] This implies that non-state parties to the ICC Statute, except for Sudan and parties to the conflict, are under no full obligation to cooperate or support the ICC in its prosecutions in the Darfur situation.[83]

The Resolution adds that non-state parties to the Rome Statute have no obligations under the Statute. This is correct under treaty law according to the maxim *pacta tertiis nec nocent nec procent.* However, when the Security Council adopted Resolution 1593, it was acting under Chapter VII and thus it can impose such obligations on all UN member states.

---

77   Condorelli, L. and Ciampi, A. 2005. Comments on the Security Council Referral of the Situation on Darfur to the International Criminal Court. *Journal of International Criminal Justice*, 3, 590-599, 596.

78   Condorelli, L. and Ciampi, A. 2005. Comments on the Security Council Referral of the Situation on Darfur to the International Criminal Court. *Journal of International Criminal Justice*, 3, 590-599, 596.

79   Happold, M. 1 January 2006. Darfur, the Security Council, and the International Criminal Court. *International and Comparative Law Quarterly*, 55, 226-238, 226.

80   See pp. 124-31 in this book, where Resolution 1497 has been analysed extensively.

81   Happold, M. 1 January 2006. Darfur, the Security Council, and the International Criminal Court. *International and Comparative Law Quarterly*, 55, 226-238, 230.

82   United Nations Security Council Resolution 1593. 31 March 2005. UN Doc. S/RES/1593, para. 2.

83   Heyder, C. 2006. The U.N. Security Council's Referral of the Crimes in Darfur to the International Criminal Court in Light of U.S. Opposition to the Court: Implications for the International Criminal Court's Functions and Status. *Berkeley Journal of International Law*, 24, 650-671, 655.

The Resolution's equivocal language may weaken the full cooperation of the states with the Court.[84] One can argue that the referral itself under Chapter VII empowers the ICC with powers similar to those of the ICTY and ICTR, and thus all states are under the obligation to cooperate fully with the ICC with respect to the Darfur referral.[85]

Fourthly, another setback in Resolution 1593 is paragraph 7, which stipulates that the costs related to investigations or prosecutions in connection with that referral shall be borne by state parties to the Rome Statute and those states that wish to contribute voluntarily, but not through the UN budget.[86] The United States was staunchly behind inserting this paragraph. The US government has even stressed that 'any effort to retrench on this principle (that all costs be borne by Statute of Rome member states) by (the United Nations) or other organizations to which (the United States) contribute(s) could result in (its) withholding funding or taking other action in response'.[87]

This raises the question of the financial relationship between the ICC and the UN, and whether the Security Council is authorized to exempt the UN members from any obligation to contribute to the budget of the ICC with respect to the referred situation.

The question is answered in the Negotiated Relationship Agreement signed in October 2004 between the ICC and the UN.[88] In this Agreement, the two institutions organized their financial relationship under the umbrella of Article 115 of the ICC Statute. The Agreement stipulates that 'the conditions under which any funds may be provided to the Court by a decision of the General Assembly of the UN pursuant to Article 115 of the Statute shall be subject to separate arrangements'.[89]

---

84   Heyder, C. 2006. The U.N. Security Council's Referral of the Crimes in Darfur to the International Criminal Court in Light of U.S. Opposition to the Court: Implications for the International Criminal Court's Functions and Status. *Berkeley Journal of International Law*, 24, 650-671, 655.

85   Udombana, N.J. Fall 2005. Pay Back Time in Sudan? Darfur in the International Criminal Court. *Tulsa Journal of Comparative and International Law*, 13, 1-57, 24.

86   United Nations Security Council Resolution 1593. 31 March 2005. UN Doc. S/RES/1593, para. 7.

87   US Ambassador to the United Nations. 31 March 2005. *Explanation of Vote on the Sudan Accountability Resolution*. Press Release. Available at: www.state.gov/p/io/44388htm [accessed: 5 June 2009].

88   Negotiated Relationship Agreement between the ICC and the UN. 4 October 2004. Available at: www.icc-cpi.int/library/asp/ICC-ASP-3-Res1English.pdf [accessed: 5 May 2009].

89   Article 13 of the Negotiated Relationship Agreement between the ICC and the UN. 4 October 2004. Available at: www.icc-cpi.int/library/asp/ICC-ASP-3-Res1English.pdf [accessed: 5 May 2009].

Further, Article 115(b) of the Rome Statute stipulates that funds provided by the United Nations, in particular those incurred due to referrals by the Security Council, are subject to the approval of the General Assembly.[90]

This means that the United Nations General Assembly is the authoritative body for deciding whether or not to provide such funds to the Court in the case of a referral.[91] This is in conformity with Article 17(1) of the UN Charter, which grants the General Assembly the power to apportion the 'expenses of the Organization'.[92]

Paragraph 7 of Resolution 1593 breaches this Agreement, as well as Article 115(b) of the ICC Statute since it deprives the General Assembly from possible contribution to the ICC regarding this referral.[93]

To conclude, Resolution 1593 was the result of a political compromise[94] rather than the outcome of an unfettered pursuit of international justice.[95] These shortcomings, however, do not minimize its significance, but draw attention to the difficulty achieving the drafters' goals, and the much work that is still needed for international justice to develop independent of political influence.

The Application of Complementarity on Darfur's Referral

Complementarity under Security Council Referrals in Abstract

When the Security Council refers a case to the ICC, the complementarity principle, as a jurisdictional principle, intersects with the top-down approach of *ad hoc* Tribunals.[96] Initially, as the Rome Statute did not include any explicit article

---

90   Article 115(b) of the Rome Statute of the International Criminal Court, UN Doc. A/CONF.183/9.

91   Happold, M. 1 January 2006. Darfur, the Security Council, and the International Criminal Court. *International and Comparative Law Quarterly*, 55, 226-238, 233.

92   Article 17(1) of the Charter of the United Nations. Available at: www.un.org/aboutun/Charter/intod.htm [accessed: 5 May 2008].

93   Article 115 of the Rome Statute of the International Criminal Court, UN Doc. A/CONF.183/9.

94   Human Rights Watch. 31 March 2005. U.N. Security Council Refers Darfur to the ICC UN Security Council Refers Darfur to the ICC Historic Step Toward Justice; Further Protection Measures Needed. Available at: http://hrw.org/english/docs/2005/03/31/sudan10408.htm [accessed: 11 May 2009].

95   Heyder, C. 2006. The U.N. Security Council's Referral of the Crimes in Darfur to the International Criminal Court in Light of U.S. Opposition to the Court: Implications for the International Criminal Court's Functions and Status. *Berkeley Journal of International Law*, 24, 650-671, 656.

96   Lipscomb, R. January 2006. Restructuring the ICC Framework to Advance Transitional Justice: A Search for a Permanent Solution in Sudan. *Columbia Law Review*, 106, 182-217, 190.

on the applicability of complementarity regarding Security Council referrals, scholars disagreed over whether or not the regime should apply.[97] This ambiguity arose from the fact that Article 18, which constitutes an integral part of the system of admissibility, does not apply to Article 13(b) referrals.[98] However, this is an erroneous understanding of the applicability of the complementarity principle regarding Security Council referral, as the exemption of the Prosecutor to notify all states parties and concerned states of his investigation is in fact due to the simple fact that these states have already been informed through the Security Council resolution.

It is clear that the complementarity regime applies in the event of a Security Council referral, as Articles 17 and 19 do not differentiate between Security Council referrals and other methods of referrals.[99] The legal language of Article 17 does not indicate any different application of the admissibility test in the event of a Security Council referral. The Statute expressly dispenses with the Article 18 notification for Council referrals, which further strengthens the conclusion *a contrario* that Articles 17 and 19 still apply even for Council referrals.[100]

This position also finds strong support in Article 53 of the Statute, which stipulates that: 'In deciding whether to initiate an investigation, the prosecutor shall: … b) consider whether the case is or would be admissible under Article 17'.[101] The Article does not speak about any specific referral, but rather abstractly organizes the Prosecutor's initiation of an investigation. This leaves no doubt that the complementarity principle remains in function. It is important to note that UN Security Council referrals have to meet the Statute requirements for admissibility, and not vice versa. It is for the Court to decide if the referral is admissible or not, as it determines its own competence, according to the principle *Kompetenz-*

---

97   Kiefer, K.P. 2005. Note, Exercising Their Rights: Native American Nations of the United States Enhancing Political Sovereignty through Ratification of the Rome Statute. *Syracuse Journal of International Law and Com*, 32, 345-372, 356; Doherty, K.L. and McCormack, T.L.H. 1999. Complementarity as a Catalyst for Comprehensive Domestic Penal Legislation. *Davis Journal of International Law and Policy*, 5, 147-180, 151.

98   Article 18 does not apply to Article 13(b) of the Rome Statute.

99   The International Criminal Court, Office of the Prosecutor. 2003. *Informal Expert Paper: The Principle of Complementarity in Practice*. ICC-OTP 2003, 1-38, 17. Available at: www.icc-cpi.int/library/organs/otp/complementarity.pdf [accessed: 11 August 2009]. The International Criminal Court, Office of the Prosecutor. 2003. *Informal Expert Paper: The Principle of Complementarity in Practice*. ICC-OTP 2003, 1-38, 20. Available at: www. icc-cpi.int/library/organs/otp/complementarity.pdf [accessed: 11 August 2009].

100   Holmes, J. 2002. Complementarity: National Courts versus the International Criminal Court, in *The Rome Statute of The International Criminal Court: A Commentary*, edited by A. Cassese, P. Gaeta and J.R.W.D. Jones. Oxford: Oxford University Press, I, 683.

101   Article 53 of the Rome Statute of the International Criminal Court, UN Doc. A/CONF.183/9.

Kompetenz.[102] It is for the Prosecutor to dismiss any situation referred to him, even those referred by the Security Council. This practice is an exception to the general powers of the Security Council under Chapter VII,[103] as usually all UN Security Council resolution, taken under Chapter VII, are binding on all states. However, the ICC is not a state, and thus Security Council actions under Chapter VII do not impose such obligation on this international organization.[104]

According to one author, Article 19 details the application of complementarity to referrals by the Security Council:

> It [Article 19] provides a second opportunity to States, even non-party States, to stop a prosecution by challenging the admissibility of a 'particular case' on the grounds set out in Article 17. By guaranteeing all those 'who have referred the situation under Article 13,' the chance to submit observations to the Court, the rule indirectly confirms the applicability of terms for admitting a case even when it is the result of a Security Council initiative.[105]

In order to avoid any exploitation of Article 13(b), the Statute imposes various requirements, which the Security Council has to fulfil. These measures include the existence of a threat to peace and security; adopting the resolution under Chapter VII; and more importantly referring a situation and not a single case.[106] The latter requirement was included to avoid allowing the Security Council to act as a judicial body, and to preserve the Court's independence in the exercise of its jurisdiction.[107]

The Pre-Trial Chamber I indicated clearly that:

> The prosecutor also has an obligation to respect the principle of complementarity
> by monitoring any ongoing investigations and prosecutions by the Government
> of Sudan itself. Subject to all the aforementioned legal duties the Statute grants

---

102   *Prosecutor* v. *Dusko Tadic A/K/A 'Dule'*, 10 August 1995. Decision on the Defence Motion on Jurisdiction, ICTY, IT-94-1.

103   El-Zeidy, M. Summer 2002. The Principle of Complementarity: A Machinery to Implement International Criminal Law. *Michigan Journal of International Law*, 23, 4, 869-978, 913.

104   The International Criminal Court, Office of the Prosecutor. 2003. *Informal Expert Paper: The Principle of Complementarity in Practice*. ICC-OTP 2003, 1-38, 21. Available at: www.icc-cpi.int/library/organs/otp/complementarity.pdf [accessed: 11 August 2009].

105   El-Zeidy, M. Summer 2002. The Principle of Complementarity: A Machinery to Implement International Criminal Law. *Michigan Journal of International Law*, 23, 4, 869-978, 913.

106   Article 13(b) of the Rome Statute of the International Criminal Court, UN Doc. A/CONF.183/9.

107   Yee, L. 2002. The International Criminal Court and the Security Council: Articles 13(b) and 16, in *The International Criminal Court: The Making of the Rome Statute, Issues, Negotiations, Results*, edited by R. Lee. The Hague: Kluwer, 144.

to the prosecutor discretion in the manner in which the investigation is carried out.[108]

Moreover, the Prosecutor, in his fourth report to the Security Council on the Darfur referral, expressed a number of important points. Firstly, he stressed the application of the complementarity principle. Secondly, he affirmed that the admissibility test applies to 'cases'; the 'case' in this regard 'represents a specific incident in which crimes within the jurisdiction of the Court have been committed by identified perpetrators'.[109] Interestingly, he indicated that, under the Statute, the admissibility test is not an assessment of the judicial system as a whole, but rather an assessment on a case-by-case level to determine if the national authorities have conducted genuine investigation or prosecution regarding the particular case.[110] Thirdly, the admissibility assessment remains 'on-going and a final determination will be made following a full investigation of the specific cases that are selected for prosecution'.[111]

Based on the above, it is incontestable that the complementarity principle frames the relation of the Security Council referrals before the ICC. The ICC must find out whether the Security Council resolution fulfils the requirement of Article 13(b), and determine the admissibility of the case under Article 17. However, the uncontested applicability of complementarity does not preclude raising the question of the nature of the complementarity principle under SC referrals.

Complementarity or primacy   As complementarity remains applicable, one cannot forget that the jurisdiction of the Court stems from a binding decision adopted by the Security Council under Chapter VII. The power of the Court in such a situation originates from Chapter VII and not from treaty law. This grants the ICC broader powers (under Chapter VII) in comparison to the cases of state referrals and *proprio motu* (treaty obligations). Under SC referral, the ICC binding

---

108   International Criminal Court, Pre-Trial Chamber I. 11 September 2006. *Situation In Darfur, Sudan: Prosecutor's Response To Cassese's Observation On Issues Concerning The Protection of Victims And The Preservation of Evidence In The Proceedings On Darfur Pending Before The ICC*, English no.: ICC-02/05.

109   International Criminal Court. February-March 2007. *The Office of the Prosecutor and its Investigation in Darfur, Sudan*, ICC News Letter, 13. Available at: www.icc-cpi.int/library/about/newsletter/files/ICC-NL13-200702_En.pdf [accessed: 16 July 2008].

110   International Criminal Court, Office of the Prosecutor. 5 June 2008. *Seventh Report of the Prosecutor of the International Criminal Court to the UN Security Council Pursuant to the UNSCR 1593(2005)*, para. 20. Available at: www.icc-cpi.int/library/organs/otp/UNSC_2008_En.pdf [accessed: 7 July 2009].

111   International Criminal Court, Office of the Prosecutor. 16 December 2006. Fourth Report of the Prosecutor of the International Criminal Court, Mr Luis Ocampo to the UN Security Council Pursuant to the UNSCR 1593(2005), 1-11, 6. Available at: www.icc-cpi.int/library/organs/otp/OTP_ReportUNSC4-Darfur_English.pdf [accessed: 25 June 2009].

power is *erga omnes* before all states, while ICC powers in the other kinds of referrals only binds state parties to the ICC Statute.

However, differences arise when analysing the role of the Security Council in the facilitation or determination of the nature and criteria of admissibility of the case before the ICC. According to one interpretation, the Security Council can facilitate admissibility through an express language in a resolution referring a situation to the Prosecutor. The Court, however, will probably reject this view, as the ICC drafters refused to grant the Council a judicial role.[112] It may be refused because the Security Council referral should meet the requirements of the Statute, and not vice versa.[113]

Another interpretation locates the power to bestow *de facto* primacy in the Security Council, since this has been manifestly true for other tribunals under Chapter VII and holds in light of Article 103 (UN Charter obligations are paramount).[114] This interpretation, however, is also inaccurate, as the referral is granted under the Statute, and thus the Statute and not the UN Charter rules it.

A third interpretation keeps Article 17 intact, but grants the Council room to express the view that a national system is unable or unwilling. The Court could consider such an opinion.[115] Yet allowing the Council, as a political entity, to make such a determination will likely be unacceptable to the Court, as a judicial body.

A fourth interpretation implies that, while Article 17 applies, the Council could direct states to defer proceedings in favour of ICC proceedings, and thus Article 17 would be satisfied due to the resulting lack of national proceedings.[116] By this logic, the OTP could interpret the referral as an indicator of the Council's

---

112   Lawyers Committee for Human Rights. August 1996. International Criminal Court Major Unresolved Issues in the Draft Statute: A Position Paper of the Lawyers Committee for Human Rights, 1-35, 18. Available at: www.iccnow.org/documents/2PrepCmtEstablishICCLCHR.pdf [accessed: 5 June 2009].

113   The Court will primary act according to Article 13 of the ICC Statute and not the UN Charter. Article 21 indicates that the Statute is the primary applicable law for the ICC. Article 21(1) of the Rome Statute of the International Criminal Court, UN Doc. A/CONF.183/9.

114   In a press release following the referral, the FIDH argued that 'although the ICC is complementary to national jurisdictions, the fact that the Security Council brought this matter to the ICC implicitly indicates that the ICC has primacy in prosecuting the suspects: the Sudanese authorities will thus have to abide by the resolution of the U.N. political body'. FIDH. 4 April 2005. *The Security Council refers the Darfur Situation to the International Criminal Court*. Available at: www.fidh.org/Article.php3?id_Article=2336 [accessed: 5 June 2009].

115   Holmes, J. 2002. Complementarity: National Courts versus the International Criminal Court, in *The Rome Statute of The International Criminal Court: A Commentary*, edited by A. Cassese, P. Gaeta and J.R.W.D. Jones. Oxford: Oxford University Press, I, 683.

116   The International Criminal Court, Office of the Prosecutor. 2003. *Informal Expert Paper: The Principle of Complementarity in Practice*. ICC-OTP 2003, 1-38, paragraphs

consideration of the lack of genuine national proceedings. It will ultimately be up to the ICC to decide on whether or not to consider such a determination a factor in its assessment. In Darfur's referral, the text of the Resolution does not provide particular assistance in facilitating admissibility. In fact, the Security Council not only left the complementarity regime intact, but also encouraged national action.[117] The Prosecutor in his reports to the Security Council applied the admissibility test on the cases of Ahmad Harun and Ali Kushayb in a similar way to that of state referrals in the case of Uganda and the DRC.[118]

Thus, the last interpretation seems to be the most appropriate for the Statute and the prosecutorial policy of the ICC. The ICC is an international organization that enjoys independence concerning other international organizations, including the UN and its Security Council. Yet while this argument is valid between the ICC and the UN, it is inapplicable with respect to states, as the UN Charter's obligations for states supersede other international obligations,[119] because state obligations under the Charter ultimately prevail over complementarity requirements under the Statute. One author affirms this by stating that 'the obligations of states under the Charter may override certain fundamental principles in the Rome Statute'.[120] For the same reason, the Group on the Principle of Complementarity in Practice agreed that the Security Council has the power to issue orders to states to comply with the requests of the ICC.[121]

The predominance of obligations under the Charter thus allows Security Council referrals, under Chapter VII, to have the practical effect of appropriating judicial primacy to the ICC, similar to that enjoyed by the ICTY and the ICTR. If the referring resolution rejects national jurisdiction in favour of the ICC, it will then have a direct effect in creating a case of 'inaction' on behalf of the national judicial system. However, it will remain for the ICC to determine the admissibility of the case. In this scenario, 'the complementarity principle would still apply,

---

67-70. Available at: www.icc-cpi.int/library/organs/otp/complementarity.pdf [accessed: 11 August 2009].

117   United Nations Security Council Resolution 1593. 31 March 2005. UN Doc. S/RES/1593, para. 4.

118   International Criminal Court, Office of the Prosecutor. 5 June 2008. *Seventh Report of the Prosecutor of the International Criminal Court to the UN Security Council Pursuant to the UNSCR 1593(2005)*, para. 20. Available at: www.icc-cpi.int/library/organs/otp/UNSC_2008_En.pdf [accessed: 7 July 2009].

119   Article 103 of the Charter of the United Nations. Available at: www.un.org/aboutun/Charter/intod.htm [accessed: 25 May 2009].

120   Lipscomb, R. January 2006. Restructuring the ICC Framework to Advance Transitional Justice: A Search for a Permanent Solution in Sudan. *Columbia Law Review*, 106, 182-217, 191.

121   The International Criminal Court, Office of the Prosecutor. 2003. *Informal Expert Paper: The Principle of Complementarity in Practice*. ICC-OTP 2003, 1-38, 20-21. Available at: www.icc-cpi.int/library/organs/otp/complementarity.pdf [accessed: 11 August 2009].

but admissibility would be upheld by the Court, given the resulting absence of competing national proceedings as a result of compliance with the order of the Council'.[122]

In terms of the Darfur referral, Resolution 1593 did not eradicate the admissibility requirements, but rather encouraged the Court to support 'international cooperation with domestic efforts to promote the rule of law, protect human rights and combat impunity in Darfur'.[123] When read together with paragraph 5 of the Resolution, it becomes clear that the Security Council respected the complementarity principle of the ICC, and encouraged every effort to improve national efforts to end impunity in Darfur.

Darfur Referral and Admissibility Requirements

It is important to note that admissibility is tested by the OTP on a case-by-case basis. Prosecutor Moreno-Ocampo stated that 'the admissibility assessment is case specific and not a judgment on the Sudanese justice system as a whole'.[124] In other words the ICC will detect if each case (that fulfils the admissibility requirements) is being investigated by the 'concerned' national judicial systems (Sudan or other states that have jurisdiction), and if so, whether these proceedings reflect the willingness and ability to prosecute international crimes. However, this is not unproblematic; in the case of inability, as defined in Article 17, all cases may potentially be affected, as the state will be suffering from 'a total or substantial collapse or unavailability of its national judicial system', preventing Sudan from carrying out its proceedings in general.[125] With respect to 'unwillingness', a differentiation can be made between complete 'unwillingness' and 'selective' unwillingness. The criterion is not legal, but rather political: 'Selective' unwillingness could occur when the state decides to prosecute certain perpetrators but not others. In this scenario, admissibility on a case-by-case basis by the ICC would be crucial for pursuing justice. Before

---

122   The International Criminal Court, Office of the Prosecutor. 2003. *Informal Expert Paper: The Principle of Complementarity in Practice.* ICC-OTP 2003, 1-38, 21, para. 69. Available at: www.icc-cpi.int/library/organs/otp/complementarity.pdf [accessed: 11 August 2009].

123   United Nations Security Council Resolution 1593. 31 March 2005. UN Doc. S/RES/1593, para. 4.

124   Moreno-Ocampo, L. Prosecutor of the International Criminal Court. 23 November 2006. Fifth Session of the Assembly of State Parties, Opening Remarks. Available at: www.icc-cpi.int/library/organs/otp/LMO_20061123_en.pdf [accessed: 5 May 2009]. This was repeated also in the Prosecutor's reports to the Security Council under Resolution 1593. See the Seventh Report to the Security Council. International Criminal Court, Office of the Prosecutor. 5 June 2008. *Seventh Report of the Prosecutor of the International Criminal Court to the UN Security Council Pursuant to the UNSCR 1593(2005)*, para. 73. Available at: www.icc-cpi.int/library/organs/otp/UNSC_2008_En.pdf [accessed: 7 July 2009].

125   Article 17(3) of the Rome Statute of the International Criminal Court, UN Doc. A/CONF.183/9.

delving into the admissibility requirements of the Darfur referral, it is important to shed light on the background of the Sudanese judicial system. After that, the chapter will address the admissibility requirements under Article 17. This entails the analysis of the complementarity principle, including looking into the existence of an investigation, unwillingness, inability and instances of 'inaction'.

The Sudanese legal system

(a) Background   The Sudanese judiciary is a judicial system with a Supreme Court at the top of the hierarchy,[126] Courts of Appeal in each state,[127] District Courts,[128] and finally Town or Rural Courts.[129] The latter mainly apply tribal law via judges chosen, from among people with good conduct, by the Chief Justice.[130] Beyond this, there is the Constitutional Court,[131] Public Order Courts,[132] Military, National Security, and Police Courts.[133] There are also other courts, usually created by executive authority, such as the special and specialized courts.[134] The latter type of courts has been adopted especially for Darfur. The Commission of Inquiry noticed that 'cases of interest to the Government appear to be referred to these

---

126   Website of the Sudanese Judiciary. Available at: www.sudanjudiciary.org [accessed: 5 June 2009].

127   The website of the Sudanese Judiciary indicates that there are 28 Appeal Courts with 133 judges. There is one in each state of Darfur. Available at: www.sudanjudiciary.org [accessed: 5 June 2009].

128   According to the website to the Sudanese Judiciary, there are 397 courts all over Sudan. Available at: www.sudanjudiciary.org [accessed: 5 June 2009].

129   According to the website to the Sudanese Judiciary, there are 1,062 courts all over Sudan. Available at: www.sudanjudiciary.org [accessed: 5 June 2009].

130   According to the US Department of State, these courts deal with land, water and family matters. US Department of State. 2004. *Report on the Human Rights Practices.* Available at: www.state.gov/g/drl/rls/hrrpt/2004/41628.htm [accessed: 12 May 2009].

131   United Nations Commission of Inquiry. 25 January 2005. *Report of the International Commission of Inquiry on Darfur to the United Nations Secretary-General, Pursuant to Security Council Resolution 1564 of 18 September 2004*, para. 438. Available at: www.un.org/News/dh/sudan/com_inq_darfur.pdf [accessed: 16 May 2009].

132   Joint Assessment Mission, Sudan. March 2005. *Cluster II Report, Governance and Rule of Law*. Available at: www.unsudanig.org/docs/Joint%20Assessment%20Mission %20(JAM)%20Volume%20II.pdf [accessed: 16 May 2009].

133   Parmar, Sh. January 2007. An Overview of the Sudanese Legal System and Legal Research, Hauser Global Law School Program, New York University School of Law, 1-16. Available at: www.nyulawglobal.org/globalex/Sudan.htm#_ednref7 [accessed: 1 July 2009].

134   Parmar, Sh. January 2007. An Overview of the Sudanese Legal System and Legal Research, Hauser Global Law School Program, New York University School of Law, 1-16. Available at: www.nyulawglobal.org/globalex/Sudan.htm#_ednref7 [accessed: 1 July 2009].

courts'.[135] The specialized courts inherited the functions and jurisdiction of the special courts, as well as their flaws and deficiencies.[136] Supporting this claim is the establishment of the Special Criminal Court on the Events in Darfur (SCCED)[137] through a decree of the Chief Justice, and the Special Criminal Courts for Nyala and El Geneina.

The effectiveness of these courts has been relatively low, if not ineffective. Very few cases of gross violations of human rights have been tackled by these courts.[138] The SCCED did not address the issue of criminal responsibility for senior-level officials in Darfur and Sudan. The single case in which a high-ranking official was charged ended with acquittal. The Human Rights Council's High-Level Mission to Darfur noticed that the 10 convicted state officials by the SCCED were low-level officers.[139] Evidence confirms a lack of respect for the due process before these specialized courts.[140]

In addition, the Sudanese president has established some extraordinary bodies for inquiring and investigating specific cases. The first of these bodies was the National Commission of Inquiry established in May 2004. The outcome of their work did not go beyond recommending 'further investigations' into specified incidents.[141] The High-Level Mission noticed that the created judicial and quasi-judicial bodies for ensuring accountability for human rights crimes in Darfur had

---

135   United Nations Commission of Inquiry. 25 January 2005. *Report of the International Commission of Inquiry on Darfur to the United Nations Secretary-General, Pursuant to Security Council Resolution 1564 of 18 September 2004*, para. 439. Available at: www.un.org/News/dh/sudan/com_inq_darfur.pdf [accessed: 16 May 2009].

136   United Nations Commission of Inquiry. 25 January 2005. *Report of the International Commission of Inquiry on Darfur to the United Nations Secretary-General, Pursuant to Security Council Resolution 1564 of 18 September 2004*, para. 442. Available at: www.un.org/News/dh/sudan/com_inq_darfur.pdf [accessed: 16 May 2009].

137   Human Rights Council. 7 March 2007. Report of the High-Level Mission on the Situation of Human Rights in Darfur pursuant to Human Rights Council Decision S-4/101, Human Rights Council Fourth Session, A/HRC/4/80, para. 50, 17.

138   Such as the mass killings of civilians, widespread burning of villages, systematic rape, and the other crimes. See United Nations Commission of Inquiry. 25 January 2005. *Report of the International Commission of Inquiry on Darfur to the United Nations Secretary-General, Pursuant to Security Council Resolution 1564 of 18 September 2004*, para. 648. Available at: www.un.org/News/dh/sudan/com_inq_darfur.pdf [accessed: 16 May 2009].

139   Human Rights Council. 7 March 2007. Report of the High-Level Mission on the Situation of Human Rights in Darfur pursuant to Human Rights Council Decision S-4/101, Human Rights Council Fourth Session, A/HRC/4/80, para. 51, 17.

140   United Nations Commission of Inquiry. 25 January 2005. *Report of the International Commission of Inquiry on Darfur to the United Nations Secretary-General, Pursuant to Security Council Resolution 1564 of 18 September 2004*, para. 445. Available at: www.un.org/News/dh/sudan/com_inq_darfur.pdf [accessed: 16 May 2009].

141   ICC, Office of the Prosecutor Report. 27 February 2007. *Situation in Darfur, the Sudan*. No. ICC-02/05.

limited results in dealing with the widespread and serious atrocities committed in the region.[142]

In terms of substantial law, Sudanese criminal laws do not proscribe the core crimes of the ICC including genocide,[143] war crimes and crimes against humanity.[144] If the Sudanese courts decide to prosecute these crimes, it has no option but to treat them as ordinary crimes, such as murder or rape. One can note that even prosecuting such crimes as ordinary ones remained limited, for example, few cases of rape have been prosecuted between 2003 and 2005.[145]

(b) The judicial system in Darfur   The Sudanese government has officially accused the rebels of weakening the effectiveness of the judiciary in Darfur.[146] However, official Sudanese sources continued to stress that the judicial system in Darfur has not collapsed substantially. Despite numerous criticisms of its impartiality and efficiency, credible reports – such as that of the International Commission of Inquiry – do not claim that the Sudanese judicial system is in a state of total or substantial collapse.[147]

On the other hand, the Sudanese judiciary seems to suffer from multiple flaws and deficiencies. Despite the existence of prisons[148] and a court structure

---

142   Human Rights Council. 7 March 2007. Report of the High-Level Mission on the Situation of Human Rights in Darfur pursuant to Human Rights Council Decision S-4/101, Human Rights Council Fourth Session, A/HRC/4/80, para. 47, 16.

143   The Genocide Convention entered into force for Sudan on 11 January 2004. Sudan does not seem to have implemented the Convention. Sudan acceded to the Convention on 13 October 2004. Available at: www.ohchr.org/english/countries/ratification/1.htm [accessed: 16 June 2009].

144   United Nations Commission of Inquiry. 25 January 2005. *Report of the International Commission of Inquiry on Darfur to the United Nations Secretary-General, Pursuant to Security Council Resolution 1564 of 18 September 2004*, para. 451. Available at: www.un.org/News/dh/sudan/com_inq_darfur.pdf [accessed: 16 May 2009].

145   Security Council. 10 May 2005. *Monthly Report of the Secretary-General on Darfur*, S/2005/305, paragraphs 19 and 20. Available at: http://daccessdds.un.org/doc/UNDOC/GEN/N05/337/43/PDF/N0533743.pdf?OpenElement [accessed: 16 June 2009]. See also Amnesty International Report. 19 July 2004. AFR 54-076/2004.

146   United Nations Commission of Inquiry. 25 January 2005. *Report of the International Commission of Inquiry on Darfur to the United Nations Secretary-General, Pursuant to Security Council Resolution 1564 of 18 September 2004*, para. 430. Available at: www.un.org/News/dh/sudan/com_inq_darfur.pdf [accessed: 16 May 2009].

147   Joint Assessment Mission, Sudan. March 2005. *Cluster II Report, Governance and Rule of Law*. Available at: www.unsudanig.org/docs/Joint%20Assessment%20Mission %20(JAM)%20Volume%20II.pdf [accessed: 16 May 2009].

148   Every state has a prison; their infrastructure is old and poor. Overcrowding is an urgent problem. See Joint Assessment Mission, Sudan. March 2005. *Cluster II Report, Governance and Rule of Law*. Available at: www.unsudanig.org/docs/Joint%20Assessment %20Mission%20(JAM)%20Volume%20II.pdf [accessed: 16 May 2009]. See also, Amnesty International. 8 June 2004. *Sudan, Darfur: Incommunicado Detention, Torture and Special*

throughout the country, regular access to justice remains very rare. This is due to the poor conditions of these structures, difficult logistical circumstances related to the judicial system, and the geography of the state.[149] A number of sources confirm that the appointment of judges is accompanied by political interferences to ensure that judges are politically loyal to the government.[150] After the coup of 1989, the followers of the National Islamic Front filled most public posts,[151] including the judicial ones. As a result, the judiciary, and the legal profession in general,[152] are perceived as subservient to the president and the security forces, especially in cases of crimes against the security of the state and the security forces.[153]

Based on the above, the Sudanese judicial system is available, and is not in a state of total or substantial collapse, yet suffers from a number of deficiencies caused by political interferences, mismanagement, corruption, and the negative impact of the conflict in Darfur.[154] The Chief Justice of West Darfur in an interview with one of the ICC Prosecution Mission to Sudan indicated that although there were difficulties for the administration of justice in the context of an ongoing conflict, the Courts under his authority completed 5,302 cases in 2006, leaving only seven cases outstanding.[155] The Report of the High-Level Mission confirms

---

Courts, AI Index: AFR 54/058/2004. Available at: http://web.amnesty.org/library/Index/ENGAFR540582004 [accessed: 22 June 2009].

149   Joint Assessment Mission, Sudan. March 2005. *Cluster II Report, Governance and Rule of Law*. Available at: www.unsudanig.org/docs/Joint%20Assessment%20Mission%20(JAM)%20Volume%20II.pdf [accessed: 16 May 2009].

150   See Kritzer, H.M. 2002. *Legal Systems of the World, A Political, Social, and Cultural Encyclopaedia*. Abc-Clio Inc, IV, 1542. Several reports by international sources highlight the Sudanese judiciary's lack of independence vis-à-vis political influence from the government. The selection of judges is based upon political loyalty rather than merits.

151   The President appoints the members of the Constitutional Courts and the Chief Justice of the Supreme Courts who controls the judiciary; see Article 104, No. 1 and 2 of the Constitution. Also, see US Department of State. 2004. *Report on the Human Rights Practices*. Available at: www.state.gov/g/drl/rls/hrrpt/2004/41628.htm [accessed: 12 May 2009].

152   In the 1997 Bar Association elections, an NIF-associated group won overwhelmingly. This happened with strong accusations of widespread fraud. See US Department of State. 2004. *Report on the Human Rights Practices*. Available at: www.state.gov/g/drl/rls/hrrpt/2004/41628.htm [accessed: 12 May 2009].

153   US Department of State. 2004. *Report on the Human Rights Practices*. Available at: www.state.gov/g/drl/rls/hrrpt/2004/41628.htm [accessed: 12 May 2009]; Kritzer, H.M. 2002. *Legal Systems of the World, A Political, Social, and Cultural Encyclopaedia*. Abc-Clio Inc, IV, 1542.

154   United Nations Commission of Inquiry. 25 January 2005. *Report of the International Commission of Inquiry on Darfur to the United Nations Secretary-General, Pursuant to Security Council Resolution 1564 of 18 September 2004*, para. 430. Available at: www.un.org/News/dh/sudan/com_inq_darfur.pdf [accessed: 16 May 2009].

155   The Office of the Prosecutor, the International Criminal Court. 27 February 2007. *Situation In Darfur, The Sudan: Prosecutor's Application under Article 58(7)*, para

this finding by indicating that 'the national court system in Sudan is functional and has jurisdiction over human rights crimes perpetrated in Darfur'.[156] However, it adds that 'these courts have been unable to resolve human rights abuses there'.[157]

The existence of an 'investigation'
Before testing whether or not the Sudanese judicial system is 'willing' and 'able' to prosecute international crimes occurring in Darfur, it is important to note that the requisite willingness and ability necessitates the presence of an investigation. The concept 'investigation', according to Article 17, refers essentially to criminal investigations. This finds grounds in paragraphs 4, 6 and 10 of the Preamble to the Statute.[158]

The Sudanese government has provided data on some cases of investigation, but, in general, there is very little evidence to suggest that investigations into crimes relevant for a complementarity assessment have yet taken place in Sudan. In terms of the jurisprudence of the Special Court for Darfur, reports show that some investigations have taken place. Until early 2006, the Special Court conducted six trials involving 26 defendants.[159] The court convicted 13 of these defendants, including one juvenile.[160] Furthermore, in February 2006, the head of the Sudanese governmental Human Rights Advisory Council submitted to the UN a list of 'individuals of the regular services who have been tried for perpetrating crimes connected with the Darfur conflict'.[161] In addition, the Commission of Inquiry has cited one case of an investigation provided by the Sudanese government in 2003 – the case of Jamal Suliman Mohamad Shayeb from the village of Halouf, and relates to the killing of 24 individuals. However, the Commission found that exceptional

---

261. Available at: www.icc-cpi.int/library/cases/ICC-02-05-56_English.pdf [accessed: 19 March 2009].

156   Human Rights Council. 7 March 2007. Report of the High-Level Mission on the Situation of Human Rights in Darfur pursuant to Human Rights Council Decision S-4/101, Human Rights Council Fourth Session, A/HRC/4/80, para. 46, 16.

157   Human Rights Council. 7 March 2007. Report of the High-Level Mission on the Situation of Human Rights in Darfur pursuant to Human Rights Council Decision S-4/101, Human Rights Council Fourth Session, A/HRC/4/80, para. 47, 16.

158   Paragraph 4, 6 and 10 of the Preamble of the Rome Statute of the International Criminal Court, UN Doc. A/CONF.183/9. See also argument *supra* in Complementarity in Abtract Chapter on on pp. 35-6.

159   Office of the Prosecutor, International Criminal Court. 13 December 2005. Second Report of the Prosecutor of the International Criminal Court, Mr. Luis Moreno Ocampo To The Security Council Pursuant to UNSC 1593 (2005), ICC-02/05, 5. Available at: www.icc-cpi.int/library/organs/otp/LMO_UNSC_ReportB_En.pdf [accessed: 15 June 2009].

160   Office of the Prosecutor, International Criminal Court. 13 December 2005. Second Report of the Prosecutor of the International Criminal Court, Mr. Luis Moreno Ocampo To The Security Council Pursuant to UNSC 1593 (2005), ICC-02/05, 5. Available at: www.icc-cpi.int/library/organs/otp/LMO_UNSC_ReportB_En.pdf [accessed: 15 June 2009].

161   Agence France Presse (AFP), 27 February 2006.

compared to the large number of cases where the government failed to take measures to prosecute since February 2003.[162] The Sudanese government recently announced that approximately 160 suspects were identified for investigation and prosecution, but the ICC Prosecutor indicated in his seventh report to the Security Council that most of the cases did not involve serious violations of international humanitarian law.[163] In a previous report to the Security Council, Prosecutor Moreno-Ocampo concluded that the Office of the Prosecutor:

> [H]as studied Sudanese institutions, laws and procedures. We have sought information on any national proceedings that may have been undertaken in relation to crimes in Darfur ... Following this analysis, I determined that there are cases that would be admissible in relation to the Darfur situation. This decision does not represent a determination on the Sudanese legal system as such, but is essentially a result of the absence of criminal proceedings related to the cases on which I focus.[164]

Furthermore, the Prosecutor indicated in his seventh report to the Security Council that the OTP found no national proceedings related to individuals and crimes investigated by the OTP in spite of the public announcement of the Sudanese government that it identified 160 suspects for investigation and possible prosecution.[165]

The information indicated *supra* shows a general lack of action on behalf of the Sudanese judicial system, although in a few cases investigations have taken place. Still, even in these cases, the quality of the investigations according to recognized international standards remain questionable. Hence, given the criterion of 'no action', the ICC will almost certainly render the case admissible; in case of investigation or prosecution, it will evaluate whether the Sudanese action meet the requirement of Article 17 according to 'willingness' and 'ability'. The Prosecutor,

---

162   United Nations Commission of Inquiry. 25 January 2005. *Report of the International Commission of Inquiry on Darfur to the United Nations Secretary-General, Pursuant to Security Council Resolution 1564 of 18 September 2004*, para. 429. Available at: www.un.org/News/dh/sudan/com_inq_darfur.pdf [accessed: 16 May 2009].

163   International Criminal Court, Office of the Prosecutor. 5 June 2008. *Seventh Report of the Prosecutor of the International Criminal Court to the UN Security Council Pursuant to the UNSCR 1593(2005)*, para. 73. Available at: www.icc-cpi.int/library/organs/otp/UNSC_2008_En.pdf [accessed: 7 July 2009].

164   Moreno-Ocampo, L. 2005. *Statement of the Prosecutor of the International Criminal Court Mr. Luis Moreno Ocampo to the Security Council on 29 June 2005 Pursuant to UNSCR 1593*, 2-3. Available at: www.icc-cpi.int/library/cases/LMO UNSC On DARFUR-EN.pdf [accessed: 24 June 2009].

165   International Criminal Court, Office of the Prosecutor. 5 June 2008. *Seventh Report of the Prosecutor of the International Criminal Court to the UN Security Council Pursuant to the UNSCR 1593(2005)*, para. 73. Available at: www.icc-cpi.int/library/organs/otp/UNSC_2008_En.pdf [accessed: 7 July 2009].

in his Application to the Pre-Trial Chamber under Article 58(7) on 27 February 2007, stated that the investigations carried out by the relevant Sudanese authorities do not target the same persons (namely Ahmad Muhammad Harun) and the same conduct (Ali Muhammad Ali Abd-Al-Rahman, known as Ali Kushayb) which was the subject at hand before the ICC. Therefore, the Prosecutor designated the case admissible on the ground of 'inaction'.[166] Yet, interestingly, he implicitly correlated the Sudanese 'inaction' to unwillingness, but without indicating that explicitly when applying the admissibility test.[167] It would have been a positive development if the Prosecutor had explicitly correlated the 'inaction' of the Sudanese judicial system to 'unwillingness' on behalf of the Sudanese government under the admissibility test. In the opinion of this author, such interpretation would be more consistent with the Preamble of the Statute and the intention of the drafters. The admissibility of cases of 'inaction' regardless of unwillingness or inability, as interpreted by the OTP in the DRC cases, will not contribute to the primary role of the states to prosecute international crimes, because it allows the Court to prosecute cases that can be prosecuted by willing and able states. Cases of 'inaction' should not be admissible except when they reflect unwillingness or inability as defined by Article 17.

Sudanese judicial system and 'unwillingness'
(a) The principles of due process   Article 17(2) stipulates that the principles of due process recognized by international law will be taken into consideration when assessing 'unwillingness'. Rule 51 of the Rules of Procedure and Evidence of the ICC permits the state invoking complementarity to provide information showing that 'its courts meet internationally recognized norms and standards for the independent and impartial prosecution of similar conduct', which helps the Court in assessing the degree of 'willingness' of the states.[168]

For instance, the criterion 'the principles of due process recognized by international law' implies the implementation of human rights standards. This brings in the application of human rights principles of fair trial and due process into the implementation of the complementarity principle.

In assessing the Sudanese judicial system, and its enforcement mechanism, one can see that it clearly suffers from gaps and practices that violate the principles of due process. For instance, a significant body of evidence shows that the National

---

166   The Office of the Prosecutor, the International Criminal Court. 27 February 2007. *Situation in Darfur, the Sudan: Prosecutor's Application under Article 58(7)*, para. 261. Available at: www.icc-cpi.int/library/cases/ICC-02-05-56_English.pdf [accessed: 19 March 2009].

167   International Criminal Court, Office of the Prosecutor. 5 June 2008. *Seventh Report of the Prosecutor of the International Criminal Court to the UN Security Council Pursuant to the UNSCR 1593(2005)*, para. 73. Available at: www.icc-cpi.int/library/organs/otp/UNSC_2008_En.pdf [accessed: 7 July 2009].

168   Rule 51 of the Rules of Procedure and Evidence. ICC-ASP/1/3, pp. 1-107, 38.

Security and the Military Intelligence systematically torture, and treat detainees inhumanely and degradingly.[169] Various practices of beating, prolonged exposure to sunlight, starvation, electrocution, candle wax burning, and *incommunicado* detention have been documented.[170] The UN Commission of Inquiry has previously reached a similar conclusion, as it managed to gather substantial evidences on the systematic use of torture against detainees in custody.[171] Regarding law, the problem is no less complex. The Presidential Decree of 2003, which established the Specialized Courts,[172] does not include any provision that rejects evidence extracted under torture or other forms of duress.[173] The use of evidence extracted under torture is a violation of the fundamental principles of due process under which an accused individual must not be compelled to testify against him or herself or confess to guilt.[174] Additionally, under human rights law, courts are obligated to investigate claims of torture and ill-treatment. Nevertheless, the practice of the Sudanese specialized courts seems inconsistent with such a duty. The UN Commission of Inquiry managed to document a number of cases where the judge declined to withdraw evidence collected under torture.[175] This is a violation of a number of international human rights instruments ratified by Sudan, such as the

---

169   Human Rights Council. 7 March 2007. Report of the High-Level Mission on the Situation of Human Rights in Darfur pursuant to Human Rights Council Decision S-4/101, Human Rights Council Fourth Session, A/HRC/4/80, para. 43, 16.

170   Human Rights Council. 7 March 2007. Report of the High-Level Mission on the Situation of Human Rights in Darfur pursuant to Human Rights Council Decision S-4/101, Human Rights Council Fourth Session, A/HRC/4/80, para. 43, 16.

171   United Nations Commission of Inquiry. 25 January 2005. *Report of the International Commission of Inquiry on Darfur to the United Nations Secretary-General, Pursuant to Security Council Resolution 1564 of 18 September 2004*, para. 368. Available at: www.un.org/News/dh/sudan/com_inq_darfur.pdf [accessed: 16 May 2009].

172   Human Rights Watch. June 2006. *Lack of Conviction the Special Criminal Court on the Events in Darfur*, 1-31, 25, 26. Available at: http://hrw.org/backgrounder/ij/sudan0606/sudan0606.pdf [accessed: 16 June 2009].

173   Amnesty International USA. Sudan Darfur: *Incommunicado* Detention, Torture and Special Courts Memorandum to the Government of Sudan and the Sudanese Commission of Inquiry. Available at: www.amnestyusa.org/document.php?lang=e&id=297D6DC9807 CB0CA80256EA50020E9A0 [accessed: 16 June 2008]; United Nations Commission of Inquiry. 25 January 2005. *Report of the International Commission of Inquiry on Darfur to the United Nations Secretary-General, Pursuant to Security Council Resolution 1564 of 18 September 2004*, para. 441. Available at: www.un.org/News/dh/sudan/com_inq_darfur.pdf [accessed: 16 May 2009].

174   Article 14(3)(g) of the International Covenant on Civil and Political Rights (1966), G.A. res. 2200A (XXI), 21 U.N. GAOR Supp. (no. 16) at 52, UN Doc. A/6316 (1966), 999 U.N.T.S. 171.

175   United Nations Commission of Inquiry. 25 January 2005. *Report of the International Commission of Inquiry on Darfur to the United Nations Secretary-General, Pursuant to Security Council Resolution 1564 of 18 September 2004*, para. 441. Available at: www.un.org/News/dh/sudan/com_inq_darfur.pdf [accessed: 16 May 2009].

ICCPR,[176] the Convention on the Rights of the Child,[177] and the African Charter on Human and Peoples' Rights.[178]

Arbitrary arrests also seem to be a common practice by the law enforcement bodies in Sudan, including Darfur, and the judicial system has thus far proven incapable of preventing such practices.[179] The UN Commission of Inquiry documented, among others, the detention of a 15-year-old epileptic boy in Nyala, in northern Darfur, in November 2004, in which the authorities did not allow the boy to inform his family about his arrest. Other detainees have been arrested for more than three months without charge.[180] All of the detainees were held *incommunicado* without trial. Such practices constitute a clear violation of Articles 9 and 10 of the ICCPR.[181]

Furthermore, a number of Sudanese laws grant broad powers to the executive at the expense of the effectiveness of the judiciary. Many of the laws in force contravene basic human rights standards.[182] For instance, the National Security Forces Act of 1999 includes many such shortcomings. Section 31 of this law, in certain cases, does not provide guarantees for immediate access to counsel. The duration of detention may sometimes exceed a 12-month period without charges, appearance in court, or visitors.[183] This is a gross violation of the rights

---

176   The International Covenant for Civil and Political Rights was ratified by Sudan on the 18 June 1986. Available at: www.ohchr.org/english/bodies/docs/status.pdf [accessed: 26 May 2009].

177   The Convention for the Right of the Child was ratified by Sudan on the 2 September 1990. Available at: www.ohchr.org/english/bodies/docs/status.pdf [accessed: 26 May 2009].

178   The African Charter on Human and Peoples' Rights was ratified by Sudan on 18 February 1986. Available at: www.africa-union.org/root/au/Documents/Treaties/List/ African%20Charter%20on%20Human%20and%20Peoples%20Rights.pdf [accessed: 16 June 2009].

179   Human Rights Council. 7 March 2007. Report of the High-Level Mission on the Situation of Human Rights in Darfur pursuant to Human Rights Council Decision S-4/101, Human Rights Council Fourth Session, A/HRC/4/80, para. 40, 15.

180   United Nations Commission of Inquiry. 25 January 2005. *Report of the International Commission of Inquiry on Darfur to the United Nations Secretary-General, Pursuant to Security Council Resolution 1564 of 18 September 2004*, para. 401. Available at: www.un.org/News/dh/sudan/com_inq_darfur.pdf [accessed: 16 May 2009].

181   United Nations Commission of Inquiry. 25 January 2005. *Report of the International Commission of Inquiry on Darfur to the United Nations Secretary-General, Pursuant to Security Council Resolution 1564 of 18 September 2004*, para. 403. Available at: www.un.org/News/dh/sudan/com_inq_darfur.pdf [accessed: 16 May 2009].

182   United Nations Commission of Inquiry. 25 January 2005. *Report of the International Commission of Inquiry on Darfur to the United Nations Secretary-General, Pursuant to Security Council Resolution 1564 of 18 September 2004*, 6. Available at: www. un.org/News/dh/sudan/com_inq_darfur.pdf [accessed: 16 May 2009].

183   United Nations Commission of Inquiry. 25 January 2005. *Report of the International Commission of Inquiry on Darfur to the United Nations Secretary-General,*

of the detainees according to Article 14(3)(c) of ICCPR.[184] In addition, section 33 provides wide immunities to members of the National Security and Intelligence Services.[185] This creates a climate of impunity that may encourage these personnel to disobey the law and breach basic principles of human rights.

Moreover, there are a number of indicators that rights of the defendants are not respected. The time to appeal death penalties does not exceed seven days, a relatively short period if one takes into consideration preparing the documents and the files necessary for appeal.[186] The right of legal representation is not fully respected under the Decree of 2003. The Counsel is granted limited time to cross-examine the prosecution witnesses and to examine defence witnesses[187] – a clear violation of Article 14 of the ICCPR.

In addition, the state of emergency is still in effect since 1999. Sudan is mainly ruled by decrees. The Specialized Court, for example, was established by an executive decree.[188]

The data above shows that the Sudanese judicial process subsumes a number of violations of principles of due process and human rights. Hence, the ICC may render them (and similar cases) admissible by considering the Sudanese judicial system in violation of Articles 17(2) and 21 of the Statute.[189]

(b) 'Genuine' investigations or prosecutions   The Rome Statute does not include a definition of the term 'genuinely'. The case law of the European Court of Human

---

Pursuant to Security Council Resolution 1564 of 18 September 2004, para. 452. Available at: www.un.org/News/dh/sudan/com_inq_darfur.pdf [accessed: 16 May 2009].

184   Article 14 of the International Covenant on Civil and Political Rights (1966), G.A. res. 2200A (XXI), 21 U.N. GAOR Supp. (no. 16) at 52, UN Doc. A/6316 (1966), 999 U.N.T.S. 171.

185   United Nations Commission of Inquiry. 25 January 2005. *Report of the International Commission of Inquiry on Darfur to the United Nations Secretary-General, Pursuant to Security Council Resolution 1564 of 18 September 2004*, para. 453. Available at: www.un.org/News/dh/sudan/com_inq_darfur.pdf [accessed: 16 May 2009].

186   United Nations Commission of Inquiry. 25 January 2005. *Report of the International Commission of Inquiry on Darfur to the United Nations Secretary-General, Pursuant to Security Council Resolution 1564 of 18 September 2004*, para. 447. Available at: www.un.org/News/dh/sudan/com_inq_darfur.pdf [accessed: 16 May 2009].

187   United Nations Commission of Inquiry. 25 January 2005. *Report of the International Commission of Inquiry on Darfur to the United Nations Secretary-General, Pursuant to Security Council Resolution 1564 of 18 September 2004*, para. 446. Available at: www.un.org/News/dh/sudan/com_inq_darfur.pdf [accessed: 16 May 2009].

188   United Nations Commission of Inquiry. 25 January 2005. *Report of the International Commission of Inquiry on Darfur to the United Nations Secretary-General, Pursuant to Security Council Resolution 1564 of 18 September 2004*, para. 450. Available at: www.un.org/News/dh/sudan/com_inq_darfur.pdf [accessed: 16 May 2009].

189   Article 17(2) of the Rome Statute of the International Criminal Court, UN Doc. A/CONF.183/9.

Rights and Inter-American Court of Human Rights held in many cases that an effective investigation should be able to identify and punish those responsible.[190]

With respect to Darfur, one could differentiate between the assessment of the effectiveness of the Sudanese judicial system in general and the assessment of how genuine investigations and prosecutions carried by the national authorities were. The former is of importance when assessing at the early stages if the referral meets the admissibility criteria. The latter pertains to a case-by-case assessment basis.

On the effectiveness of the Sudanese judicial system, there are various criticisms to the independence and efficiency of the system. One jurist argued that the Sudan judiciary has failed to prosecute serious crimes occurring in Darfur; 'it has made no genuine effort to investigate – much less discipline or prosecute – any of the individuals responsible. Instead, it has created a facade of accountability through sham prosecutions and created *ad hoc* government committees that produce nothing'.[191]

The five created judicial and quasi-judicial bodies for accountability for human rights violations in Darfur continue to have limited results and questionable outcome.[192] Credible and reliable sources – such as the UN Commission of Inquiry, the Human Rights Council's High-Level Mission, the then UN High Commissioner for Human Rights, Louise Arbour, the then UN Special Adviser on the Prevention of Genocide, Juan Mendez, and the UN Special Representative of the Secretary-General for Sudan, Jan Pronk – have indicated that the Sudanese government bears substantial responsibility for crimes committed in Darfur, directly or indirectly, through proxy forces. Another 21 independent experts have drawn similar conclusions.[193] The report of the UN Commission of Inquiry was

---

190   See ECHR cases: *Yasa* v. *Turkey*, ECHR App. no. 22281/93, 27 June 2002, not published, para. 98; *Assenov* v. *Bulgaria*, ECHR App. no. 24760/94, 28 October 1998, ECHR 1998-VIII, para. 102. Also, ACHR cases: *Velasquez Rodriguez* v. *Honduras*, 29 July 1988, I-ACHR Series C, no. 4, para. 174.

191   Udombana, N.J. Fall 2005. Pay Back Time in Sudan? Darfur in the International Criminal Court. *Tulsa Journal of Comparative and International Law*, 13, 1-57, 16.

192   Human Rights Council. 7 March 2007. Report of the High-Level Mission on the Situation of Human Rights in Darfur pursuant to Human Rights Council Decision S-4/101, Human Rights Council Fourth Session, A/HRC/4/80, 17.

193   The Representative of the Secretary-General on internally displaced persons, Francis M. Deng, Inter alia Report of the Representative of the Secretary-General on internally displaced persons, Mission to the Sudan – The Darfur Crisis, 27 September 2004, E/CN.4/2005/8; Report of the Representative of the Secretary-General on internally displaced persons, Francis M. Deng, submitted pursuant to Commission on Human Rights Resolution 2002/56, 27 November 2002, E/CN.4/2003/86/Add.1; the Representative of the Secretary-General on the human rights of internally displaced persons, Walter Kaelin, United Nations Press Release, UN Human Rights Expert Deplores Ongoing Displacement in Darfur, 11 November 2004, UN Press Release, GA/SHC/2795, Expert on Human Rights Cites Strong Indications of Commission of War Crimes in Darfur, as Third Committee Continues Dialogue with Experts, 29 October 2004; the Independent Expert on the situation of human

very explicit about the lack of genuineness of national proceedings, indicating that measures taken so far by the government are 'grossly inadequate and ineffective ... [contributing] to the climate of almost total impunity for human rights violations in Darfur'.[194] The Commission reached the conclusion that the current judicial system has effectively led to impunity for possible perpetrators.[195] It is therefore highly

---

rights in the Sudan, Emmanuel Akwei Addo; the Special Rapporteur on violence against women, its causes and consequences, Yakin Ertürk; United Nations High Commissioner for Human Rights, UN Women's Rights Expert Concludes Visit to Sudan, 6 October 2004 the Director of the UN's Internal Displacement Division, Dennis McNamara; UN News Service, Darfur's Displaced Remain Traumatized and at Risk of Rape, Harassment – UN Official, 30 August 2004, the Special Rapporteur of the Commission on Human Rights on the situation of human rights in the Sudan, Gerhart Baum; Interim Report of the Special Rapporteur of the Commission on Human Rights on the Situation of Human Rights in the Sudan, A/57/326, 20 August 2002, the Special Rapporteur on extrajudicial, summary or arbitrary executions, Asma Jahangir, and her successor, Philip Alston; Civil and Political Rights, including the Question of Disappearances and Summary Executions: Extrajudicial, Summary or Arbitrary Executions: Addendum, Mission to Sudan, E/CN.4/2005/7/Add.2, 6 August 2004 the Special Rapporteur on Torture, Theo van Boven; the Special Rapporteur on contemporary forms of racism, racial discrimination, xenophobia and related intolerance, Doudou Diene; the Special Rapporteur on the right of everyone to the enjoyment of the highest attainable standard of physical and mental health, Paul Hunt; the Special Rapporteur on the sale of children, child prostitution and child pornography, Juan Miguel Petit; the Special Rapporteur on the right to food, Jean Ziegler, United Nations High Commissioner for Human Rights, Eight UN Human Rights Experts Gravely Concerned About Reported Widespread Abuses in Darfur, Sudan, 26 March 2004 the Special Rapporteur on the situation of human rights in the occupied Palestinian territory, John Dugard; the Independent Expert on the protection of human rights and fundamental freedoms while countering terrorism, Robert K. Goldman; the Special Rapporteur on adequate housing, Miloon Kothari; the Special Rapporteur on the promotion and protection of the right to freedom of opinion and expression, Ambeyi Ligabo; the Special Rapporteur on the right to education, Vernor Muñoz Villalobos; the Independent Expert to update the set of principles for the promotion and protection of human rights through action to combat impunity, Diane Orentlicher; the Special Rapporteur on the situation of human rights and fundamental freedoms of indigenous people, Rodolfo Stavenhagen; the Chairperson of the Working Group on enforced or involuntary disappearances, Stephen Toope. UN Press Release, AFR/1126 and HR/4822, United Nations Human Rights Experts Call for Urgent, Effective Action on Darfur, Sudan, 16 March 2005. United Nations Under-Secretary-General for Humanitarian Affairs, Jan Egeland. UN Press Release, AFR/1122 and IHA/1020, Emergency Relief Coordinator Jan Egeland Concludes Trip to Sudan: Says 2005 Country's 'Make or Break' Year, 8 March 2005.

194   United Nations Commission of Inquiry. 25 January 2005. *Report of the International Commission of Inquiry on Darfur to the United Nations Secretary-General, Pursuant to Security Council Resolution 1564 of 18 September 2004*, executive summary. Available at: www.un.org/News/dh/sudan/com_inq_darfur.pdf [accessed: 16 May 2009].

195   Quénivet, N. July-September 2006. The Report of the International Commission of Inquiry on Darfur: The Question of Genocide. *Human Rights Review*, 38-68, 54.

doubtful that, in such circumstances, the investigations into the Darfur crimes were genuine. As indicated earlier, these circumstances include the alleged participation of the Sudanese government in serious crimes, the absence of independence of the judiciary,[196] the general climate of impunity, the institutionalized immunity of state actors, and the obstruction of justice, the intimidation of witnesses, and lastly, the alleged destruction of evidence.

On carrying out investigations and prosecutions genuinely, it is important to examine the level of effectiveness of investigations or prosecutions. It must be determined whether the investigation or prosecution genuinely aims to identify and punish those responsible. The few cases that were prosecuted before Sudanese courts were criticized for not carrying out the proceedings genuinely, and these cases are hence subject to the scrutiny of the ICC Prosecutor, who 'would reassess whether those cases were the subject of "genuine national investigations or prosecutions"'.[197]

In terms of case-by-case investigation and prosecutions, the UN Commission of Inquiry indicated that, except for two cases, the Sudanese system has failed to prosecute the perpetrators of the crimes that occurred after February 2003.[198] The ICC Prosecutor himself indicated in his seventh report to the Security Council that although the Sudanese government announced that approximately 160 suspects were identified for investigation and prosecution, no cases related to individuals and crimes investigated by the OTP were taking place by June 2008. The National Commission investigation, whose purpose involves a quasi-criminal investigation under Article 17, investigated and gathered proof of killings of civilians, crimes of rape and sexual violence, and forced displacement of civilian populations.[199] However, the National Committee systematically failed to complete genuine investigations in an independent manner. Instead, its report attempted to justify the violations rather than provide effective measures to provide accountability for such crimes.[200] This happened while some NGOs accused the members of the

196   Udombana, N.J. Fall 2005. Pay Back Time in Sudan? Darfur in the International Criminal Court. *Tulsa Journal of Comparative and International Law*, 13, 1-57, 16.

197   Moreno-Ocampo, L. 29 June 2005. *Statement of the Prosecutor of the International Criminal Court Mr. Luis Moreno Ocampo to the Security Council on 29 June 2005 Pursuant to UNSCR 1593*, 3. Available at: www.icc-cpi.int/library/cases/LMO UNSC On DARFUR-EN.pdf [accessed: 16 June 2009].

198   United Nations Commission of Inquiry. 25 January 2005. *Report of the International Commission of Inquiry on Darfur to the United Nations Secretary-General, Pursuant to Security Council Resolution 1564 of 18 September 2004*, para. 428. Available at: www.un.org/News/dh/sudan/com_inq_darfur.pdf [accessed: 16 May 2009].

199   United Nations Commission of Inquiry. 25 January 2005. *Report of the International Commission of Inquiry on Darfur to the United Nations Secretary-General, Pursuant to Security Council Resolution 1564 of 18 September 2004*, para. 459. Available at: www.un.org/News/dh/sudan/com_inq_darfur.pdf [accessed: 16 May 2009].

200   United Nations Commission of Inquiry. 25 January 2005. *Report of the International Commission of Inquiry on Darfur to the United Nations Secretary-General,*

National Committee of having continuous contacts with the Presidential Office.[201] Clearly, measures taken by the National Commission did not fulfil the requirement of Article 17 of the Rome Statute to carry out 'genuine' proceedings.

The national Judicial Investigations Committee (JIC), established on 19 January 2005 to address certain crimes highlighted in the reports of the National Commission of Inquiry and UN Commission of Inquiry, indicated that it was investigating several incidents and crimes. It investigated Ali Kushayb, who, according to the JIC, had been arrested by the police due to the warrant issued for him in April 2005. However, Ali Kushayb returned to active duty and a spokesman of the Sudanese government indicated that Kushayb and Harun 'are not up for trial because there is no evidence against them'.[202]

In addition, the Committee against Rape failed to hold accountable perpetrators of alleged rapes.[203] It committed several irregularities regarding the Rape Committee's investigations, such as disrespecting the confidentiality of interviews,[204] and exercising passiveness by the members of the Committee during their investigations.[205] Even if its work is elevated to a criminal proceeding under Article 17, such an investigation cannot pass Article 17's 'genuineness test' due to the lack of independence, impartiality and effectiveness of these proceedings.

Furthermore, contrary to the ICC Prosecutor's current policy, it seems reasonable to posit that the ICC Prosecutor is here entitled to deduce the genuineness of the proceedings from the general legal and institutional context in which national proceedings may or would have taken place, to be better able to assess if the proceedings were genuine. This brings to bear considering the

---

Pursuant to Security Council Resolution 1564 of 18 September 2004, para. 462. Available at: www.un.org/News/dh/sudan/com_inq_darfur.pdf [accessed: 16 May 2009].

201   Amnesty International noticed that the staff initially assigned to the commission came from the presidential office. Amnesty International. 14 May 2004. Sudan: *Commission of Inquiry must be Effective, Protect Witnesses and Report Publicly*. AI Index: AFR 54/049/2004. Available at: http://web.amnesty.org/library/Index/ENGAFR540492004 [accessed: 1 June 2009].

202   International Criminal Court, Office of the Prosecutor. 5 June 2008. *Seventh Report of the Prosecutor of the International Criminal Court to the UN Security Council Pursuant to the UNSCR 1593(2005)*, para. 40. Available at: www.icc-cpi.int/library/organs/otp/UNSC_2008_En.pdf [accessed: 7 July 2009].

203   United Nations Commission of Inquiry. 25 January 2005. *Report of the International Commission of Inquiry on Darfur to the United Nations Secretary-General, Pursuant to Security Council Resolution 1564 of 18 September 2004*, para. 465. Available at: www.un.org/News/dh/sudan/com_inq_darfur.pdf [accessed: 16 May 2009].

204   Human Rights Watch. November 2004. *If We Return, We Will Be Killed: Consolidation of Ethnic Cleansing in Darfur, Sudan*. Available at: http://hrw.org/backgrounder/africa/darfur1104/darfur1104.pdf [accessed: 9 May 2008].

205   Human Rights Watch. November 2004. *If We Return, We Will Be Killed: Consolidation of Ethnic Cleansing in Darfur, Sudan*. Available at: http://hrw.org/backgrounder/africa/darfur1104/darfur1104.pdf [accessed: 9 May 2008].

effectiveness of the Sudanese judicial system in general, along with the genuineness of the investigations and prosecutions. Combined, these considerations permit the Prosecutor to deduce whether the 'genuineness test' under Article 17 is met.

(c) The presence of one of the requirements: shielding the person or unjustified delay or lack of independence or impartiality

i.   *Shielding the person from criminal responsibility*
Article 17(2)(a) allows the ICC to challenge the good faith of a state if there is evidence that the state proceedings or prosecutions are sham, designed to defeat the jurisdiction of the ICC. This includes, among others, the presence of investigations or prosecutions of some perpetrators that lead to sham proceedings or obvious departures from the legal procedures of the state.[206]

As mentioned in previous chapters,[207] relevant facts and proof that could assist in determining if proceedings were intended to shield the person concerned from criminal responsibility can be obtained through one of the following non-exhaustive means: through a testimony from an insider within the system; through evidence included in documents such as legislation, orders, amnesty decrees, instructions and correspondence; or through procedural gaps and malfunctions, such as unjustified delay (delay inconsistent with an intent to bring the person concerned to justice), lack of impartiality, longstanding knowledge of crimes without action. Proof of shielding could be also deduced from the politicized nature of the national system concerned.[208]

With respect to Sudan, in terms of legislation, the UN former Commission on Human Rights pointed out that the 1994 National Security Act, and its amendments, provide a framework for impunity and lawlessness, and falls far short of the standards provided for in the Bill of Rights enshrined in the 1998 Constitution,[209] let alone international human rights standards. The Act grants security forces virtual immunity from prosecution and provides them with investigative powers that allow arbitrary arrest, incommunicado

---

206   Holmes, J. 2002. Complementarity: National Courts versus the International Criminal Court, in *The Rome Statute of The International Criminal Court: A Commentary*, edited by A. Cassese, P. Gaeta and J.R.W.D. Jones. Oxford: Oxford University Press, I, 667-75.

207   See Chapter 3.

208   The International Criminal Court, Office of the Prosecutor. 2003. *Informal Expert Paper: The Principle of Complementarity in Practice*. ICC-OTP 2003, 1-38, 27-28. Available at: www.icc-cpi.int/library/organs/otp/complementarity.pdf [accessed: 11 August 2009].

209   Commission on Human Rights, Economic and Social Council. 17 May 1999. Situation of Human Rights in the Sudan – Addendum. Fifty-fifth Session.

detention, lengthy detention without judicial review, and arbitrary search.[210] The National Security Act affirms that the prosecution of security forces requires the permission of the relevant minister or that of the director-general of national security.[211] Thus, the Act effectively grants the executive the authority to decide on the role of the judiciary. Furthermore, as shown supra, the National Security Law itself includes a number of flaws and deficiencies that subsumes violation to the right to fair trial.

Moreover, Sudan has been under a state of emergency since 1999 with important constitutional guarantees suspended and numerous laws adopted by executive decree.[212] The state of emergency has expanded the powers of the president considerably, allowing him to rule through decrees and to suspend powers related to the administration of the country.[213] The exceptional time of emergency became the general norm that constituted a major obstacle for a functioning criminal justice system.[214]

This raises valid concerns about the compatibility of Sudanese laws with international standards.[215] Some of these laws include restrictions that limit the ability to prosecute international crimes impartially and efficiently in Darfur.[216] While this is inadequate for judging Sudan's aims, these gaps and deficiencies provide possible grounds for shielding possible perpetrators.

---

210   Sudan Human Rights Organization. 26 March 2003. The Situation of Human Rights in Sudan 2003, Cairo. Available at: www.shro-cairo.org/reports.htm [accessed: 25 June 2009].

211   Article 33 of the National Security Act; Article 61 of the Police Forces Act and the Army Act respectively. See in Sudan Human Rights Organization. 26 March 2003. The Situation of Human Rights in Sudan 2003, Cairo. Available at: www.shro-cairo.org/reports. htm [accessed: 25 June 2009].

212   United Nations Commission of Inquiry. 25 January 2005. *Report of the International Commission of Inquiry on Darfur to the United Nations Secretary-General, Pursuant to Security Council Resolution 1564 of 18 September 2004*, para. 450. Available at: www.un.org/News/dh/sudan/com_inq_darfur.pdf [accessed: 16 May 2009].

213   United Nations Commission of Inquiry. 25 January 2005. *Report of the International Commission of Inquiry on Darfur to the United Nations Secretary-General, Pursuant to Security Council Resolution 1564 of 18 September 2004*, para. 450. Available at: www.un.org/News/dh/sudan/com_inq_darfur.pdf [accessed: 16 May 2009].

214   Joint Assessment Mission, Sudan. March 2005. *Cluster II Report, Governance and Rule of Law*. Available at: www.unsudanig.org/docs/Joint%20Assessment%20Mis sion%20(JAM)%20Volume%20II.pdf [accessed: 16 May 2009]; Sudan Human Rights Organization, Cairo. 20 January 2004. Memorandum to Sudan Government, Judiciary, and Bar Association.

215   United Nations Commission of Inquiry. 25 January 2005. *Report of the International Commission of Inquiry on Darfur to the United Nations Secretary-General, Pursuant to Security Council Resolution 1564 of 18 September 2004*, para. 450. Available at: www.un.org/News/dh/sudan/com_inq_darfur.pdf [accessed: 16 May 2009].

216   United Nations Commission of Inquiry. 25 January 2005. *Report of the International Commission of Inquiry on Darfur to the United Nations Secretary-General,*

With respect to granting amnesty or pardons, the president has broad powers to grant amnesty or pardon to any accused/convicted person,[217] and he has exercised these powers frequently.[218] Some of the amnesties granted were intended to recruit prisoners to fight against the rebels.[219] As the Rome Statute is silent on pardons, the Sudanese president can pardon perpetrators of international crimes after a proper national trial, which undermines the ICC jurisdiction. If such a situation occurs, it will count as a de facto shielding.

ii. *'Unjustified delay inconsistent with the intention to bring the person to justice'*
Unjustified delay' is the second criterion to be taken into consideration in determining 'unwillingness'. Within this criterion, three factors must be considered in order to fulfil the requirements of Article 17(2)(b): the existence of a delay, the delay is unjustified, and the delay is inconsistent with intent to bring the person to justice.[220]

In terms of undue delay, the African Commission has stated that 'the actual application of the law was also made difficult due to the state of emergency obtaining in the country [Sudan] during this period'.[221] The complainants had difficulty achieving justice due to the political situation in the country. In this case, 'it is reasonable to assume that not only the procedure of local remedies will be unduly prolonged, but also that it will yield no results'.[222] These are indicators that the Sudanese judicial system suffers from a delay in proceedings. However, it would be premature to conclude that the chronic delay could constitute an intention inconsistent with bringing the person to justice. Even when the specialized criminal courts were created in Darfur and Kordofan, the UN Commission of Inquiry reasoned that the real reason for their establishment was most probably 'fast tracking' rather than 'expediency', especially as the Commission noticed that the hearing

---

Pursuant to Security Council Resolution 1564 of 18 September 2004, para. 450. Available at: www.un.org/News/dh/sudan/com_inq_darfur.pdf [accessed: 16 May 2009].

217   Articles 208 and 211 (1) of the Sudanese Code of Criminal Procedure.

218   See for example, Global Security. 7 July 1999. Sudan Pardons. Available at: www.globalsecurity.org/military/library/news/1999/12/991207-sudan1.htm [accessed: 19 June 2009].

219   International Crisis Group. 8 March 2005. *Darfur: The Failure to Protect*, 8; International Crisis Group. 23 August 2004. *Darfur Deadline: A New International Action Plan*, 8.

220   Article 17(2)(b) of the Rome Statute of the International Criminal Court, UN Doc. A/CONF.183/9.

221   African Commission. 15-29 May 2003. African Commission Communication 228/99 Law Office/Sudan.

222   African Commission. 15-29 May 2003. African Commission Communication 228/99 Law Office/Sudan.

of a charge punishable by the death penalty sometimes did not exceed one hour![223] On command responsibility, Sima Samar, the UN Special Rapporteur on Human Rights in Sudan, told the press that '[t]here has been not much accountability for the serious crimes that have been committed in Darfur. A special court established to bring people to justice has so far not accused or prosecuted anyone with command responsibility'.[224]

iii. *Proceedings not conducted independently or impartially*

As indicated in Chapter 3, the requirements for independence and impartiality include three factors: independent proceedings, impartiality of proceeding, and in a manner inconsistent with an intent to bring the person concerned to justice. The first two factors are alternatives: it is sufficient that one of the two obtains. The proceedings must at minimum be conducted either impartially or in a non-independent manner. However, the lack of intent to bring the person concerned to justice is also required for the 'unwillingness' test to be satisfied.

With respect to impartiality or independence, the literature below will shed light on the legal requirements for these terms. According to human rights law, there are two requirements for judging the impartiality of a national judicial system. Firstly, tribunals must be objective, which requires offering guarantees that appease any legitimate doubt parties may have. Secondly, the proceedings must not be biased, and should be free from any personal prejudice.[225] The ICC will look into the process of selecting the judges and the trial chambers to determine the degree of independence of the judiciary.

In terms of objectivity, various sources show that the Sudanese judicial system suffers from political interference. The High-Level Mission concluded that the Sudanese Judicial system 'is compounded by a general lack of independence and resources, an ill-equipped police force and legislation'.[226] The judiciary and the legal profession are generally

---

223   United Nations Commission of Inquiry. 25 January 2005. *Report of the International Commission of Inquiry on Darfur to the United Nations Secretary-General, Pursuant to Security Council Resolution 1564 of 18 September 2004*, para. 444. Available at: www.un.org/News/dh/sudan/com_inq_darfur.pdf [accessed: 16 May 2009].

224   Coalition for the International Criminal Court. 7 March 2006. Sudan: UN Special Rapporteur on Human Rights in Sudan's Recent Assessment of Darfur Courts: Obasanjo Envoy and Sudan MoJ Discuss ICC. Available at: www.iccnow.org/?mod=newsdetail&news=391 [accessed: 18 June 2009].

225   *McGonnell* v. *United Kingdom*. 8 February 2000. ECHR App. No. 28488/95, ECHR 2000-II, para. 52.

226   Human Rights Council. 7 March 2007. Report of the High-Level Mission on the Situation of Human Rights in Darfur pursuant to Human Rights Council Decision S-4/101, Human Rights Council Fourth Session, A/HRC/4/80, para. 46.

portrayed as liable to the influence of the president or the security forces,[227] especially in cases of crimes committed by members of the security forces.[228] Furthermore, some of the possible perpetrators of the atrocities have themselves admitted that the Sudanese government and institutions backed and directed militia activities in northern Darfur.[229] Some jurists went so far as to accuse the Sudanese government of initiating a war against its population.[230] One author noted that 'the independence of the courts in Sudan exists in rhetoric than reality'.[231] These facts undermine the credibility of the Sudanese judicial system as an objective legislative body that can rule justly between the applicants and the defendants. The Sudanese judicial system, hence, cannot pass Article 17 requirements if the situation remains as is.

In terms of the requirement 'proceedings inconsistent with the intention to bring the person to justice', it is a subjective criterion that requires the ICC to prove the presence of a mens rea to conduct the proceedings for the purpose of shielding the perpetrators. This may be difficult to prove, as top commanders and officials frequently do not leave tangible evidence of such intentions. However, such mens rea can be deduced from contextual facts that surround the crimes.[232] The Sudanese government took a series of actions that could provide a valid ground for the ICC to determine such an intention. The UN Commission of Inquiry noticed, for example, that '[t]he judiciary appears to have been manipulated and politicised during the last decade. Judges disagreeing with the Government often suffered

---

227   US Department of State. 2004. *Report on the Human Rights Practices*. Available at: www.state.gov/g/drl/rls/hrrpt/2004/41628.htm [accessed: 12 May 2009].

228   US Department of State. 2004, 2003, 2002, 2001, 2000, 1999. *Report on the Human Rights Practices*. Available at: www.state.gov [accessed: 8 June 2009].

229   Human Rights Watch. 2 March 2005. *Militia Leader Implicates Khartoum – Janjaweed Chief Says Sudan Government Backed Attacks*. Available at: http://hrw.org/english/docs/2005/03/02/darfur10228.htm [accessed: 18 June 2009].

230   Udombana, N.J. Fall 2005. Pay Back Time in Sudan? Darfur in the International Criminal Court. *Tulsa Journal of Comparative and International Law*, 13, 1-57, 3.

231   Udombana, N.J. Fall 2005. Pay Back Time in Sudan? Darfur in the International Criminal Court. *Tulsa Journal of Comparative and International Law*, 13, 1-57, 16.

232   In *Jelisic* Case the Appeals Chamber noted that 'as to proof of specific intent, it may, in the absence of direct explicit evidence, be inferred from a number of facts and circumstances, such as the general context, the perpetration of other culpable acts systematically directed against the same group, the scale of atrocities committed, the systematic targeting of victims on account of their membership of a particular group, or the repetition of destructive and discriminatory acts'. International Tribunal for the Prosecution of Persons Responsible for Serious Violations of International Humanitarian Law Committed in the Territory of the Former Yugoslavia since 1991. 5 July 2001. *Prosecutor v. Goran Jelisic*, paragraph 47. Case No. IT-95-10-A. Available at: www.un.org/icty/jelisic/appeal/judgement/jel-aj010705.pdf [accessed: 28 June 2009].

harassment including dismissals'.[233] Given such circumstances, Sudanese policy obstructs justice, and this reflects an intention inconsistent with delivering justice.

(d) Concluding remarks on 'unwillingness'   It is important to reaffirm that the OTP assess unwillingness case-by-case[234] and not according to the Sudanese system in general.[235] However, the will of the Sudanese judiciary to prosecute has to be taken into consideration when assessing the admissibility of the cases of concern to the ICC.[236]

With respect to the proceedings already initiated by the Sudanese authorities, the ICC found the cases of Harun and Kushayb admissible on the grounds of absence of national proceedings against the two suspects, although it implicitly correlated that to the possible high-level officials' 'involvement' in the crimes and the 'failure to punish'. Even if national prosecutions take place, the ICC remains under the challenge of testing the degree of respect of the principle of due process and the genuineness of the proceedings. The ICC Prosecutor can conclude that the Sudanese judicial system does not respect the principle of due process as recognized in international law.[237] In addition, some of the proceedings are not genuine or effective according to the requirements of Article 17 of the Statute.[238] Moreover, there are a number of indicators that the Sudanese authorities are reluctant to take effective measures against alleged perpetrators. Even the judicial

---

233   United Nations Commission of Inquiry. 25 January 2005. *Report of the International Commission of Inquiry on Darfur to the United Nations Secretary-General, Pursuant to Security Council Resolution 1564 of 18 September 2004*, para. 432. Available at: www.un.org/News/dh/sudan/com_inq_darfur.pdf [accessed: 16 May 2009].

234   International Criminal Court, Office of the Prosecutor. 5 June 2008. *Seventh Report of the Prosecutor of the International Criminal Court to the UN Security Council Pursuant to the UNSCR 1593(2005)*, para. 20. Available at: www.icc-cpi.int/library/organs/otp/UNSC_2008_En.pdf [accessed: 7 July 2009]. See also Aptel Williamson, C. 1 March 2006. Justice Empowered or Justice Hampered: The International Criminal Court in Darfur. *African Security Review*, 15, 20-32, 25.

235   United Nations Commission of Inquiry. 25 January 2005. *Report of the International Commission of Inquiry on Darfur to the United Nations Secretary-General, Pursuant to Security Council Resolution 1564 of 18 September 2004*, para. 450. Available at: www.un.org/News/dh/sudan/com_inq_darfur.pdf [accessed: 16 May 2009].

236   International Criminal Court. February-March 2007. *The Office of the Prosecutor and its Investigation in Darfur, Sudan*, ICC NewsLetter, 13. Available at: www.icc-cpi.int/library/about/newsletter/files/ICC-NL13-200702_En.pdf [accessed: 28 June 2009].

237   See pp. 228-30.

238   The Commission of Inquiry reached such a conclusion. United Nations Commission of Inquiry. 25 January 2005. *Report of the International Commission of Inquiry on Darfur to the United Nations Secretary-General, Pursuant to Security Council Resolution 1564 of 18 September 2004*, para. 450. Available at: www.un.org/News/dh/sudan/com_inq_darfur.pdf [accessed: 16 May 2009].

and quasi-judicial measures adopted by Sudan came after immense international pressure and adoption of series of UN resolutions, including Resolution 1593.[239] Hence, the ICC can consider the proceedings conducted by Sudan to be for the purpose of shielding the perpetrators, a claim consistent with those sources which assert that the Sudanese government and the Janjaweed are jointly responsible for the atrocities in Darfur.[240] Furthermore, the lack of independence and impartiality of the Sudanese judicial system is evident.[241] The above implies that the cases will also be admissible under Article 17 and 20(3) of the ICC Statute (in case of existence of national proceedings).

However, Pre-Trial Chamber I, in its 27 April 2007 decision, concluded that no national proceedings were taken until then regarding the cases of Ahmad Harun and Ali Kushayb. The Prosecutor reaffirmed that in his seventh report to the Security Council.[242]

The Sudanese judicial system and 'inability'
(a) Total or substantial collapse or unavailability   In terms of substantial or total collapse, despite its weaknesses and malfunctions,[243] the Sudanese judicial system does not suffer from substantial or total collapse. Some jurists designated the Sudanese judicial system in a state of near-collapse, and thus unable to obtain key evidences and testimonies.[244] The Sudanese government has claimed that

---

239   Aptel Williamson, C. 1 March 2006. Justice Empowered or Justice Hampered: The International Criminal Court in Darfur. *African Security Review*, 15, 20-32, 24; on 7 and 11 June 2005, only a few weeks after the adoption of Resolution 1593, Sudan created a Special Court for Darfur. See Office of the Prosecutor, International Criminal Court. 13 December 2005. *Second Report of the Prosecutor of the International Criminal Court, Mr. Luis Moreno Ocampo To The Security Council Pursuant to UNSC 1593 (2005)*, ICC-02/05, 5. Available at: www.icc-cpi.int/library/organs/otp/LMO_UNSC_ReportB_En.pdf [accessed: 15 June 2009].

240   United Nations Commission of Inquiry. 25 January 2005. *Report of the International Commission of Inquiry on Darfur to the United Nations Secretary-General, Pursuant to Security Council Resolution 1564 of 18 September 2004*, 3. Available at: www.un.org/News/dh/sudan/com_inq_darfur.pdf [accessed: 16 May 2009].

241   Udombana, N.J. Fall 2005. Pay Back Time in Sudan? Darfur in the International Criminal Court. *Tulsa Journal of Comparative and International Law*, 13, 1-57, 15.

242   International Criminal Court, Office of the Prosecutor. 5 June 2008. *Seventh Report of the Prosecutor of the International Criminal Court to the UN Security Council Pursuant to the UNSCR 1593(2005)*, para. 24. Available at: www.icc-cpi.int/library/organs/otp/UNSC_2008_En.pdf [accessed: 7 July 2009].

243   United Nations Commission of Inquiry. 25 January 2005. *Report of the International Commission of Inquiry on Darfur to the United Nations Secretary-General, Pursuant to Security Council Resolution 1564 of 18 September 2004*, para. 586. Available at: www.un.org/News/dh/sudan/com_inq_darfur.pdf [accessed: 16 May 2009].

244   Udombana, N.J. Fall 2005. Pay Back Time in Sudan? Darfur in the International Criminal Court. *Tulsa Journal of Comparative and International Law*, 13, 1-57, 16; Lipscomb, R. January 2006. Restructuring the ICC Framework to Advance Transitional

rebel activities have weakened the effectiveness of the judiciary in Darfur,[245] yet it insisted that the judiciary remains willing and able to identify and bring any perpetrators to justice.[246] The judicial system in Darfur seems to suffer from 'partial collapse', but not a substantial or total one. It was argued at the Rome Conference that 'partial collapse' is not necessary a sufficient criterion to determine inability. A partial collapse of the national judicial system could occur, and yet the state may remain able to enforce the law in various other regions of the country.[247] Most courts in Darfur remain functional, although sometimes with difficulty. The High-Level Mission stated that the national court system in Sudan is functional despite ignoring human rights abuses. In fact, the Sudanese government has established a number of Special Courts for Darfur,[248] a national commission of inquiry,[249] *ad hoc* committees,[250] and committees against rape.[251] These bodies, despite various criticisms for their role, remain functional and cannot be designated as in a state of substantial or total collapse.

In west Darfur, the caseload has increased since March 2003, but at that time, there was no backlog of cases. According to the ICC Prosecutor's Report to the

---

Justice: A Search for a Permanent Solution in Sudan. *Columbia Law Review*, 106, 182-217, 192; United Nations Commission of Inquiry. 25 January 2005. *Report of the International Commission of Inquiry on Darfur to the United Nations Secretary-General, Pursuant to Security Council Resolution 1564 of 18 September 2004*, 5. Available at: www.un.org/News/dh/sudan/com_inq_darfur.pdf [accessed: 16 May 2009].

245   United Nations Commission of Inquiry. 25 January 2005. *Report of the International Commission of Inquiry on Darfur to the United Nations Secretary-General, Pursuant to Security Council Resolution 1564 of 18 September 2004*, para. 430. Available at: www.un.org/News/dh/sudan/com_inq_darfur.pdf [accessed: 16 May 2009].

246   SUNA. 5 February 2005. First Vice-President Affirms Government Refusal to Trial of Any Individual or Official Outside Sudan.

247   Holmes, J. 2002. Complementarity: National Courts versus the International Criminal Court, in *The Rome Statute of The International Criminal Court: A Commentary*, edited by A. Cassese, P. Gaeta and J.R.W.D. Jones. Oxford: Oxford University Press, I, 677.

248   Department of State, Sudan Human Rights Report, 2003, cited in Sudan Country Report, Immigration and Nationality Directorate, Home Office, United Kingdom, October 2004.

249   Presidential Decree issued under Article 54 of the Judicial Inquiry Act published on 8 May 2004. See in Amnesty International. 14 May 2004. *Sudan: Commission of Inquiry must be Effective, Protect Witnesses and Report Publicly*. AI Index: AFR 54/049/2004. Available at: http://web.amnesty.org/library/Index/ENGAFR540492004 [accessed: 1 June 2009].

250   Office of the Prosecutor, International Criminal Court. 14 June 2005. *Third Report of The Prosecutor of The International Criminal Court To The UN Security Council Pursuant To UNSCR 1593*, 1-10, 5. Available at: www.icc-cpi.int/library/cases/OTP_ReportUNSC_3-Darfur_English.pdf [accessed: 18 June 2009].

251   United Nations Commission of Inquiry. 25 January 2005. *Report of the International Commission of Inquiry on Darfur to the United Nations Secretary-General, Pursuant to Security Council Resolution 1564 of 18 September 2004*, para. 465. Available at: www.un.org/News/dh/sudan/com_inq_darfur.pdf [accessed: 16 May 2009].

Security Council, there are three Special Prosecution Commissions and a Special Court for each district in Darfur charged with looking into 'offences that have taken place after the work of the international and national commissions of inquiry. There have been reports of investigations into incidents alleged to have taken place in El-Geneina (west Darfur)'.[252]

In north Darfur, however, only a few town courts, among the 70 existing ones, were operating during the conflict. A prosecution office operates in each locality. On 15 August 2005, the Special Criminal Court in Darfur convicted two military intelligence officers for torturing to death a 13-year-old boy while in custody in north Darfur.[253]

In south Darfur, the judicial structure remained fully functional. The national Chief Justice appointed 28 judges distributed between three appellate courts and several district courts. South Darfur has 95 functioning town courts. There have been reports of investigations into crimes that have occurred in Tama and Hamada (south Darfur).[254] Sudan's Special Court for Darfur crimes has also convicted and sentenced to death two army soldiers for torturing and killing a civilian in Nyala.[255]

The ICC Prosecutor pointed out that six trials have taken place as of June 2005 for less than 30 suspects.[256] The data provided by the Sudanese Organization against Torture (SOAT) shows that despite being unfair, some trials have taken place in Darfur,[257] indicating that the judicial system is not in a state of total or substantial collapse.

---

252   Office of the Prosecutor, International Criminal Court. 14 June 2005. *Third Report of The Prosecutor of The International Criminal Court To The UN Security Council Pursuant To UNSCR 1593*, 1-10, 5. Available at: www.icc-cpi.int/library/cases/OTP_ReportUNSC_3-Darfur_English.pdf [accessed: 18 June 2009].

253   US Department of State. 2005. *Report on the Human Rights Practices-2005*. Available at: www.state.gov/g/drl/rls/hrrpt/2005/61594.htm [accessed: 18 May 2009].

254   Office of the Prosecutor, International Criminal Court. 14 June 2005. *Third Report of The Prosecutor of The International Criminal Court To The UN Security Council Pursuant To UNSCR 1593*, 1-10, 5. Available at: www.icc-cpi.int/library/cases/OTP_ReportUNSC_3-Darfur_English.pdf [accessed: 18 June 2009].

255   Sudan Online. 17 November 2005. Sudan Darfur Court Sentences Two Soldiers to Death. Available at: www.sudaneseonline.com/enews2005/nov17-25813.shtml [accessed: 18 June 2008].

256   Office of the Prosecutor, International Criminal Court. 14 June 2005. *Third Report of The Prosecutor of The International Criminal Court To The UN Security Council Pursuant To UNSCR 1593*, 1-10, 5. Available at: www.icc-cpi.int/library/cases/OTP_ReportUNSC_3-Darfur_English.pdf [accessed: 18 June 2009].

257   Sudan Human Rights Organization. 26 March 2003. The Situation of Human Rights in Sudan 2003, 18. Available at: www.shro-cairo.org/reports/04/hr03.doc [accessed: 18 June 2008].

Information gathered from a variety of credible sources indicates that local courts continue to function.[258] However, the Sudanese judicial system continues to exhibit a number of deficiencies. Relevant concerns relating to the factual condition of the judicial system exist, as there is a general lack of financial resources.[259] While these shortages do not put the judiciary in a state of substantial or total collapse, according to the Rome Statute's criteria, they do affect the quality of justice, and hence may constitute violations of the obligation to respect due process under the Statute and international law.

The Report of the High-Level Mission supports this conclusion and indicates 'the national court system in Sudan is functional and has jurisdiction over human rights crimes perpetrated in Darfur'.[260] However, it adds that 'these courts have been unable to resolve human rights abuses there'.[261] Hence, the basic requirements for inability, under Article 17(3) (represented in substantial or total collapse of the judicial system), are not fulfilled by the Sudanese judicial system. The absence of these requirements precludes rendering this case admissible based on inability.[262] Yet despite this, the study will proceed with analysing the second requirement, 'the inability to obtain the accused, or the necessary evidence or otherwise unable to carry proceedings', for enriching the discussion on the issue. These are alternative requirements, and the presence of one of them in correlation to a substantial or total collapse of the system will render the case admissible.

(b) 'Inability to obtain the accused or necessary evidence and testimony or otherwise unable to carry out its proceedings'   The Sudanese judicial system is able 'to obtain the accused or the necessary evidence and testimony or to carry out proceedings'. However, there are number of contentious issues that primarily need to be discussed.

With respect to obtaining the accused, until late 2006, the Sudanese judiciary did not accuse any of the possible major perpetrators, or indict any of the 51

---

258   Parmar, Sh. January 2007. An Overview of the Sudanese Legal System and Legal Research, Hauser Global Law School Program, New York University School of Law, 1-16, 4. Available at: www.nyulawglobal.org/globalex/Sudan.htm#_ednref7 [accessed: 1 July 2009].

259   Joint Assessment Mission, Sudan. March 2005. *Cluster II Report, Governance and Rule of Law*. Available at: www.unsudanig.org/docs/Joint%20Assessment%20Mission %20(JAM)%20Volume%20II.pdf [accessed: 16 May 2009].

260   Human Rights Council. 7 March 2007. Report of the High-Level Mission on the Situation of Human Rights in Darfur pursuant to Human Rights Council Decision S-4/101, Human Rights Council Fourth Session, A/HRC/4/80, para. 46, 16.

261   Human Rights Council. 7 March 2007. Report of the High-Level Mission on the Situation of Human Rights in Darfur pursuant to Human Rights Council Decision S-4/101, Human Rights Council Fourth Session, A/HRC/4/80, para. 47, 16.

262   Article 17(3) of the Rome Statute of the International Criminal Court, UN Doc. A/CONF.183/9.

suspects listed by UN Commission of Inquiry.[263] Yet, even if the judiciary wanted to obtain the suspects or the accused, the courts remain unable to do so. This is not due to the substantial or total collapse of the courts, but due to the complicity of the Sudanese law enforcement bodies in committing the crimes in Darfur.[264] In the case of Harun and Kushayb, the Sudanese authorities are able to arrest the suspects. In fact, Kushayb was arrested and then released by September 2007. Harun was later appointed state minister for humanitarian affairs. Furthermore, even if the judiciary wanted to obtain the accused or the suspect it will be very difficult without the support of the law enforcement bodies. The Sudanese authorities adopted laws that granted broad powers to the executive at the expense of the effectiveness of the judiciary.[265] For instance, 'the amended Law of Criminal Procedure 1991 added additional powers to law enforcement bodies to investigate, arrest, interrogate or detain irrespective of magisterial investigation, as was lawfully required to guarantee the rights of persons in contact with the law'.[266] The outcome has been that the enforcement bodies have outweighed the power of the judiciary. The police and the security forces have acted in a climate of impunity and lack of accountability, undermining the effectiveness of the judiciary in obtaining the suspects and the accused[267] despite the fact that many suspects were well known to the Sudanese authorities who refrained from taking any measures against them. The Fédération Internationale des Droits de l'Homme (FIDH) found the following:

> The state prosecutor and other local officials were also well aware of the attacks
> on the civilian populations of Marla, Khor Abeche and other villages, but

---

263   The American Non-Governmental Organizations Coalition for the International Criminal Court; A Program of the United Nations Association of the United States of America. 16 February 2006. The Current Investigation by The ICC of The Situation In Darfur, 1-14, 7. Available at: www.amicc.org [accessed: 14 September 2008].

264   United Nations Commission of Inquiry. 25 January 2005. *Report of the International Commission of Inquiry on Darfur to the United Nations Secretary-General, Pursuant to Security Council Resolution 1564 of 18 September 2004*, para. 422. Available at: www.un.org/News/dh/sudan/com_inq_darfur.pdf [accessed: 16 May 2009].

265   United Nations Commission of Inquiry. 25 January 2005. *Report of the International Commission of Inquiry on Darfur to the United Nations Secretary-General, Pursuant to Security Council Resolution 1564 of 18 September 2004*, 5. Available at: www. un.org/News/dh/sudan/com_inq_darfur.pdf [accessed: 16 May 2009].

266   Parmar, Sh. January 2007. An Overview of the Sudanese Legal System and Legal Research, Hauser Global Law School Program, New York University School of Law, 1-16, 8. Available at: www.nyulawglobal.org/globalex/Sudan.htm#_ednref7 [accessed: 1 July 2009].

267   United Nations Commission of Inquiry. 25 January 2005. *Report of the International Commission of Inquiry on Darfur to the United Nations Secretary-General, Pursuant to Security Council Resolution 1564 of 18 September 2004*, 5. Available at: www. un.org/News/dh/sudan/com_inq_darfur.pdf [accessed: 16 May 2009].

insisted that the cases could not be taken to court because the identity of the perpetrators remained unknown. Knowledge of the identity of the perpetrators was hardly the real problem, however: Mussa Hilal and other militia leaders had been publicly accused of crimes for months, and were even included on a U.S. State Department list of militia leaders.[268]

Senior regime officials not only denied international accusation against suspects like Mussa Hilal, but also refused to investigate or interrogate these suspects.[269]

In terms of 'inability to obtain the necessary evidence and testimony', some courts in Darfur suffered from serious setbacks due to the ongoing conflict. For instance, by June 2006, there was still no progress resolving the case of the 100 civilians killed in Hamada, which was brought before the South Darfur Special Court on January 2005. The President of the Court highlighted the lack of access to the witnesses located in rebel-controlled areas.[270] There are also credible allegations that the Sudanese government has attempted to obstruct the course of justice at the national and international level. This can be inferred from political interferences in accountability efforts, intimidation and arrest of victims and witnesses, and seizure or destruction of materials perceived to be supportive of such efforts. In order to prevent victims and witnesses from speaking to those furthering accountability efforts, the Sudanese government and its supporters intimidated witnesses and victims. For instance, those who succeeded in contacting human rights observers were harassed and threatened by local authorities,[271] and some who reported crimes were subsequently harassed or arrested by official entities.[272] The International Commission of Inquiry also reported that some victims and witnesses were too scared to report the incidents

---

268   Human Rights Watch. December 2005. *Entrenching Impunity Government Responsibility for International Crimes in Darfur*, 17, no. 17(A), 1-79, 59. Available at: http://hrw.org/reports/2005/darfur1205/darfur1205text.pdf [accessed:16 June 2009].

269   Reeves, E. 29 April 2005. *Darfur and the International Criminal Court*, Middle East Report. Available at: www.merip.org/mero/mero042905.html [accessed: 18 January 2009].

270   Office of the Prosecutor, International Criminal Court. 14 June 2005. *Third Report of The Prosecutor of The International Criminal Court To The UN Security Council Pursuant To UNSCR 1593*, 1-10, 4. Available at: www.icc-cpi.int/library/cases/OTP_ ReportUNSC_3-Darfur_English.pdf [accessed: 18 June 2009].

271   Report of the Secretary-General on the Sudan Pursuant to Paragraphs 6, 13 and 16 of Security Council Resolution 1556 (2004), Paragraph 15 of Security Council Resolution 1564 (2004), and Paragraph 17 of Security Council Resolution 1574 (2004); S/2004/947, para. 40; 3 December 2004.

272   Security Council. 12 April 2005. *Monthly Report of the Secretary-General on Darfur*, S/2005/240. See also, Inter alia Report of the Secretary-General on the Sudan Pursuant to Paragraphs 6, 13 and 16 of Security Council Resolution 1556 (2004), Paragraph 15 of Resolution 1564 (2004) and Paragraph 17 of Resolution 1574 (2004), S/2005/140, 4 March 2005, para. 17; Amnesty International, Report 2005, Sudan.

to them, following intimidation by National Security forces.[273] A number of witnesses disappeared or were transferred when the National Commission indicated its intention to speak to them. One police officer, who had given evidence to the National Commission, went missing.[274] The Sudanese authorities have also intimidated aid workers or NGOs interested in fostering justice and accountability in Darfur.[275]

There are also indications that government forces and the Janjaweed have deliberately destroyed mass graves and other evidence. There are many examples that have shown that the actions of the police have led to the obstruction or destruction of evidence, leaving the courts unable to obtain the accused or the necessary evidence and testimony.[276] Human Rights Watch researchers visited two alleged mass graves at Abu Gamra in July 2005. Researchers saw a field strewn with skeletons, some still wearing clothes. It did confirm the occurrence of numerous cleansing operations. In March 2005, Human Rights Watch 'heard credible reports that mass graves in and near the town containing the bodies of victims of the March 2004 executions were dug up and the remains burned'.[277] It indicated that it has obtained copies and documents, without confirming authenticity, addressed from Mussa Hilal to security agencies and Sudanese officials, which included orders to dispose of evidences of mass graves.[278]

---

273   United Nations Commission of Inquiry. 25 January 2005. *Report of the International Commission of Inquiry on Darfur to the United Nations Secretary-General, Pursuant to Security Council Resolution 1564 of 18 September 2004.* Available at: www. un.org/News/dh/sudan/com_inq_darfur.pdf [accessed: 16 May 2009].

274   United Nations Commission of Inquiry. 25 January 2005. *Report of the International Commission of Inquiry on Darfur to the United Nations Secretary-General, Pursuant to Security Council Resolution 1564 of 18 September 2004,* 5. Available at: www.un.org/News/dh/sudan/com_inq_darfur.pdf [accessed: 16 May 2009]; see also Human Rights Watch. 21 January 2005. *Targeting the Fur: Mass Killings in Darfur,* 14; Human Rights Watch. November 2004. *If We Return, We Will Be Killed; Consolidation of Ethnic Cleansing in Darfur, Sudan,* 26. Available at: http://hrw.org/backgrounder/africa/darfur1104/darfur1104.pdf [accessed: 9 May 2008].

275   United Nations Security Council. 12 April 2005. *Monthly Report of the Secretary-General on Darfur,* UN SC/2005/240, para. 20. Available at: http://daccessdds.un.org/doc/UNDOC/GEN/N05/303/55/PDF/N0530355.pdf?OpenElement [accessed: 16 May 2009].

276   Office of High Commissioner of Human Rights. 29 July 2005. *Report of the United Nations High Commissioner for Human Rights: Access to Justice for Victims of Sexual Violence.* Available at: www.ohchr.org/english/press/docs/20050729Darfurreport.pdf [accessed: 16 June 2009].

277   Human Rights Watch. December 2005. *Entrenching Impunity Government Responsibility for International Crimes in Darfur,* 17, No. 17(A), 1-79, 62-63. Available at: http://hrw.org/reports/2005/darfur1205/darfur1205text.pdf [accessed: 16 June 2009].

278   Human Rights Watch. December 2005. *Entrenching Impunity Government Responsibility for International Crimes in Darfur,* 17, No. 17(A), 1-79, 62-63. Available at: http://hrw.org/reports/2005/darfur1205/darfur1205text.pdf [accessed: 16 June 2009].

These practices and policies have created an intimidating atmosphere that could be considered as an obstruction of justice. As a result, there has been widespread fear among crime survivors to file official reports on crimes committed.[279] The judiciary has been affected by this atmosphere and, at best, has not been able to ensure any official cooperation to obtain evidence or witnesses' testimonies. The Commission of Inquiry already confirmed that many witnesses have feared reprisals and thus have not resorted to the national justice system.[280]

As the starting point to access justice, the police seemed unable to protect the victims and the civilians.[281] In some cases, the police explicitly refused to protect those asking for assistance.[282] In terms of obtaining testimonies, there was a general lack of trust in the impartiality and efficiency of the police. A number of cases were not reported to the police,[283] as victims and witnesses claim that they were terrified that the police 'will punish them even more'.[284]

---

279   United Nations Security Council. 12 April 2005. *Monthly Report of the Secretary-General on Darfur*, UN SC/2005/240. Available at: http://daccessdds.un.org/doc/UNDOC/GEN/N05/303/55/PDF/N0530355.pdf?OpenElement [accessed: 16 June 2009]; United Nations Security Council. 10 May 2005. *Monthly Report of the Secretary-General on Darfur*, S/2005/305. Available at: http://daccessdds.un.org/doc/UNDOC/GEN/N05/337/43/PDF/N0533743.pdf?OpenElement [accessed: 16 June 2009]; United Nations Security Council: Secretary General Report. 3 December 2004. Report of the Secretary-General on the Sudan Pursuant to Paragraphs 6, 13 and 16 of Security Council Resolution 1556 (2004), Paragraph 15 of Security Council Resolution 1564 (2004), and Paragraph 17 of Security Council Resolution 1574 (2004), S/2004/947. Available at: http://daccessdds.un.org/doc/UNDOC/GEN/N04/633/97/PDF/N0463397.pdf?OpenElement [accessed: 16 June 2009]; Paragraph 17 of United Nations Security Council Resolution 1574 (2004). See also Médecins Sans Frontières. 8 March 2005. *The Crushing Burden of Rape: Sexual Violence in Darfur*, 6. Available at: www.doctorswithoutborders.org/publications/reports/2005/sudan03.pdf [accessed: 16 June 2009].

280   United Nations Commission of Inquiry. 25 January 2005. *Report of the International Commission of Inquiry on Darfur to the United Nations Secretary-General, Pursuant to Security Council Resolution 1564 of 18 September 2004*, 5. Available at: www.un.org/News/dh/sudan/com_inq_darfur.pdf [accessed: 16 May 2009].

281   Report of the UN Commissioner for Human Rights. 7 May 2004. E/CN.4/2005/3, para. 34.

282   See Human Rights Watch Briefing Paper. 12 April 2005. Sexual Violence and its Consequences among Displaced Persons in Darfur and Chad, 3.

283   United Nations Security Council: Secretary General Report. 3 December 2004. Report of the Secretary-General on the Sudan Pursuant to Paragraphs 6, 13 and 16 of Security Council Resolution 1556 (2004), Paragraph 15 of Security Council Resolution 1564 (2004), and Paragraph 17 of Security Council Resolution 1574 (2004), S/2004/947, S/2004/947, para. 17; S/2004/787, para. 34. Available at: http://daccessdds.un.org/doc/UNDOC/GEN/N04/633/97/PDF/N0463397.pdf?OpenElement [accessed: 16 June 2008].

284   Amnesty International Report. 2 December 2004. *No-One to Complain To*. AFR 54/138/2004.

Based on the above, it is evident that serious obstacles face the Sudanese judiciary in trying to 'obtain the accused or the necessary evidence and testimony or to carry out proceedings properly'. Due to these various flaws, deficiencies and obstacles indicated *supra*, the Sudanese judicial system is 'unable' to obtain the accused or the necessary evidence and testimony. However, in this author's opinion, this inability is not related to the substantial or total collapse of the judiciary. Although the insurgency affected the work of some of the courts in Darfur,[285] it did not lead to a substantial or total collapse of the judicial system in the region. Therefore, the requirements of 'inability' under Article 17(3) of the Statute are not fulfilled, and unwillingness rather than inability better describes the Sudanese judiciary.

'Inaction'

The ICC can activate and trigger its jurisdiction in the instance that national courts do not take action.[286] These are called 'uncontested jurisdiction' cases, meaning that the ICC will exercise an uncontested jurisdiction over cases that are of interest to the Court if there are no national proceedings focusing on the most serious crimes and on those who bear the greatest responsibility for those crimes.[287]

The Prosecutor defined the term 'case' as representing 'a specific incident in which crimes within the jurisdiction of the Court have been committed by identified perpetrators'.[288] It is important here to note that the OTP, in determining admissibility, does not assess the whole Sudanese judicial system but rather conducts case-specific assessments.[289] The Prosecutor's *Report to the Security*

---

285   United Nations Commission of Inquiry. 25 January 2005. *Report of the International Commission of Inquiry on Darfur to the United Nations Secretary-General, Pursuant to Security Council Resolution 1564 of 18 September 2004*, para. 430. Available at: www.un.org/News/dh/sudan/com_inq_darfur.pdf [accessed: 16 May 2009].

286   Olasolo, H. 26 March 2004. *The Triggering Procedure of the International Criminal Court, Procedural Treatment of the Principle of Complementarity, and the Role of Office of the Prosecutor*. Guest Lecture Series of the Office of the Prosecutor, The Hague, 1-22, 14.

287   International Criminal Court, Office of the Prosecutor. 14 June 2005. *Third Report of The Prosecutor of The International Criminal Court To The UN Security Council Pursuant To UNSCR 1593*, 1-10, 6. Available at: www.icc-cpi.int/library/cases/OTP_ReportUNSC_3-Darfur_English.pdf [accessed: 18 June 2009].

288   International Criminal Court, Office of the Prosecutor. 14 June 2005. *Third Report of The Prosecutor of The International Criminal Court To The UN Security Council Pursuant To UNSCR 1593*, 1-10, 3. Available at: www.icc-cpi.int/library/cases/OTP_ReportUNSC_3-Darfur_English.pdf [accessed: 18 June 2009].

289   International Criminal Court, Office of the Prosecutor. 14 June 2005. *Third Report of The Prosecutor of The International Criminal Court To The UN Security Council Pursuant To UNSCR 1593*, 1-10, 6. Available at: www.icc-cpi.int/library/cases/OTP_ReportUNSC_3-Darfur_English.pdf [accessed: 18 June 2009].

Council Pursuant to Resolution 1593 has shown a sample of his assessment to a case that was under investigation. He assessed the incident in Hamada where a number of crimes took place.[290]

With respect to 'inaction', the ICC Prosecutor, in his fourth report to the Security Council, noticed developments in the national proceedings on behalf of the Special Courts, the Judicial Investigation Committee, and the Special Prosecution Commission.[291] The Prosecutor concluded, after evaluating these 'proceedings', that no action was taken against those who bear the greatest responsibility for the most serious crimes in the case.[292] This was also stated in previous reports, where the Prosecutor noted the president of the Special Court's statement indicating that 'no cases involving serious violations of international humanitarian law were ready for trial and that the six cases selected were in fact chosen from the case files lying before the ordinary Courts'.[293] This was highlighted again in the Prosecutor's seventh report to the Security Council on 5 June 2008.[294] He indicated that among the approximately 160 suspects identified for national investigation and prosecution, no cases related to individuals and crimes investigated by the OTP were taking place.

Despite recent developments and attempts by the Sudanese authorities to take steps to investigate and prosecute in order to avoid having those cases fall under the ICC's jurisdiction,[295] the OTP has adopted the position that investigations into

---

290   International Criminal Court, Office of the Prosecutor. 14 June 2005. *Third Report of The Prosecutor of The International Criminal Court To The UN Security Council Pursuant To UNSCR 1593*, 1-10, 4. Available at: www.icc-cpi.int/library/cases/OTP_ReportUNSC_3-Darfur_English.pdf [accessed: 18 June 2009].

291   International Criminal Court, Office of the Prosecutor. 16 December 2006. Fourth Report of the Prosecutor of the International Criminal Court, Mr Luis Ocampo to the UN Security Council Pursuant to the UNSCR 1593(2005), 1-11, 6. Available at: www.icc-cpi.int/library/organs/otp/OTP_ReportUNSC4-Darfur_English.pdf [accessed: 6 June 2009].

292   International Criminal Court, Office of the Prosecutor. 16 December 2006. Fourth Report of the Prosecutor of the International Criminal Court, Mr Luis Ocampo to the UN Security Council Pursuant to the UNSCR 1593(2005), 1-11, 6, 7. Available at: www.icc-cpi.int/library/organs/otp/OTP_ReportUNSC4-Darfur_English.pdf [accessed: 6 June 2009].

293   International Criminal Court, Office of the Prosecutor. 14 June 2005. *Third Report of The Prosecutor of The International Criminal Court To The UN Security Council Pursuant To UNSCR 1593*, 1-10, 5. Available at: www.icc-cpi.int/library/cases/OTP_ReportUNSC_3-Darfur_English.pdf [accessed: 18 June 2009].

294   International Criminal Court, Office of the Prosecutor. 5 June 2008. *Seventh Report of the Prosecutor of the International Criminal Court to the UN Security Council Pursuant to the UNSCR 1593(2005)*, para. 22. Available at: www.icc-cpi.int/library/organs/otp/UNSC_2008_En.pdf [accessed: 7 July 2009].

295   *Sudanese Online*. 4 April 2007. Sudan to Try Darfur Crime Suspects. Available at: www.sudaneseonline.com/en2/publish/Latest_News_1/SUDAN_TO_TRY_DARFUR_CRIME_SUSPECTS.shtml [accessed: 3 July 2009].

allegations of serious crimes committed in Darfur since July 2002 have not taken place.

However, the ICC's assessment of the Sudanese legal system in dealing with serious crimes committed in Darfur is an ongoing process,[296] and since the ICC Prosecutor is under no obligation to inform the states of his investigations,[297] it will be for the state that has jurisdiction (Sudan) or the concerned person (an accused or a person for whom a warrant of arrest or a summons to appear is issued) to challenge the admissibility of the case prior to or at the commencement of the trial.[298]

The assessment *supra* of some of the initiatives established by the Sudanese government showed that they would not be considered as investigations under Article 17 if the ICC were to investigate these cases. For instance, the National Commission of Inquiry cannot initiate criminal investigations without explicit permission from the Attorney General.[299] Without permission, such activities cannot be considered 'genuine' investigations under Article 17. The Committees against Rape have been denied any power to carry out prosecutions,[300] and if their activities are not followed by accountability measures, they cannot be labelled as 'investigations' under Article 17. If this scenario occurs, the ICC will most probably render the case admissible on account of the absence of proceedings.

The Pre-Trial Chamber has already considered the cases of Harun and Kushayb admissible, as no national investigations or prosecutions have taken place for them.[301] The same applies to the case of al-Bashir. The Court did not view the national investigation and release of Kushayb as a genuine criminal investigation against the suspect. It rather considered that in fact no action has been taken by the Sudanese authorities against the same person and conduct investigated by the court. Nevertheless, the Sudanese authorities can still initiate a genuine

---

296   Aptel Williamson, C. 1 March 2006. Justice Empowered or Justice Hampered: The International Criminal Court in Darfur. *African Security Review*, 15, 20-32, 25.

297   Article 18 of the ICC Statute does not apply to SC Referrals. Article 18 of the Rome Statute of the International Criminal Court, UN Doc. A/CONF.183/9.

298   Article 19 of the Rome Statute of the International Criminal Court, UN Doc. A/CONF.183/9.

299   Amnesty International. 14 May 2004. *Sudan: Commission of Inquiry must be Effective, Protect Witnesses and Report Publicly.* AI Index: AFR 54/049/2004. Available at: http://web.amnesty.org/library/Index/ENGAFR540492004 [accessed: 16 June 2009].

300   United Nations Commission of Inquiry. 25 January 2005. *Report of the International Commission of Inquiry on Darfur to the United Nations Secretary-General, Pursuant to Security Council Resolution 1564 of 18 September 2004*, para. 465. Available at: www.un.org/News/dh/sudan/com_inq_darfur.pdf [accessed: 16 May 2009].

301   International Criminal Court, Office of the Prosecutor. 14 June 2005. *Third Report of The Prosecutor of The International Criminal Court To The UN Security Council Pursuant To UNSCR 1593*, 1-10, 7. Available at: www.icc-cpi.int/library/cases/OTP_ReportUNSC_3-Darfur_English.pdf [accessed: 18 June 2009].

investigation and prosecution and pre-empt the ICC's jurisdiction at any time before the commencement of the trial.[302]

Gravity as an Admissibility Criterion

Gravity is a pivotal requirement for the admissibility of the case before the ICC.[303] As mentioned in previous chapters,[304] the gravity of a case may be assessed firstly according to the particular circumstances of each of the crime committed (gravity *in concreto*) and secondly according to the person concerned (gravity *in personam*). The element of gravity of the crimes and the level of responsibility of the accused has to be taken into account.[305]

The gravity of cases, in Article 17, is narrower than the gravity criterion in selecting situations. There has been no contestation over whether the gravity criterion for the Darfur situation was satisfied. Prosecutor Moreno-Ocampo has labelled the Darfur situation as one of the gravest situations in Africa, taking into consideration the quantitative criteria deduced, *inter alia*, from the number of victims of the most serious crimes committed in Darfur.[306]

In terms of gravest incidents, various credible resources, such as the International Commission of Inquiry Report,[307] the High-Level Mission and international NGOs,[308] have confirmed the occurrence of numerous incidents where serious international crimes have occurred, causing death, torture, rape

---

302   However, Article 19(4) of the Rome Statute stipulates that; 'In exceptional circumstances, the Court may grant leave for a challenge to be brought more than once or at a time later than the commencement of the trial'. Article 19(4) of the Rome Statute of the International Criminal Court, UN Doc. A/CONF.183/9.

303   Article 17(1)(d) of the Rome Statute of the International Criminal Court, UN Doc. A/CONF.183/9.

304   See Chapter 3.

305   Rule 11 *bis* of Rules of Procedure And Evidence of The International Criminal Tribunal for the former Yugoslavia, Revised 30 September 2002, amended 28 July 2004, amended 11 February 2005. IT/32/Rev. 37. Available at: www.un.org/icty/legaldoc-e/index-t.htm [accessed: 16 June 2008].

306   Moreno-Ocampo, L. 2006. Symposium: International Criminal Tribunals in the 21st Century: Keynote Address: Integrating the Work of the ICC into Local Justice Initiatives. *American University International Law Review*, 21, 497-503, 499.

307   United Nations Commission of Inquiry. 25 January 2005. *Report of the International Commission of Inquiry on Darfur to the United Nations Secretary-General, Pursuant to Security Council Resolution 1564 of 18 September 2004*, para. 450. Available at: www.un.org/News/dh/sudan/com_inq_darfur.pdf [accessed: 16 May 2009].

308   Human Rights Council. 7 March 2007. Report of the High-Level Mission on the Situation of Human Rights in Darfur pursuant to Human Rights Council Decision S-4/101, Human Rights Council Fourth Session, A/HRC/4/80; Human Rights Watch. 11 August 2004. *Empty Promises? Continuing Abuses In Darfur, Sudan: A Human Rights Watch Briefing Paper*, 1-37. Available at: www.hrw.org/backgrounder/africa/sudan/2004/sudan0804.pdf [accessed: 16 May 2009].

and the forced displacement of thousands of civilians. Data has showed the occurrence of several counts of war crimes and crimes against humanity.[309]

Moreover, the fulfilment of the second criterion of gravity requires identifying (and then prosecuting) those most criminally responsible for committing crimes in the case investigated. Hence, the Summons to Appear that was requested by the Prosecutor has named three of those believed to be most responsible for committing crimes within a case under investigation by the ICC. The ICC Prosecutor has named in the Summons to Appear the State Minister for Humanitarian Affairs Ahmed Haroun, the 'Janjaweed' militia leader 'Ali Kushayb,[310] and more importantly President Omar al-Bashir.[311]

Political and Practical Challenges

The analysis *supra* of the complementarity principle with respect to the Darfur referral is conducted solely from a legal approach. However, the application of international criminal law does not occur in a vacuum, but rather in a complex medium where numerous factors interact and affect the application of international justice, chief among them being the political dimension. Cecile Aptel indicates that:

> The challenges faced by the ICC in Darfur demonstrate that international criminal justice does not operate in a political vacuum. On the contrary, its success depends very much on the good will and cooperation of states. The ICC experience illustrates that political expediency weighs heavily in the balance of international justice.[312]

Resolution 1593 imposes an obligation on the Sudanese government and all other parties to the conflict in Darfur to cooperate fully with, and provide necessary

---

309 International Criminal Court, Office of the Prosecutor. 27 February 2007. ICC Prosecutor Presents Evidence on Darfur Crimes, The Hague, ICC-OTP-20070227-206-En. Available at: www.icc-cpi.int/pressrelease_details&id=230&l=en.html [accessed: 16 June 2009].

310 Human Rights Watch. February 2007. *ICC Prosecutor Identifies Suspects in First Darfur Case Questions and Answers*, 1-9, 2. Available at: http://hrw.org/english/docs/2007/02/25/darfur15404_txt.htm [accessed: 6 July 2009].

311 International Criminal Court, Office of the Prosecutor. 14 July 2008. ICC Prosecutor Presents Case against Sudanese President, Hassan Ahmad Al Bashir, for Genocide, Crimes against Humanity and War Crimes in Darfur, ICC-OTP-20080714-PR341-ENG. Available at: www.icc-cpi.int/press/pressreleases/406.html [accessed 28 July 2009].

312 Aptel Williamson, C. 1 March 2006. Justice Empowered or Justice Hampered: The International Criminal Court in Darfur. *African Security Review*, 15, 20-32, 29.

assistance to, the ICC and the Prosecutor.[313] However, the Resolution could be criticized for using weak language regarding all other states. It 'urges' them and other concerned regional and international organizations to cooperate fully with the ICC, as opposed to requesting Sudanese government to cooperate fully.[314] The language of Resolution 1593 bears some confusion on this level. Some interpreted the Resolution as stipulating that only Sudan and other parties to the Darfur conflict are obliged to cooperate fully with and provide necessary assistance to the Court and the Prosecutor, while other states are merely urged to cooperate.[315] Security Council referrals, as indicated above, do not abolish the complementarity principle, but rather boost it through Chapter VII's enforcement powers. Here, the ICC counts on states' cooperation under the UN Charter to meet any obligation (if present) under the Rome Statute.

Yet the above is purely a legal analysis of the power of the UN Charter versus another treaty. When political aspects are taken into consideration, the success of the ICC in exercising its jurisdiction in Darfur, along with the application of the complementarity test, become dependent on a number of political variables, which themselves work against the facilitation of ICC jurisdiction.

Firstly, while interested human rights activists welcomed the Security Council referral, there have been indicators that the referral has acted to shift the political burden away from the Security Council, which was reluctant to interfere in Darfur to prevent the ongoing atrocities.[316] Most major powers appeared unwilling to get involved in a humanitarian intervention to stop the massacres. Three of the five permanent Security Council members have major investments in the Sudanese oil sector. In addition, four of the five members have been brokering arms contracts with the Sudanese government.[317] Moreover, all five permanent members remain staunch defenders of state sovereignty, and none wants to embolden precedents that might diminish state sovereignty. These factors all work against exerting intense

---

313 Moreno-Ocampo, L. 29 June 2005. *Statement of the Prosecutor of the International Criminal Court Mr. Luis Moreno Ocampo to the Security Council on 29 June 2005 Pursuant to UNSCR 1593* (2005), 5. Available at: www.icc-cpi.int/library/cases/ LMO_UNSC_On_DARFUR-EN.pdf [accessed: 24 June 2009].

314 United Nations Security Council Resolution 1593. 31 March 2005. UN Doc. S/ RES/1593.

315 Udombana, N.J. Fall 2005. Pay Back Time in Sudan? Darfur in the International Criminal Court. *Tulsa Journal of Comparative and International Law*, 13, 1-57, 16; Lipscomb, R. January 2006. Restructuring the ICC Framework to Advance Transitional Justice: A Search for a Permanent Solution in Sudan. *Columbia Law Review*, 106, 182-217, 205.

316 Lindberg, T. 15 March 2005. ICC Offers Darfur Hope, *Washington Times*. Available at: http://washingtontimes.com/op-ed/20050314-090221-2751r.htm [accessed: 7 May 2009].

317 Lipscomb, R. January 2006. Restructuring the ICC Framework to Advance Transitional Justice: A Search for a Permanent Solution in Sudan. *Columbia Law Review*, 106, 182-217, 188.

pressures on Sudan for taking severe actions and fully implementing Resolution 1593.

Secondly, Sudan remains uncooperative with the ICC despite being under legal obligation to do so. The ICC Prosecutor indicated explicitly in his sixth and seventh report to the Security Council of Sudan's non-cooperation without any measure taken by the Security Council.[318] Sudan has repeatedly indicated that it will not allow any Sudanese citizen to be tried before the ICC or outside Sudan.[319] The only 'concession' Sudan has made was allowing the ICC to visit its national courts in Darfur to assess national proceedings in relation to the alleged crimes. However, it refused to allow ICC investigators to work within Sudanese territory.[320] The maximum Sudan granted was allowing ICC-OTP investigative staff to conduct formal interviews with two senior officials of the Sudanese government regarding the conflict in Darfur.[321] The result has been that the ICC remains incapable of conducting investigations on the Sudanese territories, and is thus forced to conduct investigations outside Sudan.[322] This is a huge setback for delivering justice; even if the ICC succeeds in conducting an efficient investigation, it will be extremely difficult, if not impossible, for it to call on witnesses in Sudan or The Hague. Thus, it will be very difficult for the ICC to achieve its goals in Darfur if major political players do not exert further political, economic and military pressure on Sudan to abide by Resolution 1593. The ICC success relies heavily on Sudan's

---

318   International Criminal Court, Office of the Prosecutor. 5 June 2008. *Seventh Report of the Prosecutor of the International Criminal Court to the UN Security Council Pursuant to the UNSCR 1593(2005)*, para. 4. Available at: www.icc-cpi.int/library/organs/otp/UNSC_2008_En.pdf [accessed: 7 July 2009]. See also, International Criminal Court, Office of the Prosecutor. 5 December 2007. *Sixth Report of the Prosecutor of the International Criminal Court to the UN Security Council Pursuant to the UNSCR 1593(2005)*, para. 4. Available at: www.icc-cpi.int/library/organs/otp/OTP-RP-20071205-UNSC-ENG.pdf [accessed: 11 February 2009].

319   According to AFP and Reuters Sudan's President Omar al-Bashir vowed in April 2005 never to hand over any Sudanese national to international jurisdiction. See in Aptel Williamson, C. 1 March 2006. Justice Empowered or Justice Hampered: The International Criminal Court in Darfur. *African Security Review*, 15, 20-32, 25.

320   Office of the Prosecutor, International Criminal Court. 13 December 2005. *Second Report of the Prosecutor of the International Criminal Court, Mr. Luis Moreno Ocampo To The Security Council Pursuant to UNSC 1593 (2005)*, ICC-02/05, 5. Available at: www.icc-cpi.int/library/organs/otp/LMO_UNSC_ReportB_En.pdf [accessed: 15 June 2009].

321   International Criminal Court, Pre-Trial Chamber I. 11 September 2006. *Situation In Darfur, Sudan: Prosecutor's Response To Cassese's Observation on Issues Concerning The Protection of Victims And The Preservation of Evidence In The Proceedings on Darfur Pending Before The ICC*, English no.: ICC-02/05, para. 20.

322   Office of the Prosecutor, International Criminal Court. 13 December 2005. *Second Report of the Prosecutor of the International Criminal Court, Mr. Luis Moreno Ocampo To The Security Council Pursuant to UNSC 1593 (2005)*, ICC-02/05, 5. Available at: www.icc-cpi.int/library/organs/otp/LMO_UNSC_ReportB_En.pdf [accessed: 15 June 2009].

cooperation,[323] a normal fact for international criminal justice, which ultimately depends on the cooperation of the state to execute its mandate.[324]

Furthermore, the ICC is aware of the importance of cooperation with other international and regional organizations, particularly the African Union and the United Nations. The ICC has emphasized that cooperation of the African Union Mission in Sudan (AMIS), despite its narrow and limited mandate,[325] is crucial for the ICC investigation in Darfur. However, the ICC Prosecutor has indicated in his reports that there is slow progress in the cooperation between the OTP and AMIS, although there are signals that cooperation will improve in the future.[326] The Prosecutor stated that in June 2006 he received the first set of reports from AMIS in response to a request for assistance submitted in February 2006.[327] As for cooperation with the United Nations, it may become more effective after the adoption of Resolution 1706, which extended the mandate of the United Nations Mission in Sudan (UNMIS) to include Darfur. Resolution 1706 expanded the UNMIS deployment to include Darfur as a means for supporting the restoration of peace and the effective implementation of the Darfur Peace Agreement.[328] The UNMIS deployment in Darfur could be a turning point for the ICC vis-à-vis acquiring evidences, witnesses and accused.[329] The UNMIS, as part of the UN

---

323   AMICC, A Program of The United Nations Association of The United States of America. 16 February 2006. The Current Investigation by The ICC of The Situation In Darfur, 1-14, 7-9. Available at: www.amicc.org [accessed: 3 June 2009].

324   Aptel Williamson, C. 1 March 2006. Justice Empowered or Justice Hampered: The International Criminal Court in Darfur. *African Security Review*, 15, 20-32, 26.

325   Aptel Williamson, C. 1 March 2006. Justice Empowered or Justice Hampered: The International Criminal Court in Darfur. *African Security Review*, 15, 20-32, 27.

326   Until June 2008, the Memorandum of Understanding between the ICC and the AU has not been signed. See the International Criminal Court, Office of the Prosecutor. 5 June 2008. *Seventh Report of the Prosecutor of the International Criminal Court to the UN Security Council Pursuant to the UNSCR 1593(2005)*. Available at: www.icc-cpi.int/ library/organs/otp/UNSC_2008_En.pdf [accessed: 7 July 2009]. See also, International Criminal Court, Office of the Prosecutor. 14 June 2005. *Third Report of The Prosecutor of The International Criminal Court To The UN Security Council Pursuant To UNSCR 1593*, 1-10, 5. Available at: www.icc-cpi.int/library/cases/OTP_ReportUNSC_3-Darfur_English. pdf [accessed: 18 June 2009].

327   International Criminal Court, Office of the Prosecutor. 16 December 2006. Fourth Report of the Prosecutor of the International Criminal Court, Mr Luis Ocampo to the UN Security Council Pursuant to the UNSCR 1593(2005), 1 – 11, 9. Available at: www.icc-cpi. int/library/organs/otp/OTP_ReportUNSC4-Darfur_English.pdf [accessed: 6 June 2009].

328   United Nations Security Council. 31 August 2006. *Security Council Expands Mandate of UN Mission in Sudan to Include Darfur, adopting Resolution 1706 by Vote of 12 in Favour, with 3 Abstaining*. Department of Public Information, News and Media Division. New York: Security Council 5519th Meeting.

329   Aptel Williamson, C. 1 March 2006. Justice Empowered or Justice Hampered: The International Criminal Court in Darfur. *African Security Review*, 15, 20-32, 28.

peacekeeping forces, are under the 'urge' of Security Council Resolution 1593 to cooperate with the ICC.

It seems as though in order to ensure better cooperation, it will be necessary for the Security Council to adopt another resolution that imposes explicit obligation on concerned 'international organization and all states' to cooperate fully with the ICC in Darfur. The ICC could follow the path of the ICTY and seek the cooperation of peacekeeping forces; their assistance proved vital for the ICTY to function in the forum of the crimes in the former Yugoslavia.[330] Whatever the ICC's course, it will undoubtedly remain complex, requiring greater consensus among the major powers, especially since China, Russia and Qatar abstained from voting on Resolution 1706.[331] Yet this deficit is a key concern since two major powers (Russia and China) maintain strong economic ties with Sudan.[332]

Moreover, Sudan itself remained for a while unenthusiastic for the UN deployment. The High-Level Mission on the Situation of Human Rights in Darfur stated previously that 'the Government of the Sudan publicly opposed Resolution 1706 and has actively resisted the deployment of UN peacekeeping forces in Darfur'.[333] After intensive diplomatic efforts and pressures, Sudan accepted a three-phased hybrid approach in Addis Ababa in November 2006.[334] However, since then the arrangements for the application of the three-hybrid approach

---

330   The United Nations Protection Force (UNPROFOR), The European Union Force in Bosnia and Herzegovina (EUFOR), and the North Atlantic Treaty Organisation (NATO) Missions assisted in searching and arresting several suspects in Bosnia-Herzegovina. See Aptel Williamson, C. 1 March 2006. Justice Empowered or Justice Hampered: The International Criminal Court in Darfur. *African Security Review*, 15, 20-32, 27.

331   United Nations Security Council. 31 August 2006. *Security Council Expands Mandate of UN Mission in Sudan to Include Darfur, adopting Resolution 1706 by Vote of 12 in Favour, with 3 Abstaining*. Department of Public Information, News and Media Division. New York: Security Council 5519th Meeting.

332   Lipscomb, R. January 2006. Restructuring the ICC Framework to Advance Transitional Justice: A Search for a Permanent Solution in Sudan. *Columbia Law Review*, 106, 182-217, 187,188.

333   Human Rights Council. 7 March 2007. Report of the High-Level Mission on the Situation of Human Rights in Darfur pursuant to Human Rights Council Decision S-4/101, Human Rights Council Fourth Session, A/HRC/4/80, para. 67.

334   The Human Rights Council high-level mission to Darfur took notice of that the 'AU Peace and Security Council endorsed a three-phased UN support package for AMIS, and extended the mandate to 1 January 2007. Phase one would provide a light support package with a small number of UN advisors and some vital material assets. The second phase represents a heavy support package with a number of critical enabling capabilities, including 2,250 military personnel and a number of civilian personnel to undertake substantive tasks related to the implementation of the DPA. The third phase would bring a fully-hybrid AU-UN operation. Phase one has been completed and Phase Two is set to begin'. Human Rights Council. 7 March 2007. Report of the High-Level Mission on the Situation of Human Rights in Darfur pursuant to Human Rights Council Decision S-4/101, Human Rights Council Fourth Session, A/HRC/4/80, para. 67.

have remained under discussion, leading to an ongoing delay.[335] In the meantime, Sudanese officials remain wary and opposed to further international intervention in Darfur. President Omar al-Bashir announced that any UN takeover of security responsibility from the African Union in Darfur could be dangerous and warned that Darfur would become a 'graveyard' for any foreign military, present against Sudan's will.[336] The compromise landed on a UN–AU joint mission in Darfur. The African Union/UN Hybrid operation in Darfur UNAMID was established on 31 July 2007 with the adoption of Security Council Resolution 1769.[337]

The above shows that Sudanese cooperation with the ICC in Darfur, although an obligation under Resolution 1593, is not guaranteed in reality. There are number of political factors that work against achieving full cooperation between certain states and the Court. The international community and the major powers have been called upon not only to refer the situation in Darfur to the ICC, but also to follow this up with a strong political will to support the ICC's investigations and prosecutions. Intense pressure on Sudan is required to secure its cooperation with the ICC. It is a deep paradox for the ICC, whose jurisdiction is triggered by the lack of action or unwillingness of Sudan, to rely heavily on the support of Sudan to carry out its mandate.[338] The complementarity principle cannot have the intended impact if the efficiency of the ICC is diminished, and this depends on the cooperation of all concerned states and organizations.[339]

Conclusion

The argument raised previously leads to the conclusion that the ICC subsumes the same unfortunate character of international criminal courts as 'giant(s) without legs and arms'.[340] These arms and legs are states and international organizations cooperating with the Court, and this cooperation, at heart, is unfortunately liable to political considerations. It is unfortunate that international justice remains affected

---

335   Human Rights Council. 7 March 2007. Report of the High-Level Mission on the Situation of Human Rights in Darfur pursuant to Human Rights Council Decision S-4/101, Human Rights Council Fourth Session, A/HRC/4/80, para. 67.

336   AFP, 4 March 2006.

337   On 31 July 2008, the Security Council extended UNAMID's mandate for a further 12 months to 31 July 2009 and then again on 6 August 2009, for a further 12 months to 31 July 2010. Available at: www.un.org/en/peacekeeping/missions/unamid [accessed: 24 January 2010].

338   Aptel Williamson, C. 1 March 2006. Justice Empowered or Justice Hampered: The International Criminal Court in Darfur. *African Security Review*, 15, 20-32, 26.

339   Aptel Williamson, C. 1 March 2006. Justice Empowered or Justice Hampered: The International Criminal Court in Darfur. *African Security Review*, 15, 20-32, 26.

340   An expression coined by Professor Cassese, cited from Aptel Williamson, C. 1 March 2006. Justice Empowered or Justice Hampered: The International Criminal Court in Darfur. *African Security Review*, 15, 20-32, 26.

by conflicting political interests that limit the parameters of its application of justice, undermine its efficiency, and in some cases damage its credibility.

From the face of it, the Darfur referral under Chapter VII gives the ICC powers similar to that of the ICTY and ICTR.[341] The actions of the *ad hoc* Tribunals under Chapter VII enjoyed jurisdictional primacy over national courts. The ICC, although it should theoretically enjoy such power in relation to Sudan, has to respect its Statute and apply the complementarity principle.[342] It will still recognize the primary jurisdiction of Sudan to prosecute international crimes, except when there is no genuine action by the Sudanese system or when the actions taken reflect unwillingness or inability.[343] Security Council Resolution 1593 recognizes the importance of domestic efforts to promote the rule of law, protect human rights and combat impunity in Darfur.[344]

This raises an important question about the legal nature of complementarity under a Security Council referral in comparison to complementarity under the pure ambit of the Rome Statute. Some jurists argue that 'the obligations of states under the Charter may override certain fundamental principles in the Rome Statute from a strict legal perspective. This referral could be seen as having the practical effect of creating judicial primacy for the ICC similar to that enjoyed by the ICTY and the ICTR'.[345] This could be the case only if the Security Council adopts a resolution, under Chapter VII, that defers the national jurisdiction in favour of the ICC.

However, Resolution 1593 does not in fact alter the nature of the complementarity principle, as it remains for complementarity to be assessed by the articles of the ICC Statute, and not by the UN Charter. Hence, complementarity under Security Council referrals remains of the same nature as referrals by state parties, and the Prosecutor's *proprio motu* investigations. The fundamental difference occurs in the source of the power of enforcement of the ICC jurisdiction. Whereas in the case of state referral or *proprio motu* cases, the power of enforcement of ICC decisions, investigations and requests relies on the Rome Statute obligations; the enforcement power of the ICC regarding Darfur's referral rests on Chapter VII of the UN Charter. One could argue that the power of enforcement of the ICC in this situation rests on the primacy of Security Council resolutions with respect to

---

341 Udombana, N.J. Fall 2005. Pay Back Time in Sudan? Darfur in the International Criminal Court. *Tulsa Journal of Comparative and International Law*, 13, 1-57, 24.

342 Article 21 of the Rome Statute of the International Criminal Court, UN Doc. A/CONF.183/9.

343 Article 17 of the Rome Statute of the International Criminal Court, UN Doc. A/CONF.183/9.

344 United Nations Security Council Resolution 1593. 31 March 2005. UN Doc. S/RES/1593, para. 4.

345 Lipscomb, R. January 2006. Restructuring the ICC Framework to Advance Transitional Justice: A Search for a Permanent Solution in Sudan. *Columbia Law Review*, 106, 182-217, 191.

national jurisdictions. This enforcement power of the ICC and the duty to cooperate with the Court are therefore similar to that of the ICTY and the ICTR.

In practice, Resolution 1593 is the result of a political compromise[346] rather than the outcome of international legal logic.[347] A number of major states remain reluctant to exert more pressure on Sudan to cooperate with the ICC pursuant to Resolution 1593. Cooperation with the ICC in Darfur, while being an obligation under Resolution 1593, is not guaranteed in reality. In the opinion of this author, it is not enough for the international community and the major powers to refer the situation in Darfur to the ICC, but rather to proceed with a strong political will to support ICC investigations and prosecutions. Intense pressure on Sudan remains indispensable for changing Sudan's position vis-à-vis the Court, as Sudan's reluctance to cooperate with the ICC is a setback to possible successes for the ICC in its mandate to deliver justice in Sudan.

This does not mean that Sudan is not already experiencing pressure due to the implication of the referral. The measures taken by Sudan ranging from the establishment of Special Courts for Darfur, committees to investigate human rights violations and various other measures to reform the judicial system,[348] are indicators of some kind of pressure. The most likely reason behind such measures is avoiding ICC jurisdiction.[349] One cannot claim that up until now the ICC succeeded to encourage the Sudanese judicial system to conduct impartial and effective prosecutions. The Prosecutor's seventh report to the Security Council seemed pessimistic about the Sudanese steps regarding those most responsible or even low-level perpetrators.

An international court with weak enforcement means cannot exert the necessary pressure on the Sudanese government to either exercise its primary jurisdiction to prosecute international crimes in Darfur, or to surrender possible perpetrators to the ICC for prosecution. These 'means' are the cooperation of the states and the support of the international community. This political dimension remains vital in order for the ICC to exercise its jurisdiction and to empower its

---

346   Human Rights Watch. 31 March 2005. *UN Security Council Refers Darfur to the ICC U.N. Security Council Refers Darfur to the ICC Historic Step Toward Justice; Further Protection Measures Needed.* Available at: http://hrw.org/english/docs/2005/03/31/ sudan10408.htm [accessed: 6 June 2009].

347   Heyder, C. 2006. The U.N. Security Council's Referral of the Crimes in Darfur to the International Criminal Court in Light of U.S. Opposition to the Court: Implications for the International Criminal Court's Functions and Status. *Berkeley Journal of International Law*, 24, 650-671, 656.

348   International Criminal Court, Office of the Prosecutor. 16 December 2006. Fourth Report of the Prosecutor of the International Criminal Court, Mr Luis Ocampo to the UN Security Council Pursuant to the UNSCR 1593(2005), 1-11. Available at: www.icc-cpi. int/library/organs/otp/OTP_ReportUNSC4-Darfur_English.pdf [accessed: 6 June 2009].

349   AMICC, A Program of the United Nations Association of the United States of America. 16 February 2006. The Current Investigation by the ICC of the Situation in Darfur, 1-14. Available at: www.amicc.org [accessed: 16 January 2009].

complementarity principle to 'pressure' the Sudanese government to prosecute genuinely international crimes rather than gaining more referrals to The Hague. If this materializes, it will be the ultimate proof of the ICC's success.

Although it remains difficult, at this stage, to draw final conclusions as to whether the Sudanese efforts to prosecute a number of alleged perpetrators in Darfur (other than Harun, Kushayb, and definitely al-Bashir) are genuine and reflect willingness, it can at least affirm that the ICC's impact regarding Sudan's prosecution of Harun, Kushayb and al-Bashir has not been effective. Sudan continues to resist the ICC's pressure to conduct genuine proceedings against Harun, Kushayb and al-Bashir or surrender them to the Court.

Chapter 7

Conclusion

The drafters of the ICC created the complementarity principle as a compromise between the legal duty to prosecute international crimes and the principle of state sovereignty. States were careful not to grant the ICC, as an international organization, the power to supersede their sovereignty over territories and citizens.[1] This aimed to strike a balance between sovereign privileges and world community responsibilities.

However, it has become clear that a balance between these two concepts is unrealistic. The short experience of the ICC and the embryonic application of the complementarity principle are subject to certain realities that cannot be ignored.

The hope that the ICC would change the dynamics of international relations, creating a global body that transcends state interests to enforce an *erga omnes* duty to prosecute international crimes, has not been yet realized. The ICC continues to face significant obstacles in moving towards a world order premised on the pillars of respect for human rights, the rule of law, and accountability for international crimes.

The close textual analysis of the Rome Statute and a critical analysis of the work of the ICC, including the development of its prosecutorial policy in selected cases, all support the conclusions above. With respect to the substantive content of Article 17, the ICC Prosecutor's policy on the admissibility of 'inactions' could encourage in theory national systems to prosecute core crimes; however, in reality it could lead to the opposite. From a preliminary reading of Article 17, the Prosecutor's policy is consistent with the Rome Statute – a logical outcome of the reluctance of states to take action. However, such a prosecutorial policy could have a negative impact on the ICC's role in encouraging national legal systems to prosecute international crimes. The admissibility of all 'inaction' scenarios regardless of inability or unwillingness could encourage states to be 'lazy' in prosecuting core international crimes. A state that is 'willing and able' can still relieve itself of the burden of prosecuting international crimes under the Statute by refraining from taking any action. In such a situation, states will pass off the financial burden and the political difficulties inherent to trials of those most responsible for international crimes. The Ugandan referral exemplified such a scenario and provided an example of a state party with an 'able' and 'willing' judicial system as stipulated under Article 17, yet nonetheless managed to transfer the burden to the ICC.

---

1   Bassiouni, M.Ch. 1 July 2006. The ICC – Quo Vadis? *Journal of International Criminal Justice*, 4, 421-428, 423.

Despite the ability of the Ugandan judicial system and its willingness to prosecute LRA criminals, the ICC rendered Uganda's case erroneously admissible on the ground of 'unavailability' of the Ugandan judicial system to capture the accused. The ICC's position in the DRC situation raises other concerns, particularly with regard to the Court's approach to cases of 'inaction'. Lubanga and Germain Katanga were already in Congolese custody awaiting trial for more serious crimes when the ICC requested their surrender considering that the DRC was not investigating the crimes the Court has been investigating. The Congolese judicial system, at least in certain areas of the DRC (including Kinshasa) was 'able and willing'. It was only for Mathieu Ngudjolo Chui who was not in custody when the ICC issued his arrest warrant,[2] but he was arrested and surrendered to the ICC by the (willing and relatively able) Congolese judicial system. Given these developments, the ICC has been more concerned over launching its first trials than supporting the Congolese national system in exercising its primary jurisdiction. For a Court promoting positive complementarity it would have been understandable if the ICC had become involved in bilateral discussions with the Congolese judicial system, which was already willing (and at least 'able' regarding Lubanga and Katanga – they were captured and detained in Kinshasa) to amend the national indictments to cover the conducts that were under investigation by the ICC. The ICC's contribution to national prosecutions in a case where DRC authorities were already able and willing to conduct proceedings in Kinshasa, albeit with some support from the ICC, has been relatively low. Probably, the prosecutions by the DRC would have faced numerous challenges since human rights guarantees provided for an accused in a fragile judicial system, like that of the DRC, will be lower than that provided by the Statute and human rights standards.[3] Nevertheless, the ICC could have made a more effective contribution to the Congolese judicial system if it encouraged the judiciary to take primary responsibility, with the ICC functioning to monitor the trials for their degree of conformity with international standards.

In the Darfur case, the complementarity principle rests on the Security Council referral under Chapter VII, where states' cooperation is presumed. The application of the complementarity principle in the Darfur referral did have some impact on Sudan, as the Sudanese authorities took some judicial measures: establishing Special Courts for Darfur, the Judicial Investigations Committee (JIC),[4] setting

---

2   Human Rights Watch. 7 February 2008. *ICC/DRC: New War Crimes Suspect Arrested.* Available at: http://hrw.org/english/docs/2008/02/07/congo17996.htm [accessed: 24 March 2009].

3   See the UN Independent Expert on Human Rights for the DRC Titinga Frederic Pacere comments during his visit to the DRC in December 2007. Available at: www.reliefweb.int/rw/rwb.nsf/db900SID/EGUA-79LQQF?OpenDocument&RSS20=02-P [accessed: 23 March 2009].

4   The JIC investigated number of cases, but no further developments were observed. See International Criminal Court, Office of the Prosecutor. 27 February 2007. *Situation*

up other committees to investigate human rights violations,[5] and renewing the investigation by the Sudanese Attorney General of Minister Ahmad Harun and Ali Kushayb, after claiming that new evidence had been discovered.[6] However, Sudan released Kushayb in September 2007 considering that there were no sufficient evidences against him. After that, the ICC Prosecutor took a bold step in his 'Application for Arrest Warrant Under Article 58 against President Omar Al Bashir'.[7] In spite of the importance of such an action, it is too early to determine its impact on the Sudanese judicial system, especially since Sudan continues to refuse to cooperate with the ICC.

A textual analysis of the Rome Statute cannot reveal, in itself, the many factors that influence the relations between the ICC and state parties. Despite the progress made by its establishment, the ICC – similar to previous international courts – lacks a strong enforcement mechanism.[8] The ICC enforcement system is even weaker than the other *ad hoc* Tribunals. This has implications for the application of the complementarity principle and for its potential to contribute to reforms in national legal systems.

This structural weakness is unfortunate, as it weakens the potential for a progressive role for the ICC. The case studies discussed in previous chapters suggest that the ICC, during its short experience, has struggled to find its place in the existing international order. It has been more a passive rather than a leading actor. The 'teething' problems, which Antonio Cassese has outlined regarding the ICC and other international courts,[9] are likely to continue, which will leave the ICC struggling to find its path within the current world order rather than creating its own.

The Court's contribution to the national judicial systems for the prosecution of core crimes will vary from one place to another: from one suitable political context to another less suitable one, from a supporting balance-of-power setting to an 'unsupportive' one. The 'stateless' Prosecutor of the ICC, to succeed, must take into consideration the political circumstances of any situation as he analyses the

in Darfur, the Sudan: Annex 12 to the Prosecutor's Application under Article 58(7). ICC-02/05-56-Anx12 27-02-2007 1/3 EO PT. Available at: www.icc-cpi.int/library/cases/ICC-02-05-56-Anx12_English.pdf [accessed: 16 March 2009].

5   International Criminal Court. February-March 2007. *The Office of the Prosecutor and its Investigation in Darfur, Sudan*. ICC News Letter, 13.

6   Aljazeera Arabic. 23 March 2007. New Investigation with a Sudanese Minister. Available at: www.aljazeera.net [accessed: 9 April 2009].

7   International Criminal Court, Office of the Prosecutor. 14 July 2008. *Prosecutor's Application for Warrant of Arrest under Article 58 against Omar Hassan Ahmad Al Bashir*. Available at: www.icc-cpi.int/library/organs/otp/ICC-OTP-ST20080714-ENG.pdf [accessed: 14 July 2009].

8   Cassese, A. 1 July 2006. Is the ICC Still Having Teething Problems? *Journal of International Criminal Justice*, 3, 434-441, 435.

9   Cassese, A. 1 July 2006. Is the ICC Still Having Teething Problems? *Journal of International Criminal Justice*, 3, 434-441, 435.

legal requirements for jurisdiction and admissibility under the Statute. Apparently, the ICC will continue to be constrained by a world order that remains defined primarily by state sovereignty and state interests.

The Ugandan initial referral has reflected a willing system that supported the ICC jurisdiction without reservation. Other international and regional actors, including major powers, showed no objection or opposition to Uganda's referral and the ICC's role in the conflict. However, it is the Acholi local community and the victims who showed less trust in the ICC.[10] Thus, the ICC can continue to function in a supportive setting without opposition by major stakeholders, as many international NGOs and like-minded states remain vigilant to encourage concerned parties to cooperate with the ICC in its investigation of the Ugandan referral. Hence, the situation cannot be analysed without taking into consideration the international and regional circumstances. The impact of the ICC could have been different if important players (such as Uganda, the DRC, Sudan, African Union and the European Union) opposed the ICC's role in the conflict, or were uncooperative. The ICC enforcement system by itself is not able, without the support of the important actors, to have a substantial effect at the national level.

This argument *supra* is not to belittle the positive achievements of the ICC, accomplished by the establishment and existence of the Court and through its embryonic experiences. Rather it is intended to highlight the continuing constraints within which the Court operates and which continue to limit its potential. More support from below (local and domestic) and from above (international) is needed for the ICC to strengthen prosecutions at the national level. The criticisms of the ICC cannot be separated from the broader shortcomings of the international legal system. The ICC reflects those shortcomings that have continuously frustrated those seeking to end impunity for international crimes through more effective enforcement of international criminal law. Until that change, the ICC is like a mirror subsuming some of these obstacles rather than being a true vehicle for change.

Taking the aforementioned into consideration, the impact of the ICC's complementarity regime will depend on the level of support and cooperation available at the particular moment of the situation. In a situation where effective, international, regional and local stakeholders support accountability vis-à-vis international justice, the ICC's chances of success in contributing to indirect enforcement at the national level are higher than in those situations that lack this support.

Finally, although expectations remain high, the ICC's short experience serves to highlight the weaknesses of the Court's enforcement mechanisms, and that has implications for the complementarity principle in relation to national legal

---

10   Human Rights Center, International Center for Transitional Justice and Payson Center for International Development. December 2007. When the War Ends: A Population-Based Survey on Attitudes about Peace, Justice, and Social Reconstruction in Northern Uganda.

systems. The ICC's existence and practice has created some contribution on the national level, but it has not reached a systematic level. Despite this, the ICC is still in its embryonic stages. Time is needed to allow the ICC to create room within the international legal system. It remains a challenge for the ICC, not only to create its own place in this system, but also to create a new dynamic for change, to contribute to a new world order where respect for human rights prevails.

Bibliography

Abbas, A. Winter 2005. The Competence of the Security Council to Terminate Jurisdiction of The International Criminal Court. *Texas International Law Journal*, 4, 263-309.

Abdulqawi, Y. 1995. Reflections on the Fragility of State Institutions in Africa. *African Yearbook of International Law*, 2, 3.

Africa News. 9 February 2005. Sudan; African Union Tribunal Proposed for War Crimes in Darfur.

African Commission. 15-29 May 2003. African Commission Communication 228/99 Law Office/Sudan.

Agence France-Presse. 25 February 2004. Museveni Pledges to Cooperate with ICC to Probe Uganda War Crimes. Available at: www.spacewar.com/2004/040225143401.8peoxfh1.html [accessed: 25 March 2009].

Ahmedani, M., Barba, C., Mcgonigle, B., Heindel, A. and Thompson, L. Fall 2005. Updates From the International Criminal Courts. *Human Rights Brief*, 13, 37-52.

Akande, D. December 2003. The Jurisdiction of the International Criminal Court over Nationals of Non-Parties: Legal Basis and Limits. *Journal of International Criminal Justice*, 618-656.

Akhavan, P. April 2005. Developments at the International Criminal Court: The Lord's Resistance Army Case: Uganda's Submission of the First State Referral to the International Criminal Court. *The American Journal of International Law*, 99, 403-429.

Akhbar Alyoum Daily. 2004. Deputy Governor of Southern Darfur State Says the State is Stable. 3 August.

Al-Anbaa Newspaper. 2004. President Al-Bashir Gives Interview to Lebanese Al Mustaqbal Newspaper on Darfur. 14 August.

Aliro, O. 2003. Why Museveni and Byanyima Divorced, Interview with the former Director at the Movement Secretariat, Winnie Byanyima, *The Monitor*, 23-30 July.

Aljazeera Arabic. 23 March 2007. New Investigation with a Sudanese Minister. Available at: www.aljazeera.net [accessed: 9 April 2009].

Amanpour, C. 12 May 2004. Sudan's Hellish Humanitarian Crisis. *CNN*. Available at: http://edition.cnn.com/2004/WORLD/africa/05/12/sudan.crisis [accessed: 16 June 2009].

The American Non-Governmental Organizations Coalition for the International Criminal Court A Program of the United Nations Association of the United

States of America. 16 February 2006. First Arrest Warrants Issued for Lord's Resistance Army. Available at: www.amicc.org [accessed: 9 March 2009].

The American Non-Governmental Organizations Coalition for the International Criminal Court; a Program of the United Nations Association of the United States of America. 16 February 2006. The Current Investigation by the ICC of the Situation in Northern Uganda. Available at: www.amicc.org [accessed: 16 March 2009].

Amnesty International. November 1997. *The International Criminal Court: Making the Right Choices- Part III. Ensuring Effective State Cooperation.* AI Index: IOR40/13/97.

Amnesty International. May 2003. *International Criminal Court: Security Council Must Refuse to Renew Resolution 1422.* AI index: IOP 40/008/2003.

Amnesty International. November 2003. *Sierra Leone: Special Court for Sierra Leone: Denial of Right to Appeal and Prohibition of Amnesties for Crimes under International Law.* Available at: http://web.amnesty.org/library/index/engafr510122003 [accessed: 5 July 2009].

Amnesty International. 2004. *Uganda Annual Report 2004.* Available at: http://web.amnesty.org/report2004/uga-summary-eng [accessed: 16 March 2009].

Amnesty International. 25 February 2004. *Uganda: Soldiers Executed after Unfair Trial.* AFR 59/004/2003.

Amnesty International. 14 May 2004. *Sudan: Commission of Inquiry must be Effective, Protect Witnesses and Report Publicly.* AI Index: AFR 54/049/2004. Available at: http://web.amnesty.org/library/Index/ENGAFR540492004 [accessed: 1 June 2009].

Amnesty International. 8 June 2004. *Sudan, Darfur: Incommunicado Detention, Torture and Special Courts.* AI Index: AFR 54/058/2004. Available at: http://web.amnesty.org/library/Index/ENGAFR540582004 [accessed: 22 June 2009].

Amnesty International. June 2004. *Open Letter To The Security Council Regarding Renewal of Security Council Resolution 1487.* Available at: http://web.amnesty.org/library/index/ENGIOR400092004 [accessed: 11 June 2009].

Amnesty International. 27 July 2004. *Africa: Uganda, Uganda Concerns about the International Criminal Court Bill.* Available at: http://web.amnesty.org/library/Index/ENGAFR590052004?open&of=ENG-UGA [accessed: 16 March 2009].

Amnesty International. 13 October 2004. *Civilians Still under Threat in Darfur: An Agenda for Human Rights Protection,* AFR 54/131/2004. Available at: http://web.amnesty.org/library/index/engafr541312004 [accessed: 3 May 2009].

Amnesty International. 2 December 2004. *No-One to Complain To.* AFR 54/138/2004.

Amnesty International. 3 February 2006. *Democratic Republic of Congo: Parliament must Reform and Enact International Criminal Court Bill.* AI Index: AFR 62/002/2006. Available at: http://web.amnesty.org/library/Index/ENGAFR620022006?open&of=ENG-COD [accessed: 24 June 2009].

Amnesty International. 4 August 2006. *Public Statement: Uganda: Amnesty International Calls for an Effective Alternative to Impunity.* AI Index: AFR 59/004/2006, News Service No: 203. Available at: www.amnestyusa.org/regions/africa/document.do?id=ENGAFR590042006 [accessed: 9 December 2008].

Amnesty International. 13 December 2006. *Press Release: UN: Human Rights Council Resolution a Lukewarm Response to Deepening Crisis in Darfur.* Available at: http://news.amnesty.org/index/ENGIOR410292006 [accessed: 21 March 2009].

Amnesty International USA. 6 September 2005. *Sudan: Human Rights Concerns.* Available at: www.amnestyusa.org/countries/sudan/index.do [accessed: 19 May 2009].

Amoru, P. 18 September 2008. Uganda: Local War Crimes Court Excludes UPDF From Trial. *The Monitor.* Available at: http://allafrica.com/stories/200809180042.html [accessed: 21 February 2010].

Andersson, H. 2004. Screams of Sudan's Starving Refugees. BBC News. 26 June. Available at: http://www.bbc.co.uk/2/hi/programmes/from our correspondent/3840 427.stm [accessed: 16 May 2009].

Aptel Williamson, C. 1 March 2006. Justice Empowered or Justice Hampered: The International Criminal Court in Darfur. *African Security Review*, 15, 20-32.

Apuuli, K.P. 1 March 2006. The ICC Arrest Warrants for the Lord's Resistance Army Leaders and Peace Prospects for Northern Uganda. *Journal of International Criminal Justice*, 49, 179-188.

Arbour, L. 13 May 1999. Press Release: Statement by the Prosecutor of the ICTY and ICTR, The Hague, JL/PIU/401-E, as quoted in Kovacs, P. Intervention Armee des Forces de l'OTAN au Kosovo. *International Review of the Red Cross*, 837, 103-128. Available at: www.icrc.org/web/fre/sitefre0.nsf/html/5FZEXP [accessed: 12 January 2009].

Arsanjani, M.H. May 1999. Reflections on the Jurisdiction and Trigger Mechanism of the International Criminal Court, in *Reflections on the International Criminal Court*, edited by H. von Hebel, J.G. Lammers and J. Schukking. Cambridge: Cambridge University Press.

Arsanjani, M.H. and Reisman, W.M. April 2005. The Law-in-Action of the International Criminal Court. *The American Journal of International Law*, 99, 2, 385-403.

Asia Africa Intelligence Wire. 16 December 2003. *Uganda: New Amnesty Act to Exclude Rebel LRA Leaders.* Available at: www.accessmylibrary.com/comsite5/bin/pdinventory.pl?pdlanding=1&referid=2930&purchase_type=ITM&item_id=0286-19714599 [accessed: 16 September 2009].

Barnett, J.D. February 1927. The Grounds of Pardon. *Journal of American Institute of Criminal Law and Criminology*, 17, 4, 490-530.

Bassiouni, M.Ch. 1987. *International Extradition: United States Law and Practice.* United States: Oceana Publications, fourth edition.

Bassiouni, M.Ch. 1992. *Crimes against Humanity*. Dordrecht/Boston/London: Martinus Nijhoff Publishers.

Bassiouni, M.Ch. 1996. *International Extradition: United States Law and Practice*. Dobbs Ferry: Oceana.

Bassiouni, M.Ch. Winter 1997. Observations Concerning the 1997-1998 Preparatory Committee Work. Nouvelles, 13, 25, *Denver Journal of International Law and Policy*, 397.

Bassiouni, M.Ch. (ed.). 1998. *International Criminal Law; Procedural and Enforcement Mechanism*. New York: Transnational Publishers, second edition.

Bassiouni, M.Ch. 1999. Symposium: Negotiating the Treaty of Rome on the Establishment of the International Criminal Court. *Cornell International Law Journal*, 443.

Bassiouni, M.Ch. (ed.). 2002. *Post-Conflict Justice*. Ardsley: Transnational Publishers.

Bassiouni, M.Ch. 2003. *Introduction to International Criminal Law*. Ardsley: Transnational Publishers.

Bassiouni, M.Ch. 1 July 2006. The ICC – Quo Vadis? *Journal of International Criminal Justice*, 4, 421-428.

Bassiouni, M.Ch. and Wise, E. 1995. *Aut Dedare Aut Judicare, the Duty to Extradite or Prosecute in International Law*. Dordrecht: Martinus Nijhoff Publishers.

BBC News. 30 September 2004. *Who are Sudan's Darfur Rebels?* Available at: http://news.bbc.co.uk/2/hi/africa/3702242.stm [accessed: 16 May 2009]

Beale, A. and Geary, R. January 1994. Subsidiarity Come of Age? *New Law Journal*, 144, 12-15.

Benzing, M. 2003. The Complementarity Regime of the International Criminal Court: International Criminal Justice between State Sovereignty and the Fight against Impunity. *Max Planck Yearbook of United Nations Law*, 7, 591-632.

Beres, L.R. 1998. Israel's Freeing of Terrorists Violates International Law. Available at: www.gamla.org.il/english/article/1998/dec/1002.htm [accessed: 19 March 2008].

Bergsmo, M. and Pejic, J. 1999. Article 15, in *Commentary on the Rome Statute of the International Criminal Court: Observer's Note, Article by Article*, edited by Otto Triffterer. Baden-Baden: Nomos Verlagsgesellschaft, 359-363.

Bergsmo, M. and Pejic, J. 1999. On Article 16, in *Commentary on the Rome Statute of the International Criminal Court: Observer's Note, Article by Article*, edited by Otto Triffterer. Baden-Baden: Nomos Verlagsgesellschaft, 377.

Boos, A. 2002. From the International Law Commission to the Rome Conference (1994-1998), in *The Rome Statute of the International Criminal Court: A Commentary*, edited by A. Cassese, P. Gaeta and J.R.W.D. Jones. Oxford: Oxford University Press, I, 36.

Broomhall, B. 2003. *International Justice and the International Criminal Court: Between Sovereignty and the Rule of Law*. Oxford: Oxford University Press.

Brown, B.S. Summer 1998. Primacy or Complementarity: Reconciling the Jurisdiction of National Criminal Tribunals. *The Yale Journal of International Law*, 23, 2, 383-436.

Brubacher, M.R. 2004. Prosecutorial Discretion within the International Criminal Court. *Journal of International Criminal Justice*, 2, 1, 71-95.

Cárdenas, C. 25-26 June 2004. The Admissibility Test Before The International Criminal Court Under Special Consideration of Amnesties and Truth Commissions, in *Complementary Views on Complementarity Proceedings of the International Roundtable on the Complementary Nature of the International Criminal Court*, edited by J. Kleffner and G. Kor. May 2006. Amsterdam: Cambridge University Press.

Carozza, P. January 2003. Subsidiarity as a Structural Principle of International Human Rights Law. *The American Journal of International Law*, 97, 1, 38-79.

Cassese, A. 2003. *International Criminal Law*. Oxford: Oxford University Press.

Cassese, A. 1 July 2006. Is the ICC Still Having Teething Problems? *Journal of International Criminal Justice*, 3, 434-441.

Cassese, A., Gaeta, P. and Jones, J.R.W.D (eds). 2002. *The Rome Statute of the International Criminal Court: A Commentary.* Oxford: Oxford University Press, two volumes.

Chan, E. 2003. One Country, Two Systems. The Decision To Investigate and Prosecute in China and Special Administrative Region of Hong Kong. Paper submitted to the Seventh Conference of the International Society for the Reform of Criminal Law held in The Hague, the Netherlands, 24-28 August 2003. Available at: www.isrcl.org [accessed: 25 January 2009].

Citizens for Global Solutions. 23 June 2004. US Withdrew It Demands for Peacekeeping Exemption Renewal. Available at: http://globalsolutions.org/programs/lawjustice/news/nounscrenewal.html [accessed: 14 June 2009].

Citizens for Global Solutions. 30 June 2004. US Policy on the ICC. Available at http://globalsolutions.org/programs/lawjustice/icc/resources/uspolicy.html [accessed: 11 June 2009].

Citizens for Global Solutions. June 2004. In Uncharted Waters: Seeking Justice before the Atrocities Have Stopped, the International Criminal Court in Uganda and the Democratic of the Congo, 1-43.

Coalition for the International Criminal Court. 7 March 2006. Sudan: UN Special Rapporteur on Human Rights in Sudan's Recent Assessment of Darfur Courts; Obasanjo Envoy and Sudan MoJ Discuss ICC. Available at: www.iccnow.org/?mod=newsdetail&news=391 [accessed: 18 June 2009].

Coalition to Stop the Use of Child Soldiers. 21 February 2001. *UN Finds Congo Child Soldiers*. Child Soldiers 1379 Report. Available at: www.childsoldiers.org/cs/childsoldiers.nsf/0/c560bb92d962c64c80256c69004b0797?OpenDocument [accessed: 16 September 2008].

Coalition to Stop the Use of Child Soldiers. 25 June 2003. *Child Soldiers Coalition Reports Alarming Levels of Abductions and Recruitment of Children by LRA and UPDF in Northern Uganda.* Available at: www.child-soldiers.org/home [accessed: 14 May 2009].

Cocks, Tim. 16 January 2007. *Sudanese President Omar Hassan al-Bashir Vowed to 'Get Rid of the LRA from Sudan' In Reuters: Uganda LRA to Go Home, Army Says Would Be 'War'.* Available at: http://sg.news.yahoo.com/070115/3/45zeg.html [accessed: 6 March 2009].

Commission on Human Rights, Economic and Social Council. 17 May 1999. Situation of Human Rights in the Sudan – Addendum. Fifty-fifth Session.

Committee of the Whole. 10 July 1998. *Jurisdiction, Admissibility and Applicable Law*, Bureau Proposal, Part 2. A/CONF.183/C.1/L.59.

Condorelli, L. and Ciampi, A. 2005. Comments on the Security Council Referral of the Situation on Darfur to the International Criminal Court. *Journal of International Criminal Justice*, 3, 590-599.

Cote, L. March 2005. Reflections on the Exercise of Prosecutorial Discretion in International Criminal Law. *Journal of International Criminal Justice*, 162-185.

Czaretzky, J.M. and Rychlack, R.J. December 2003. An Empire or Law? Legalism and the International Criminal Court. *Notre Dame Law Review*, 79, 55-126.

Danner, A.M. July 2003. Enhancing the Legitimacy and Accountability of Prosecutorial Discretion at the International Court. *The American Journal of International Law*, 510-572.

Dashwood, A., Wyatt, D., Arnull, A. and Ross, M. 2000. *European Union Law*. London: Sweet & Maxwell, fourth edition.

Declaration made upon ratification of the Rome Statute by Colombia. Available at: http://untreaty.un.org/ENGLISH/bible/englishinternetbible/partI/chapterXVIII/treaty10.asp [accessed: 11 September 2009].

Della Morte, G. 2002. Les Frontières De La Compétence De La Cour Pénale Internationale: Observations Critiques. *Revue Internationale De Droit Penal*, 73, 24.

Despouy, L. 30 December 2003. Report of the Special Rapporteur on the Independence of Judges and Lawyers: Civil and Political Rights, Including the Questions of: Independence of the Judiciary, Administration of Justice, Impunity. E/CN.4/2004/60.

Deutsche Presse Agentur. 9 June 2004. Ugandan Government Says 19 Die in Rebel Attack on Refugee Camp.

Doherty, K.L. and McCormack, T.L.H. 1999. Complementarity as a Catalyst for Comprehensive Domestic Penal Legislation. *Davis Journal of International Law and Policy*, 5, 147-180.

Draft Resolution of the Assembly of States Parties on the Proposed Program Budget for 2007. Annex I. ICC-ASP/5/32.

Dugard, J. 2002. Possible Conflicts of Jurisdiction with Truth Commissions, in *The Rome Statute of The International Criminal Court: A Commentary*, edited by A. Cassese, P. Gaeta and J.R.W.D. Jones. Oxford: Oxford University Press, I, 699.

Duker, W.F. 1977. The Presidents Power to Pardon: A Constitutional History. *WM and Mary Law Review*, 18, 475-479.

Dworkin, R. 1977. *Taking Rights Seriously*. Cambridge, MA: Harvard University Press.

Eckhardt, W.G. Summer 2000. Essay on the Trials of the Century: My Lai: An American Tragedy. *University of Missouri at Kansas City Law Review*, 671-708.

El-Zeidy, M. Summer 2002. The Principle of Complementarity: A Machinery to Implement International Criminal Law. *Michigan Journal of International Law*, 23, 4, 869-978.

El-Zeidy, M. November 2002. The United Nations Dropped the Atomic Bomb of Article 16 of the ICC Statute: Security Council Power of Deferrals and Resolution 1422. *Vanderbilt Journal of Trans National Law*, 35, 1503-1548.

El-Zeidy, M. 2005. The Ugandan Government Triggers the First Test of the Complementarity Principle: An Assessment of the First State's Party Referral to the ICC. *International Criminal Law Review*, 5, 83–119.

Endo, K. 2001. *Subsidiarity and its Enemies: To What Extent is Sovereignty Contested in the Mixed Commonwealth of Europe?*, EU Working Paper No. RSC 2001. Available at: http://netec.mcc.ac.uk/WoPEc/data/Papers/erpeuirscp0051.html [accessed: 14 March 2009].

Estella, A. 2002. *The EU Principle of Subsidiarity and Its Critique*. Oxford: Oxford University Press.

Falk, R. 1964. The Adequacy of Contemporary Theories of International Law Gaps in Legal Thinking. *Virginia Law Review*, 50, 2, 231-265.

Falk, R. April 1975. A New Paradigm for International Legal Studies: Prospects and Proposals. *The Yale Law Journal*, 84, 5, 969-1021.

Falk, R. 1976. The Role of Law in World Society: Present Crisis and Future Prospects, in *Toward World Order and Human Dignity*, edited by B.H. Weston and W.M. Reisman. New York: Free Press, 132-166.

Falk, R. January 1980. The Shaping of World Order Studies: A Response. *The Review of Politics*, 42, 1, 18-30.

Falk, R. January 1997. State of Siege: Will Globalization Win Out? *International Affairs (Royal Institute of International Affairs 1944-)*, 73, 1, 123-136.

Falk, R. 1999. *Predatory Globalization: A Critique*. Cambridge: Cambridge University Press.

Falk, R. 2002. Reframing the Legal Agenda of World Order in the Course of a Turbulent Century, in *Reframing The International: Law Culture, Politics*, edited by R. Falk, R.L. Edwin and R.B.J. Welker. New York and London: Routledge.

Falk, R. July 2003. What Future for the UN Charter System of War Prevention? *The American Journal for International Law*, 97, 3, 590-598.

Falk, R. 2006. Reshaping Justice: International Law and the Third World: An Introduction. *Third World Quarterly*, 27, 711-712.

Falk, R., Edwin J.R. Lester and Welker, R.B.J. (eds). 2002. *Reframing The International: Law Culture, Politics*. New York and London: Routledge.

Ferencz, B. January 2000. Book Review of *The International Criminal Court: The Making of the Rome Statute – Issues, Negotiations, Results*, edited by R. Lee. *The American Journal of International Law*, 94, 218-221. Available at: www.benferencz.org/arts/38.html [accessed: 14 October 2008].

Fernández de Gurmendi, S.A. 1999. The Role of the International Prosecutor, in *The International Criminal Court: The Making of the Rome Statute – Issues, Negotiations and Results*, edited by R. Lee. The Hague: Kluwer Law International, 55.

FIDH. 4 April 2005. *The Security Council Refers the Darfur Situation to the International Criminal Court*. Available at: www.fidh.org/article.php3?id_article=2336 [accessed: 5 June 2009].

Friesecke, U. 6 August 2004. Western Powers Seek Sudan Disintegration. *Executive Intelligence Review*, 31. Available at: www.larouchepub.com/eirtoc/2004/eirtoc_3131.html [accessed: 16 May 2009].

Gallagher, K. Fall 2000. No Justice, No Peace: The Legalities and Realities of Amnesty in Sierra Leone. *Thomas Jefferson Law Review*, 23, 149-195.

Gamer, B. (ed.). 1999. *Black Law Dictionary*. St Paul: West, seventh edition.

Gargiulo, P. 1999. The Controversial Relationship between the International Criminal Court and Security Council, in *Essays on the Rome Statute of the International Criminal Court*, edited by William Schabas and F. Lattanzi. Ripa Fagnano Alto: Editrice il Sirente, 1, 67-103.

Gavron, J. 2002. Amnesties in the Light of Developments in International Law and the Establishment of the International Criminal Court. *International and Comparative Law Quarterly*, 51, 91-126.

Ghandi, P.R. (ed.). 2002. *Blackstone's International Human Rights Documents*. Oxford: Oxford University Press, third edition.

Gilbert, M. March 2001. The Role of the Acholi Religious Leaders Peace Initiative (ARLPI) in Peace Building in Northern Uganda, in *The Effectiveness of Civil Society Initiatives in Controlling Violent Conflicts and Building Peace – A Study of Three Approaches in the Greater Horn of Africa*. USAID/Management Systems International.

Gil Gil, A. 1999. *Derecho Penal Internacional: Especial consideracion del delito de genocidio*. Madrid: Editorial Tecnos.

Gil Gil, A. 1999. Die Tatbestände der Verbrechen gegn die Menschlichkeit und des Völkermordes im Römischen Statut des Internationalen Strafgerichtshofs. *Zeitschrift für die gesamte Strafrechtswissenschaft*, 112, 381-397.

Global IDP Project. July 2003. Army Displaced 300,000 People. Available at: www.db.idpproject.org/Sites/IdpProjectDb/idpSurvey.nsf/wViewCountries/BCA796EFE6FE85C2C1256DDE0034984A [accessed: 19 March 2009].

Global Rights. August 2005. S.O.S Justice, What Justice is there for Vulnerable Groups in Eastern DRC? 1-12.

Global Security. 7 July 1999. Sudan Pardons. Available at: www.globalsecurity. org/military/library/news/1999/12/991207-sudan1.htm [accessed: 19 June 2009].

Greenawalt, A.K. 1999. Rethinking Genocidal Intent: The Case for a Knowledge-Based Interpretation. *Columbia Law Review*, 99, 2259-2294.

Grotius, H. 1624. *De Jure belli Ac Pacis*. Book 2, ch. XXI. Sections 3, 4, 5(1) and 5(3).

Hafner, G., Boon, K., Rbesame, A. and Huston, J. March 1999. A Response to the American View as Represented by Ruth Wedgwood. *The European Journal of International Law*, 10, 108-128.

Happold, M. 1 January 2006. Darfur, the Security Council, and the International Criminal Court. *International and Comparative Law Quarterly*, 55, 226-238.

Heinrich, M. December 2001. Macedonia Pardons 11 Guerrillas to Launch Amnesty. Available at: www.alb.net.com/amcc/cgi-bin/viewsnews.cgi?newsi d1007583679,97020 [accessed: 19 March 2009].

Henry Campbell, B. 1979. *Black's Law Dictionary*. St Paul: West, fifth edition.

Henry Campbell, B. 1991. *Black's Law Dictionary*. St Paul: West, sixth edition.

Heyder, C. 2006. The U.N. Security Council's Referral of the Crimes in Darfur to the International Criminal Court in Light of U.S. Opposition to the Court: Implications for the International Criminal Court's Functions and Status. *Berkeley Journal of International Law*, 24, 650-671.

Hiatt, F. July 1998. The Trouble with The War Crime Court, *The Washington Post*, 26 July 1998, 7, in *Prosecutorial Discretion Before National Courts And International Tribunals*, edited by D.D. Ntanda Nsereko. Guest lecture Series of The Office of the Prosecutor. ICC-OTP and Individual Authors. 2003, 1-15.

Holmes, J. 1999. The Principle of Complementarity, in *The International Criminal Court: The Making of the Rome Statute, Issues, Negotiations, Results*, edited by R. Lee. The Hague: Kluwer, 1-54.

Holmes, J. 2002. Complementarity: National Courts versus the International Criminal Court, in *The Rome Statute of The International Criminal Court: A Commentary*, edited by A. Cassese, P. Gaeta and J.R.W.D. Jones. Oxford: Oxford University Press, I, 674.

Hovil, L. and Lomo, Z. February 2005. Whose Justice? Perceptions of Uganda's Amnesty Act 2000: The Potential for Conflict Resolution and Long-Term Reconciliation. Refugee Law Project Working Paper No. 15. Faculty of Law of Makerere University, 1-30, Available at www.refugeelawproject.org [accessed: 12 May 2009].

Human Rights and Peace Centre and Liu Institute for Global Issues. 30 October 2003. The Hidden War: The Forgotten People – War In Acholiland and Its Ramifications for Peace and Security in Uganda. Kampala/Uganda.

Human Rights Centre, International Centre for Transitional Justice and Payson Center for International Development. December 2007. *When the War Ends:*

A Population-Based Survey on Attitudes about Peace, Justice, and Social Reconstruction in Northern Uganda.

Human Rights Council. 7 March 2007. Report of the High-Level Mission on the Situation of Human Rights in Darfur pursuant to Human Rights Council Decision S-4/101, Fourth Session, A/HRC/4/80.

Human Rights Watch. 1999. Chile Report. Available at: www.hrw.org/reports/1999/chile/Patrick-03.htm#P422_160352 [accessed: 23 January 2009].

Human Rights Watch. July 2003. *Uganda, Abducted and Abused: Renewed Conflict in Northern Uganda*, 15, 12 (A). Available at: www.hrw.org/reports/2003/uganda0703 [accessed: 16 March 2009].

Human Rights Watch. 1 October 2003. *The ICC and Security Council: Resolution 1422, Legal and Policy Analysis*. Available at: www.hrw.org/legacy/campaigns/icc/docs/1422legal.htm [accessed: 11 June 2009].

Human Rights Watch. 3 October 2003. *Uganda: Security Force Executions Reported.* Available at: http://hrw.org/english/docs/2003/10/03/uganda6428. htm [accessed: 10 March 2009].

Human Rights Watch. January 2004. *Democratic Republic of the Congo: Confronting Impunity*, 1-11. Available at: http://hrw.org/english/docs/2004/02/02/congo7230_txt.htm [accessed: 11 August 2009].

Human Rights Watch. 29 March 2004. State of Pain: Torture in Uganda, Section VI. Available at: http://hrw.org/reports/2004/uganda0404 [accessed: 16 March 2009].

Human Rights Watch. April 2004. *Darfur in Flames: Atrocities in Western Sudan*, 16, 5, 23. Available at: http://hrw.org/reports/2004/sudan0404 [accessed: 22 June 2009].

Human Rights Watch. 20 July 2004. *Darfur Documents Confirm Government Policy of Militia Support: A Human Rights Watch Briefing Paper*. Available at: http://hrw.org/english/docs/2004/07/19/darfur9096.htm [accessed: 16 May 2009].

Human Rights Watch. 11 August 2004. *Empty Promises? Continuing Abuses In Darfur, Sudan; A Human Rights Watch Briefing Paper*, 1-37. Available at: www.hrw.org/backgrounder/africa/sudan/2004/sudan0804.pdf [accessed: 16 May 2009].

Human Rights Watch. September 2004. *Making Justice Work: Restoration of the Legal System in Ituri, DRC*. Available at: www.hrw.org/backgrounder/africa/drc0904/index.htm [accessed: 11 August 2009].

Human Rights Watch. September 2004. *The International Criminal Court: How Nongovernmental Organizations Can Contribute To the Prosecution of War Criminals.* Available at: www.hrw.org/backgrounder/africa/icc0904/icc0904. pdf [accessed: 9 March 2009].

Human Rights Watch. November 2004. *If We Return, We Will Be Killed; Consolidation of Ethnic Cleansing in Darfur, Sudan*. Available at: http://hrw. org/backgrounder/africa/darfur1104/darfur1104.pdf [accessed: 16 May 2009].

Human Rights Watch. 21 January 2005. *Targeting the Fur: Mass Killings in Darfur*. Available at: www.hrw.org/en/reports/2005/01/21/targeting-fur-mass-killings-darfur [accessed: 22 June 2009].

Human Rights Watch. 2 March 2005. *Militia Leader Implicates Khartoum-Janjaweed Chief Says Sudan Government Backed Attacks*. Available at: http://hrw.org/english/docs/2005/03/02/darfur10228.htm [accessed: 18 June 2009].

Human Rights Watch. 31 March 2005. *UN Security Council Refers Darfur to the ICC U.N. Security Council Refers Darfur to the ICC Historic Step toward Justice; Further Protection Measures Needed*. Human Rights Watch. Available at http://hrw.org/english/docs/2005/03/31/sudan10408.htm [accessed: 11 May 2009].

Human Rights Watch. September 2005. *Uprooted and Forgotten: Impunity and Human Rights Abuses in Northern Uganda*, 17, 12 (A). Available at: www.hrw.org/reports/2005/uganda0905/index.htm [accessed: 16 December 2008].

Human Rights Watch. 14 October 2005. *ICC Takes Decisive Step for Justice in Uganda*. Available at: http://hrw.org/english/docs/2005/10/14/uganda11880.htm [accessed: 19 December 2008].

Human Rights Watch. December 2005. *Entrenching Impunity Government Responsibility for International Crimes in Darfur*, 17, 17(A), 1-79, 59. Available at: http://hrw.org/reports/2005/darfur1205/darfur1205text.pdf [accessed: 16 June 2009].

Human Rights Watch. June 2006. *Lack of Conviction the Special Criminal Court on the Events in Darfur*, 1-31. Available at: http://hrw.org/backgrounder/ij/sudan0606/sudan0606.pdf [accessed: 16 June 2009].

Human Rights Watch. February 2007. *ICC Prosecutor Identifies Suspects in First Darfur Case, Questions and Answers*, 1-9. Available at: http://hrw.org/english/docs/2007/02/25/darfur15404_txt.htm [accessed: 6 July 2009].

Human Rights Watch. March 2007. *A Summary of the Case Law of the International Criminal Court*. Available at: www.hrw.org/en/news/2007/03/22/summary-case-law-international-criminal-court [accessed: 24 March 2009].

Human Rights Watch. 20 January 2008. *Sudan: Notorious Janjaweed Leader Promoted*. Available at: www.hrw.org/english/docs/2008/01/20/sudan17835.htm [accessed: 22 March 2009].

Human Rights Watch. February 2008. *Analysis of the Annex to the June 29 Agreement on Accountability and Reconciliation*.

Human Rights Watch. 7 February 2008. *ICC/DRC: New War Crimes Suspect Arrested*. Available at: http://hrw.org/english/docs/2008/02/07/congo17996.htm [accessed: 24 March 2009].

Human Rights Watch Briefing Paper. 12 April 2005. Sexual Violence and its Consequences among Displaced Persons in Darfur and Chad.

Internal Displacement Monitoring Centre. May 2004. *Anti-terrorism Laws Undermine Amnesty Act of 2000*. Available at: http://www.internaldisplacement.org/8025708F004CE90B/(httpEnvelopes)/88FA701937E475A980 2570B8005AAD12?OpenDocument [accessed: 21 October 2008].

International Criminal Court. 29 January 2004. *Press Release; President of Uganda Refers Situation Concerning the Lord's Resistance Army (LRA) to the ICC.* Available at: http://www.icc-cpi.int/pressrelease_details&id=16.html [accessed: 16 March 2009].

International Criminal Court. 29 January 2004. *Background Information on the Situation in Uganda.*

International Criminal Court. 14 October 2005. *Warrants of Arrest Unsealed Against Five LRA Commanders.* Press Release. The Hague. ICC-20051014-110-En.

International Criminal Court. Feb-March 2007. *The Office of the Prosecutor and its Investigation in Darfur, Sudan.* ICC News Letter, 13. Available at: www.icc-cpi.int/library/about/newsletter/files/ICC-NL13-200702_En.pdf [accessed: 16 July 2009].

International Criminal Court, Office of the Prosecutor. 2003. *Informal Expert Paper: The Principle of Complementarity in Practice.* ICC-OTP 2003, 1-38.

International Criminal Court, Office of the Prosecutor. 2003. *Paper on Some Policy Issues before the Office of the Prosecutor.* ICC-OTP 2003, 1-9. Available at: www.icc-cpi.int/library/organs/otp/030905_Policy_Paper.pdf [accessed: 23 June 2009].

International Criminal Court, Office of the Prosecutor. 2003. *Working Group on Complementarity Issues, Final Document, Experts Group Reflection Paper for The Principle of Complementarity in Practice,* ICC-OTP.

International Criminal Court, Office of the Prosecutor. 14 June 2005. *Third Report of The Prosecutor of the International Criminal Court to the UN Security Council Pursuant To UNSCR 1593.* 1-10. Available at: www.icc-cpi.int/library/cases/OTP_ReportUNSC_3-Darfur_English.pdf [accessed: 18 June 2009].

International Criminal Court, Office of The Prosecutor. 29 June 2005. *Report of The Prosecutor of The International Criminal Court, Mr Luis Ocampo-Moreno to the UN Security Council Pursuant to UNSC 1593.* The Hague, ICC-OTP-0629-105-En, 1-11.

International Criminal Court, Office of The Prosecutor. December 2005. *Informal Meeting of Legal advisors of Ministries of Foreign Affairs in New York, 24 October 2005.*

International Criminal Court, Office of the Prosecutor. 13 December 2005. *Second Report of the Prosecutor of the International Criminal Court, Mr. Luis Moreno Ocampo To The Security Council Pursuant To UNSC 1593 (2005),* ICC-02/05, 5. Available at: www.icc-cpi.int/library/organs/otp/LMO_UNSC_ReportB_En.pdf [accessed: 16 June 2009].

International Criminal Court, Office of the Prosecutor. 14 September 2006. *The Office of the Prosecutor Report on Prosecutorial Strategy,* The Hague, 1-11.

International Criminal Court, Office of the Prosecutor. 16 December 2006. Fourth Report of the Prosecutor of the International Criminal Court, Mr Luis Ocampo to the UN Security Council Resolution Pursuant to the UNSCR 1593(Dec

14, 2006), 1-11. Available at: www.icc-cpi.int/library/organs/otp/OTP_ ReportUNSC4-Darfur_English.pdf [accessed: 25 June 2009].

International Criminal Court, Office of the Prosecutor. 27 February 2007. ICC Prosecutor Presents Evidence on Darfur Crimes, The Hague, ICC-OTP-20070227-206-En. Available at: www.icc-cpi.int/pressrelease_ details&id=230&l=en.html [accessed: 16 June 2009].

International Criminal Court, Office of the Prosecutor. 27 February 2007. *Situation in Darfur, the Sudan: Annex 12 to the Prosecutor's Application under Article 58(7)*. ICC-02/05-56-Anx12 27-02-2007 1/3 EO PT. Available at: www.icc-cpi.int/library/cases/ICC-02-05-56-Anx12_English.pdf [accessed: 16 March 2009].

International Criminal Court, Office of the Prosecutor Report. 27 February 2007. *Situation in Darfur, the Sudan*. No. ICC-02/05.

International Criminal Court, Office of the Prosecutor Report. 27 February 2007. *Situation in Darfur, the Sudan: Prosecutor's Application under Article 58(7), para 261*. Available at: www.icc-cpi.int/library/cases/ICC-02-05-56_English. pdf [accessed: 19 March 2009].

International Criminal Court, Office of the Prosecutor. 5 December 2007. *Sixth Report of the Prosecutor of the International Criminal Court to the UN Security Council Resolution Pursuant to the UNSCR 1593(2005)*. Available at: www. icc-cpi.int/library/organs/otp/OTP-RP-20071205-UNSC-ENG.pdf [accessed: 11 February 2009].

International Criminal Court, Office of the Prosecutor. 5 June 2008. *Seventh Report of the Prosecutor of the International Criminal Court to the UN Security Council Resolution Pursuant to the UNSCR 1593(2005)*. Available at: www. icc-cpi.int/library/organs/otp/UNSC_2008_En.pdf [accessed: 7 July 2009].

International Criminal Court, Office of the Prosecutor. 14 July 2008. *Prosecutor's Application for Warrant of Arrest Under Article 58 against Omar Hassan Ahmad Al Bashir*. Available at: www.icc-cpi.int/library/organs/otp/ICC-OTP-ST20080714-ENG.pdf [accessed: 14 July 2009].

International Criminal Court, Press Release. 29 January 2004. *President of Uganda Refers Situation Concerning the Lord's Resistance Army (LRA) to the ICC*. Available at: www.icc-cpi.int [accessed: 22 May 2009].

International Criminal Court, Pre-Trial Chamber I. 11 September 2006. *Situation In Darfur, Sudan: Prosecutor's Response To Cassese's Observation On Issues Concerning The Protection Of Victims And The Preservation Of Evidence In The Proceedings On Darfur Pending Before The ICC*, ICC-02/05.

International Criminal Court Prosecutor. 5 July 2004. *Letter by the Chief Prosecutor of 17 June 2004 addressed to the President of the ICC as attached to the decisions of the Presidency of ICC; The Decision of the Presidency assigning the situation in Uganda to Pre-Trial Chamber II*, ICC-02/04.

International Crisis Group. 14 April 2004. *Northern Uganda: Understanding and Solving the Conflict*, ICG Africa Report No. 77.

International Crisis Group. 22 September 2004. *Reports: Uganda, Conflict History*. Available at: www.crisisgroup.org/home/index.cfm?action=conflict_ search&l=1&t=1&c_country=111 [accessed: 24 March 2009].

International Crisis Group. 23 August 2004. *Darfur Deadline: A New International Action Plan*, 83. Available at: www.crisisgroup.org/home/index. cfm?id=2920&l=1 [accessed: 16 May 2009].

International Crisis Group. 25 March 2004. *Darfur Rising: Sudan's New Crisis*, ICG Africa Report. Nairobi/Brussels, 76.

International Crisis Group. 8 March 2005. *Darfur: The Failure to Protect*. Available at: www.crisisgroup.org [accessed: 24 March 2009].

International Educational Development to the UN Sub-Commission on the Promotion and Protection of Human Rights. July-August 2001. *Forced Displacement in Northern Uganda*, written statement submitted by International Educational Development to the UN Sub-Commission on the Promotion and Protection of Human Rights. Fifty-third Session, Agenda item 2. Available at: www.webcom.com/hrin/parker/sub01wsu.html [accessed: 16 March 2009].

International Law Commission. 1994. *Draft Statute for An International Criminal Court*, prepared by the International Law Commission, in Report of the International Law Commission on the work of its forty-sixth session, UN GAOR, 49th session supp. No. 10, at 84, UN Doc. A/49/10.

International Law Commission Report. 1996. *Draft Code of Crimes against the Peace and Security of Mankind*, Chapter II. Available at: www.un.org [accessed: 14 June 2008].

IRIN News. 23 February 2003. *Uganda: Rebels Massacre More than 200 in Lira IDPs Camp*.

IRIN News. 25 February 2004. *Uganda: Focus on LRA attack on Barlonyo IDPs Camp*.

IRIN News. 25 May 2004. *Uganda: Army Arrests Officers after Second Rebel Attack On an IDP Camp in Days*.

IRIN News. 11 January 2005. *OCHA; Uganda, Optimism That Sudanese Peace Deal Could Help Pacify Northern Uganda*. Available at: www.irinnews.org/ report.asp?ReportID=45000&SelectRegion=East_Africa&SelectCountry=U GANDA-SUDAN [accessed: 10 September 2008].

IRIN News. 13 January 2005. *How Credible is Darfur's Third Rebel Movement?* Available at: www.irinnews.org/report.aspx?reportid=52658 [accessed: 26 May 2009].

IRIN News. 9 June 2005. *The UN Office for the Coordination of Humanitarian Affairs (OCHA); Uganda, Waiting for Elusive Peace in the War-Ravaged North*. Available at: www.irinnews.org/report.asp?ReportID=47568&SelectR egion=East_Africa [accessed: 9 December 2008].

IRIN News. 9 June 2005. *Uganda: Forgiveness as an Instrument of Peace*.

IRIN News. 9 June 2005. *Uganda: Waiting For Elusive Peace in the War-Ravaged North*. Available at: www.irinnews.org/report.asp?ReportID=47568&SelectRe gion=East_Africa [accessed: 16 September 2008].

Jensen, R. 26-30 August 2001. *Complementarity: the Principle of Complementarity in the Rome Statute of the International Criminal Court*. Submitted at the 15th International Conference of the International Society for the Reform of Criminal Law held at Canberra, Australia.

Joint Assessment Mission, Sudan. March 2005. *Cluster II Report, Governance and Rule of Law*. Available at: www.unsudanig.org/docs/Joint%20Assessment%20 Mission%20(JAM)%20Volume%20II.pdf [accessed: 16 September 2008].

Jurdi, N.N. 2010. The Prosecutorial Interpretation of the Complementarity Principle: Does It Really Contribute to Ending Impunity on the National Level? *International Criminal Law Review*, 10, 73-96.

Juris Dictionary. Available at: www.jurisdictionary.com/dictionary/J.asp [accessed: 23 January 2008].

Kait, B. December 1996. Pardon Me? The Constitutional Case Against Presidential Self-Pardons! *Yale Law Journal*, 106, 3, 778-809.

Kalinauskas, M. 2002. The Use of International Military Force in Arresting War Criminals: The Lessons of the International Criminal Tribunal for the Former Yugoslavia. *U. Kan. L. Rev.*, 50, 399.

Katz Cogan, J. 2002. International Criminal Courts and Fair Trials: Difficulties and Prospects. *Yale Journal of International Law*, 27, 119.

Kelly, M. Fall 2003. Cheating Justice by Cheating Death, the Doctrinal Collision for Prosecuting Foreign Terrorist – Passage of Aut Dedare Aut Judicare into Customary International Law and Refusal to Extradite on the Death Penalty. *Arizona Journal of International and Comparative Law*, 20, 491-532.

Kelsen, H. November 1941. The Pure Theory of Law and Analytical Jurisprudence. *Harvard Law Review*, 55, 1, 44-70.

Kiefer, K.P. 2005. Note, Exercising Their Rights: Native American Nations of the United States Enhancing Political Sovereignty Through Ratification of the Rome Statute. *Syracuse Journal of International Law and Commerce*, 32, 345-372.

King, L. 2000. *Hammurabi Code of Laws*. Available at: http://eqwc.evansville. edu/anthology/hammurabi.htm [accessed: 8 May 2009].

Kirsch, P. August 2001. Negotiating On Institution for Twenty-First Century: Multilateral Diplomacy and International Criminal Court. *McGill Law Journal*, 46, 1141-1161.

Kirsch, P. and Holmes, J. January 1999. The Rome Conference on an International Criminal Court Negotiating Process. *The American Journal of International Law*, 93, 1, 2-12.

Kirsch, P. and Robinson, D. 2002. Referral by State Parties, in *The Rome Statute of The International Criminal Court: A Commentary*, edited by A. Cassese, P. Gaeta and J.R.W.D. Jones. Oxford: Oxford University Press, I, 622.

Kleffner, J. April 2003. The Impact of Complementarity on National Implementation of Substantive International Criminal Law. *Journal of International Criminal Justice*, 1, 86-115.

Kleffner, J. and Kor, G. (eds). May 2006. *Complementary Views on Complementarity Proceedings of the International Roundtable on the Complementary Nature of the International Criminal Court, Amsterdam 25-26 June 2004.* Cambridge: Cambridge University Press.

Knoops, G.J.A. 2002. *Surrendering To International Criminal Courts: Contemporary Practice and Procedure.* New York: Transnational Publishers.

Koskenniemi, M. 1991. The Future of Statehood. *Harvard International Law Journal*, 32, 397-410.

Koskenniemi, M. 2002. *The Gentle Civilizer of Nations: The Rise and Fall of International Law 1870-1960.* Cambridge: Cambridge University Press.

Kress, C. December 2004. Self-Referrals and Waivers of Complementarity. *Journal of International Criminal Justice*, 2, 4, 944-950.

Kress, C. July 2005. The Darfur Report and Genocidal Intent. *Journal of International Criminal Justice*, 3, 562-577.

Kress, C. and Sluiter, G. 2002. Imprisonment, in *The Rome Statute of the International Criminal Court: A Commentary*, edited by A. Cassese, P. Gaeta and J.R.W.D. Jones. Oxford: Oxford University Press, II, 1791.

Kritz, N.J. Autumn 1996. Coming to Terms with Atrocities: a Review of Accountability Mechanism for Mass Violations of Human Rights. *Law and Contemporary Problems*, 59, 4, 127-152.

Kritzer, H.M. 2002. *Legal Systems of the World, A Political, Social, and Cultural Encyclopaedia.* Abc-Clio Inc, vol. IV.

La Fraper Du Hellen, B. 1999. Round Table: Prospects for The Functioning of The International Criminal Court, in *The Rome Statute of the International Criminal Court: A Challenge to Impunity, Proceedings of the Trento Conference on the ICC*, edited by M. Politi and G. Nesi. Aldershot: Ashgate.

Lasok, D. 1992. Subsidiarity and the Occupied Field. *New Law Journal*, 1228.

Lasok, K.P.E. 2001. *Laws and Institutions of the European Union.* London: Butterworths.

Lasswell, H.D. and McDougal, M.S. March 1992. *Jurisprudence for a Free Society: Studies in Law, Science and Policy.* Dordrecht: Martinus Nijhoff.

Lattanzi, F. 2002. Official Capacities and Immunities, in *The Rome Statute of the International Criminal Court: A Commentary*, edited by A. Cassese, P. Gaeta and J.R.W.D. Jones. Oxford: Oxford University Press, I.

Lawyers Committee for Human Rights. August 1996. International Criminal Court Major Unresolved Issues in the Draft Statute: A Position Paper of the Lawyers Committee for Human Rights, 1-35. Available at: www.iccnow.org/documents/2PrepCmtEstablishICCLCHR.pdf [accessed: 5 June 2009].

Lee, R. 1999. The Rome Conference and its Contribution to International Law, in *The International Criminal Court, The Making of The Rome Statute. Issues, Negotiations, Results*, edited by R. Lee. The Hague: Kluwer International, 1.

Lee, R. March 2002. How the World Will Relate to the Court: An Assessment of the ICC Statute. *Fordham International Law Journal*, 25, 750-763.

Ligenti, K. 2005. Protocol of the Proceedings on Concurrent National and International Criminal Jurisdiction and the Principle of Ne Bis in Idem. *Revue Internationale De Droit Penal*, 751.

Lindberg, T. 15 March 2005. ICC Offers Darfur Hope, *Washington Times*. Available at: http://washingtontimes.com/op-ed/20050314-090221-2751r.htm [accessed: 7 May 2009].

Lindenmann, J. 2001. The Rules of Procedure and Evidence on Jurisdiction and Admissibility, in *International and National Prosecution of Crimes under International Law*, edited by H. Fischer, C. Kress and S.R. Lueder. Berlin: Berlin Verlag Arno Spitz GmbH/Berliner Wissenschaftsverlag, 181-182.

Lipscomb, R. January 2006. Restructuring the ICC Framework to Advance Transitional Justice: A Search for a Permanent Solution in Sudan. *Columbia Law Review*, 106, 182-217.

Liu Institute for Global Issues. February 2003. *Update on the Human Security Situation in Northern Uganda – Report of the Liu Institute Mission to Northern Uganda 7-27 January 2003*. Vancouver: Liu Institute for Global Issues.

Lucima, O. (ed.). 2002. *Protracted Conflict, Elusive Peace: Initiatives To End The Violence In Northern Uganda*. Accord No. 11.

McGoldrick, D., Rowe, P. and Donnelly, E. 2004. *The Permanent Criminal Court, Legal and Policy Issues*. Portland: Hart Publishing.

MacPherson, B. July 2002. Authority of the Security Council Exempt Peace Keepers from International Criminal Court Proceedings. *ASIL Insights*. Available at: www.asil.org/insights.htm [accessed: 11 April 2009].

Maddux, C. 5 July 2006. *International Court Wants Uganda Rebel Leader Despite Amnesty Offer.* Blogger News Net. Available at: www.bloggernews. net/2006/07/International-court-wants-uganda-rebel.html [accessed: 9 March 2009].

Médecins Sans Frontières. 8 March 2005. *The Crushing Burden of Rape: Sexual Violence in Darfur*. Available at: www.doctorswithoutborders.org/publications/ reports/2005/sudan03.pdf [accessed: 16 June 2009].

Moir, Lindsay. 2002. *The Law of Internal Armed Conflict*. Cambridge: Cambridge University Press.

The Monitor. 11 November 2003. Statement made by Jan Egeland during his Mission to Uganda on 7–10 November 2003.

The Monitor. 24 April 2004. Rights Activists Accuse State Organs of Torture.

The Monitor. 9 May 2004. Military Courts get Underway in Pader.

The Monitor. 5 June 2004. 23 Soldiers for Trial on Murder.

The Monitor. 8 October 2004. UPDF Arrests 26 over LRA Links.

The Monitor. 3 November 2004. Priest Held over LRA Links.

The Monitor. 5 November 2004. Catholic Priest to be Prosecuted.

The Monitor. 6 July 2006. Museveni Amnesty to Kony Illegal – ICC.

Moreno-Ocampo, L. March 2005. *The International Criminal Court: Hopes and Fears*, Coca-Cola World Fund at Yale Lecture, New Haven.

Moreno-Ocampo, L. 29 June 2005. *Statement of the Prosecutor of the International Criminal Court Mr. Luis Moreno Ocampo to the Security Council on 29 June 2005 Pursuant to UNSCR 1593*. Available at: www.icc-cpi.int/library/cases/LMO UNSC On DARFUR-EN.pdf [accessed: 24 June 2009].

Moreno-Ocampo, L. 14 October 2005. *Statement by Chief Prosecutor Luis Moreno Ocampo*. Available at: www.icc-cpi.int/library/organs/otp/Uganda-LMOSpeech14102005.pdf [accessed: 9 December 2008].

Moreno-Ocampo, L. 2006. Symposium: International Criminal Tribunals in the 21st Century: Keynote Address: Integrating the Work of the ICC into Local Justice Initiatives. *American University International Law Review*, 21, 497-503.

Moreno-Ocampo, L. 23 November 2006. Fifth Session of the Assembly of State Parties, Opening Remarks, The Hague, 1-7. Available at: www.icc-cpi.int/library/organs/otp/LMO_20061123_en.pdf [accessed: 5 May 2009].

Morris, M. Autumn 1996. International Guidelines against Impunity: Facilitating Accountability. *Law and Contemporary Problems*, 59, 29-39.

Morris, M. 2000. Complementarity and Its Discontents: States, Victims and the International Criminal Court, in *International Crimes, Peace, and Human Rights: The Role of the International Criminal Court*, edited by D. Shelton, 189-190.

Moy, H.A. Spring 2006. Recent Development: The International Criminal Court's Arrest Warrants and Uganda's Lord's Resistance Army: Renewing the Debate Over Amnesty and Complementarity. *The Harvard Environmental Law Review*, 19, 267-277.

MSF-Netherlands. 7 December 2004. The People of Darfur Have the Right to Ask Why. Available at: www.msf.org/msfInternational/invoke.cfm?objectid=27A81758-C4B6-4FD9-81EDE9D9266E3519&component=toolkit.Article&method=full_html&CFID=314357&CFTOKEN=73920792 [accessed: 16 May 2009].

Mueller, G. 1983. International Criminal Law: *Civitas Maxima* – An Overview. *Case Western Reserve Journal of International Law*, 1.

Musoke, C. 19 December 2006. Uganda: Museveni Offers LRA's Kony Way Out. *New Vision*. Available at: http://allafrica.com/stories/200612190045.html [accessed: 9 March 2009].

Neha, J. April 2005. A Separate Law for Peace Keepers: The Clash between the Security Council and the Court. *The European Journal of International Law*, 16, 239-255.

New Vision. 22 November 2002. LRA Man on Treason.

New Vision. 5 April 2003. Treason Suspects Apply for Amnesty.

New Vision. 10 September 2003. Museveni Rules Out Forceful Takeover.

New Vision. 23 April 2004. Soldier Gets 10 Years for Rape.

New Vision. 5 May 2004. Anti-Torture Body Formed.

New Vision. 27 May 2004. UNICEF Warns On Air Strikes.

New Vision. 28 May 2004. Uganda Human Rights Commission Tells Govt to Pay Family 25m.

New Vision. 9 June 2004. Government to Probe Amnesty File.

New Vision. 4 August 2004. Eight LRA Agents Arrested.

New Vision. 5 August 2004. Arrest Rebel Agents.

New Vision. 7 September 2004. Airport Personnel Linked to LRA Rebels.

New Vision. 14 September 2004. Army Catches Kony Guard.

New Vision. 8 October 2004. Suspected LRA Rebel Partners Detained.

New Vision. 15 October 2004. Army Nets 19 LRA Spies.

New Vision. 1 December 2004. UPDF Absorbs 932 LRA Rebels and LDUs.

New Vision. 19 December 2006. Uganda: Museveni Offers LRA's Kony Way Out, Kampala.

Newman, D.G. 2005. The Rome Statute, Some Reservations Concerning Amnesties, and a Distributive Problem. *American University International Law Review*, 293-246.

Newton, M.A. 2001. Comparative Complementarity: Domestic Jurisdiction Consistent with the Rome Statute of the International Criminal Court. *Military Law Review*, 167, 20-73.

Ntanda Nsereko, D.D. 2003. *Prosecutorial Discretion before National Courts and International Tribunals*. Guest Lecture Series of The Office of the Prosecutor. ICC-OTP and Individual Authors 2003, 1-15.

Olasolo, H. 2003. The Prosecutor of the ICC before the Initiation of Investigations: A Quasi-Judicial or a Political Body? *International Criminal Law Review*, 3, 87–150.

Olasolo, H. 26 March 2004. *The Triggering Procedure of the International Criminal Court, Procedural Treatment of the Principle of Complementarity, and the Role of Office of the Prosecutor*. Guest Lecture Series of the Office of the Prosecutor, The Hague, 1-22.

Olasolo, H. 2005. The Triggering Procedure of the International Criminal Court, Procedural Treatment of the Principle of Complementarity, and the Role of Office of The Prosecutor. *International Criminal Law Review*, 5, 121–146

Orentlicher, D.F. June 1991. Symposium: International Law: Article: Settling Accounts: The Duty To Prosecute Human Rights Violations of a Prior Regime. *Yale Law Journal*, 2537-2630.

Parmar, Sh. January 2007. An Overview of the Sudanese Legal System and Legal Research. Hauser Global Law School Program, New York University School of Law, 1-16.

Pejic, J. Winter 2001. The United States and the International Criminal Court: One Loophole Too Many. *University of Detroit Mercy Law Review*, 78, 267-297.

Pena, M. and Kocabayoglu, S. 13 October 2005. *The ICC And Alternative Justice Mechanisms in Africa Introduction.* The American Non-Governmental Organizations Coalition for the International Criminal Court; a Program of the United Nations Association of the United States of America, 1-10. Available at: www.amicc.org/docs/ICC%20Alternative%20Justice%20Africa.pdf [accessed: 16 March 2009].

Pestojova, K. Fall 2004. Was The United States Justified In Renewing Resolution 1487 In Light of Abu Ghraib Prison Abuse Scandal. *ILSA Journal of International and Comparative Law*, 11, 195-121.

Philip, T.R., Deputy Spokesman. 6 December 2001. *US State Department, Press Statement: Terrorist Exclusion List Published by US State Department.* Available at: www.immigrationlinks.com/news/news1204.htm [accessed: 10 December 2008].

Policy and Operation Department of the Dutch Ministry of Foreign Affairs. The Definitions of Complementarity and their Evolution. Working Document. Available at: www.euforic.org/iob/publ/workdocs/complimentarity3.html [accessed: 10 March 2008].

Politinfo US. 11 November 2004. Country Reports on Human Rights Practices; Human Rights in Uganda, Released on 31 March 2003.

Power, S. 2004. Dying in Darfur. Can the Ethnic Cleansing in Sudan be Stopped? *The New Yorker*. Available at: www.newyorker.com/archive/2004/08/30/040830fa_fact1 [accessed: 16 May 2009].

Pronk, J. 4 November 2004. The UN Special Representative of the Secretary-General's Statement to the UN Security Council.

Provost, R. 30 September 2005. *International Human Rights and Humanitarian Law*. Cambridge: Cambridge University Press.

Quénivet, N. July-September 2006. The Report of the International Commission of Inquiry on Darfur: The Question of Genocide. *Human Rights Review*, 38-68.

Raz, J. 1980. *The Concept of a Legal System: An Introduction to The Theory of Legal System*. Oxford: Clarendon Press, second edition.

Reeves, E. 2005. *Darfur and the International Criminal Court*, Middle East Report on Line. 29 April 2005. Available at: www.merip.org/mero/mero042905.html. [accessed: 18 June 2009].

Reeves, E. 18 April 2006. UN Takes its Turn at Posturing on Genocide in Darfur, *Sudan Tribune*. Available at: www.sudantribune.com/spip.php?article15146 [accessed: 18 January 2009].

Refugee Law Project. February 2004. *Behind the Violence: Causes, Consequences and the Search for Solutions to the War in Northern Uganda*. Working Paper No. 11.

Refugee Law Project. 28 July 2004. *The Refugee Law Project's Position Paper On The Announcement Of Formal Investigations Of The Lord's Resistance Army By The Chief Prosecutor Of The International Criminal Court And Its Implications On The Search For Peaceful Solutions To The War In Northern Uganda.* Faculty of Law, Makerere University, 1-12. Available at: www. refugeelawproject.org/resources/papers/archive/2004/RLP.ICC.investig.pdf [accessed: 18 September 2008].

Regan, F. 1994. Legal Resources Development in Uganda. *International Journal of Sociology of Law*, 22, 203.

Renteln, A. 1999. The Child Soldier: The Challenge of Enforcing International Standards. *Whittier Law Review*, 21, 191-205.

Report of the Ad Hoc Committee on the Establishment of an International Criminal Court, UN GAOR, 50th Session, Supp. No. 22, para. 47, UN Doc. A/50/22 (1995).

Report of the Committee on International Criminal Court Jurisdiction. 1952. UN Doc. A/2135.

Report of the International Law Commission. 6 May-26 July 1996. 48th session. UN Doc. A/51/10, 1996.

Report of the Preparatory Committee on the Establishment of an International Criminal Court. 14 April 1998. A/conf.183/2/add1, 40-42.

Report of the Preparatory Committee on the Establishment of an International Criminal Court. Proceedings of the Preparatory Committee during March, April and August 1996. Available at: www.npwj.org/netrep/cdrpm/prepcom/prepcom.pdf [accessed: 15 May 2009].

Republic of Uganda, the Courts of Uganda. *The Judicial System.* Available at: www.judicature.go.ug/index.php [accessed: 16 March 2009].

Reuters. 29 December 2005. Sudan Says Darfur Rebel Groups Involved in Attack. Available at: www.sudantribune.com/spip.php?mot34&debut_affiche_news=10 [accessed: 26 May 2009].

Robertson, G. 1999. *Crimes against Humanity*. New York: Penguin Inc.

Robertson QC, G. August 2000. *Crimes against Humanity: The Struggle for Global Justice*. United Kingdom: Penguin.

Robinson, D. June 2003. Serving the Interest of Justice: Amnesties, Truth Commissions and the International Criminal Court. *The European Journal of International Law*, 14, 481-509.

Robinson, M. 2001. The Principles on Universal Jurisdiction, Program in Law and Public Affairs, Princeton University. Princeton, New Jersey.

Rodney, D. and Khan, K. 2003. *Archbold, International Criminal Courts Practice, Procedure and Evidence.* London: Sweet & Maxwell Limited.

Roht-Arriaza, N. 2000. Amnesty and the International Criminal Court, in *International Crimes, Peace, and Human Rights: The Role of the International Criminal Court*, edited by D. Shelton, 77.

Ruaudel, H. and Timpson, A. 12 December 2005. *Situation Report; Northern Uganda from a Forgotten War to an Unforgivable Crisis – The War against Children.* Institute for Security Studies.

Russel, R.B. 1958. *A History of the United Nations Charter 1940-1945.* Brookings Institution.

Sadat, L. and Carden, S.R. March 2000. The New International Criminal Court: An Uneasy Revolution. *Georgetown Law Journal*, 88, 381-474.

Sarooshi, D. December 2004. Editorial Comments: The ICC Takes Off – Prosecutorial Policy and the ICC – Prosecutor's *Proprio Motu* Action or Self-Denial? *Journal of International Criminal Justice*, 2, 4, 940-944.

Schabas, W. 2001. *An Introduction to the International Criminal Court.* Cambridge: Cambridge University Press.

Schabas, W. 2002. The Rwanda Case, Sometimes its Impossible, in *Post-Conflict Justice*, edited by M.Ch. Bassiouni and M. Ardsley. New York: Transnational Publishers, 499-522.

Schabas, W. 2003. National Courts Finally Begin to Prosecute Genocide, the Crime of Crimes. *Journal of International Criminal Justice*, 39-66.

Schabas, W. September 2004. United States Hostility to the International Criminal Court: it's all about the Security Council. *The European Journal of International Law*, 15, 701-721.

Schabas, W. December 2004. The Special Court for Sierra Leone: Testing the Waters – Conjoined Twins of Transnational Justice? – The Sierra Leone Truth and Reconciliation Commission and the Special Court. *Journal of International Criminal Justice*, 1082-1092.

Schabas, W. 23 June 2007. *Complementarity in Practice: Some Uncomplimentarity Thoughts*. Presentation at the 20th Anniversary Conference of the International Society for the Reform of Criminal Law, Vancouver, 1-28.

Scharf, M. 1999. Symposium: The Amnesty Exception to the Jurisdiction of the ICC. *Cornell International Law Journal*, 32, 507-531.

Scharf, M. Spring 1999. Clear and Present Danger: Enforcing the International Ban on Biological and Chemical Weapons Through Sanctions, Use of Force, and Criminalization. *Michigan Journal of International Law*, 20, 477-521.

Scheffer, D. The US Ambassador at Large For War Crimes. 1998. Is an UN International Criminal Court in the Interest of the United States National? *Hearing before the Subcommittee on International Foreign Relations*. Tenth Congress.

Scotland on Sunday. 30 January 2005. No Relief for Sudan's Agony as UN Quibbles over the Case for Genocide.

Security Council. 3 December 2004. Report of the Secretary-General on the Sudan Pursuant to Paragraphs 6, 13 and 16 of Security Council Resolution 1556 (2004).

Security Council. 12 April 2005. *Monthly Report of the Secretary-General on Darfur*, UN SC/2005/240. Available at: http://daccessdds.un.org/doc/UNDOC/GEN/N05/303/55/PDF/N0530355.pdf?OpenElement [accessed: 16 May 2009].

Security Council. 10 May 2005. *Monthly Report of the Secretary-General on Darfur*, S/2005/305. Available at: http://daccessdds.un.org/doc/UNDOC/GEN/N05/337/43/PDF/N0533743.pdf?OpenElement [accessed: 16 June 2009].

Security Council, Department of Public Information, News and Media Division. 14 June 2006. *International Criminal Court Prosecutor Briefs Security Council On Darfur: Says Will Not Draw Conclusions On Genocide Until Investigation*

Complete; Luis Moreno-Ocampo Tells Council, Given Scale, Complexity of Crimes, Anticipates Prosecuting Sequence of Cases, Rather Than a Single Case, Security Council, 5459th Meeting. Available at: www.un.org/News/ Press/docs/2006/sc8748.doc.htm [accessed: 26 June 2009].

Sirica, J. 1979. *To Set The Record Straight: The Break-in, The Tapes, The Conspirators, The Pardon.* New York: Norton.

Slaughter, A. April 1993. International Law and International Relations: A Dual Agenda. *The American Journal of International Law*, 87, 2, 205-239.

Slye, R. Fall 2002. The Legitimacy of Amnesties under International Law and General Principles of Anglo-American Law: Is a Legitimate Amnesty Possible? *Virginia Journal of International Law*, 173-241.

Slye, R. Winter 2004. The Cambodian Amnesties: Beneficiaries and the Temporal Reach of Amnesties for Gross Violations of Human Rights. *Wisconsin International Law Journal*, 99-117.

Smith, A. Summer 2004. Book Review: *From Nuremberg to The Hague: The Future of International Criminal Justice. Harvard International Law Journal.*

Sohn, J. 25 July 2005. *UNICEF Executive Director Ann M. Veneman Highlights the Plight of Children Caught in Uganda's Conflict.* The United Nations Children's Fund. Available at: http://www.unicef.org/infobycountry/uganda_ 27744.html [accessed: 16 September 2008].

Southwick, K. Fall 2005. Investigating War in Northern Uganda: Dilemmas for the International Criminal Court. *Yale Journal of International Affairs*, 105-119.

Ssenyonjo, M. November 2005. Accountability of Non-State Actors in Uganda for War Crimes and Human Rights Violations: Between Amnesty and the International Criminal Court. *Journal of Conflict and Security Law*, 10, 405-433.

Stahn, C. February 2003. The Ambiguities of Security Council Resolution 1422. *The European Journal of International Law*, 14, 85-108.

Strohmeyer, H. January 2001. Collapse and Reconstruction of a Judicial System: The United Nations Missions in Kosovo and East Timor. *The American Journal of International Law*, 95, 1, 46-63.

Sudan Human Rights Organization. 26 March 2003. The Situation of Human Rights in Sudan 2003, Cairo. Available at: www.shro-cairo.org/reports.htm [accessed: 25 June 2008].

Sudan Human Rights Organization. 20 January 2004. Memorandum to Sudan Government, Judiciary, and Bar Association.

Sudanese Human Rights Organization. 16 April 2005. *Press Release.* Available at: www.shro-cairo.org/pressreleases/05/16april.htm [accessed: 16 June 2009].

Sudan Vision Daily Newspaper. 24 February 2010. Government, JEM Sign Ceasefire Framework Agreement in Doha.

Sudanese Online. 4 April 2007. Sudan to Try Darfur Crime Suspects. Available at: www.sudaneseonline.com/en2/publish/Latest_News_1/SUDAN_TO_TRY_ DARFUR_CRIME_SUSPECTS.shtml [accessed: 3 July 2009].

SUNA. 14 August 2004. Celebrations of Golden Jubilee of the Armed Forces.

SUNA. 22 September 2004. General Al-Dabi Affirms Stability of Security Situations in Darfur States.

SUNA. 1 November 2004. President Al-Bashir Addresses Celebrations of PDF Anniversary, Affirms Readiness To Complete Peace Process.

SUNA. 5 February 2005. First Vice-President Affirms Government Refusal to Trial of Any Individual or Official Outside Sudan.

Surlan, T. 2005. Ne bis in idem in Conjunction with the Principle of Complementarity in the Rome Statute. The European Society of International Law: 'Agora' Papers presented at the 2005 Florence Founding Conference of the European Society of International Law, 1-8. Available at: www.esil-sedi.eu/english/pdf/Surlan.PDF [accessed: 1 October 2009].

Swaak-Goldman, O. 25 September 2006. Second Public Hearing of the Office of the Prosecutor; Outlining the Three-Year Report. The Hague. Available at: www.icc-cpi.int/organs/otp/otp_public_hearing/otp_ph2/otp_ph2_HGstates.html [accessed: 9 March 2009].

Syrpis, P. June 2004. In Defence of Subsidiarity. *Oxford Journal of Legal Studies*, 323-334.

Tait, D. 2002. Pardons in Perspective: The Role of Forgiveness in Criminal Justice. *Vera Institute of Justice, Inc. Federal Sentencing Reporter*, 134-143.

Tallgren, I. 1999. Article 20: Ne bis in idem, in *Commentary on the Rome Statute of the International Criminal Court: Observer's Note, Article by Artic*le, edited by O. Triffterer. Badeb-Baden: Nomos Verlagsgesellschaft, 431.

Third Session of the Assembly of States Parties. 6 September 2004. *Address by Luis Moreno-Ocampo, Prosecutor of the ICC*. ASP.

Triffterer, O. (ed.). 1999. *Commentary on the Rome Statute of the International Criminal Court: Observer's Note, Article by Article*. Baden-Baden: Nomos Verlagsgesellschaft.

Tutrone, G. 2002. Powers and Duties of The Prosecutor, in *The Rome Statute of The International Criminal Court: A Commentary*, edited by A. Cassese, P. Gaeta, and J.R.W.D. Jones. Oxford: Oxford University Press, 2, 1141.

Udombana, N.J. Fall 2005. Pay Back Time in Sudan? Darfur in the International Criminal Court. *Tulsa Journal of Comparative and International Law*, 13, 1-57.

Uganda Human Rights Commission. 18 April 2003. *UHRC Annual Report January 2001 – September 2002*, Kampala. Available at: www.uhrc.org/archive.php [accessed: 11 December 2008].

Uganda Law Society. 2003. *Review of Military Justice under the UPDF Bill*, Larkin Reynolds, Section 6.

UK Discussion Paper on Complementarity. 29 March 1996. Available at: www.iccnow.org/documents/UKPaperComplementarity.pdf [accessed: 11 December 2008].

UN Diplomatic Conference on the Establishment of an International Criminal Court, Volume I and II.B. *Report of the Preparatory Committee on the Establishment of an International Criminal Court*. Available at: www.un.org/

law/icc/rome/proceedings/E/Rome%20Proceedingsv3e.pdf [accessed: 11 June 2008].

UN High Commissioner for Human Rights. 2003. *Report on the Mission Undertaken by Her Office, Pursuant to Commission Resolution 2000/60, to Assess the Situation on the Ground with Regard to the Abduction of Children from Northern Uganda.* UN Doc. E/CN.4/2002/86 (2001). Available at: www.ohchr.org/english [accessed: 16 September 2008].

UN Press Release. 16 March 2005. *United Nations Human Rights Experts Call for Urgent, Effective Action on Darfur, Sudan,* AFR/1126 and HR/4822.

UN Security Council. 31 January 2003. *Child Soldiers: Letter from Uganda to the UN President of the Security Council.*

United Nations Commission of Inquiry. 25 January 2005. *Report of the International Commission of Inquiry on Darfur to the United Nations Secretary-General, Pursuant to Security Council Resolution 1564 of 18 September 2004*, paragraph 3, Geneva. Available at: www.un.org/News/dh/sudan/com_inq_darfur.pdf [accessed: 16 May 2009].

United Nations Office of High Commissioner for Human Rights. 7 May 2004. *Report of the United Nations High Commissioner for Human Rights*, E/CN.4/2005/3.

United Nations Office of High Commissioner for Human Rights. 29 July 2005. *Report of the United Nations High Commissioner for Human Rights: Access to Justice for Victims of Sexual Violence.* Available at: www.ohchr.org/english/press/docs/20050729Darfurreport.pdf [accessed: 16 June 2009].

United Nations News Service. 23 February 2004. *Annan Condemns Rebel Massacre of Nearly 200 Civilians in Northern Uganda.* Available at: www.un.org/english [accessed: 16 March 2009].

United Nations News Service. 31 August 2006. *Security Council Expands Mandate of UN Mission in Sudan to Include Darfur, Adopting Resolution 1706 by Vote of 12 in Favour, with 3 Abstaining.* Security Council 5519th Meeting, New York.

US Ambassador to the United Nations. 31 March 2005. *Explanation of Vote on the Sudan Accountability Resolution.* Press Release. Available at: www.state.gov/p/io/44388htm [accessed: 5 June 2009].

US Department of State. February 2001. *Human Rights Report 2000.* Available at: www.state.gov/g/drl/rls/hrrpt/2000 [accessed: 8 March 2009].

US Department of State. 2004. *Report on the Human Rights Practices.* Available at: www.state.gov/g/drl/rls/hrrpt/2004/41628.htm [accessed: 12 May 2009].

US Department of State. 25 February 2004. *Bureau of Democracy, Human Rights, and Labour, Country Reports on Human Rights Practices – Uganda 2003 Section 1(e).* Available at: www.state.gov/g/drl/rls/hrrpt/2003/27758.htm [accessed: 16 March 2009].

US Department of State. January 2005. *Background Note on Uganda.* Available at: www.State.Gov/R/Pa/Ei/Bgn/2963.htm [accessed: 16 March 2009].

US Department of State. 2005. *Report on the Human Rights Practices-2005.* Available at: www.state.gov/g/drl/rls/hrrpt/2005/61594.htm [accessed: 18 May 2009].

Van den Wyngaert, C. and Ongena, T. 2002. Ne bis in idem Principle, Including the Issue of Amnesty, in *The Rome Statute of The International Criminal Court: A Commentary*, edited by A. Cassese, P. Gaeta and J.R.W.D. Jones. Oxford: Oxford University Press, I, 706-726.

Van den Wyngaert, C. and Stessens, G. October 1999. The International Non Bis In Idem Principle: Resolving Some of the Unanswered Questions. *The International and Comparative Law Quarterly*, 48, 4, 779-804.

Vest, H. 2002. *Genozid durch organisatorische Machtapparate.* Baden-Baden: Nomos Verlagsgesellschaft.

Walker, D.M. 1980. *The Oxford Companion to Law.* Oxford: Clarendon Press.

Wartanian, A. Summer 2005. The ICC Prosecutor's Battlefield: Combating Atrocities While Fighting For States' Cooperation Lessons From The U.N. Tribunals Applied To The Case of Uganda. *Georgetown Journal of International Law*, 36, 1289-1314.

Wedgwood, R. 1998. International Criminal Tribunals and State Sources of Proof: The Case of Tihomir Blaškic. *Leiden Journal of International Law*, 11, 635-654.

Weston, B.H. and Reisman, W.M. (eds). 1976. *Toward World Order and Human Dignity.* New York: Free Press, 132-166.

Wetsh'okondo Kosos, M. February 2005. *Human Rights and Justice Sector Reform in Africa: Why Congo Need the ICC?.* Open Society Justice Initiative, 58-62. Available at: justiceinitiative.org/db/resource2/fs?...&rand=0.849487244243 [accessed: 5 June 2009].

Wheaton, H. 1866. *Elements of International Law.* London: R.H. Dana, eighth edition.

Williams, P.R. and Waller, K.M. 2002. Coercive Appeasement: The Flawed International Response to the Serbian Rogue Regime. *New England Law Review*, 36, 825-898.

Williams, Sh.A. 1999. Article 17: Issues of Admissibility, in *Commentary on the Rome Statute of the International Criminal Court: Observer's Note, Article by Article*, edited by O. Triffterer. Baden-Baden: Nomos Verlagsgesellschaft, 383-394.

Williams, Sh.A. Summer 2000. The Rome Statute on the International Criminal Court: From 1947-2000 and Beyond. *Osgoode Hall Law Journal*, 38, 2, 297-330.

Wilmshurst, E. 1999. Jurisdiction of the Court, in *The International Criminal Court: The Making of the Rome Statute: Issues, Negotiations and Results*, edited by R. Lee. The Hague: Kluwer Law International, 131-134.

Wise E.D. 1998. Aut Dedare aut Judicare: The Duty to Prosecute or Extradite, in *International Criminal Law; Procedural and Enforcement Mechanisms*, edited by M.Ch. Bassiouni. New York: Transnational Publishers, second edition.

World Health Organization. 15 October 2004. *WHO Media Briefing: Mortality Projections for Darfur*. Available at: www.who.int/disasters/repo/14985.pdf [accessed: 6 June 2009].

Working Group on Complementarity and Trigger Mechanism. 13 August 1997. *Preparatory Committee on the Establishment of an International Criminal Court*. 4-15 August 1997. A/Ac.249/1997/Wg.3/Crp.2. Available at: www. iccnow.org/documents/IssuesofAdmissibility.pdf [accessed: 3 July 2008].

Yannis, A. 1997. State Collapse and Prospects for Political Reconstruction and Democratic Governance in Somalia. *African Yearbook of International Law*, 5.

Yee, L. 2002. The International Criminal Court and the Security Council: Articles 13(b) and 16, in *The International Criminal Court: The Making of the Rome Statute – Issues, Negotiations, and Results*, edited by R. Lee. The Hague: Kluwer, 144.

Yemi, O. 1996. Legality in a Collapsed State: the Somali Experience. *International and Comparative Law Quarterly*, 45, 910.

Young, G. January 2002. Amnesty and Accountability. *University of California Davis Law Review*, 35, 427-486.

Zappalà, S. 2001. Do Heads of State in Office Enjoy Immunity from Jurisdiction for International Crimes? The Ghaddafi Case Before the French Cour de Cassation. *European Journal of International Law*, 12, 3, 595-612.

Zappalà, S. 2003. The Reaction of the US to the Entry into Force of the ICC Statute: Comments on UN SC Resolution 1422 (2002) and Article 98 Agreements. *Journal of International Criminal Justice*, 1, 114-134.

Zimmermann, A. 1998. The Creation of a Permanent International Criminal Court. *Max Planck Yearbook of United Nations Law*, 12, 169.

Index

www.ingramcontent.com/pod-product-compliance
Ingram Content Group UK Ltd.
Pitfield, Milton Keynes, MK11 3LW, UK
UKHW020400010325
455677UK00021B/554